HISPANIC PHILOSOPHY IN THE AGE OF DISCOVERY

**STUDIES IN PHILOSOPHY
AND THE HISTORY OF PHILOSOPHY**

General Editor: Jude P. Dougherty

**Studies in Philosophy
and the History of Philosophy   Volume 29**

Hispanic Philosophy in the Age of Discovery

edited by Kevin White

THE CATHOLIC UNIVERSITY OF AMERICA PRESS
Washington, D.C.

Copyright © 1997
The Catholic University of America Press
All rights reserved
Printed in the United States of America

The paper used in this publication meets the minimum requirements of American National Standards for Information Science—Permanence of Paper for Printed Library materials, ANSI Z39.48-1984.
∞

LIBRARY OF CONGRESS CATALOGING-IN-PUBLICATION DATA
Hispanic philosophy in the age of discovery / edited by Kevin White.
    p. cm. — (Studies in philosophy and the history of
philosophy ; v. 29)
  Includes bibliographical references and index.
  1. Philosophy, Spanish. 2. Spain—Intellectual life—16th
century. 3. Spain—Intellectual life—17th century. I. White,
Kevin. II. Series.
B776.S7H57   1996
196'.1—dc20
96-14797
ISBN 978-0-8132-3058-0 (pbk)

Contents

Introduction   vii

PART I

1. JORGE J. E. GRACIA, Hispanic Philosophy: Its Beginning and Golden Age   3

PART II

2. MAURICIO BEUCHOT, The Philosophical Discussion of the Legitimacy of the Conquest of Mexico in the Sixteenth Century   31
3. JOHN P. DOYLE, Vitoria on Choosing to Replace a King   45
4. MARCELO SÁNCHEZ-SORONDO, Vitoria: The Original Philosopher of Rights   59
5. EDUARDO ANDÚJAR, Bartolomé de Las Casas and Juan Ginés de Sépulveda: Moral Theology versus Political Philosophy   69
6. RAFAEL ALVIRA AND ALFREDO CRUZ, The Controversy between Las Casas and Sepúlveda at Valladolid   88

PART III

7. WILLIAM A. WALLACE, Domingo de Soto and the Iberian Roots of Galileo's Science   113
8. JUAN ANTONIO WIDOW, The Economic Teachings of Spanish Scholastics   130
9. JEAN DE GROOT, Teresa of Avila and the Meaning of Mystical Theology   145
10. YVES FLOUCAT, The Christian Mysticism of St. John of the Cross and the Metaphysics of Being   160

11. MIRKO SKARICA, The Problem of God's Foreknowledge
    and Human Free Action in Spanish Philosophy   181

PART IV

12. NORMAN WELLS, Suárez and a Salamancan Thomist:
    A Tale of a Text   201
13. STEPHEN MENN, Suárez, Nominalism, and Modes   226
14. CARLOS G. NOREÑA, Francisco Suárez on Democracy and
    International Law   257

PART V

15. JOHN DEELY, A New Beginning in Philosophy: Poinsot's
    Contribution to the Seventeenth-Century Search   275

    Contributors   315
    Index   321

Introduction

I

The present volume gathers together fifteen philosophical studies occasioned by the commemoration of the five hundredth anniversary of Columbus's discovery of America. Although several of the studies directly concern the significance of the initial encounter between Native Americans and the Spanish, the scope of the volume goes beyond this event to take in the golden age of Hispanic philosophy which followed upon it. Accordingly, a wide range of philosophical topics is discussed, including political philosophy, philosophy of nature, economics, mysticism, natural theology, metaphysics, and semiotics. Presenting the results of ground-breaking historical research and careful philosophical reflection, the essays together constitute a rich and varied resource for scholars interested in the field.

The introductory paper, by *Jorge J. E. Gracia*, provides both a definition and a brief but expert survey of the period. Gracia begins by arguing that the notion "Hispanic philosophy"—which focuses attention on the close relations among philosophers in the Iberian peninsula and the Iberian colonies of the New World—is more satisfactory than less-inclusive national designations, and by defending this notion against charges of emptiness, Eurocentrism, and inaccuracy. He then turns to "the beginning and golden age" of Hispanic philosophy (approximately 1500–1650), suggesting that the period is "golden" because of the number, brilliance, and influence of its protagonists; and that it is the first period of properly "Hispanic" philosophical development both because of the new political, religious, and corresponding intellectual unity then distinguishing the Iberian peninsula and Iberian colonies from Europe, and because it is largely the response of a native Iberian Scholastic tradition to issues arising from the discovery and colonization of the New World. Gracia discusses four challenges—the discovery of the New World, the rise of Renaissance humanism, the spread of the Reformation, and the growth of skepticism—and two other significant factors—the relatively late emergence of Iberian Scholasticism and the close relations between church and state in the Iberian peninsula—which combined to unify Hispanic philosophy in this period and set it apart from European thought. He concludes by reflecting on the forgottenness of this period of philosophy, and by arguing for the originality of the period, which raised new issues, transcended earlier Scholasticism, and took bold and conscious steps to separate philosophy from theology.

II

The subjects of the following five essays proposed philosophical responses to urgent and unprecedented practical questions arising from European conquest of the New World.

Reflections on the legitimacy of the conquest by two Spanish scholars living in Mexico are discussed by *Mauricio Beuchot*. Juan de Zumárraga (1468/9–1548), the first archbishop of Mexico, argued that it was not legitimate to enslave the Indians, and declared the war of conquest to be illegitimate because it was hindering the just aim of converting the natives to Christianity. Vasco de Quiroga (late 1480s–1565), bishop of Michoacán, similarly argued that the war of conquest as carried out was unjust. The *De debellandis indis* that is sometimes attributed to Vasco, which presents the harsher position that infidels have no right to power, seems in fact not be his work; the authentic position of Vasco appears in the resumé prepared by Miguel de Arcos. Beuchot concludes that most early theoreticians did legitimate the conquest, but only as far as was necessary for evangelizing the Native Americans; and that the principled sense of an obligation to convert the natives must be distinguished from the twisted application of reasoned principles by the conquistadors.

The following two essays concern the thought of Francisco de Vitoria (1492/3–1546), who never published his works, but whose innovative teaching in the Faculty of Theology at the University of Salamanca was widely influential.

John P. Doyle discusses Vitoria's remarks on the choice by a people to replace a king. After noting Vitoria's Aristotelian and Thomistic view of man as a political animal, Doyle points out that, according to Vitoria, political community is both natural and a consequence of a human free choice to transfer power to some authority. Unanimity being too rare, agreement of a majority suffices for this transfer. Can a monarchical republic by majority vote limit the power it has granted to a king, or choose to replace a king? In the *Relectio de potestate civili* (1528), Vitoria holds that while the power of a king is from God, authority to exercise it is conferred by the republic. In the *Relectio de Indis recenter inventis*

(1539), he considers the transfer of power by the Indians as a title for Spanish domination of the New World, arguing in one place that such transfer would in the circumstances be vitiated inasmuch as the Indians would be acting in fear and ignorance, but in another place that majority rule as such would in principle make such transfer a possible justification of Spanish domination. In this acknowledgment of the legitimacy of majority rule Doyle finds the first stirrings of democracy in the modern sense: Vitoria's consistent doctrine of a single power conferred by a majority tends towards not an absolutism of divine right, but a recognition of majority rule.

Marcelo Sánchez-Sorondo reflects on the unique role of Vitoria in the history of man's progressively emerging consciousness of persons, rights, and duties. Drawing both on Thomistic anthropology and on the biblical teaching of natural human goodness, Vitoria suggested that the determination of the precepts of natural law is a historical process which accompanies the unfolding of human nature to itself. Vitoria's point of departure is the person in human nature, from which he developed a theory of equality in the family and the political community. The state, in turn, is inserted in the world of international community. The consciousness of a universal humanity, already present in Christian teaching and developed by St. Augustine but made newly urgent by the discovery of the peoples of America, was given form by Vitoria's notion of a community of nations governed by international law, a community in which wars of religion would give way to religious tolerance. Vitoria, it would seem, was the original philosopher of rights.

The last two essays in this section offer different perspectives on a famous *disputatio* held in Valladolid in 1550–51 between Bartolomé de Las Casas (1474–1566) and Juan Ginés de Sepúlveda (1490–1573) concerning procedures of evangelization and establishment of legitimate Spanish sovereignty in the New World.

Eduardo Andújar carefully describes the circumstances of the debate, the traditional characterization of the opponents (Las Casas the liberator versus Sepúlveda the enslaver), and the historical background of the debate in the early years of the discovery and conquest. To the question, "Is it right for his majesty to fight before preaching to the natives occurs?," Sepúlveda answered in the negative and Las Casas in the affirmative. Both opponents drew on Aristotle's account of natural slavery, Las Casas arguing that natural slaves must be few in number, Sepúlveda responding that numbers were irrelevant in the present case, where certain practices, notably human sacrifice and cannibalism, suggested that the precepts of the natural law had become obscured. Andújar suggests that Las Casas's call for an absolute absence of coercion was optimistic but unrealistic, while Sepúlveda's more realistic philosophico-political perspective was based on principles of natural right.

While extending the contrast between the evangelizing, "medieval" approach of Las Casas and the humanistic, "renaissance" approach of Sepúlveda, *Raphael Alvira* and *Alfredo Cruz* at the same time argue for a commonality and complementarity between the two disputants at Valladolid. Each contributed a necessary element to the debate, namely, a concern with prudence and justice, respectively, and the two were often closer than one might imagine. In contrast to Vitoria, neither examined the problem strictly within the limits of natural law, and both accepted the papal bull. The opponents were divided not by the facts, but by their evaluation of them, Sepúlveda's humanism stressing the cultural difference between Europeans and Americans, and Las Casas's Christianity minimizing it. The debate produced a confrontation of two great historical forces, pagan (Aristotelian) culturalist elitism and Christian metaphysical egalitarianism. Whereas Aristotle had considered man's "historicized" nature, Christianity underlined the "innate" nature to which all men are called, and hence the unity of man, and thus proposed a solution to the political problem in terms of equality.

III

The next group of papers draws our attention from the conquest to a variety of other philosophical themes arising in Hispanic thought of the sixteenth and early seventeenth centuries.

William A. Wallace offers a valuable addition to his distinguished researches in the history of science by uncovering a link between the thought of Domingo de Soto (1494–1560) and that of Galileo (1564–1642) on the subject of uniformly accelerating motion. After contrasting the scientific and logical Soto with his contemporary and fellow student at Paris, the Catalan humanist Juan Luis Vives (1492–1540), and discussing the summulist tradition at Paris, Wallace presents the "twofold enigma" of Soto. The first question is why Soto, unlike his immediate predecessors, gave the example of a falling body and projectile to illustrate motion which is *uniformiter difformis;* Wallace shows that Soto likely learned of experimental work on falling bodies from Italian Dominicans on his journey to the Council of Trent in 1545–50. The other question is whether Soto's work was in fact known to Galileo. Duhem's thesis of continuity between the two thinkers is both right and wrong. Galileo did appropriate Soto's teaching, but through the intermediary of Jesuit teachers in Rome: Soto's Jesuit student Toletus brought Soto's teaching to Rome; the Jesuit Menu followed Toletus; and Menu was succeeded by the Jesuits Vallius, Vitelleschi, and Rugerius, three thinkers whose works find parallels throughout Galileo's notebooks; in 1604, Vallius and Eudaemon were teaching in Padua. Another point of influence may be discerned from Galileo's frequent use of the term *ex suppositione*, which refers to the demonstrative regressus, in which a cause is discerned from its effect, and then the effect is demonstrated from its cause. Wallace presents the momentous discovery that Galileo's source here—again via Toletus and the Roman Jesuits—was Soto's fusion of nominalism and realism.

Juan Antonio Widow draws attention to the central moral aspect of the economic teachings of Vitoria, Martin de Azpilcueta (1493–1586), Soto, Juan De Lugo (1583–1660), Vives, and Luis de Molina (1535–1600). The fundamental point is that for these thinkers economic activity, involving dominion over external goods—a dominion which is less absolute than is implied by the modern notion of "property"—is intrinsically voluntary, and therefore human and moral. Such dominion involves responsibility, and therefore calls for virtue and appropriate use. Widow shows how, proceeding from the premise that economic actions are inevitably just or unjust, these thinkers dealt with the classical problems of the just price and usury. Regarding the fixing of an unjust price as possibly a mortal sin, they discussed the circumstances of variations in price and disputed as to whether the just price is to be determined by "the wise" or "the many." Vitoria identified three principles of the just price, namely, absence of fraud, of involuntariness, and of compulsion. Usury was also regarded as a serious crime, one offending against the feudal bond of personal loyalty. With the exceptions of Sombart and Keynes, modern economists have misunderstood the economic doctrine of these thinkers. Widow closes by noting that, in contrast to these doctrines, the classical modern economic doctrine proceeds on the assumption that man does *not* have free will.

The following two papers offer philosophical reflections on the writings of the two great Spanish mystics.

Jean De Groot's discussion of some passages by St. Teresa of Avila (1515–82) clarifies the meaning of mystical theology and corrects a contemporary misconception concerning the nature of mystical experience. As understood by both patristic authors and Teresa, the elements of such experience cannot be reduced to merely private and subjective events, but must rather be seen as effects of divine causes. These effects both serve as signposts on the soul's road to union with God and represent the verbally inexpressible divine life; hence, mystical experience is something like a map, that is, a schematized representation needing a key. The constriction imposed by modern interpretations of mystical experience emerges in the assertion that Teresa's claim to have felt God's presence expresses a belief requiring the justification of empirical evidence. Teresa herself suggests another kind of evidence in the will's act of love. Aristotle's reasoning that, since loving is an activity, one cannot love without knowing it, helps to make clear that Teresa did not have a "belief" that God was present to her. We should not, then, ask how her belief can be justified, but rather whether she is a competent judge of her love. Teresa's loving is something like evidence that God is present, and loving constitutes evidence because of the mutual involvement of lover and object. This involvement entails "the typical inversion" of loving, in which what begins as activity is converted into an undergoing—in the case of mystical experience, "the undergoing of divine things." De Groot concludes by suggesting that contemporary study of mystical experience should, in a Platonic spirit, include the lover's apprehension of the beloved within the notion of objectivity.

Yves Floucat examines the correspondences between two forms of Christian experience, namely, mystical union as described by St. John of the Cross (1542–91) and metaphysics. He begins by conceding that it is difficult to see the relation between mystical wisdom, which involves love, faith, unknowing, and connaturality, and metaphysical knowledge. While spiritual experience is not absent from philosophy, the latter is more an affair of intellectual and even rational knowledge, although the intuition of being and the discovery of the incapacity of finite beings to account for their intelligibility indeed involve mystery. Christian mysticism and Christian metaphysics are irreducibly distinct, although both are contemplative, and the two may be united in a thinker. The mysticism of John of the Cross contains a number of metaphysical implications. Like metaphysical thinking, this mysticism involves a certain purification of images and an attentiveness to being. John's mysticism points not to resorption in the One, but to a sense of the analogy of being, the distinction between created and uncreated being, and the primacy of being over mind. John's mysticism is thus distinct from anticontemplative mystical ruptures frequently proposed in the history of metaphysical thought. In brief, the expression of Christian wisdom in John's mysticism and that in Thomas's metaphysics are in deep accord.

Mirko Skarica discusses the famous problem of the compatibility between God's foreknowledge and free human action in the thought of four Hispanic thinkers, focusing on the question of how God knows future free acts. Domingo Báñez (1528–1604) follows Aquinas and Cajetan in arguing that everything existing is present to eternity, and that God knows future contingents ("futuribles") by that presence, so that he knows future and past by knowledge of vision. Luis de Molina, on the other hand, objecting that Aquinas's position requires both a temporal and an eternal existence of the contingent, proposes a "middle knowledge" of futuribles standing between the natural knowledge of all possibles and the free knowledge of creation. Francisco Suárez (1548–1617) defends Molina, but speaks of "conditioned" rather than "middle" knowledge, and adds that middle knowledge, and even knowledge by vision, are "natural" to God in a broad sense. Suárez differs from Molina in focus, asking whether future acts are knowable in themselves or determinately true, and disagreeing with Molina's conclusion that they are not. The Chilean Franciscan Alonso Briceño (1587–1669), known as *Alter Scotus* and *Scotulus*, disagreed with all of the foregoing, arguing in particular against Gabriel Vásquez (1549–1604), the originator of the doctrine that God knows future contingents with determinate truth. Briceño argued that the origin of this determinate truth is not the intrinsic conformity of the thing known, but rather comes from outside the thing in a decree of the divine will. Briceño follows Scotus in asserting that divine foreknowledge is God's knowledge of his own will; conformity to the object is not essential.

IV

The next three papers are centrally concerned with the most famous and influential philosopher of the period, Francisco Suárez.

Norman Wells discusses the influence on Suárez and Descartes of the Thomist Francisco Zumel's (1541–1607) position on the status of the essences of creatures prior to their creation. With Aquinas, Nedellec, and Soncinas, and against Henry of Ghent and Capreolus, Zumel argues that there are no essences, no eternal propositions, and no contingent truths outside the divine intellect and power, and thus far Suárez would agree. But, Zumel adds, it is probable that essential propositions are true perpetually *and intrinsically;* here he is not rejecting Aquinas, but rather Henry, Capreolus, and even their critics, all of whom fail to acknowledge the eternity of existential truths. Suárez is well aware of the Henry-Capreolus tradition of eternal essences possessing *esse essentiae*, to which his response is like that of Zumel, whose text he certainly knows. Suárez is not giving his own position, but a critical account, just or not, of Zumel's. Descartes, who was unaware of Zumel but knew of Suárez, rejects uncreated eternal essences and truths, as did Suárez. Did Descartes read Suárez's text on the *moderni theologi* as expressing Suárez's own opinion? There are no grounds for the claims of Cartesian scholars: the text is *not* a statement of Suárez's own opinion, but his critical account of an adversary's position, that is, that of the *moderni theologi,* including Zumel.

Stephen Menn discusses Suárez, nominalism, and modes. He begins by distinguishing the "liberal Jesuit realism" of Pedro da Fonseca (1528–99) and Suárez from "conservative Dominican realism." He then discusses explanations of relations of union by Scotus, Ockham, Fonseca, and Suárez. Suárez is the "shameless" person of Scotus's fears who denies that things one of which can remain without the other are really distinct. Suárez is unique in taking a modal account of relations of union as a model for solving many difficulties of the realist theory of categories; for example, he takes figure to be only a mode of quantity. Fonseca's systematic discussion of the distinctions of modes provided a model for Suárez's *Disputationes Metaphysicae.* Suárez departs deeply from Fonseca on the distinction of three classes of modes. Fonseca's discussion of *Metaphysics* IV–V resembles and is the precursor of Suárez's *Disputationes.* Fonseca and Suárez pursue a realist agenda and voluntarist principles; Suárez is distinguished by his clear vision, thoroughness, and mercilessness.

Carlos G. Noreña discusses Suárez's contribution to reflections on democracy and international law. Suárez followed a path between the Thomist "objectivists" and the Ockhamite "voluntarists." He saw the central problem as how the commands of natural law are rendered specific, and the element of voluntarism involved a recognition of the source of authority in commanding and obeying wills. Suárez argued that coercion is necessary, but not because of sin; he is sober and eclectic, considering both moral grounds and natural self-interest. He stresses that after transfer of power to a king, the people have no power, the transfer being not a delegation, but an alienation. But mixed with his antipopulist caution are potentially more democratic views that emerge when he considers the need to preserve the state and self-defense against tyrants. He was pioneering in the concept of international community, and had lasting influence in this regard; he considered *ius gentium* not as a part of natural law, but as an extension of it. Suárez's achievement was to integrate political philosophy and ethics into the philosophy of law, giving a role to human intellect and reason. Suárez on democracy is both traditional and modern. He is a champion of cosmopolitan solidarity and of pluralism.

V

The concluding paper, by *John Deely*, argues that the last great figure of the period, Descartes's contemporary, John Poinsot, or John of St. Thomas (1589–1644), discovered a new philosophical starting-point in a doctrine of signs which both synthesized the Latin past and gave it a future bearing which extends beyond modernity itself. Poinsot's respect for the past contrasts with Descartes's desire for a radical break. Having been influenced by the theory of signs developed by Soto at Paris, Poinsot took the innovative step of publishing a separate treatise on signs in place of a commentary on the *De interpretatione*. With his doctrine of signs, Poinsot produced from within the resources of the Latin tradition an answer to the modern question concerning "in what way particular things are susceptible of investigation by the human mind." Considered both within the context of Poinsot's *Cursus Philosophicus Thomisticus* and independently, the doctrine of signs provides a new starting point for philosophy. Based as it is on Aquinas's account of relations, the doctrine of the *Treatise on Signs* establishes nothing less than a comprehensive role for signs in which they provide the fabric and structure both for experience as a whole and for the full range of acts of understanding. Poinsot indicates that the doctrine of signs must take its departure from a standpoint that transcends the division of being into *ens reale* and *ens rationis*. The *Treatise on Signs* calls for a reexamination of philosophy's starting-point, and an admission that that starting-point is rooted in the operation of signs that determine the nature and extent of our knowledge. The most surprising thing about the treatise is how modern it is. Locke's concern with semiotic, anticipated by Poinsot, was later taken up by C. S. Peirce. Poinsot's claim that the doctrine of signs transcends in its starting point the division of being into *ens reale* and *ens rationis* implies that semiotic transcends the opposition between realism and idealism.

All but one of these essays were originally presented at a conference entitled "Hispanic Philosophy in the Age of Discovery," held at The Catholic University of America in October of 1992. It is hoped that this publication will stimulate further researches into a rich but still too little-known period in the history of philosophy.

Finally, I wish to mention my gratitude to Mark Hurley for his work as copy-editor of this volume.

PART I

1 Hispanic Philosophy: Its Beginning and Golden Age
JORGE J. E. GRACIA

I. HISPANIC PHILOSOPHY

The notion of Hispanic philosophy is a useful one for trying to understand certain historical phenomena related to the philosophy developed in the Iberian peninsula, the Iberian colonies in the New World, and the countries that those colonies eventually came to form.[1] It is useful for two reasons: first, it focuses attention on the close relations among the philosophers in these geographical areas, and second, other historical denominations and categorizations do not do justice to such relations. This becomes clear when one examines the standard general categorizations according to which the philosophical thought of the mentioned geographical areas is divided and studied: Spanish philosophy, Portuguese philosophy, Catalan philosophy, Latin American philosophy, Spanish-American philosophy, and Ibero-American philosophy.

The category "Spanish philosophy" usually includes only the philosophy that has taken place in the territory occupied by the modern Spanish state, whether before or after the state was constituted in the fifteenth century as a result of the efforts of Ferdinand of Aragón and Isabella of Castile. Thus, most histories of Spanish philosophy discuss the thought of Roman, Islamic, and Jewish philosophers who worked in that territory, as well as of medieval and subsequent authors who did likewise. In some cases, these accounts concentrate on Castilian-speaking philosophers, and at other times they also include those who spoke in

---

1. The term "Hispanic" is a derivative from *Hispania*, the name used by Romans for the Iberian peninsula. Its use was popularized by the members of the Generation of 1898, a Spanish group of intellectuals who flourished at the turn of the century and who can be considered the progenitors of modern Iberian thought. In philosophy, the term "Hispanic" has been used to refer to the philosophy of Spain and Spanish America by Eduardo Nicol. See his *El problema de la filosofía hispánica* (Madrid: Editorial Tecnos, 1961).

Catalan and Portuguese. They generally ignore, however, the work of Latin American authors and seldom explore the close ties of those authors to philosophers working in the Iberian peninsula.[2] Something similar can be said about other peninsular histories of philosophy, with the added disadvantage that they, like those histories of Spanish philosophy that deal exclusively with Castilian-speaking philosophers, tend to ignore the developments in the Iberian peninsula that take place in linguistic and cultural contexts other than their own.[3] The reasons for these sometimes conscious oversights are rooted in nationalistic feelings dating back to historical conflicts and antagonisms that have little to do with philosophical, historical reality but nonetheless affect historical accounts of that reality.

New World histories of philosophy concerned with Latin America suffer similar shortcomings, although in this case their neglect concerns the thought of Iberian authors and their close relations with, and the impact they have had on, Latin American philosophers.[4] Histories of Latin American or Ibero-American philosophy and thought tend to concentrate on developments in the New World, ignoring the strong relations that tie such developments to the thought of Spanish and Portuguese authors.[5] In the case of histories dealing specifically with Spanish American philosophy, the situation is even worse, as they tend to ignore the Portuguese side of Latin America and the cultural and intellectual ties that relate it to the rest of the area.[6]

---

2. Cf. Alain Guy, *Histoire de la philosophie espagnole*, 12th ed. (Toulouse: Université de Toulouse-Le Mirail, 1985); Marcial Solana, *Historia de la filosofía española: Época del Renacimiento (siglo XVI)*, 3 vols. (Madrid: Real Academia de Ciencias Exactas, Físicas y Naturales, 1941); and José Luis Abellán, *Historia crítica del pensamiento español*, 7 vols. (Madrid: Espasa-Calpe, 1979–91).

3. Cf. José Marinho, *Estudos sobre o pensamento português contemporâneo* (Lisbon: Biblioteca Nacional, 1981); and José Marinho, *Verdade, condição e destino no pensamento português contemporâneo* (Porto: Lello and Irmão, 1976). There are occasional attempts, however, at establishing the influence of some peninsular authors on Latin America. See, for example, María del Carmen Rovira, *Ecléticos portugueses del siglo XVIII y algunas de sus influencias en América* (Mexico: Colegio de México, 1958). These attempts however, are usually specialized and do not seem to influence general histories of philosophy of peninsular nations.

4. I am conscious that my use of the term "New World" to refer to North and South America is Eurocentric, but there is no other adequate term available. "America," which works in Spanish and Portuguese, does not work in English because it has been appropriated by the United States; moreover, one might argue that "America" is also Eurocentric to some extent.

5. Cf. Harold E. Davis, *Latin American Thought: A Historical Introduction* (New York: The Free Press, 1974); Manfredo Kempff Mercado, *Historia de la filosofía en Latinoamérica* (Santiago: Zig Zag, 1958); and Francisco Larroyo and Edmundo Escobar, *Historia de las doctrinas filosóficas en Latinoamérica* (Mexico: Editorial Porrúa, 1968).

6. Cf. Ramón Insúa Rodríguez, *Historia de la filosofía en Hispanoamérica* (Guayaquil,

General histories of philosophy seldom, if ever, do justice to the historical relations between Iberian and Latin American philosophers or to the philosophy of Spain, Catalonia, Portugal, and Latin America.[7] Indeed, it is particularly rare to find any reference to Latin American contributions to philosophy in histories other than histories of Latin American philosophy.[8] This becomes quite evident when one turns to particular periods of the history of philosophy, such as the period that will especially occupy us, the sixteenth century and part of the seventeenth century. This period is studied under such labels as "Renaissance Philosophy," "Counter-Reformation Philosophy," "Late Scholasticism," "Late Medieval Philosophy," "Second Scholastic," and "Silver Age of Scholasticism," to mention just the most frequently used. Some historians may want to argue that there is justification for this oversight in some cases. Indeed, one could argue that the impact of the Renaissance in Latin America came too late to be incorporated into a general history of the Renaissance, and also that the vector of influence went only one way, from Europe to Latin America, and not vice versa.[9] It is not true, however, that the impact of European Renaissance thought on Latin America came too late to be considered in histories of Renaissance thought; humanism influenced Latin American thought via Iberian thought beginning in the first half of the sixteenth century. Moreover, although it is true that Latin American humanism did not influence European humanism, it does nonetheless present some in-

---

Ecuador: Universidad de Guayaquil, 1945). The tendency to isolate Spanish America from Portuguese America is present in many authors of very different persuasions. See, for example, José Mariátegui, *Obras*, ed. Francisco Baeza (Havana: Casa de las Américas, 1982), 2:250.

7. For example, Wilhelm Windelband's influential *A History of Philosophy*, 2 vols. (New York: Harper and Brothers, 1958), which covers the sixteenth century in some detail, makes no reference to Francisco de Vitoria and only two passing references to Francisco Suárez. W. T. Jones's extensive, multivolume *A History of Western Philosophy*, 4 vols. (New York: Harcourt Brace Jovanovich, 1970), does not have a single reference to Iberian or Latin American philosophers.

8. Even histories of Western philosophy which take into account Iberian developments suffer from this fault. See, for example, Frederick Copleston, *A History of Philosophy* (New York: Image Books, 1950). It is only recently and sporadically that general dictionaries and encyclopedias of philosophy include references to Latin American philosophy. Only general histories of philosophy produced by Latin American philosophers contain materials on Latin American thought. See, for example, José Vasconcelos, *Historia del pensamiento filosófico* (Mexico: Imprenta Universitaria, 1937).

9. Among histories and studies of Renaissance thought that ignore Latin America, see, for example, Paul Oskar Kristeller, *Renaissance Thought and Its Sources* (New York: Columbia University Press, 1979); Kristeller, *Renaissance Thought: The Classic, Scholastic, and Humanistic Strains* (New York: Harper and Brothers, 1961); and Charles B. Schmitt et al., eds., *The Cambridge History of Renaissance Philosophy* (Cambridge: Cambridge University Press, 1988).

teresting characteristics that should not be ignored in an overall history of Renaissance philosophy.[10] Moreover, just like histories and studies of Renaissance thought, histories of the Counter-Reformation, late Scholastic philosophy, and so on, generally neglect Latin America and often fail to represent the particularly vibrant tone of the intellectual life of the Iberian peninsula during this time, even though they do make reference to Iberian contributions to philosophy.[11]

The general neglect of Iberian and Latin American thought outside Iberian and Latin American countries makes no historical sense. What is particularly distressing is to see the failure to take into account the close relations of the philosophy of Latin America and the countries of the Iberian peninsula even within studies produced in Latin America and the Iberian peninsula. For texts dislodged from the tradition which produced them are silent, and many of the texts produced by Latin America and Iberian philosophers are the product of close relations between Latin America and the Iberian peninsula. This is especially clear in the case of Latin American scholastics, because their link to the authors of the thirteenth and fourteenth centuries they emulated was mediated by Iberian scholastics. Alonso de la Vera Cruz (1504?–84) and Alonso Briceño (1587?–1669?) cannot properly be understood when one does not take into account the work of Iberian Thomists and Scotists on whom they partly relied or through whom they approached the work of Thomas Aquinas and Duns Scotus.[12] But this

10. Cf. José M. Gallegos Rocafull, *El pensamiento mexicano en los siglos XVI y XVII*, 2d ed. (Mexico: Universidad Nacional Autónoma de México, 1974); Guillermo Furlong, *Nacimiento y desarrollo de la filosofía en el Río de La Plata, 1536–1810* (Buenos Aires: Guillermo Kraft, 1952); Alain Guy, *Panorama de la philosophie Ibero-Américaine du XVIe siècle a nos jours* (Geneva: Patiño, 1989); Mauricio Beuchot, *La filosofía en el México colonial* (Mexico: Universidad Nacional Autónoma de México, in press); Beuchot, "La influencia del Renacimiento en la Colonia," in *Estudios de historia y filosofía en el México colonial* (Mexico: Universidad Nacional Autónoma de México, 1991), 73–106; and Gabriel Méndez Plancarte, *Humanismo mexicano del siglo XVI* (Mexico: Universidad Nacional Autónoma de México, 1946). It should also be noted that, as we shall see later, the nonhumanistic thought of the period in Latin America did influence European thought.

11. Carlo Giacon's *La seconda scolastica*, 2 vols. (Milan: Fratelli Bocca, 1946), and Schmitt's *The Cambridge History of Renaissance Philosophy* pay considerable attention to Iberian philosophy (see in particular the chapters by Charles H. Lohr and E. J. Ashworth in the latter). Other histories which cover the period do not do so. Cf. Norman Kretzman et al., eds., *The Cambridge History of Later Medieval Philosophy* (Cambridge: Cambridge University Press, 1982).

12. See, for example, Mauricio Beuchot, "Panorama de la historia de la filosofía novohispana," in *Estudios de historia y filosofía*, 22–36. Concerning Alonso de la Vera Cruz and his relations to Iberian thought, see in particular Walter Redmond and Mauricio Beuchot, *Pensamiento y realidad en Alonso de la Vera Cruz* (Mexico: Universidad Autónoma de México, 1987). Concerning Briceño, see Walter Hanisch Espíndola, *En torno a la filosofía en Chile 1594–1810* (Santiago: Universidad Católica de Chile, 1963), 24–30.

problem is not restricted to this period. The work of some Latin Americans in the twentieth century who looked at Nicolai Hartmann and Max Scheler as intellectual mentors, for example, is incomprehensible unless one keeps in mind that they first learned about them through José Ortega y Gasset (1883–1955). Indeed, there is an Orteguean "color" to the Germanism of Samuel Ramos (1897–1959) and others who relied on Hartmann and Scheler for many of their ideas.[13] Although this color fades somewhat as Latin Americans learn German and become directly acquainted with German texts, it never quite disappears, for the patterns of interpretation and emphasis established at the beginning left discernible traces.[14]

The same can be said about studying Iberian philosophy apart from Latin American philosophy, for even in cases in which the philosophy of Latin America did not explicitly influence Iberian philosophers, the Latin American reality did. Consider the case of sixteenth-century Iberian philosophers, like Francisco de Vitoria (1492/3–1546). Can we ignore the fact that much of what they thought about philosophically was prompted by the new reality they confronted as a result of the discovery?[15] Did they not see that new reality through the eyes of those who lived in and travelled to the colonies? It was Latin Americans, whether adopted or native, who provided these Iberian philosophers with many of the issues and themes they were to explore. Again, this need not be restricted to that age. The most distinguished group of Spanish philosophers in the twentieth century, the *transterrados* (fugitives from the Spanish Civil War), moved to Latin America and were as influenced by the philosophers they found or helped develop there as they influenced them.[16]

---

13. Cf. Samuel Ramos's *Hacia un nuevo humanismo: Programa de una antropología filosófica* (Mexico: Fondo de Cultura Económica, 1962).

14. Cf. Francisco Romero's *Theory of Man*, trans. William Cooper (Berkeley: University of California Press, 1964); and Risieri Frondizi's *What Is Value? An Introduction to Axiology*, trans. Solomon Lipp (La Salle, Ill.: Open Court, 1963).

15. In the case of Vitoria the discovery seems to be an important concern, as is evident in *Relectio de indis* (1538) and *Relectio de iure belli* (1539). In fact, there is substantial evidence that colonial Latin American thinkers not only influenced Iberian authors but also European philosophers like Descartes. See Mauricio Beuchot, "Aportaciones de pensadores novohispanos a la filosofía europea y universal," in *Estudios de historia y filosofía*, 43–51.

16. On the *transterrados*, see José Luis Abellán, *Filosofía española en América (1936–1966)* (Madrid: Ediciones Guadarrama, 1967). The concern of José Gaos, Eduardo Nicol, and other *transterrados* with the relation of Latin American thought to Iberian thought is evident in their writings and can be explained only by the influence that Latin Americans and the Latin American reality had on them. Gaos's *Historia del pensamiento de lengua española en la edad contemporánea (1744–1944)* (Mexico: Séneca, 1945) and Nicol's *El problema de la filosofía hispánica* make no sense plucked from the Latin American experience.

For all these reasons it should be clear that we need a general category to bring out the philosophical reality encompassed by the Iberian peninsula and Latin America. The category of Hispanic philosophy responds to this need, focusing attention on historical relations and phenomena which are generally ignored in histories which use other categories and divisions. I have not considered the national histories of philosophy of individual Latin American countries, for it should be obvious that they are even more restrictive than the sorts of histories I have mentioned.[17] Moreover, they are sometimes marred by nationalistic concerns which distort the historical record, although one must grant that, like most historical accounts, they have their uses.

Having noted the advantages of using the category of Hispanic philosophy in the historical account of the development of philosophy in the Iberian peninsula and Latin America, I must warn that use of such a category does not imply that there is something peculiar, some idiosyncratic feature or features, which characterize such philosophy throughout its history.[18] Much Spanish and Latin American thought of the last one-hundred years has devoted itself to the search for the unique features which characterize Spanish, Latin American, and national philosophies, distinguishing them from each other and from the philosophies of other countries and cultures.[19] This effort, however, has been to a great extent fruitless, for it has been difficult to identify even one feature that can serve to characterize any of these philosophies, let alone what I have referred to here as Hispanic philosophy. There are no doubt certain concerns, approaches, and methods in philosophy that characterize one or more periods of the history of His-

---

17. A couple of examples will serve as illustrations: Samuel Ramos, *Historia de la filosofía en México* (Mexico: Imprenta Universitaria, 1943); and Guillermo Francovich, *La filosofía en Bolivia* (La Paz: Juventud, 1966).

18. In this I must differ with Nicol and those who have tried to see some common element to all Hispanic philosophy. See Eduardo Nicol, "Meditación del propio ser: La hispanidad," in *Filosofía e identidad cultural en América latina*, ed. Jorge J. E. Gracia and Iván Jaksić (Caracas: Monte Avila, 1988).

19. Iván Jaksić and I have gathered the most important texts of this controversy concerning Latin American philosophy in the collection cited in the previous note. The controversy was fueled in part by the peninsular quest for a cultural ethos so evident in the Generation of 1898 and in subsequent authors, and received philosophical justification through Ortega y Gasset's perspectivism. It was explicitly formulated as the problem of Latin American philosophical identity by Leopoldo Zea in 1942 and, although it found immediate detractors, such as Risieri Frondizi, the controversy still survives in various forms. For Frondizi's objections, see "Hay una filosofía iberoamericana?" *Realidad* 3 (1948), 158–70. Zea's original article, "En torno a una filosofía americana," and Frondizi's article are reproduced in Gracia and Jaksić, eds., *Filosofía e identidad cultural*, 187–207 and 211–27, respectively. Ofelia Schutte explores the issue of cultural identity in Latin America in her recent *Cultural Identity and Social Liberation in Latin American Thought* (Albany: SUNY Press, 1993).

panic philosophy, a fact which is well established in numerous studies.[20] But there is no definitive evidence that indicates this may be true for all the philosophy that may be included under the epithet "Hispanic."

The category of Hispanic philosophy needs to be understood differently. I propose to understand it as the philosophy produced by a group of philosophers who span diverse political, territorial, linguistic, and ethnic and racial boundaries, but who are closely tied historically. It is not language that ties these philosophers, for some of them write in Latin, whereas others write in Catalan, Spanish, or Portuguese. Nor do they come from the same country. Some of them were born in Spain or Catalonia, but others were born in Portugal and the various Spanish and Portuguese colonies and countries of Latin America. Indeed, in many cases they taught and wrote in lands other than their native countries. Finally, they cannot be regarded as having the same ethnic or racial background, since their origins differ, some being European, others being descendants of Africans or native American, and still others representing a mixture of various races and ethnic groups. What these philosophers have in common is not language, country, race, or ethnic background, but rather a history. It is the events of that history, the historical reality they share, that provides the unity which brings them together.

Naturally, historical ties tend to generate common characteristics, but those characteristics may not extend beyond certain periods of time or geographical areas. There can be continuity without commonality. *A* may follow *B*, and *B* may follow *C*, and *C* may follow *D*, thus implying a connection between *A* and *D* even though *A* may have nothing in common with *D*. This is the kind of unity that Hispanic philosophy has. It is not a unity of common elements. Francisco Suárez (1548–1617) may not have anything in common with Francisco Romero (1891–1962), but both Suárez and Romero are tied by a series of events that places them together and separates them from Descartes, Hume, and Kant. It is not necessary, then, to find common characteristics to all Hispanic philosophers for them to be justifiably categorized as Hispanic. What unites them is the same sort of thing that unites a family, as Wittgenstein would say.[21] There may not be common features among

---

20. See, for example, *La filosofía en América: Trabajos presentados en el IX Congreso Interamericano de Filosofía*, 2 vols. (Caracas: Sociedad Venezolana de Filosofía, 1979); *Ideas en torno de Latinoamérica*, 2 vols. (Mexico: Universidad Nacional Autónoma de México, 1986); Jorge J. E. Gracia, ed., *Latin American Philosophy in the Twentieth Century* (Buffalo: Prometheus Books, 1986); and *América Latina: Historia y destino*, 2 vols. (Mexico: Universidad Nacional Autónoma de México, 1992).

21. Wittgenstein, *Philosophical Investigations* (New York: Macmillan, 1953), secs. 66–67.

all of them, but they belong together because somehow they are all historically related, as a father is to a son, an aunt to a niece, and grandparents to grandchildren. The Wittgensteinian metaphor of the family is particularly appropriate in this case, for a history of philosophy is always the history of the philosophical thought of a community. Beginning in the sixteenth century, the Hispanic community includes not only the inhabitants of the Iberian peninsula but also those of Latin America.

Still, one may question the need or benefit of using the category of Hispanic philosophy to study the philosophers from the Iberian peninsula and Latin America. If there are no common characteristics to all Hispanic philosophers, what can an account of Hispanic philosophy add to accounts of periods or countries which more clearly have characteristics in common? In short, what do we gain from the study of Hispanic philosophy that we do not already know and know better from the study of, say, Spanish, Catalan, Portuguese, and Latin American philosophy? My claim is that we gain a greater understanding of the historical reality of a particular area of the history of philosophy which is otherwise missed.

A history of philosophy is an account of how ideas developed and thus involves an account of how philosophers influenced each other. For an account to be historical it must pay careful attention to the events and figures which played roles in history, avoiding the introduction of artificial divisions among them. My claim is that the notion of a Hispanic philosophy, more than any other notion, reflects the historical reality of the philosophy produced in Spain, Catalonia, Portugal, and Latin America, for it recognizes that there are no fast boundaries among the philosophers of these territories. Consider Francisco Suárez, who was born in Spain but taught in Portugal for many years, or Antonio Rubio (1548–1615), who worked in Mexico but whose *Logic* became a textbook in Spain.[22] More recently, the case of Ortega y Gasset stands out, for his influence in Latin America was perhaps greater than in Spain.[23] These are just a few examples of the many that reveal the historical unity of Hispanic philosophy. To parcel out Hispanic philosophy into various compartments according to political, territorial, racial, or lin-

---

22. Concerning Suárez, see Raoul Scorraille, *François Suárez de la Compagnie de Jésus*, 2 vols. (Paris: P. Lethielleux, 1912). Concerning Rubio, see Gallegos Rocafull, *El pensamiento mexicano*, 262–78; and Walter Redmond and Mauricio Beuchot, *La lógica mexicana en el siglo de oro* (Mexico: Universidad Nacional Autónoma de México, 1985).

23. Any good history of Latin American philosophy will refer to this influence, but there are also more specialized studies. See, for example, Abellán, *Filosofía española en América (1936–1966)*, 103–92; and José Gaos, *Sobre Ortega y Gasset* (Mexico: Imprenta Universitaria, 1952).

guistic groups is to miss many of the historical ties which bind the diverse elements which make up the philosophy of Spain, Catalonia, Portugal, and Latin America.

There are still two other objections that may be raised against the use of the term "Hispanic" to characterize the philosophy of the countries of the Iberian peninsula and Latin America. One may wish to object, for example, that the term "Hispanic" is not only Eurocentric but in fact indicates the relation of dominator-dominated which for several centuries characterized the relations between the countries in the peninsula and their colonies in America. Would not the use of this term, then, tend to perpetuate a spirit of domination which would stand in the way of the intellectual liberation of Latin America?

Notice that this objection does not challenge the accuracy or usefulness of this term for describing the actual historical reality of Latin America. The objection challenges its use because it regards the term as dangerous insofar as it can be used to perpetuate a situation which is morally wrong and thus intolerable. Could the use of the expression "Hispanic philosophy" promote the dominance of Iberian philosophy, thus leading to further intellectual enslavement in Latin America?

My response to this objection is twofold. First I would like to respond as a historian. Even if it were the case that in fact the term "Hispanic" carried with it the kind of baggage which could stand in the way of the intellectual liberation of Latin America, the use of the term would still be justified as long as it were applied to a historical period where it served to characterize accurately the historical situation. The historian is not concerned with what it should have been but with what actually was the case. My claim is precisely that the history of Iberian and Latin American philosophy up to the present, and particularly in the period that concerns us, supports the use of such a term, bringing to the fore historical connections which otherwise would remain hidden.

Second, although the term may at some point have been used in a way which gave support to the objection, I believe this is no longer the case. As it is generally used today, I believe the term simply refers to anything that has to do with Spain, the Spanish language, Latin America, or the Iberian peninsula.[24] Thus, I do not think its use can result

---

24. In Latin America and Spain, the term is frequently used to refer to things Spanish, thus excluding the Portuguese or Brazilian; see note 6 above. There are some subgroups of the Hispanic community in this country, moreover, who object to the use of the term to refer to themselves. Whether they are justified or not is irrelevant for the historiographical thesis of this paper. Nonetheless, it should be noted that most of the arguments adduced in this direction are based on limited knowledge of the history of the Iberian peninsula or of Latin America. See "Chicanos, not Hispanics" (anonymous

in the perpetuation of a relation of dominator-dominated in a way that would promote the continuance of a subservient role for Latin America.

The second objection is that the use of this term is misleading because it suggests that Latin American philosophy depended throughout its history on the thought of the Iberian peninsula, whereas in fact this is not so. Indeed, so the argument goes, after the colonial period Latin America turned toward France, England, and Germany for philosophical inspiration, ignoring what went on in the peninsula.

In response I must first agree that at least since around 1750, Latin America has been heavily influenced by the thought of philosophers from France, England, and Germany. But this does not militate against the notion of a Hispanic philosophy for two reasons. First, the term "Hispanic philosophy" as used here is not meant to convey a sense of philosophical dependence of Latin America on the peninsula. My point in using the term does not concern philosophical dependence, but historical relations in general. Second, it is not only in Latin America that the influence of France, England, and Germany has been felt, but also in the Iberian peninsula itself.[25] In this sense, there is much that looks the same in Latin America and in the Iberian peninsula. Finally, much of the influence of French, English, and German thinkers, whether we Latin Americans like it or not, did come through Iberia. The case of Ortega's introducing German thought in Argentina and elsewhere, and the influence of the *transterrados* in Mexico and other countries, should suffice as illustrations.

In short, the category of Hispanic philosophy is a useful one for the description and understanding of the history of the philosophical thought of Latin America and the countries of the Iberian peninsula. Whether it will continue to be so is, of course, a matter to be determined by the future. For the present it serves well the purpose of those who wish to understand the thought of the world created by the European discovery of America.

---

paper from the Third World forum, Montréal, 14 March 1990); Earl Shorris, "Latino Sí. Hispanic, No," *New York Times*, 28 October 1992; Shorris, *Latinos: A Biography of the People* (New York: W. W. Norton, 1992), xv–xvii; and David González, "What's the Problem with 'Hispanic'," *New York Times*, 15 November 1992.

25. See Abellán's monumental history of Spanish thought (see note 2), where such influences are recorded.

II. THE BEGINNING AND GOLDEN AGE

Having clarified the notion of Hispanic philosophy, I must turn now to the part of it which concerns us in particular. The period in question covers, like the *Siglo de Oro* of Spanish letters, more than a century: from the beginning of the sixteenth century to the middle of the seventeenth. Its first notable figure is Juan de Zumárraga (1468?–1548) and its last is Juan de Santo Tomás (Jean Poinsot) (1589–1644). In between are Bartolomé de Las Casas (1484–1566), Vasco de Quiroga (1487?–1568), Juan Luis Vives (1492–1540), Francisco de Vitoria (1492/3–1546), Domingo de Soto (1494–1560), Alfonso de Castro (1495–1558), Alonso de la Vera Cruz (1504?–1584), Francisco de Salazar (1505–1575), Melchior Cano (1509–1560), Pedro da Fonseca (1528–1599), Domingo Báñez (1528–1604), Tomás de Mercado (1530?–1575), Francisco Toletus (1532–1596), Luis de Molina (1535–1600), Benito Pereira (1535?–1610), Juan de Mariana (1536–1624), Antonio Rubio (1548–1615), Francisco Suárez (1548–1617), Gabriel Vázquez (1549–1604), Antonio Arias (1564–1603), and Alonso Briceño (1587?–1669?), among many others. Territorially, it covers the Iberian peninsula and the Iberian colonies in the New World. In the Iberian peninsula certain universities stand out, such as Salamanca and Coimbra, but others, like Valladolid, Segovia, Alcalá, and Evora, follow closely. In the New World, the most important centers of activity are found in Mexico and Peru, particularly in the capital cities of Mexico City and Lima, although there are also developments in other areas.

It is important to note both that this period deserves to be regarded as the golden age of Hispanic philosophy because of the number and brilliance of its members and the influence they exerted on others, and that it is also the first period of philosophical development that properly merits being called Hispanic. It merits the name for two reasons. First, this is the first time that a new intellectual unity that can be distinguished from European philosophy is formed by the Iberian peninsula and the Latin American colonies. There is for the first time in history a political unity of the kingdoms of the Iberian peninsula and thus of the colonies of those kingdoms. There is also religious unity after the expulsion of the Muslims and the Jews. In addition, there is a strong sense of mission that permeates the activities and thinking at the time. This is the period during which the international medieval intellectual union which had characterized Europe for over a thousand years breaks up under the stresses of humanism, the Reformation, and the political pressures exerted by modern European states. Moreover, the Iberian world, in spite of its strong political and ideological interests in Europe, gradually directs its attention toward the colonies of the New World, the extraordinary opportunities they make available, and the enormous demands those colonies exert on the peninsula. Iberia, then, not only becomes unified in various ways but at the same time becomes increasingly separated from the rest of Europe and closer to the New World. This is reflected in the intellectual life of both the peninsula and the colonized territories and thus justifies for the first time the category "Hispanic."

Prior to this time it makes no sense to employ this category in historical accounts. The Roman philosophers of Iberian origin, such as Seneca, belonged culturally and intellectually to a unit that was centered elsewhere and extended well beyond Iberia. Likewise, Islamic philosophers of Iberian origin, such as Averroës, belonged to a world which gravitated toward a different axis. Something similar can be said of Maimonides and other Jewish philosopher-theologians of the medieval period, for their history grouped them in ways which had little to do with the Iberian peninsula. Likewise, medieval Scholastics from the peninsula were part of the greater unit represented by European Scholasticism. They were at home in that philosophy and their historical and intellectual relations were not so much to each other as to the common heritage of the age. Indeed, the agenda that moves them is centered primarily elsewhere, in Paris, Oxford, Cambridge, and Rome. All this changes in the sixteenth century. Although the Iberian and Latin American philosophers of the time continue to address issues of general concern to Europeans and to be influenced by sources that originate outside the peninsula and Latin America, there is a strong surge of interest in problems and issues which arise from the historically unique situation posed by the discovery, colonization, and evangelization of the New World. Moreover, there is also, in part as a result of common interests, but also as a result of other factors, a tightening of the relations among philosophers of these various lands, who exchange ideas and dispute among themselves in ways which were not enacted before. Indeed, some studies show a strong predilection in some of the Hispanic authors of this period for their Hispanic contemporaries.[26]

This leads me to the second reason why this is the first historical period for which the term "Hispanic philosophy" is justified. The philosophy produced in the Iberian countries and their colonies between 1500 and 1650 springs forth to a great extent as a response of a well-

---

26. See, for example, Hanisch Espíndola, *En torno a la filosofía en Chile (1594–1810)* (Santiago: Universidad Católica de Chile, 1963), 36–37.

established Iberian Scholastic tradition to the issues that confront Iberian and Latin American intellectuals at the time and that result from the discovery and colonization of the New World. It is a philosophy, then, grounded in an Iberian tradition and in the consideration of issues and problems of which Iberian and Latin American philosophers had first-hand experience in most cases. This lends their philosophy an autochthonous character which is missing in most subsequent Iberian and Latin American thought. Indeed, many Iberian and Latin American philosophers have complained repeatedly about the derivative nature of more recent Iberian and Latin American philosophical thought. They charge, often with reason, that philosophical thought in these areas has resulted from uncritical borrowing from non-Hispanic, European, and Anglo-American sources, and thus lacks originality and authenticity.[27] The reasons for this lacking are to be found precisely in the fact that Iberian and Latin American philosophers have forgotten their roots and that philosophy must begin in human experience. It does not pay to talk about what others say if we have no first-hand experience of what gave rise to what they say. This is, of course, what makes the sixteenth and early seventeenth centuries different. The thinkers of that period were not only well-grounded historically in their intellectual traditions, but concerned themselves with what they knew best. That is why they can be accurately regarded as Hispanic philosophers and why they were able to excel to the degree they did.

The development of the kind of intellectual unity in the sixteenth century which I have used to justify the category of Hispanic philosophy can be understood if one considers the four challenges faced by the period in question: the discovery of the New World, the rise of Renaissance humanism, the spread of the Reformation, and the growth of skepticism. The discovery of the New World had a profound and lasting impact on the thinking of Europeans. It posed for Iberians in particular a set of problems that were new and required immediate solution. They were confronted with hitherto unknown peoples with different cultures and religious beliefs who nonetheless possessed enormous riches and who quickly became subject to them. What were the rights of these people? Should Christianity be imposed on them? Should they be treated as slaves? Who was the rightful owner of the riches that hitherto had belonged to them? What should the conquerors make of the natives' laws and traditions? Questions such as these were

27. The most eloquent articulation of this criticism is provided by Augusto Salazar Bondy in his ¿ *Existe una filosofía de nuestra América?* (Mexico: Siglo XXI, 1968); and his *Sentido y problema del pensamiento hispano-americano*, with English translation by Arthur Berdtson (Lawrence: University of Kansas Center for Latin American Studies, 1969).

raised and had to be answered concerning most aspects of the lives of the conquered peoples, from general aspects of the relations among peoples considered as nations to particular aspects of daily living. Issues ranged from international mercantile laws to the validity of pre-Columbian marriages.[28]

Obviously, the discovery of America represented an enormous challenge to intellectuals in the Iberian peninsula, forcing them to raise and deal with issues that they had not confronted before. This oriented their thinking toward new issues, away from traditionally travelled European areas and into new territories. The impact of the discovery on philosophy was an awakening to the need to deal with legal and ethical issues which were new to the times and which tended both to form a core of concerns which tied Iberian and Latin American thinkers together and at the same time to distance them from their European counterparts who had other concerns and agendas.[29]

The other three challenges faced by Iberian and Latin American philosophers and theologians at this time had a similar effect of strengthening the ties among them and distancing them from the rest of Europe, supporting their historical interrelations and thus the development of a Hispanic philosophical universe. But this effect was not accomplished in the same way as was accomplished by the discovery of the New World. The challenges of humanism, the Reformation, and skepticism did not open the exploration of new themes that would draw Iberian and Latin American philosophers closer. What these challenges did was to alert them to the need to come together in order to collect their forces and repel those whom most of them perceived as enemies. The need to defend what they considered to be the true Faith, to purge it from contamination by unorthodox or dangerous doctrines, and to vanquish those who threatened it, had the effect of drawing these philosophers together in a way that had not happened prior to this time.[30]

28. The rest of this discussion follows in part a section of my "Scholasticism: A Bridge between Classical Antiquity and Colonial Latin American Thought," in *The Classical Tradition and the Americas*, ed. W. Haase et al., vol. 2, forthcoming.

29. There is much literature on this topic. Among the most recent publications that give an idea of the issues in question is Luciano Pereña, *The Rights and Obligations of Indians and Spaniards in the New World* (Salamanca: Universidad Pontificia de Salamanca and Catholic University of America, 1992). The issues in question were not only moral and legal, but extended to matters of commerce and economics. See, for example, M. Grice-Hutchinson, *The School of Salamanca. Readings in Spanish Monetary Theory, 1544–1605* (Oxford: Clarendon Press, 1952); and R. Sierra Bravo, *El pensamiento social y económico de la escolástica desde sus orígenes al comienzo del catolicismo social*, 2 vols. (Madrid: Consejo Superior de Investigaciones Científicas, 1975).

30. Cf. Luis Gil Fernández, *Estudios de humanismo y tradición clásica* (Madrid: Editorial Complutense, 1984), 15–94.

The impact of humanism on the Iberian peninsula and its colonies was felt quite early and, although some Iberian and Latin American intellectuals were receptive to humanism, the movement was generally perceived by ecclesiastical and governmental authorities as a threat to the orthodox Faith.[31] The discovery of new literary, philosophical, and artistic works from the ancient world had given rise not only to a renewed interest in pagan ideas, but to a change of attitude in the intellectual community that was taken by many to pose a threat to the integrity of Christianity. Humanism was considered a threat, then, because it looked to pagan antiquity as an ideal era whose values had to be emulated. The Christian Middle Ages and in particular Scholasticism also had looked to antiquity for enlightenment, but the attitude of the humanists was broader and less cautious. Scholastics borrowed from the past selectively, filtering what they borrowed through the sieve of Christian doctrine, and accepting only what they thought could be harmonized with that doctrine.[32] In spite of the borrowing *en masse* that took place in the thirteenth century, a suspicious attitude concerning pagan antiquity was never absent, as the repeated condemnations of heretical and pagan doctrines illustrate.[33] The humanists, by contrast, were attracted to the ancients and emulated less discriminately the forms and values of the period as displayed in art and literature. Their concern with beauty, the human body, ancient rites, literary style, and pagan religious ideas was a source of concern to ecclesiastical authorities. Although some humanists were devoted Christians and used their textual and linguistic skills for the service of the Faith, many were interested in the recovery of classical knowledge and art, not for the sake of enriching the Christian faith, but for their own sake. This was certainly different from the attitude of medieval Scholastics and, moreover, appeared potentially dangerous to those in the Iberian peninsula and its colonies who wished to preserve the medieval worldview.[34]

Another challenge, the Reformation, had an effect on Iberian and Latin American philosophers and theologians similar to that of humanism. Indeed, it posed an even greater threat than humanism to the

---

31. J. Fuster, *Rebeldes y heterodoxos* (Barcelona: Edicions Ariel, 1972), 72.

32. Bonaventure, *Collationes in Hexaemeron* 19, in *Opera omnia*, vol. 5 (Ad Claras Aquas: Collegium S. Bonaventurae, 1882–1902), 422.

33. The most important of these condemnations took place in Paris, in 1277. See Etienne Gilson, *History of Christian Philosophy in the Middle Ages* (New York: Random House, 1954), 402–10.

34. The conduct of Renaissance popes like Leo X did not help to assuage the fears of such people. For a readable account of Leo X and other Renaissance popes, see E. R. Chamberlin, *The Bad Popes* (New York: Dorset Press, 1969).

Church, for it was a challenge within the Church's own ranks and involved theology, the Church's conceptual foundation. Moreover, this rebellion against institutionalized Christianity gained considerable political support in some parts of Europe. There had been heretical challenges to the Church from within its ranks during the Middle Ages. Large revolts had occurred in southern France, as happened with the Albingensians, for example. There had also been serious threats to Christianity from without, primarily from Islam. But the Reformation was a different sort of movement for various reasons, three of which stand out: first, it was a challenge based on criticisms concerning the corruption prevalent at the Papal court; second, it had strong political overtones, which lent it power in a way that some of the earlier reform movements had lacked; third, it was a theological challenge arising from within the Church itself. These factors combined to make the Reformation a most powerful threat and one that endangered the stability and future of the Church.

The final challenge that helped to draw Iberians and Latin Americans together is less defined than the others, but not for that reason less effective. This was the rise of skepticism. Skepticism had not been strong in the Middle Ages. It was known primarily through Augustine, who had argued against it in *Contra academicos* in particular. In fact, skepticism had a bad name among Scholastics, who used it to accuse and condemn their opponents.[35] Yet, there were many Scholastics who adopted a skeptical or somewhat skeptical stance in order to defend those tenets of the faith that they thought could not be defended if reason were held to be the ultimate arbiter of belief. Thus, there was a background to the skepticism that developed in the sixteenth century with authors like Montaigne, and which was so decisively to affect the course of early modern philosophy. The skepticism of Montaigne, however, went far beyond that adopted by some Scholastics and did not aim to support the Faith. Montaigne's question, *Que sais-je?* combined with a tolerance of what ecclesiastical authorities considered an easy morality, was regarded as an unwelcome development by those who considered themselves champions of the Christian faith.[36]

35. See John Duns Scotus's charge of skepticism against Henry of Ghent in *Opus oxoniense* I, dist. 3, q. 4, a. 1, in Duns Scotus, *Philosophical Writings*, ed. Allan Wolter (London: Nelson, 1963), 103–6. For discussions of skepticism in the Middle Ages, see K. Michalski, *La philosophie au XIVe siècle. Six études* (Frankfurt: Minerva, 1969); and Mauricio Beuchot, "Escepticismo en la edad media: El caso de Nicolás de Autrecourt," *Revista Latinoamericana de Filosofía* 15, no. 3 (1989): 307–19.

36. For a treatment of the growth of the skeptical movement in the sixteenth century and the beginning of the reaction to it, see Richard Popkin, *The History of Scepticism from Erasmus to Descartes* (Assen: Van Gorcum, 1964).

The response of the Church to humanism, the Reformation, and skepticism was swift. First, there was a movement toward reform led by members of the Church hierarchy which aimed to stamp out corruption and also to regularize Christian doctrine, rites, and laws. The most effective instruments used to achieve these aims were the Council of Trent (1545–1563) and the Inquisition. The Council took care of doctrinal matters, whereas the Inquisition was charged with the task of enforcing the new standards. Second, the movement of renewal affected also the rank-and-file members of the Church. Among grassroots efforts the most successful was the foundation of the Society of Jesus by Ignatius of Loyola (1491–1556). This religious order became the symbol of reformed Roman Catholicism and one of the most effective instruments of the Counter-Reformation.

In the Iberian peninsula and the Iberian colonies, the reaction to the use of humanistic, Reformation, and skeptical ideas by the ecclesiastical establishment was also quick. Humanists, reformers, and skeptics were portrayed as mixtures of grammarians and heretics whose influence had to be eradicated.[37] This was achieved in various ways, including the exercise of strict controls on the publication and distribution of books and the general discouragement of book learning.[38]

The intellectual climate at the time in which the Iberian thought of the sixteenth and seventeenth centuries flourished, therefore, was a defensive one. The Church was under siege and felt it had to fight its assailants. The result among Roman Catholic intellectuals was a great effort to rethink and defend traditional Christian theology. Thus we find an abundance of literature dealing with doctrinal controversies cast both in apologetic and theological modes. Both modes are amply documented in the history of the Church prior to this time, but in the sixteenth and seventeenth centuries there was a renewed interest in them. Moreover, the polemical and defensive tone of some of these writings contrasts with the tone of many earlier Scholastics. The Iberian and Latin American thought of the period mirrors these characteristics. The effect of humanism, the Reformation, and skepticism in the sixteenth and seventeenth centuries, then, was to make Iberian and Latin American philosophers and theologians close ranks so that they might overcome these challenges to the established Church.

37. See notes 30 and 31 above.
38. See M. de la Pinta Llorente, *La Inquisición española y los problemas de la cultura y de la intolerancia* (Madrid: Ediciones Cultura Hispánica, 1953–58); M. Defourneaux, *Inquisición y censura de libros en la España del siglo XVIII* (Madrid: Taurus, 1973); and Vicente G. Quesada, *La vida intelectual en la América española durante los siglos XVI, XVII, y XVIII* (Buenos Aires: Arnoldo Moen y Hermano, 1910), 3–33.

As noted, the attitude developed by the Roman Church in response to the challenges of humanism, the Reformation, and skepticism was not peculiar to the Iberian countries and their colonies, but the leadership of the Church's response fell largely to the Iberians—to the government of the peninsula where arms were required, and to its philosophers and theologians where intellectual weapons were in order. Latin Americans, of course, did not participate as actively in this affair, but their activities were regulated to a great extent by what was taking place in the peninsula, making them dependent on and subsidiary to it. Nowhere is this more evident, for example, than in the control of reading materials allowed into the colonies. Although there have been some exaggerated claims concerning the control exercised by peninsular authorities over the circulation of books in the New World, it is evident that efforts were made in this direction and that to a certain extent the peninsula established the intellectual parameters within which intellectuals from the New World were supposed to work.[39] This, naturally, tended to separate the New World from intellectual developments occurring beyond the Pyrenees, and to tie it closely to peninsular concerns and news.

Apart from the four challenges discussed, there are two other factors that need to be mentioned because they also helped shape the course of Iberian and Latin American thought and thus the development of Hispanic philosophy. These two factors are the relatively late emergence of Iberian Scholasticism and the close relations between Church and State that developed in the Iberian peninsula.

The relatively late emergence of Iberian Scholasticism meant that this movement was influenced by well-established traditions associated with various religious orders. From the thirteenth century onwards, religious orders, particularly the powerful Franciscans and Dominicans, had appropriated certain ideas and authors, and they promoted them with extraordinary zeal. The Franciscans devoted themselves to the study and dissemination of the thought of Augustine and Duns Scotus, whereas the Dominicans worked under the doctrinal tutelage of Thomas Aquinas and, through him, Aristotle. This commitment to a certain set of ideas and to certain authors became accentuated in some writers as time went on, lending the later Middle Ages an overall ideological tone. There was, however, a break from this feeling of partisanship in the early sixteenth century, perhaps as a result of the influence of humanism and the overall rebellion against the excessive technicism that characterized the practice of philosophy in most European uni-

39. See note 38 above.

versities, particularly in Paris, at the time.⁴⁰ But this reprieve ended quickly after the rise of the Jesuits and the subsequent growth of rivalry between them and the Dominicans.

The respect for well-established conceptual traditions, together with the large literature inherited from the thirteenth and fourteenth centuries, helped develop, moreover, an encyclopedic attitude in which recovery and exposition became central to the scholastic enterprise. Not that this attitude had been lacking in earlier stages of Scholasticism. From the very beginning, the Middle Ages displayed a concern with the recovery and preservation of the past. Thus we find throughout the period many encyclopedias of knowledge. The earliest successful attempts in this direction were *De institutione divinarum litterarum* of Cassiodorus (477?–570?) and *Etymologiae* of Isidore of Seville (d. 636). Both of these owed debts to earlier classical sources—as is the case of Isidore with Suetonius Pratum, for example—and both works were greatly successful, the first owing to its elegant and easy style, and the second because of the mass of material it contained.⁴¹ This kind of effort went on, as is clear from the *Speculum majus* of Vincent of Beauvais (1190/1200?–1264?), produced in the thirteenth century, and the *Crestià*, undertaken by Francesc Eiximenis (1340–1409) at the end of the fourteenth century.

In the sixteenth and seventeenth centuries, the encyclopedic emphasis on gathering all available information surrounding a topic became more pronounced. So much had been produced, and was of such high quality, that it was natural for late Scholastics to feel they had to preserve it and at least take it into account in their own thinking. For this reason we find during the period much that is primarily expository, and many works whose character is informative. This attitude is displayed even in the work of the most original Iberian Scholastics, such as Francisco Suárez. In many ways, and in spite

---

40. For the technical character of the philosophy of this period, see Carlos Noreña, *Studies in Spanish Renaissance Thought* (The Hague: Nijhoff, 1975); R. García Villoslada, *La Universidad de París durante los estudios de Francisco de Vitoria, O.P. (1507–1522)* (Rome: Universitas Gregoriana, 1938); V. Muñoz Delgado, *La lógica nominalista en la universidad de Salamanca (1510–1530)*; V. Muñoz Delgado, "La lógica en Salamanca durante la primera mitad del siglo XVI," *Salmanticensis* 14 (1967): 171–207; V. Muñoz Delgado, "La obra lógica de los españoles en París (1500–1525)," *Estudios* 26 (1970): 209–80; V. Muñoz Delgado, "Lógica hispano-portuguesa hasta 1600 (notas bibliográfico-doctrinales)," *Repertorio de historia de las ciencias eclesiásticas en España* 4 (1972): 9–122; and E. J. Ashworth, *Language and Logic in the Post-Medieval Period* (Dordrecht: Reidel, 1974). There were some good reasons for the criticism of humanists like Luis Vives and others.

41. See Peter L. Schmidt's "Suetons 'Pratum' seit Wessner (1917)," in W. Haase et al., eds., *The Classical Tradition and the Americas*. See also Gilson, *History of Christian Philosophy*, 107.

of their originality in many areas, Suárez's *Disputationes metaphysicae* (1597) constitute an encyclopedia of metaphysics in which every topic, every author of importance, and every relevant argument is carefully presented, examined, and evaluated.[42] Unfortunately, this emphasis on the past sometimes obscures the brilliant contributions of the period and has mistakenly led some historians to characterize the period as sterile.

The second factor that played a major role in shaping the Hispanic thought of the period was the close relationship that developed between the Roman Church and the Iberian states, particularly the Spanish state. In the fifteenth century the Roman Church became the state church in Spain and the Pope granted the Spanish kings the right to appoint the highest members of the hierarchy in the country. This extraordinary development made Spain a *de facto* theocracy in which the interests of the state and the interests of the Church were identified. It is easy to understand the reasons for this situation. First, Spain had become the main defender of the Faith against the threat of Islam. Having successfully expelled the Moors from Iberian soil after a seven-hundred-year struggle, Spain was in a favorable position to continue the defense of Christianity throughout the Mediterranean. Moreover, Spain was poised to become, and in fact did become, the first and most powerful modern European nation. Its kings, who became also emperors of the Holy Roman Empire for a time, controlled not only the Iberian peninsula but also territories in Italy, France, the Netherlands, and Germany, and thus exercised extraordinary power.

Second, the Spanish struggle against Islam had been both national and religious; the Spanish kings had fought in the name of the Cross both for territory and the spread of Christianity. Therefore, it made sense to extend this political, military, and religious struggle against the reformers.

Third, Spain had recently discovered America and this provided an unusual opportunity for both colonization and missionary work. Since the Church had no means to organize the indoctrination of the newly discovered lands, it was natural that the Spanish crown be entrusted with the task, enforcing once more the bonds that united Church and state in the peninsula.

Fourth, the preoccupation with the *Reconquista* had to some extent kept Spain away from the intellectual developments associated with the

---

42. Other examples are the *Cursus Conimbricensis* and Juan de Santo Tomás's *Cursus philosophicus*. See John Trentman, "Scholasticism in the Seventeenth Century," in Kretzman et al., eds., *The Cambridge History of Later Medieval Philosophy*, 835–37.

early Renaissance, making it an ideal place of operations for the defense against humanists, reformers, and skeptics. A militant faith was needed to defeat the challenges faced by the Church, and Spain certainly had such a faith. Spain had the faith, the power, and the means to conduct the struggle, and so it was to Spain that the task fell. Consequently, philosophical thought in the Iberian peninsula became subject to political influence and functioned in many instances as a tool of the Spanish government.

As a result of the two factors identified (the late emergence of scholasticism and the close relations between Church and state) and the four challenges it faced (the discovery of the New World, humanism, the Reformation, and skepticism), the philosophy of this period in Iberia and in its colonies developed close ties, which separated it from the rest of Europe and made it chart a course on its own, but it also developed some characteristic features which tended to distinguish it from prior and subsequent European thought. It was, for example, more encyclopedic, expository, and eclectic; it had a defensive, apologetic, and theological emphasis; it had the state and its power behind it and thus was partly influenced by political considerations that affected the state; and it developed a set of new issues dealing with international law and human rights.

III. HISPANIC PHILOSOPHY AND EUROPEAN PHILOSOPHY

For our purposes, the most significant aspect of all this is the separation of Hispanic philosophy from the mainstream of European thought, for in spite of considerable popularity at the time, most of the Hispanic philosophers of this period have been largely forgotten. Suárez, Vitoria, Molina, and some of the other authors listed earlier were common names in the philosophical controversies of the time. Suárez's *Disputationes metaphysicae,* for example, was printed in more than seventeen editions outside the Iberian peninsula between 1597 and 1636, whereas Descartes's *Meditations* were edited only nine times between 1641 and 1700.[43] Yet Descartes is considered a major figure in the history of philosophy, whereas Suárez is hardly known. Indeed, if we were to ask the more than eleven thousand philosophers who teach in the United States today to tell us a few facts about Suárez, I am sure only a couple hundred, if that many, would be able to reply. Yet Suárez is without a doubt the most important and well-known His-

---

43. See J. Iriarte, "La proyección sobre Europa de una gran metafísica, o Suárez en la filosofía en los días del Barroco," *Razón y Fe,* número extraordinario (1948): 236.

panic philosopher of the period. Only a dozen American philosophers have ever heard of Fonseca or Rubio.

We may ask, then, two questions: first, Why have these philosophers been forgotten? Second, How can their thought constitute a golden age, as I have claimed?

The answer to the first question is to be found in the very points I have been making concerning the development of Hispanic philosophy. For the reasons given, the philosophy of the Iberian peninsula and its Latin American colonies became increasingly isolated from European philosophy, thus losing the historical ties it had had with it. Hispanic philosophy turned in upon itself, concerned about the peculiar and pressing problems faced by Hispanic society, and, in fear of European developments that threatened its political and religious stability, it looked for support in the past. Thus, it not only became isolated from the mainstream philosophical developments in the West, but consciously rejected these developments in favor of its medieval foundations. The result was to be expected. European philosophy continued on its own way and came to regard the philosophy practiced in the Iberian peninsula and its colonies as marginal and regressive. For a while, the political and military power of Spain ensured that Iberian voices were taken seriously outside the peninsula, but the decline in political and military power in the seventeenth century contributed to the view of Iberian philosophy as stagnant and retrograde. This view slowly extended to all Hispanic philosophy and thought, leading to the general perception that there is little of importance to be found in it.[44] Thus were forgotten the original and extraordinary contributions to philosophy of the Hispanic authors of the sixteenth and seventeenth centuries.

This brings me to the answer to the second question, namely, how can the thought of the Hispanic philosophers of this period constitute a golden age? Hispanic philosophy in the period we have been exploring stands out not only in the history of Hispanic philosophy as a whole, but also in the complete history of Western philosophy. It is true that Hispanic philosophy has its roots in medieval philosophy and that its Scholastic language and theological concerns make it look as if it belonged in an earlier age, from which it is but a derivative development. But these characteristics are in many ways deceiving, for the philosophy

---

44. Indeed, Hispanic philosophers themselves are relentless in their repetition of this view. Cf. E. Villanueva, "Philosophical Analysis in Mexico," in *Philosophical Analysis in Latin America*, ed. Jorge J. E. Gracia et al. (Dordrecht: Reidel, 1984), 170; and Salazar Bondy, "The Meaning and Problem of Hispanic American Thought," in Gracia, ed., *Latin American Philosophy in the Twentieth Century*, 234.

of this period makes possible much that was to come in early modern philosophy and breaks with medieval thought in significant ways. I will mention only three of the many areas in which this is evident.

First, as is clear from what was said earlier, the philosophy of this period formulated and tried to address many philosophical issues which were new to the history of Western philosophy. These issues had to do with the discovery and colonization of the New World and later came to form a permanent part of the concerns that Western philosophy has addressed. Authors like Las Casas and Vitoria were pioneers who opened up new areas of investigation in philosophy. Not only that, but their views formed the basis for the kind of humane and liberal thinking that was to become mainstream in European philosophy.

Second, Hispanic philosophers from this period often went beyond the limits of what had been achieved in Scholastic thought prior to this century, deepening their analyses and extending the parameters established by earlier Scholastics. This is evident in most of the authors of the period. Mariana's notorious doctrine of tyrannicide and Molina's much-discussed view of middle knowledge are just two dramatic examples of how far the thinking of these authors exceeded anything taught in the previous ages.

Finally, and perhaps most importantly, these Hispanic philosophers, despite a deep faith and a desire to preserve and support traditional Christian teaching, took bold and conscious steps to keep philosophy separate from theology. Perhaps the most stark example of this phenomenon is to be found in Suárez, who not only was a devout Christian, but saw his primary role as the understanding and defense of Christian doctrine. In spite of this, he consciously separated metaphysics from theology. Suárez's contribution in this regard can be seen in both the stated intention of his *Disputationes metaphysicae* and the method that he employs in it. The fact that he calls himself a philosopher, that he avoids arguments based on faith in philosophical contexts, and that he apologizes for dealing, even incidentally, with theological matters in a work of philosophy, should be sufficient to make the point.[45] Although many of the masters who taught liberal arts in the Middle Ages were not theologians, and taught subjects independently of theology, the most famous Scholastics of the age considered themselves theologians and their philosophical views were generally presented within theological works. Moreover, even though many Scholastics distinguished between

---

45. I have dealt with these points in more detail in my "Francisco Suárez: The Man in History," *American Catholic Philosophical Quarterly* 65, no. 3 (1991): 262–65; and my "Suárez and Later Scholasticism," in *The Routledge History of Medieval Philosophy*, ed. John Marenbon, forthcoming.

theology and philosophy, none of them would have apologized for the introduction of theological matter in a philosophical context, and most of them used both faith and reason to argue for both philosophical and theological views. But such a procedure is abandoned in Suárez's *Disputationes*. Occasionally, he does bring up a theological point, but in such cases the aim is to show the reader how to apply metaphysical principles to theology rather than to use theology to prove philosophy. This secular emphasis in metaphysics both sets Suárez apart from his medieval predecessors and situates him at the beginning of the modern tradition.[46]

What has been said about Suárez's views concerning the relation of philosophy and theology, together with the formulation of new issues and the development of original views mentioned earlier, illustrates the importance of Hispanic philosophy in the sixteenth and seventeenth centuries for the development of European philosophy. Indeed, the influence of Hispanic philosophy on European philosophy at this time was substantial.[47] Early modern philosophers from Locke and Descartes to Wolff and Leibniz are full of the language used, and sometimes introduced, by Hispanic philosophers of this period and often explicitly refer to Hispanic philosophers.

As to this period's enduring philosophical importance, I believe that time will vindicate it. In my own experience, I have dealt with no philosophical issue for which I have not found much help in the writings of these philosophers. Consider the problem of individuation, to which I have devoted considerable time in recent years. I have yet to find a treatment of this issue in the history of philosophy before the twentieth century that, measured by philosophical sophistication and comprehensiveness, even approaches Suárez's discussion of it in his fifth *Disputation*.[48] This is but one example. In areas of contemporary interest, such as semiotics, the philosophy of language, and logic, the work of Hispanic philosophers in the golden age holds vast reservoirs of inter-

---

46. For further discussion of the relation of Suárez's metaphysics to early modern philosophy, see my "Suárez's Conception of Metaphysics: A Step in the Direction of Mentalism?" *American Catholic Philosophical Quarterly* 65, no. 3 (1991): 287–310; Jean-François Courtine, "Le project Suárezien de la metaphysique," *Archives de Philosophie* 42 (1979): 236; and Charles Lohr, "Metaphysics," in Schmitt et al., eds., *The Cambridge History of Renaissance Philosophy*, 611ff.

47. See notes 15 and 43 above; and William A. Wallace, "The Early Jesuits and the Heritage of Domingo de Soto," *History and Technology* 4 (1987): 301–20. There was also influence outside of philosophy; see William A. Wallace, *Galileo and His Sources* (Princeton: Princeton University Press, 1984).

48. See my "Francisco Suárez," in *Individuation in Scholasticism: The Later Middle Ages and the Counter-Reformation* (Albany: SUNY Press, 1994), 475–510; and my *Suárez on Individuation* (Milwaukee: Marquette University Press, 1982).

esting, original, and valuable materials.⁴⁹ Most of these materials, however, are not easily accessible; they are available only in old and difficult-to-find editions. And, of course, the materials are in Latin, a language with which very few philosophers are familiar today. Thus, the job of those who wish to bring to light the contributions of this period to the history of philosophy is not easy, but I believe the enterprise should nonetheless deliver ample rewards. I finish, then, with a call to renew the effort to recover the contributions of Hispanic philosophy in its golden age.⁵⁰

49. See, for example, *"Tractatus de signis": The Semiotic of John Poinsot*, translated and presented in bilingual format by John Deely in consultation with Ralph A. Powell (Berkeley: University of California Press, 1985).

50. A shorter version of this paper was read at the conference "Hispanic Philosophy in the Age of Discovery," The Catholic University of America, October 1992. The paper, except for minor modifications, was printed in *Review of Metaphysics* 46 (March 1993): 475–502. I am grateful to Edward Mahoney and William Irwin for offering some useful criticisms on an early version of the paper.

PART II

2 The Philosophical Discussion of the Legitimacy of the Conquest of Mexico in the Sixteenth Century

MAURICIO BEUCHOT
Translated by Concepción Abellán

The purpose of this study is to review some of the speculations about the conquest of Mexico, written by two of the scholars who lived there at the time. There were in New Spain thinkers who discussed the legitimacy of the conquest, and who were either contemporary to or slightly older than Francisco de Vitoria. These two theoreticians are Juan de Zumárraga, the first archbishop of Mexico, and Vasco de Quiroga, the first bishop of Michoacán. Their opinion regarding the conquest will be examined and their doctrine will be interpreted and evaluated.

JUAN DE ZUMÁRRAGA

Juan de Zumárraga, born in 1468 or 1469 at Tabira de Durango in Vizcaya, was a great Franciscan missionary. He became the first archbishop of Mexico and was always a defender of the Indians.[1] When he left Spain in 1528, he held the post of elected bishop, but was not formally consecrated until he returned in 1533 to clarify some accusations against him because of his defense of the natives.[2] In 1534 he came back to Mexico, and continued to defend the rights of the Indians, but now as a consecrated bishop. He founded the first *Colegio Mayor* in Mexico, the Santa Cruz de Tlaltelolco College, to provide education to the natives. He also started the San Juan de Letrán College and created

---

1. See J. García Icazbalceta, *Fray Juan de Zumárraga, primer obispo y arzobispo de México* (Buenos Aires: Espasa-Calpe, 1952); and F. de J. Chauvet, *Fray Juan de Zumárraga* (México: Ed. Jus, 1948).
2. See A. M. Carreño, "Un insigne protector de los indios," in his *Misioneros en México* (México: Jus, 1961), 44–48.

and supported the Hospital de San Juan de Dios. He promoted the foundation of the university and the importance of the printing press. He died in 1548.

During his lifetime, not only did Zumárraga concretely practice the defense of the Indians, but he also wrote theoretical works in which he defended doctrinally the human rights of the natives in a Scholastic fashion, as his *Segundo parecer sobre la esclavitud* shows.[3] While in some of his other writings he has a humanistic attitude, in this work he follows a clearly Scholastic approach, which is, in fact, the tendency of most missionaries. The work includes, however, some Renaissance influences, but in a derivative manner. It is most curious that, in this *parecer*, he gives the impression of agreeing with the main views of the School of Salamanca, at whose head were Vitoria and Soto. Herrejón dates Zumárraga's *parecer* of 1536, and it is known that Vitoria's *Relectio de indis* was composed between 1538 and 1539, thus making it impossible for Zumárraga to have drawn on Vitoria's *Relectio*. In fact, the first writings in which Vitoria deals with the subject of the Indians were written no earlier than 1534, two years before Zumárraga's *parecer*, making it difficult to believe that Zumárraga knew them, particularly since he returned to Mexico in 1534.[4] It is however possible that Zumárraga drew on the arguments under discussion while he was in Spain.

Arguments about the Legitimacy of the Conquest

Zumárraga faced, from very early on, the theorizing about the legitimacy of the conquest. The Viceroy Antonio de Mendoza sent him a questionnaire with three queries, one of which asked whether it was legitimate to make slaves of war and another asking if, since the Indian chiefs had declared the war, they could be threatened with being sentenced to slavery and branded as slaves. It must be pointed out that the viceroy assumes that the declaration of war, which does not seem to be anything more than the famous *requerimiento* (request) invented by Palacios Rubio and ferociously fought against by Las Casas, is completely just and sufficient. In this declaration, the Indians were invited to accept Christianity and to submit to the kings of Spain, under the threat of war. Viceroy Mendoza asks the first archbishop of Mexico if it is also legitimate to soften the Indians through slavery, not so much to

3. See Juan de Zumárraga, *Segundo parecer sobre la esclavitud*, in *Textos políticos en la Nueva España*, ed. C. Herrejón Peredo (México: Universidad Nacional Autónoma de México, 1984), 173–183.
4. See Escuela de Salamanca, *Carta magna de los indios* (Madrid: C.S.I.C., 1988), 35.

frighten them as to hasten things, since slavery had been imposed regularly and could be included in the request.

Zumárraga's answer to these two questions are contained in two *pareceres*. I will refer to the second *parecer*, in which the answers are the same as in the first one, but they are presented in a more careful and studied way. It also has the advantage of referring directly to the problem of the legitimacy of the conquest.

To the question about the legitimacy of making slaves of war, in relation to the illegitimacy of the war of conquest, the answer is negative. Zumárraga supports his denial based on six arguments. The first argument is that the war that has been declared against the Indians "is unfair and iniquitous."[5] It does not matter which authority allowed it, particularly considering that those infidels lived peacefully and quietly. He is distinguishing here between the infidels who are so based on ignorance from those who are not ignorant, as Cardinal Cajetan does. If they are infidels through ignorance, they cannot be attacked; preaching should be practiced in this case. On the contrary, if they are infidels with full knowledge, then a distinction must be made between those who do not attack Christians and those who do attack and insult them. In the case of those who live peacefully, even when they are infidels with full knowledge, they should not be attacked; it is only just to bring war to those who insult the Christians, as is the case with the Muslims, for instance. Zumárraga implies that the American Indians were neither infidels with full knowledge, nor did they attack Christians; therefore, the war brought against them cannot be considered just. He declares that, since the Indians live peacefully, they cannot be attacked. On the other hand, the Spaniards have attacked and robbed them, having thus committed injustice against them. The Indians themselves have not even attacked Christianity, neither with blasphemy nor with persecution; furthermore, they have even converted to Christianity of their own will in most cases.

The second argument is that evangelizing should be favored and not impeached. It is, therefore, unjust to bring war against the Indians, and even more unfair to enslave them, because what is looked for is to benefit preaching, and this impeaches preaching of the faith and makes it hateful. The preaching must be done peacefully and through persuasion;[6] whatever is acquired under the pretext of preaching is stealing and demands restitution.

The third argument is that the aim of the pope, when he put the

5. Zumárraga, *Segundo parecer*, 180. All translations are my own.
6. Ibid., 181.

Spanish kings in charge of the Indies, was preaching. This aim has not been maintained; on the contrary, it has been replaced by robbery, thus perverting and turning into an unjust cause the presence of the Spaniards in America.

The fourth argument is that the king of Spain is required to accomplish the aim of the papal commission, that is, preaching through appropriate methods; this also implies that the kingdoms of the Indies have been put under his charge so that the gospel is preached, and his dominion over the Indians is reduced to that preaching.

The fifth argument is that the Church has a unique way to call the Indians to the faith (in this, Zumárraga coincides with Las Casas), which is "in peace, with wisdom, instruction, humility, kindness, meekness, liberality."[7] It is the way in which Christ and the apostles preached, that is, through living in a saintly manner and not converting the hearers of the word either by force or by robbery.

The sixth argument is that the infidelity of the Indians is due to unyielding ignorance. The idea behind this statement is that such a sin is not a valid cause for a just war; and, even though they have all the sins, not each and every one of the Indians has all those sins; they are, therefore, neither *salvajes* (savages) nor *bárbaros* (barbarians). If they are not savages, they are not serfs by nature, and cannot be enslaved. He also mentions this because some persons thought that sins deprived those who committed them of their rights, but he says that not even the accumulation of sins—which they had in an ordinary way, like other peoples—could deprive them from their rights in such a way that there would be a just war. Zumárraga denies, thus, that the war against the Indians may be just, and concedes only that Spanish domination over the Indians is reduced to the necessity to evangelize. Therefore, even though he does not state it, he suggests that once the evangelization has been accomplished, the Spaniards do not have any rights over the Indians.

Consistent with his first answer, Zumárraga also replies negatively to the question about the declaration of war and the threat to enslave and to brand the Indians. The archbishop asks the Spanish government to remember that the only reason for their presence in the Indies is to preach. He rebukes them, in the name of the blood of Christ: so that "These ambitious, greedy, miserable men forget about the conquering ventures, since they are shameful insults to our holy faith and to the sacred name of Christ, which has been denied and blasphemed by these unhappy men before they even knew it and received its announce-

---

7. Ibid., 182.

ment."[8] Zumárraga also complains that none of the judicial provisions of the king of Spain has helped to prevent injustices to the Indians.

Zumárraga declares thus that the war of conquest is illicit, because it is not the way to conversion to Christianity, and because it hinders preaching instead of helping it. However, the shortness of this work does not allow one to say that he opposes the war of conquest in itself, other than opposing it because of the way in which it was undertaken. He maintains, as Vitoria—but only two years after Vitoria's first writings, making it difficult to think Zumárraga was inspired by him—that the only reason to justify the presence of the Spaniards in America is the task of evangelizing, and it does not authorize either enslaving the Indians or stealing from them. But he does not say anything sufficiently explicit about whether evangelizing in itself, in the sense of requiring the defense of the preachers and the converted, justifies the war of conquest as a warlike intervention by Spain in favor of those men.

VASCO DE QUIROGA

Vasco (or Blasco) de Quiroga was born towards the end of the 1480s, at Madrigal de las Altas Torres in Spain. He travelled to New Spain in 1531, as a bachelor of law; he was part of the *Segunda Audiencia* of Mexico, which had to mend the abuses of the first one.[9] He was a layman, but his enterprise was so successful that he was elected bishop of Michoacán even though he was not a priest. This is why Juan de Zumárraga awarded him all the clerical orders besides consecrating him archbishop in 1538.

When he was "oidor," he wrote his famous letter about the social experiment of the hospitals in Santa Fe (1531). He defended the human rights of the Indians against the previous *Audiencia* in his *Información en Derecho* (1535); his ideas about justice, in particular about the right of conquest and of just colonization and proper evangelization, are reflected in this piece.[10] Once consecrated bishop of Michoacán, Quiroga erected in 1543 the hospital of Santa Fe, which would become his social work for the hospital-villages. Besides this, he built the Colegio de San Nicolás, with the intention of educating future priests. In it, the Indian languages known by Quiroga were taught. He also

---

8. Ibid., 183.
9. See F. Miranda, "Vasco de Quiroga, artífice humanista de Michoacán," in *Humanismo y ciencia en la formación de México*, ed. C. Herrejón Peredo (Zamora, México: El Colegio de Michoacán, 1984), 131–49, esp. 133.
10. See F. B. Warren, *Vasco de Quiroga y sus hospitales-pueblo de Santa Fe* (Morelia: Universidad Michoacana, 1977).

founded the Colegio de Niñas and other schools, both for children and for adults.[11] He made plans for the cathedral and the diocesan city; these would favor the fusion of the Spanish and Indian races, and become a laboratory of racial mixtures. Viceroy Mendoza objected to the Spaniards and Indians mixing and asked for two cities, one for each race.

In the meetings at Valladolid in Spain (1550), he opposed Bartolomé de las Casas—honestly following his conscience—and voted in favor of the *repartimientos* and *encomiendas* being given for life to the conquistadors. This is not due to his trying to cover up injustice, but because he thought that splitting the Indians and the Spaniards—as in fact las Casas wanted—would prevent racial and cultural mixing:

> For Quiroga, using the simile of the human body, the Indians and the Spaniards being elements of a new society, it was impossible to keep them separate; and, in his realism, he sees the convenience of the Spaniards taking the ruling role, but, as with the human body, they would constitute the skeleton, being capable of providing the structure, taken care of and sustained by the Indians, in the same way as the flesh does in the human body.[12]

In 1554, he returned to Michoacán, in his seat of Pátzcuaro, where he worked until he died. He devoted himself to consolidating the founding of hospitals and centers of instruction for Indians. In 1555 he attended the first Provincial Council in Mexico, where he succeeded in making it compulsory to build a hospital near the church in every village. He printed a catechism or doctrine, promoted new agricultural enterprises, improved handcrafts, and organized markets. While devoted to these altruistic activities (as may be seen in his will), he died at Uruapan on 14 March 1565.

Discussion of the Conquest

In his letter of 1531, addressed to the Council of Indies, Vasco asserts that the only legitimization of the presence of the Spaniards in the Indies is based on evangelization, and therefore he condemns the wars of conquest and the enslaving undertaken as a result of them.[13]

The main work written by Vasco de Quiroga is his *Información en derecho*, dated 1535. In this *Información*, Vasco says again that the war

---

11. See R. Valdéz, *Estudio sociopedagógico de la obra educativa de don Vasco de Quiroga* (México: Secretaría de Educación Pública, 1975).
12. Miranda, "Vasco de Quiroga," 142–43.
13. See Vasco de Quiroga, "Carta al Consejo de Indias," in Aguayo Spencer, *Don Vasco de Quiroga, taumaturgo de la organización social, seguido de un apéndice documental* (México: Ed. Oasis, 1970), 75–83, esp. 78.

brought against the Indians is unjust.[14] He follows Cajetan in the classification of infidels, and he sees that the Indians gave no reason for an unfair war. Cajetan identified three kinds of infidels: ones that were subjects of the Christians in fact and by right (that is, the Jews and Moors who live in Christian territory); others who were subjects by right but not in fact (that is, the Muslims who occupied the Sacred Land); and the third ones who were subjects neither in fact nor by right (that is, those who live in the lands which have never been owned by the Christians). The Indians belong to the third class, and, therefore, the war that enslaved them was never just.

Vasco de Quiroga, in a way similar to that of Vitoria and Las Casas and the same as Zumárraga, says that the only justification for the war against the Indians would be their resisting the evangelization or causing difficulties for those who had converted. He believes that they have not refused preaching and that they have converted voluntarily, and even agreeably, thus coinciding with Zumárraga's point of view; he thinks, however, that their form of government did not favor this new Christian life, and thus it was justified that the Spaniards should be placed above them, even through war. His approach is unique on this point. As a matter of fact, according to him, it is very clear that there exists the obligation of preaching the gospel, which gives the right to remove the obstacles found, and that the Indian government opposed such preaching, thus making it necessary to undertake the war of conquest and put Spanish governors above Indian ones. Vasco wanted the native governors to be kept, but they had to be subordinated to some superior Spanish governors, in order to protect and favor evangelizing. This is why he called it a "mixed government."

It should be pointed out that Vasco, in the same way as most of the theoreticians of the conquest and in accordance with Thomas Aquinas, says that the Indians should not be converted by force, but that preaching should be protected and favored. It was only just to enter into a war for the success of the compulsory evangelizing mission. But the conquistadors used this to say that the war of conquest was also necessary to take over the power and the wealth of the Indians; they thus justified it and took advantage of the situation to attack the Indians. Vasco, however, insists on the fact that conversion must be undertaken voluntarily and preaching must be peaceful and pursued through charitable persuasion. Only in the case of a government that prevents peaceful preaching of the largest imaginable benefit, that is, faith, does he justify war. Indian governors, by preventing the peaceful preaching and prose-

---

14. Ibid., 68.

cuting those who converted to Christianity, provoked a fair war and were justly deposed from their functions, which were handed to the Spaniards; but this was done only to accomplish the aims of evangelizing. Vasco again bases his arguments on Cajetan, who follows Thomas Aquinas's theories on tyranny and says that based on such an oppressive situation, the Indians had tyrant governors and there was a right to intervene and free them from their own sovereigns. Since the Indians and their governors used violence against evangelization, the war against them was intended as a "pacification."

In any case, Vasco makes it clear that such a war was not intended to destroy or to enslave the Indians. This is why he fights against the perverse and twisted way in which the conquest had been made. The conquistadors, in fact, used the just cause for conquering the Indians— evangelization—to seize them and their properties, and, thus, the war of conquest became unjust. Vasco insists that enslaving was never among the fair aims of this pacifying war, and that their possessions and freedom had to be restored to the Indians, "since it is more forbidden for the faithful to have something through oppression and in a wrong way, than for the barbarian and infidel, especially the freedom of the free man, which is so inestimably precious."[15]

Vasco suggests that the Spanish governors and judges imposed on the Indians be removed and replaced by Indian governors and judges, who could be under the superior supervision of the Spaniards, always dependent on evangelizing.[16] He also proposes racial and cultural mixing, and traces different social lines to obtain the coexistence of the Indians and the Spaniards justly and peacefully. While Bartolomé de las Casas wanted to separate them, because of the difficulties the Indians caused the Spaniards, Vasco wanted to unite them, so that they were charitable to one another and learned to live in fraternity.

The Attack on the Indians in a Short Work Arguably Attributable to Vasco de Quiroga

It is possible to find a very harsh approach in a treatise, or *parecer*, which has been attributed to Vasco de Quiroga. Entitled *De debellandis indis*, it deals with the legality of the conquest undertaken by the Spaniards and with the war against the Indians.[17] Its main subject matter is

---

15. Ibid., 140.
16. Ibid., 219ff.
17. See Vasco de Quiroga, *De debellandis indis*, ed. R. Acuña (México: Universidad Nacional Autónoma de México). The editor, René Acuña, attributes this treatise to Vasco. The thesis about the authorship is opposed by Silvio Zavala in his article "En busca del

the war that should be brought against the Indians: the author thinks that the Spaniards have acquired the obligation of transmitting European culture to the Indians, even through violence. In what concerns the authorship of the work, I prefer to speak of the "author," since I believe the attribution to Vasco de Quiroga is not yet definitive. The reasons adduced by Silvio Zavala have to be taken into consideration: the use of authors that are not found in other works undoubtedly written by Quiroga, the diversity of opinions, and so on. I believe strongly what Zavala says: *De debellandis indis* by Vasco de Quiroga was judged by the Spanish Dominican provincial, Miguel de Arcos, and the résumé he makes of this book provides doctrines that are contrary to the ones advanced in the anonymous manuscript of the Colección Muñoz from the Academia de la Historia at Madrid (where it is written that it might be by Vasco), which is the treatise under discussion here.[18] We should wait, therefore, until the authorship attributed to Quiroga is decided, and, meanwhile, we will have to abstain from attributing it to Vasco.

The author of this short work, when he establishes the opinions that are contrary to his own, says that some maintain that the war against the Indians cannot be undertaken, and he quotes Cajetan, who states that, by natural right as well as by human right, the Indians cannot be deprived of their possessions, since they voluntarily converted to the gospel.[19] Furthermore, by divine right, there exists the obligation of charity, which requires the Spaniards to help them. According to this, the war against the Indians is unjust, since their possessions belong to them, and the Spaniards cannot take away their kingdoms, as they have incorrectly done. Even less just is this war since they have converted and been baptized. But the author opposes this opinion, and says that it is, in fact, legal. He bases his position on the famous Hostiensis, for whom the infidels are not worthy of having any power. He also argues, through forced exegesis, that all the kingdoms belong to Christ, and that he would take them from the infidels. Besides, he says, adducing the twisted authority of Torquemada on this point, Christ gave them to Peter, and, therefore, to the papacy. Even more, it is the pope who concedes them to the emperor, and so he has conceded the government

---

tratado *de debellandis indis* de Vasco de Quiroga," *Historia Mexicana* 17, no. 68 (1968): 485–515; on the other hand, in "Don Vasco de Quiroga y su tratado *de debellandis indis*," in *Historia Mexicana* 18, no. 72 (1969): 615–22, B. Biermann defends the suggestion that Vasco is the author of this work. Zavala responds to Biermann and defends his position in "En torno del tratado *de debellandis indis* de Vasco de Quiroga," in *Historia Mexicana* 18, no. 72 (1969): 623–26.

18. See Silvio Zavala, "Algo más sobre Vasco de Quiroga," in *Evangelización y teología en América (Siglo XVI)*, ed. J. I. Saranyana et al. (Pamplona: Eunsa, 1990), 1:395–411.

19. Quiroga, *De debellandis indis*, 145.

of the Indies. Thus the Spanish emperor has taken justly the power of those kingdoms.[20] And the pope did not give him those kingdoms for spiritual aims, since those he keeps for himself, but for material aims, as it is the competence of the secular people.

He says that the reasons advanced by Cajetan do not work, since they would apply only if the kings of Spain had taken the Indies by their own initiative; but they did it with the authorization of the pope. He mentions Cajetan's distinction of infidels, discussed earlier, between those who admit the dominion of the Church, and thus should be tolerated, and those who do not have any contact with the Christians. About the latter he says that they do not have dominion, because they do not recognize either the pope or the emperor. They can possess particular things, but they cannot have kingdoms.[21] The author adds to infidelity:

Besides, because they practiced idolatry, they adored idols, being unjust among themselves, killing and stealing from one another and offering themselves to the devils, as is manifest in so many things of their history which have been written by those who conquered them.[22]

He believes that he has answered his main opponents, Cajetan and his followers. In fact, he has only succeeded in maintaining the papist view of the two swords, which is untenable, as well as the insensible opinion of the Hostiensis that the infidels lose dominion because of their sins, without being excused by their ignorance.

This short treatise is so contrary to the doctrines expressed by Quiroga and inspired mostly by Cajetan, that it would seem it was not written by Vasco. Furthermore, the argument is so unsound and weak that it reinforces the doubts about it having been composed by Vasco de Quiroga. He spent most of his life, like Las Casas, defending the Indians against the injustices of the conquistadors.[23]

Vasco's Doctrine as Described in the Résumé by Miguel de Arcos

According to Silvio Zavala, the contents of the authentic short work by Vasco appears in the résumé written by Miguel de Arcos.[24] The com-

---

20. Ibid., 157.
21. Ibid., 173.
22. Ibid., 175.
23. See F. Martín Hernández, "Don Vasco de Quiroga, protector de los indios," *Salmanticensis* 34 (1987): 61–85.
24. This compendium can be found in the compilation by Lewis Hanke, *Cuerpo de documentos del siglo XVI sobre los derechos de España en las Indias y las Filipinas* (reprint, México: Fondo de Cultura Económica, 1977).

pendium by Arcos shows that Vasco maintains as his main thesis not only that it is legal to make war against the Indians who they are going to dispossess, but also that the pope and the Spanish crown of Castile are obliged to retain them. The reason is that the obligation of charity to free them from their ignorance of the gospel exists; but they cannot be freed from that ignorance without being retained, and if that has to be done violently, it has to be done thus.

Arcos objects that it has not to be done through violence, since in the times of the apostles the pagans converted by peaceful persuasion. But he accepts that, given the characteristics of these Indians, they are not constant in the faith that they receive so easily. They transform from infidels into heretics, in a negative way, which is even more dangerous than those who are infidels in the contrary way. But he reflects that, if this adversity to the faith is due to the atrocities committed by the Spaniards, then they are really responsible for the lack of faith in the Indians. Arcos also objects that there is no obligation for the king of Spain to retain the Indians who have not yet been retained (he does not refer to those who are already retained) in order to convert them, since he has no jurisdiction over them. He argues that this does not appear in the commission given by Pope Alexander VI to the Catholic kings.

On the other hand, Arcos thinks that the pope can send a Christian king to war only if the Indians oppose evangelization, but not a grossly disproportionate war: above all, even if they are vanquished, the Indians cannot be deprived of their lands and properties, unless they are given some tributes that compensate for what has been spent during the war. In fact, according to Arcos, the pope is not the temporary owner of these worldly goods, and so he can only dispose of them with a spiritual aim. Arcos thinks that the pope has been fooled in matters regarding the New World, and sometimes puts forth documents that concede powers that would better not be conceded. In the same way, he insists on the bad intention to become rich that most of those who travel to America have (and in no manner is it the intention to evangelize, which only a few really have).

Arcos says that the author of this short work also argues that making war against the Indians to subject them is not primarily to make war against them, but to prevent them from the many wars that they fight amongst themselves, and very cruel ones. But Arcos objects that this argument does not justify its conclusion, because harm should not be done in order to obtain good. Not everything that can bring success and good effects is appropriate, therefore, this war continues to be unjust. For Arcos, the only just war against the Indians is the one undertaken against those who have yet to be conquered:

If all or most of them or their rulers do not consent that the gospel is preached in their lands and provinces. If some of the Indians, having converted to the Catholic faith, are perverted and returned to their mistakes by their rulers, their masters or other Indians. . . . If some of the Indians are badly treated in a manifestly unjust way by others who are more and more powerful, mainly if the oppressed ask for help. . . . If some who voluntarily have become friends and allies to the Christians are badly treated by others, the king of Spain is obliged by the laws of friendship and alliance to return and take them, making war against those who commit some grievance, so that his friends live in peace.[25]

Arcos, like Las Casas, seems more radical than Vasco in his proclamation of the injustice of the wars of conquest. In fact, each one of them expressed it in his own way following different principles. Even though on occasion it may seem paradoxical, Vasco was a defender of the Indians, despite his defense of the legitimacy and even the forcefulness of the war of conquest in order to instill European civilization and the gospel in the Indians.[26] He saw this imposition as necessary to provide the Indian with an autonomy and a freedom that were his own as a result of the new culture he was receiving.

CONCLUSION

It has been said that the theoreticians of the conquest devoted themselves to justifying it, to providing doctrinal or ideological support in order to legitimate it. When it is presented thus, it may sound true, but it is misleadingly simplified. It is obvious that in their fundamental premise, namely, that the best that could be given to the Indians was the Christian faith (and, furthermore, that the Spaniards had the obligation of transmitting it and the Indians of receiving it), it is only possible to see anything other than an enslaving ideology. It is necessary, however, to be impartial and not to oversimplify matters, as well as to try to fix the boundaries of responsibility. Most of the theoreticians of the conquest legitimated it only as far as it was necessary for evangelizing, but no further. They did not consider it, as some scholars think, legitimate in itself or as the right to bring war against the infidels because they were infidels. (It must be said that some agreed with this last idea, as is the case with the short work attributed to Vasco de Quiroga.) They subjected the conquest to the preaching of the faith, and

25. Ibid., 9.
26. See M. Bataillon, "Vasco de Quiroga et Bartolomé de las Casas," *Revista de Historia de América* 33 (1952): 83–95; and G. Vargas Uribe, "La influencia de la *Utopía* de Moro en los hospitales fundados por Don Vasco de Quiroga," *Boletín de la Coordinación de la Investigación Científica de la Universidad Michoacana* 10 (1986): 16–23.

as far as necessary to allowing that preaching to be brought to the Indians.

It has to be taken into account, besides, that there were also twisted intentions in the conquistadors who applied those principles. Anything seemed to them a cause for violence in order to guarantee the life and efficiency of the preachers. In the same way, the conquest was legitimated if it was necessary to keep the Indians already converted from being incited by their governors to return to infidelity, or for preventing the persecution of the new Christians. Those who were interested not so much in evangelizing as in oppression saw the symptoms and indications that it was necessary, or at least very convenient, to intervene with violence and to conquer in order to avoid the persecution and disturbance of the newly converted who practiced their faith. This was not judged, in fact, by the theological philosophers of the conquest, but rather enforced to the advantage of those who had material interests in the enterprise.

It is necessary to understand before judging. If it is not very clear that the Christian priests thought about their obligation of preaching and of converting the Indians, it is not possible to understand what moved them, all their principles and acts being seen as misguided. Besides, it has to be taken into consideration that the practical application was made by some in an excessive and twisted manner (such as those who professed that the "letra con sangre entra"—the alphabet has to be learned with blood if necessary—and thus they wanted to convert the Indians with violence, if necessary, against Thomas Aquinas, Cajetan, and Vitoria) and by others it was made meekly, peacefully, very humbly, through use of the good word, with no physical violence. The theoreticians, however, wanted to mark very well, following Thomas Aquinas and Vitoria, that conversion cannot be forced and that the only thing that could be forced upon the Indians was that they listened to the preaching, and if, once listened to calmly and in abundance, it did not convince them, they should be left in peace. This was put down in their writings, but clearly it was not respected in most cases and conversion was forced, if not with violence, then at least with threats and fear. The principles were there—written but violated, more moderate but disobeyed—establishing that it was not possible to force anyone to receive the faith. But it is most important to point out here precisely those principles: the tone and the structure with which they were expressed, the logical connection that they had, the discrepancies and emphasis among the theoreticians, and the different ways in which they speculated.

It is evident that they were not followed as they were speculated upon, and that it produced a disaster in practice. But from this situation to the claim that they were ideologists who justified the oppression, there is a long way. It may even be said that their attempts, carefully looked at and weighed, were intended as a search for the common good and justice, even liberation. This depends, however, on the attitude and the objectivity with which history is seen and interpreted.

3   Vitoria on Choosing to Replace a King
JOHN P. DOYLE

I. A NOTE ON VITORIA'S IMPORTANCE AND INFLUENCE

Anyone familiar with the development of Hispanic philosophy in the Age of Discovery must be aware of the importance of Francisco de Vitoria (c. 1492–1546). Perhaps, however, that person will be surprised to hear that Vitoria, the holder of the *Catedra de Prima* in theology at the University of Salamanca, never published any of his own works.[1] Instead, it was through his teaching that, during and after Spain's golden century, Vitoria influenced countless disciples, especially in areas of ethical and political thought. There are estimates of up to one thousand auditors attending some of his lectures.[2] He himself in one place comes close to confirming that figure.[3] But more than this, in the decades that followed, almost all the great moralists of the age looked back to Vitoria as their foremost authority. Their names read like the honor roll of Spanish and Counter-Reformation Scholasticism.[4] But also outside Spain and Catholic Scholastic circles, in the dawning age of international jurisprudence, Vitoria exercised patent influence on

---

1. Luis Alonso Getino (*El Maestro Fr. Francisco de Vitoria: su vida, su doctrina e influencia* [Madrid, 1930], 299), has grouped Vitoria's works as follows: "La Bibliografía del P. Vitoria abarca tres grupos de obras: 1° las que él publicó de otros autores; 2° las que otros publicaron de él; 3° las que se encuentran manuscritas en los archivos." For a convenient listing of the works of others which Vitoria was instrumental in publishing, cf. Teofilo Urdánoz, ed., *Obras de Francisco de Vitoria: Relecciones teologicas*, ed. crítica (Madrid, 1960), 83; unless otherwise noted, Vitoria's *Relectiones* and the corresponding page numbers will be cited from this edition. Also, see Marcial Solana, *Historia de la Filosofía Española. Época del Renacimiento* (Madrid, 1940), 3:47. Among these works was Peter Crockaert's 1512 redaction (for the first time in France) of St. Thomas Aquinas's *Summa theologiae* II-II; on this, see Ricardo G. Villoslada, *La Universidad de Paris durante los estudios de Francisco de Vitoria, O.P. (1507–1522)*, 264–65; for Vitoria's dedicatory preface, see app. 2, "Primer escrito de Francisco de Vitoria (Paris 1512)," 422–25.
2. Urdánoz, *Obras*, 68.
3. Cf. Francisco de Vitoria, *Comentarios a la Secunda Secundae de Santo Tomás*, ed. Vincente Beltrán de Heredia, 6 vols. (Salamanca, 1932–35, 1952), in q. 89, a. 7; vol. 5, p. 20.
4. For some of their testimonies, see Getino, *El Maestro*, 281–84, and app. 1, esp. 421–28; also Solana, *Historia*, 84–85.

important figures such as Hugo Grotius (1583–1645) and Alberico Gentili (1552–1608).[5] Looking at all his influence and at the dearth of work published while he lived, it was with perfect truth that Domingo Báñez (1528–1604) could refer to him as "another Socrates."[6]

II. VITORIA'S GENERAL POLITICAL PHILOSOPHY

In his political philosophy, Vitoria himself was evidently and unabashedly a disciple of Aristotle and St. Thomas Aquinas. With St. Thomas, he emphasized the rational, free nature of human beings, created by God in His own image.[7] And with both Aquinas and Aristotle, he would agree that man is by that same nature "a political animal."[8] There is thus in every human being a power of discernment and self-determination as well as a natural teleology toward life together with his fellows in society. This teleology is first toward life in the domestic society of the family. But this is not enough.[9] Beyond the family, human beings are *by nature inclined* toward that civil society which is the *polis*, the city-state *(civitas)* or the republic *(respublica).*[10]

III. THE ORIGINAL TRANSFER OF PUBLIC AUTHORITY

It was clear then to Vitoria that states and republics were not merely an invention of men. They were not to be numbered among artificial things. Instead, they have proceeded from nature, which has prompted men to this way of living for their protection and conservation.[11] From

---

5. See, e.g., the listings of parallel passages between Vitoria and Grotius, and then Gentili, as given by Luis Alonso Getino, *Relecciones teológicas de Maestro Fray Francisco de Vitoria* (Madrid, 1935), 3:ix–xliii.
6. Getino, *El Maestro*, 283.
7. Cf., e.g., *Relectio de Indis recenter inventis* (hereafter, *De Indis*), I, n. 21; p. 663, and *Relectio de homicidio* (hereafter, *De homicidio*), n. 2; p. 1091.
8. "Quapropter et in 1 *Politicorum* Aristoteles ostendit hominem naturaliter esse civilem, sociabilemque" (*Relectio de potestate civili* [hereafter, *De potestate civili*], n. 4; p. 155); "... est enim homo animal civile, ..." (*De Indis*, II, n. 1; p. 670); "... cum homo sit animal civile, ..." (*De Indis*, III, n. 5; p. 711); and *Relectio de eo ad quod tenetur homo* (hereafter, *De eo ad quod tenetur*), II, n. 7; p. 1344.
9. "Quamquam enim mutua officia sibi praestent, non tamen familia una sufficiens est sibi et maxime adversus vim iniuriamque propulsandam" (*De potestate civili*, n. 4; p. 157).
10. Cf. ibid.; pp. 154–57. On this, consider Urdánoz: "Con esto se sitúa Vitoria en un orden de valoración perfectiva, no en el orden genético o más originario, si se compara la sociedad civil con la familia. Pero es justa y acertada la idea sociológica que apunta aquí Vitoria, de que el Estado no surge históricamente como una prolongación de la familia, sino muchas veces nace de la necesidad de convivir y agruparse individuos y comunidades heterogéneas" (p. 116).
11. "Patet ergo fontem et originem civitatum rerumque publicarum non inventum

here it immediately follows that the same purpose and the same necessity exist for public power. For if the good condition *(incolumitas)* of men requires their association and gathering together, it is also a fact that no society can persist without some force *(vis)* and power *(potestas)* governing it and providing for it:

> For if all men would be equal and subject to no power, with each one tending by his own choice and opinion in a different direction, without some providence which would have common care and concern for the common good, the republic would necessarily be pulled apart and the state would be destroyed.... Just as the human body could not remain whole without some ordering force which would compose its individual members for the advantage of other members and especially for the good of the whole man, so it is in the state if everyone would be worried about his own advantage and everyone would neglect the public good. We have in this the final and principal cause of civil and secular power....[12]

Something to note here is that Vitoria is not embracing some Hobbesian "state of nature" doctrine.[13] He is not saying that the original condition of mankind, the "natural" condition, was a war of every man against every other man—that man is by nature a wolf to man. Quite the contrary.[14] While Vitoria would not discount original sin and the need of God's grace,[15] in Catholic fashion he believes in the innate goodness of all God's creatures, especially human beings.[16] Coupled with that, he thinks human beings have a natural drive not toward conflict, but toward God and the common good even more than towards themselves and their private advantage.[17] Consistently, he believes that

---

esse hominum, neque inter artificiata numerandum, sed tanquam a natura profectum, quae ad mortalium tutelam et conservationem hanc rationem mortalibus suggessit" (*De potestate civili*, n. 5; p. 157).

12. "Nam si omnes aequales essent et nulli potestati subditi, unoquoque ex sua sententia et arbitrio in diversitatem tendente, necessario distraheretur respublica, dissolveretur civitas, nisi aliqua esset providentia quae in communi curaret consuleretque communi bono.... Sicut corpus hominum in sua integritate conservari non posset nisi esset aliqua vis ordinatrix quae singula membra in usus aliorum membrorum, maxime in commodum totius hominis componeret. Sane ita in civitate contingere necesse esset, si unusquisque pro suarum rerum utilitate sollicitus esset, et unusquisque civis publicum bonum negligeret. Habemus igitur finalem et potissimam causam potestatis civilis et saecularis..." (ibid.; pp. 157–58). All translations, unless otherwise noted, are my own.

13. This is true despite the translation of the just quoted passage given by Anthony Pagden and Jeremy Lawrance, *Francisco de Vitoria: Political Writings* (Cambridge, 1991), 9–10.

14. *De Indis*, III, n. 3; p. 709.
15. Ibid., II, n. 8; p. 687; and *De eo ad quod tenetur*, n. 6; p. 1340.
16. *De homicidio*, n. 2; pp. 1090–91.
17. "... ego vero nego hominem inclinari ad diligendum se plus quam Deum, vel proprium bonum plus quam commune. Sicut enim membrum plus inclinatur ad bonum totius quam ad bonum proprium, periclitatur enim manus pro salute totius; ita etiam ex

one of the main spurs to the political community is an inclination to bear one another's burdens.[18] What he is teaching in the passage given just above is that individual human beings, each a free center of activity, left to themselves would go their separate ways. This does not mean that they would necessarily kill or rob one another. But they would be unlikely to found and maintain states or republics. In order, therefore, that such naturally good republics exist, with all their benefits to men, some directive (or at times even coercive) public power seems necessary.

In accord with this, to avoid a life "at sixes and sevens" and to effect laws and other things needed in society, human beings had to limit their freedom as individuals by a voluntary transfer of power to a ruler.[19] At this point, the actual state emerged.[20] In this way the actual state is both natural and also derived from human free choice. It is natural for human beings to live in a political community. But the historical state arises from a free transfer of power or authority.[21] Depending on the character of the original transfer, states may be monarchical, aristocratic, democratic, or some mixture of these.[22] As a matter of experienced fact, there are different states.[23] Vitoria's own preference is for a monarchy or a mixed monarchical state, such as that in Spain.[24] But

---

naturali inclinatione homo, quem Deus fecit partem reipublicae, natura inclinatur ad bonum publicum plus quam ad privatum. Et cum Deus sit bonum universale, plus etiam homo diligit Deum quam seipsum" (ibid., n. 10; pp. 1103–04).

18. "... ut alter alterius onera portaret, ..." (*De potestate civili*, n. 4; p. 156).

19. "... haec autem potestas per ipsam multitudinem exerceri non potest (non enim commode posset leges condere atque edicta proponere, lites dirimere et transgressores punire) necesse ergo fuit ut potestatis administratio alicui aut aliquibus commendaretur, qui huiusmodi curam gererent" (*De potestate civili*, n. 8; p. 162); "... convenientibus in unum aliquibus in unam rempublicam, ex consensu communi sibi constituerunt principem" (*De Indis*, II, n. 1; p. 672); also see *In II-II*, q. 47, a. 10 (Beltrán, 2:368) and q. 62, a. 1, n. 21 (Beltrán, 3:78).

20. "Certum est enim vel his, vel aliis non dissimilibus modis dominia et imperia incoepisse in mundo, ..." (*De Indis*, II, n. 1; p. 672).

21. On the Aristotelian character of this twofold provenance of the state and its distinction from a "social contract" theory, see Emilio Naszalyi, *El Estado según Francisco de Vitoria* (Madrid, 1948), 168.

22. See *De potestate civili*, n. 11; pp. 166–67; also, *In II-II*, q. 47, a. 10 (Beltrán, 2:368).

23. On the contrast here between Vitoria and St. Thomas, Pierre Mesnard notes, "A l'inverse de saint Thomas qui, après Aristote, étudie dans l'abstrait chaque mode de gouvernement avant de conclure en faveur du régime mixte, Vitoria raisonne à partir de cas concrets qui entraînent son assentiment. 'Ce sont le royaume de France ou d'Aragon, ou la République de Venise qui se présentent d'abord dans leur réalité concrète, à l'esprit du moraliste, et c'est sur elle qu'il est toujours tenté de raisonner. Sujet de Charles-Quint, il ne songe pas à dissimuler ses préférences monarchiques'" (Pierre Mesnard, *L'Essor de la philosophie politique au XVI⁰ siècle* [Paris, 1969], 460; citing Hubert Beuve-Méry, *La théorie des pouvoirs publics d'après François de Vitoria* [Paris, 1928], 32).

24. Cf. "Optimum ergo regnum est unius, sicut totus orbis ab uno principe et domino sapientissimo gubernatur. Verum est autem quod tutissimus principatus et administratio videtur esse mixtus ex tribus, qualis videtur esse hispaniorum" (*De potestate civili*, n. 11;

inasmuch as each state has the same natural origin, there is a fundamental equality among them. It matters not whether public power is transferred to one person or to many;[25] it is the same in all instances, with the same obligation for those subject to it.[26]

In Vitoria's time, there might be doubt about the powers by which the republics of non-believers *(infideles)* are governed. Are there legitimate princes and judges among the pagans?[27] It might seem not. Earlier, Richard Fitzralph, Archbishop of Armagh (d. 1360), in his *De paupertate Christi*, had denied public power not only for nonbelief or infidelity, but even for any mortal sin. Richard argued that the basic title to or foundation for all power, dominion, and jurisdiction, whether these be public or private, is in Grace.[28] This doctrine, as renewed by Wycliff and Hus, had been condemned in 1415 at the General Council of Constance.[29]

Speaking in 1528, in his *Relectio de potestate civili,* Vitoria declined to give what he regarded as the very weak reasons supporting this view. He would give the same reasons given by Fitzralph and others a decade later in his *Relectio de Indis recenter inventis.* But in 1528 he contents himself with stating that, beyond doubt, among pagans there are legitimate princes and "lords" *(domini).*[30] In support of this contention, with its implication of a natural equality between Christian and pagan rulers as well as states, he cites St. Paul (Rom. 13:1-2) counseling obedience to pagan rulers of his time. He also recalls Joseph (Gn 41:39-57) and

---

p. 167); also, "Et optima politia videtur nunc quae est mixta, ut Doctor dicit. Et sic aliquomodo est inter christianos ubi sunt reges" *(In I-II,* q. 105, a. 1 [Beltrán, 6:481]).

25. "... nihil refert uni an pluribus commendetur" *(De potestate civili,* n. 8; p. 162).

26. "Quia cum eadem sit potestas, ... sive in uno sive in pluribus sit, et tantum uni melius sit subiici quam pluribus (tot enim domini quot sunt superiores) ergo non est minor libertas ubi omnes uni sunt subditi quam pluribus" (ibid., n. 11; pp. 166-67).

27. "... an inter paganos sint legitimi principes et alii magistratus" (ibid., n. 8; p. 165). This question is central to Vitoria's treatment of Spanish claims to the New World; cf. *De Indis,* I, nn. 4-21; pp. 650-66.

28. Noted by Vitoria at *De potestate civili,* n. 9; p. 165. Note that Naszalyi (*El Estado,* 97n27) and later, Ramón Hernández (*Un Español en la ONU: Francisco de Vitoria* [Madrid, 1977], 146) have erroneously identified Vitoria's opponent here as Richard of Middleton. This seems to be a mistake, inasmuch as (1) Richard of Middleton, to my knowledge, did not author a treatise *De paupertate,* whereas Richard Fitzralph ("Armachanus") did write a *"De pauperie Christi"* (cf. *The Catholic Encyclopedia* [1913], s.v. "Fitzralph, Richard"); and (2) Vitoria rejects the same doctrine in *De Indis,* I, n. 5; pp. 652-53, and there ascribes it to Fitzralph in two works. On this last ascription, see Francisco de Vitoria, *Relectio de Indis o libertad de los Indios,* ed. L. Pereña and J. M. Perez Prendes (Madrid, 1967), 15nn. 20-21.

29. See H. Denzinger and A. Schönmetzer, *Enchiridion symbolorum definitionum et declarationum de rebus fidei et morum,* ed. 32 (Barcinonae, 1963), nn. 1165 and 1230.

30. "Nec omnino est dubitandum quin apud ethnicos sint legitimi principes et domini, ..." *(De potestate civili,* n. 9; p. 165).

Daniel (Gn 47:6–28), who were themselves princes, procurators, or ministers of pagans. Accordingly, he continues, Christian princes and ecclesiastical leaders should not deprive nonbelievers of power and government *(principatus)* for the sole reason that they are unbelievers. If these are to be stripped of such power, it ought to be for some other injury that they have perpetrated.[31]

IV. MAJORITY RULE

In the same *Relectio de potestate civili*, Vitoria has clearly noted that in order originally to transfer power and thus to establish an actual state there is no requirement of unanimous consent. Instead, a majority (if hardly egalitarian)[32] vote will suffice. If for its own advantage a republic can entrust power to one person, it is certain that the dissent of a single person or of a few people cannot block the rest from thus providing for the common good. Otherwise, that is, if the consent of everyone were required, the republic would not be sufficiently provided for, since such unanimous agreement rarely or never occurs in a mass of people. Therefore, in order that public matters be done rightly, it is enough that the greater part agree.[33]

Likewise, he says, this is proven from actual practice *(efficaciter)*, for whenever two factions contradict one another about a matter of public policy, it is necessary that one of their views prevail. But the view of the smaller faction should not prevail. Therefore, the view of the majority should be followed.[34] Then, in an enigmatic two sentences, he

31. "Nec aut principes christiani saeculares aut ecclesiastici huiusmodi potestate et principatu privare possent infideles, eo dumtaxat titulo quia infideles sunt, nisi ab eis alia iniuria profecta sit" (ibid.). For application of this in the context of Spanish actions in the New World, cf. "Si ergo nulla praecessit a barbaris iniuria, nulla est causa iusti belli" *(De Indis,* II, n. 11; p. 691).

32. On this, Ramón Hernández writes, "En los tiempos de Francisco de Vitoria, el pueblo carecía de sentido politico, no se sentía llamado a participar en la concesión del poder; eran los altos funcionarios de la corte los que por sí mismos efectuaban la elección" (Hernández, *Un Español en la ONU,* 150).

33. "Si enim respublica suam potestatem uni alicui mandare potest et hoc propter utilitatem reipublicae, certum est non obstare dissensus unius aut paucorum, quominus ceteri providere possint bono reipublicae. Alias non esset sufficienter consultum reipublicae, si consensus omnium exigeretur, cum ille in multitudine aut vix aut nunquam contingat. Satis ergo est ut maior pars conveniat in unum, ut jure aliquid fiat" *(De potestate civili,* n. 14; p. 179).

34. "Item probatur efficaciter. Nam duabus partibus dissentientibus in administratione reipublicae, oportet ut praevaleat sententia alterius partis necessario si volunt contradictoria. Non autem debet valere sententia minoris partis. Ergo sequenda est maioris partis sententia" *(De potestate civili,* n. 14; this is my transcription of the text of the Palencia manuscript, folio 36r, as photographically reproduced by Getino, *Relecciones,* I, p. 61; for Urdánoz, see p. 179). Pagden and Lawrance *(Vitoria: Political Writings,* 30), obviously fol-

highlights the impasse which would result without majority rule: "If in order to create a king the consent of all is required, why is it not also required in order not to create a king? For why is there required unanimous consent more for the affirmative part than for the negative?"[35] But beyond its being what works in practice, majority rule in political transactions, Vitoria says in another place, is necessary for peace and is a matter of natural law.[36]

V. THE QUESTION OF A VOLUNTARY CHANGE OF GOVERNMENT

Once a regime has been established by majority vote with full power to govern the republic, can that vote be altered or reversed? Can the regime or government so established be changed or even abolished?

Vitoria would never sanction the abrogation of all political power, a condition he would regard as basically unnatural.[37] He tells us, even if all the citizens resolve not to exercise the republic's power to administer itself, for which office kings have been established, this power nonetheless remains.[38] In other words, civil power as such is not dependent on the will of those subject to it and an anarchical state is unacceptable or even impossible.[39]

To be sure, not even by consent of "the whole world" *(totus orbis)* can political power be completely abrogated.[40] He reasons, if a man cannot renounce his right to defend himself and his right or faculty of using his own members for his own utility,[41] neither can he renounce power

---

lowing the Palencia manuscript, have translated this passage well. On the manuscripts of Vitoria, see Vincente Beltrán de Heredia, *Los manuscritos del Maestro Fray Francisco de Vitoria, O.P. Estudio crítico de introducción a sus lecturas y Relecciones* (Madrid-Valencia, 1928).

35. "Nam si ad creandum regem requiritur consensus omnium, quare etiam non requiritur ad non creandum? Quare enim magis requiritur consensus omnium ad affirmativam quam ad negativam?" *(De potestate civili,* n. 14; p. 179).

36. "Et illud est necessarium ad pacem, quod ubi agitur de utilitate communi, sententia majoris partis praevaleat et superet. Et hoc est de jure naturali, quod etiamsi nollent alii, quod major pars dixit, illud teneatur" *(In II-II,* q. 62, a. 1 [Beltrán 3:79n22]).

37. "... dicebamus, nullam huiusmodi potestatem hominum consensu abrogari posse" *(De potestate civili,* n. 10; p. 166); also see note 43 below.

38. "Constituta est enim in republica, omnibus etiam civibus invitis, potestas seipsam administrandi, in quo officio civiles reges constituti sunt" *(De potestate civili,* n. 8; p. 164).

39. "El estado anárquico, sin gobierno ni organización autoritaria, no es concebible, según nuestro teólogo" (Urdánoz, *Obras,* 125).

40. "... ut nec orbis totius consensu tolli aut abrogari possit" *(De potestate civili,* n. 1; p. 151).

41. For a more extended discussion on not exercising such rights, with attention paid to circumstances, the rights of others, the common good, charity, and so on, see *De homicidio,* nn. 24–37; pp. 1118–30.

since that belongs to him by divine and natural right. In like manner, the republic cannot rightly be deprived of the public power needed to administer itself and to defend itself against injury *(injuriam)*, both "from its own citizens and from those outside it" *(suorum et exteriorum)*.[42] This would be so, even if all citizens were to agree to abolish that power and agree to be ruled by no laws and to rule over no one. For such an agreement would be null and void inasmuch as it would be contrary to natural law.[43]

The question then is more limited. Once established by the majority, can a particular regime or government be abrogated or exchanged for another? Obviously, much here will depend upon the nature of the original contract or establishment. If we are dealing with a government established as democratic, one which continues to function by majority vote, there is no apparent reason in principle why a majority of its members could not vote for a senate or a king to rule over them. Equally, in the case of an aristocratic government (for example, in the sixteenth-century free city-states of Venice or Florence), there seems to be no reason why the majority, say, of a senate could not vote for a king. Thus, by similar majority votes, democracies or aristocracies could modify themselves or adopt some other form of government, even if that form would not be an absolute best form.[44]

The principal problem regards *monarchy*, which, as we have mentioned, the Aristotelian Vitoria did consider a better form of government than either aristocracy or democracy. In a true monarchy there would be no appeal from the king to the republic.[45] But then can a monarchical republic by majority vote limit the power it has granted unconditionally to its king? Against his will, can it depose that king? Can it replace him with another king, or with other rulers? Such questions are very relevant to Vitoria's thinking about political power in general and about the establishment of Spanish rule in the New World in particular.[46]

---

42. *De potestate civili*, n. 10; p. 166.

43. "Atque ita si cives omnes in hoc convenirent, ut omnes has potestates amitterent, et ut nullis tenerentur legibus, nulli imperarent, pactum esse nullum et invalidum, utpote contra jus naturale" (ibid).

44. Cf. "... infertur corollarium, quod in liberis civitatibus, ut sunt Venetiae, Florentinae, posset maior pars eligere sibi regem aliis contradicentibus. Et hoc verum videtur non solum quia hoc manifeste expedit reipublicae, sed dato quod magis expediret politia aristocratica, aut democratica. Nam postquam respublica habet jus se administrandi et id quod facit maior pars, facit tota, ergo potest accipere politiam quam voluerit, etiam si non sit optima, sicut Roma habuit aristocraticam, quae non est optima" (ibid., n. 14; p. 181). See also *In I-II*, q. 105, a. 2 (Beltrán 6:481–82).

45. "Item non appellatur a rege ad rempublicam" (*De potestate civili*, n. 14; p. 180).

46. For another, more detailed development of this theme a dozen or so years later by Alonso de la Vera Cruz in 1553–54 at the nascent University of Mexico, see *The Writ-*

VI. VITORIA'S DOCTRINE IN THE *RELECTIO DE POTESTATE CIVILI*

As Vitoria sees it, a king chosen by the majority is king over the whole republic. In the case of a royal regime, the king does not just rule over individual citizens, but over all together, that is, over the whole republic as such.[47] Otherwise, the republic would be above the king and the regime in question would be democratic rather than royal.[48] Thus, even though kings owe their election to the republic, once elected, they stand in its place and exercise its authority so totally that "without them nothing can be done publicly in war or in peace."[49]

At the same time, Vitoria is never in any doubt about the subject of political power—in Aristotelian terminology, its material cause *(to hypokeimenon)*. Both before and after the transfer, such power is in the republic as such.[50] Rulers, even kings, do not have a different power from that of the republic. What they have is the authority to exercise the single power given to the republic by nature, and ultimately by nature's God.[51] The power would be one and the same whether the republic would be a democracy, an aristocracy, or a monarchy.[52] As such it would be of natural and ultimately divine origin. Its exercise, however, would be immediately a matter of the republic's choice. Thus he can hold with perfect consistency that the *power* of the king (or of the senate) is from God rather than the republic,[53] while the authority to exercise it is conferred by the republic.[54]

---

ings of Alonso de la Vera Cruz: II, Defense of the Indians: Their Rights, original text with English translation, ed. Ernest J. Burrus (Rome, 1968), nn. 856–99, pp. 428–48.

47. "Volo dicere quod, in regio principatu, rex est non solum supra singulos, sed etiam supra totam rempublicam, id est etiam supra omnes simul" *(De potestate civili*, n. 14; p. 179).

48. "Quia si respublica esset supra regem, ergo esset principatus democraticus, id est popularis, et sic non est monarchia et principatus unius" (ibid., pp. 179–80).

49. "Quia princeps non est nisi ex electione reipublicae. Ergo gerit vicem et auctoritatem illius. Imo iam ubi sunt legitimi principes in republica, tota auctoritas residet penes principes, neque sine illis aliquid publice aut bello aut pace geri potest" *(Relectio de jure belli*, n. 6; p. 821).

50. "Causa vero materialis, in qua huiusmodi potestas residet jure naturali et divino, est ipsa respublica, cui de se competit gubernare seipsam et administrare, et omnes potestates suas in commune bonum dirigere" *(De potestate civili*, n. 7; p. 159). See also, n. 8; p. 164 (text in note 51, below). On the republic's retention of power, cf. Urdánoz, *Obras*, 133–34.

51. "Videtur quod regia potestas sit non a republica, sed ab ipso Deo, . . . Quamvis enim a republica constituatur (creat namque respublica regem) non potestatem, sed propriam auctoritatem in regem transfert, nec sunt duae potestates, una regia, altera communitatis" *(De potestate civili*, n. 8; p. 164).

52. See note 26 above.

53. ". . . dico reges etiam a jure divino et naturali habere potestatem, et non ab ipsa republica, aut prorsus ab hominibus" *(De potestate civili*, n. 8; pp. 161–62).

54. See note 51. "Respublica non transtulit dominium suarum rerum in regem, sed gubernationem" *(In I-II*, q. 105, a. 2 [Beltrán, 6:483]).

VII. THE DOCTRINE IN THE *RELECTIO DE INDIS RECENTER INVENTIS*

There are two principal places in the first *Relectio de Indis*, dating from January of 1539, in which Vitoria has considered a post-original voluntary transfer of political power by citizens of a republic. More specifically, this would be a transfer which would involve a change of sovereignty wide enough to encompass the replacement of a king. In the first place, he has rejected the assertion of such a transfer by the Indians as a title for Spanish domination of the New World.[55] By contrast, in the second place he accepted such a voluntary transfer as a possible justification of Spanish domination.[56]

The immediate difference between the two places has to do with the circumstances of the transfer as they would affect its voluntary character. In the first instance, the transfer would be vitiated inasmuch as the Indians would be acting in fear and ignorance.[57] But in the second case, which is immediately relevant to us, Vitoria allows in principle for a majority vote of the people of a republic deposing their king and replacing him with another. He says:

ANOTHER TITLE could be through a genuine voluntary election, for example, if these barbarians, both rulers and others, knowing the wise administration and the civilization *[humanitatem]* of the Spaniards, would in consequence wish to accept the king of Spain as their prince. For this could be done and it would be a lawful title, even by natural law. Indeed, every republic can set up its own ruler—and to do this universal consent would not be necessary, but instead the consent of a majority seems sufficient. For, as we have argued elsewhere [cf. *Relectio de potestate civili*, n. 14], in matters relating to the good of the republic, things agreed upon by the majority are of obligation, even when others oppose them. Otherwise, nothing could be done for the benefit of the republic, since it is difficult for all to be of one mind.[58]

---

55. *De Indis*, II, n. 16; p. 701.
56. Ibid., III, n. 16; pp. 721–22.
57. Cf. "Nec iste titulus est idoneus. Patet primo, quia deberet abesse metus et ignorantia quae vitiant omnem electionem. Sed haec maxime intervenit in illis electionibus et acceptationibus" (ibid., II, n. 16; p. 701).
58. "ALIUS TITULUS posset esse per veram voluntariam electionem, puta si barbari ipsi intelligentes prudentem administrationem et humanitatem hispanorum, ultro vellent accipere in principem regem Hispaniae, tam domini quam alii. Hoc enim fieri posset et esset legitimus titulus etiam de lege naturali. Quaelibet enim respublica potest sibi constituere dominum, nec ad hoc esset necessarius consensus omnium, sed videtur sufficere consensus maioris partis. Quia, sicut alias disputavimus in his quae spectant ad bonum reipublicae, illa quae constituuntur a maiori parte, tenent, etiam aliis contradicentibus: alias nihil posset geri pro utilitate reipublicae, cum difficile sit ut omnes conveniant in unam sententiam" (ibid., III, n. 16; pp. 721–22).

So far, no problem. Leaving aside comment on whether Vitoria was speaking with tongue in cheek about the Spaniards, the phrase "both rulers and others" is striking. First, it implies that, *in the absence of further reasonable cause,* the people alone or their rulers alone would not be sufficient to effect a lawful change of government.[59] And, second, it would take in a host of different situations. While the majority voting might not be egalitarian, such a vote of rulers and others would allow a lawful new transfer of power and a replacement of rulers in an aristocracy or even in a monarchy if the king agreed to abdicate.

At this point the text continues:

Accordingly, if in some state or province Christians would be a majority and in the interest of Faith and for the common good they would want a Christian prince, I believe that they could elect one, even when it entails rejection of other infidel rulers, and even in face of opposition from the minority. In this way the French for the good of their republic changed princes and, having taken their kingdom away from Childeric, handed it over to Pippin, the father of Charlemagne, which change Pope Zacharias approved.[60]

With this Vitoria no longer seems to be talking about a willing aristocracy deposing itself or about a king voluntarily stepping aside. Instead, this looks like a push which can come from below. While it is hardly democracy in the modern sense, it looks like a first stirring in that direction. Granted that he speaks of "Christians" and granted that he has in mind something like "the Pauline privilege" (cf. 1 Cor 7:15), where the Church for the good of the faith of a Christian spouse may dissolve his or her marriage to an implacable pagan,[61] nevertheless, the election of a new ruler or king and the rejection of former rulers or kings would be by majority vote, for the common good or for the good of the republic. Even though in the case of Pippin replacing Childeric, Pope Zacharias approved,[62] a close reading of Vitoria

---

59. ". . . non potest populus sine alia rationabili causa accersere novos dominos, quod est in detrimentum priorum. Item nec e contrario ipsi domini possunt novum principem creare sine assensu populi" (ibid., II, n. 17; p. 702). Note the phrase here, "sine alia rationabili causa."

60. "Unde si in aliqua civitate aut provincia maior pars esset christianorum et illi in favorem fidei et pro bono communi vellent habere principem christianum, credo quod possent eligere, aliis invitis, etiam relinquendo alios dominos infideles. Et dico quod possent eligere principem non solum sibi, sed toti reipublicae. Sicut et galli pro bono suae reipublicae mutaverunt principes et ablato regno a Childerico tradiderunt Pipino, Caroli magni patri. Quam mutationem Zacharias Pontifex comprobavit" (ibid., III, n. 16; p. 722).

61. For Vitoria's employment of the Pauline privilege, see *De Indis,* III, n. 14; p. 720. On the privilege today, see *Code of Canon Law: Latin-English Edition* (Washington, D.C., 1983), canons 1143–47, pp. 412–15.

62. On this example, cf.: "Vitoria fait allusion au coup d'état de 751 par lequel Pépin

suggests that the change would have been lawful even without papal approval.

This suggestion is confirmed by a passage from Vitoria's lectures on the *Summa theologiae* at Salamanca during the academic year 1533–1534. For in that place, directly to the present question, we read:

> In a case where the republic has given authority to a king, if it has given it unconditionally and in perpetuity to him and to his successors, it cannot demand it back. Even if it be expedient, it is no longer lawful to change the government. But it is true that if the king would be a tyrant in governing, the republic could depose him. For even though the republic has given its authority, it retains its right to defend itself. And if it cannot do so in any other way, it may remove its king.[63]

In principle, therefore, the republic, by majority vote, can lawfully remove even an absolute monarch, if he is ruling in a tyrannical fashion.[64] On the other hand, Vitoria's support of royal power would not yield for reasons of simple expediency. Bad decisions by the king or his general incompetence would hardly justify his replacement.[65] Perhaps better said, they would not do so ordinarily. For one can conceive a situation where the king's decisions or level of competence would so imperil the republic as to threaten its existence. In such a case, I have little doubt that Vitoria's monarchism would allow his removal. The argument would be to the effect that the *raison d'être* of all public power would be for the common good. But in the situation under consideration the common good could not be preserved without the removal of the king. For in that situation the king, by the level of his incompetence, would be ruling against the common good, in effect (if not by

---

le Bref (714–768) père de Charlemagne, mit fin à la dynastie mérovingienne en déposant Childéric III (d. 754), fils de Chilpéric II, incapable de gouverner. Cette sustitution de dynastie se fit avec l'accord de l'Église et du pape Zacharie. En fait dit un historien, 'L'Eglise a couvert l'usurpation.' (J. Calmette, *Le Monde féodal*, P.U.F., p. 99)" (M. Barbier, *Francisco de Vitoria, leçons sur les Indiens et sur le droit de guerre* [Geneve, 1966], 99n1).

63. "Vel respublica dedit auctoritatem regi, quam non potest repetere, si sine conditione dedit in perpetuum illi et suis successoribus. Etiamsi expediat non licet tunc mutare principatum. Verum est quod, si esset rex tyrannus quantum ad gubernationem, posset respublica illum deponere. Nam etsi respublica dederit auctoritatem suam, tamen manet apud eam ius defendendi se; et si aliter non potest, potest reicere regem" (*In I-II*, q. 105, a. 2 [Beltrán, 6:482]).

64. On the difference between the rule of a true king and the rule of a tyrant, cf.: "Hoc enim interest inter rem legitimum et tyrannum, quod tyrannus ordinat regimen ad proprium quaestum et commodum; rex autem ad bonum publicum ut tradit Aristoteles 4 *Politicorum* c. 10" (*De jure belli*, n. 12; p. 824). For Aristotle, see *Politics* IV.10, 1295a20–23; III.7, 1279b6–7; and V.10, 1311a1–4.

65. On this, I agree with Hernández, *Un Español en la ONU*, 148.

intent) ruling tyrannically. In this instance, the republic could exercise its right to self-defense and the majority would have "a further reasonable cause" for his removal.[66]

One more note is necessary. Even though the removal of a tyrant is lawful, Vitoria will not leap to its accomplishment. Ever the judicious doctor, anxious to preserve law, order, and stability in the republic, he tells us that to the extent that they are suitable for the republic even a tyrant's laws oblige—not indeed from his enacting them but rather from the consent of the republic itself.[67] In line with this, obedience to a tyrant is evidently preferable to lawless anarchy.[68]

VIII. CONCLUSION

On the question of royal power and the removal of a king, Vitoria is not without his modern critics. Bernice Hamilton, for example, thinks that his doctrine of one power of the republic administered by the king has contradictory implications. "It is, and it is not," she says, "a theory of divine right."[69] Pierre Mesnard, in his well-known work on the "soaring" of political philosophy in the sixteenth century, while acknowledging merit in Vitoria, has seen him moving toward the "L'État, c'est moi" of Louis XIV (1638–1715).[70] Regrettably, I cannot comment in detail here on their criticism. I have indicated in section VI my own belief in the consistency of Vitoria's doctrine of one power. And while he would certainly stress the divine origin of that power, this is a long way from the divine-right absolutism of Louis XIV.

In fact, I would argue, Vitoria was moving in the opposite direction. Granted, his sixteenth-century steps were modest by twentieth-century standards. Nevertheless, they plainly led toward recognizing a majority's right to remove even a total monarch when there was reasonable cause to do so. In the Age of Discovery of new lands and peoples, which was also a period of religious turmoil, of rising nation states, and of

---

66. See note 59 above.
67. "Certe videtur quod leges quae sunt convenientes reipublicae obligent si ferantur a tyranno, non quidem quia a tyranno latae, sed ex consensu reipublicae, cum sanctius sit ut serventur leges a tyranno lata quam quod nullae serventur" (*De potestate civili*, n. 24; p. 193).
68. "Et profecto esset in apertam perniciem reipublicae, si principes qui non habent iustum titulum occuparent regnum, quod nulla essent iudicia nec aliquomodo possent malefactores puniri, aut coerceri, cum non sit tyrannus iudex legitimus, si leges eius non obligant" (ibid.).
69. Bernice Hamilton, *Political Thought in Sixteenth-Century Spain* (Oxford, 1963), 37–38.
70. Mesnard, *L'Essor de la philosophie politique*, 472.

growing monarchical claims, this was no mean achievement. Finally, against such diverse and sundry background, our Salamancan professor's steps gain special importance from the fact that he took them on a ground of clear thinking about the nature of human beings and the natural teleology of their political associations.

4   Vitoria: The Original Philosopher of Rights
MARCELO SÁNCHEZ-SORONDO

It is known that Hegel saw the philosophy of universal history as the progressive development of the essence of man, his liberty. The Orient, the land of the sunrise *(Morgenland)*, the arising of humanity, was the first step. There, only one was free: the one who from time to time has power, the tyrant who is not even conscious of being one. With Greece we have the anthropological turn: "Man is the measure of all things" (Protagoras). Greece produced anthropomorphism, even to the extent that the gods are like men. There one considered the spirit as thought, as *nous*. Man is man, insofar as he is cultured, is a philosopher, is a citizen of the *polis*. Many are free, that is to say, those who are citizens. Through the message of Jesus Christ, which says that all men have an absolute relationship with God the Father, insofar as they are the object of His personal love, it is Christianity alone that makes one aware of radical liberty. Men are free insofar as they are men, because they are destined to have an absolute relationship with God. All men have an aptitude for God, an aptitude for being inhabited by His Spirit, which is the greatest freedom.[1]

Within this progressive consciousness of the message of Christian liberty, Thomas Aquinas has a singular place, as his great disciple, Francisco de Vitoria, also has. It is Vitoria on whom we will expound. But first, let it be said: It is not possible to present the modern awareness of man and of his rights without considering the anthropological doctrine of Thomas Aquinas, which has its practical diffusion with the discovery of America and the courageous position of the Dominicans of the second Scholastic, among whom the guiding figure of Vitoria emerges. To be even clearer one might say that the positive values which the French Revolution and liberalism claim to vindicate were al-

---

1. See G. W. F. Hegel, *Enz.*, para. 482. See also *Vorl. über d. Phil. d. Gesch.* (Hamburg: J. Hoffmeister, 1955), 155–56 and 61–62.

ready present, in a more balanced way, in the doctrine of Francisco de Vitoria. It was only with the discovery of America and the debate which it aroused in Europe that one became conscious of man as man, while before this the consciousness of man was presented as divided in diverse religious cultural forms; the Greek, the Roman, the European, the East Indian, the African, but man as man, the subject of universal salvation, did not exist. We affirm immediately that the discovery of America is the discovery of man and of his universality. It is man becoming conscious of himself and of his dignity by the very fact of his being man, a son of God and capable of being saved by Christ.

For Vitoria the reality of man and of the universe has an autonomy and force which begins with creation and not only with re-creation. Like Leonardo da Vinci, St. Francis of Asissi, and Thomas Aquinas, Vitoria calls out to nature: "daughter of God." Without doubt the human being has a primary dignity which separates him from and elevates him above all the other beings of creation. Man has therefore a most privileged position. This echoes the thinking of St. Thomas, so many times recalled by John Paul II, according to whom the human person is: "Id quod est perfectissimum in tota natura."[2] For Vitoria, it is the power of reason which expresses most profoundly this emergence of man, within all of nature, that makes him into an image of God: "Homo est imago Dei per naturam, scilicet per potentias rationales."[3] This image of God was made immediately proper to man by the first creation, by that which our author calls *naturam*. It is written, engraved by God, in the nature of man. Therefore, one is not concerned with a sacred nature or a nature which is fallen because of sin, but rather with a nature which, despite original sin, is an image of God because it is crowned by reason and liberty from the very first moment.

In man there is no Platonic, Augustinian, or Cartesian dualism. The human person is considered in the whole dimension of its humanity, that is to say, in the entirety of its nature with the sensitive and intellective dimensions. Thus when Vitoria speaks of the inclination of man, he is indicating with it the whole man "in so far as he is man," which embraces all of his reality: "Inclinatio hominis absolute est inclinatio hominis inquantum homo est."[4]

The vision of nature and of man is profoundly optimistic in Vitoria. He repeatedly cites Gen. 1:31: "And God saw everything that He had made, and behold, it was very good." This optimism from a biblical

2. Thomas Aquinas, *Summa theologiae* I, q. 29, a. 1.
3. Francisco de Vitoria, *De Indis*, in *Obras de Francisco de Vitoria*, ed. Teófilo Urdanoz (Madrid: B.A.C., 1960), n. 6, p. 654.
4. Francisco de Vitoria, *De Homicidio*, in *Obras*, n. 3, p. 1097.

fount is what allows him to reject with decisiveness any Lutheran interpretation about the radical corruption of nature. The departing point of the philosophy of Vitoria is the affirmation of the divine origin of man, with respect to both the soul as well as the body. Man, by his creation, is good and "man's inclination as man is good," because "the inclination of human nature comes immediately from God, and consequentially it cannot be oriented towards evil."[5]

In order to know man and his activity, the evaluating of the nature of man with its requirements and its inclinations, with its rights and duties, is indispensable. Human nature, we can say, writes its own law for itself, interprets its progress, makes its own way, unfolds its perfection and presents within itself its self-comprehension. Man realizes his perfection by unfolding his nature. The moral law and the working of man is not therefore, as it is in Ockhamism, the projection in history of atemporal decrees, but it is a reality to be discovered by human reason and by the experience of history as the profound requirement of the being of man.

Man by his reason can and should know this law. All the work of Vitoria tends towards this finality. Our author writes, "In practical things there are principles known to all, such as 'Good is to be done and sought after, evil is to be avoided.' But there are others not known to all."[6] At this point Vitoria cites a Thomistic text which says: "A thing is said to belong to the natural law in two ways. First, because nature inclines thereto: for example, that one should not do harm to another. Secondly, because nature did not introduce the contrary: thus we might say that for man to be naked is of the natural law, because nature did not give him clothes, but art invented them. In this sense 'the possessing of all things in common and universal freedom' are said to be of the natural law, because subordination and the division of goods were not introduced by nature, but devised by human reason for the benefit of human life. Accordingly the law of nature has not been changed in this respect, except by addition."[7] It is in this Thomistic doctrine of mutation by addition that Vitoria sees human rights (*ius gentium*), which participate in the natural and the positive and which represent man's progressive cognizance of his own being and his social life. For Vitoria,

---

5. "Defendo inclinationem hominis, quatenus quidem homo est, bonam esse ... Inclinatio naturae humanae est immediate ab ipso Deo. Ergo non potest esse ad malum" (ibid., 1091).

6. "Ita in practicis sunt principia nota omnibus, ut bonum est faciendum; alia quae non sunt omnibus" (Francisco de Vitoria, *Comentarios a la Secunda secundae*, ed. Beltrán de Heredia [Salamanca, 1952], 6:426). When in doubt, one consults the wise; cf. *De Indis*, nn. 1–3, pp. 648–50.

7. Aquinas, *Summa theologiae* I-II, q. 94, a. 5.

nature and history, as the maturing of the experience of man, pertain inseparably to human rights. Because of this, it is possible to say that the natural law is susceptible to progress (by addition) and one could speak of a "natural law of progressive content."[8]

Thus, in the determination of the law and its requirements, insofar as it is human, Vitoria does not conform with the principles of an abstract philosophy nor with the mere repetition of classical authors without having grounded his position on an analysis of the experience of man travelling the difficult road of understanding himself. This reflection upon the human experience along the historical road of the determination of natural precepts is so accentuated in Vitoria that he sometimes seems not to leave space for the specificity of Christian morality, which almost presents itself as the most intimate aspect of the same nature. Thus he proposes, for example, friendship and solidarity as the fundamental precepts which should govern the relations between men. In his important commentary on the *Summa* of St. Thomas Aquinas, Vitoria advises confessors to keep very much in mind these precepts of the natural law: "The confessor should not preoccupy himself with the precepts of the new law but with the natural law."[9]

In order to work well, it is not necessary to place our actions in relationship to God, as our ultimate end, it is sufficient rather to fulfill precepts according to one's nature. Therefore, those who do not know God can act morally.[10] Consequently, for Vitoria human realities insofar as they are human acquire all their weight. "God did not command us to honor our parents for God, but only to honor them. And thus also with the other precepts, that is to say, God commanded that in each case they be fulfilled in a suitable way."[11]

Thus Vitoria constructs his theory of the rights and duties of man on the basis of human nature, and not faith alone nor grace alone. That is why these rights and duties are the same for all men. In effect, for Vitoria, one of the fundamental characteristics of human rights is that of equality. This is the great principle expressed in the famous letter written in 1534 at the end of his career to Fr. Miguel de Arcos: "If the

---

8. "Dico ergo in summa quod nihil est de iure naturali nisi quod naturaliter potest sciri ab homine.... S. Thomas ... expresse determinat quod illa sunt de iure naturali quae ab omnibus cognosci possunt, nisi impediantur ex mala consuetudine vel ex prava affectione vel mala doctrina vel studio" (Vitoria, *Comentarios*, q. 57, a. 2, n. 5).

9. "Non oportet confessorem esse sollicitum de praeceptis legis novae, sed naturae" (Vitoria, *Comentarios*, 6:493).

10. "Omnis homo cum primum ad usum rationis pervenerit, etiam si Deum neque cognoscat neque possit cognoscere, potest bene moraliter agere" (Vitoria, *De eo ad quod* ..., in *Obras*, n. 7, p. 1344).

11. Ibid., p. 1345.

Indians are not men but rather apes.... But if they are men, they are our neighbors."[12] Every human person has a right to human dignity as well as all that which is necessary to guarantee it, precisely because each is a human being.[13] Man's political equality follows from the equality of men as such. This proceeds from the fecund principle maintained by Vitoria. The state enjoys by a divine and natural privilege the power to govern and administer itself. Yet before this same natural law and the abstraction made from human laws, "there is no reason why such a power should reside in one or another subject... because before men came together, nobody was superior to another, nor is there a reason why in the same society somebody should attribute to himself power over others."[14]

Francisco de Vitoria, parting from these principles, articulates his propositions as one would concentric circles, indicating the principal rights of the human person, such as equality, liberty, and solidarity. Thus the rights of the person are compromised in the primordial form of human association: marriage and the family. Doing something extremely rare for the literature of the time, Vitoria indicated the necessity of love within marriage: "The mutual duties and services of matrimony cannot be done if they are not done through and only through love. This is something that cannot be realized if the matrimony is the result of force."[15]

Vitoria also indicates the social dimension of man: "Homo natura est animale civile et sociale."[16] Following the authoritative Aristotelian fragments concerning man as "a naturally social and political animal,"[17] the Salamancan professor thus establishes the natural foundation of political society. The nature of man, fragile and weak, is such that he cannot subsist without the help of his equals and without mutual relationships and a social life. But sociability does not realize itself

---

12. This important letter was discovered by Beltrán de Heredia, who published it in *Ciencia Tomista* (Salamanca, 1930). Alberto María Torres also refers to this letter in his book, *El padre Valverde, ensayo biográfico y crítico* (Quito, Ecuador, 1932).
13. P. V. Beltrán de Heredia, *Francisco de Vitoria* (Barcelona, 1939), 123.
14. "Non sit maior ratio ut potestas illa sit in uno quam in altero ... si enim priusquam in civitatem homines convenirent, nemo erat aliis superior, non est aliqua ratio cur in ipso coetu, seu conventu civili, quisque sibi super alios potestatem vendicaret" (Vitoria, *De potestate civile*, in *Obras*, n. 7, p. 159).
15. "Officia et mutua obsequia, nisi ex amore proficisci non possunt. Qui contingere aut vix aut nunquam posset, si matrimonia inter invitos constituerentur" (Vitoria, *De Matrimonio*, in *Obras*, n. 7, p. 894). See also: "Primus enim finis matrimonii, scilicet procreatio prolis et educatio, certe esse non posset inter invitos, et se non invicem amantes, cum commercium matrimoniale sit magnum signum amoris" (ibid.).
16. Vitoria, *De éo ad quod*, n. 7, p. 1344.
17. Aristotle, *Politics* I.2.1253a2.

as only an inexorable necessity of the physical condition of man, but also of all the aspects of his spiritual being: that is, as a necessity of his intellectual development and then of the virtuous fruits of justice and friendship for which the will is responsible. And Vitoria, anticipating the "modern philosophy of language," proves sociability by the gift of the word, "the announcement of the understanding."[18]

The justification of all the social degrees and forms originates from this naturalness and basic requirement of sociability for the realization of man. Yet this is also especially true for the political community as we can see in the following text: "It is clear that the source and the origin of the city and of republics are not of human invention, nor should one consider them as something artificial, but rather as something that proceeds from human nature to defend and preserve itself it suggested this reason to mortals."[19] Such a political society among all social groupings "is the most natural to man, the most convenient" within the entirety of natural creation.[20] With this Vitoria places himself in an order of perfective valorization, and not in the genetic order. This might be better understood by comparing civil society with the family. However, the sociological idea touched on here by Vitoria seems to be confirmed by modern ethnology, according to which the state does not arise as a prolongation of the family, but many times it is born out of the necessity for heterogeneous people and communities to form groups and to live together.

That is why Vitoria does not consider the state isolated as an ultimate political entity. In reality, just as man is inserted into the state, the states are inserted into the total perspective of the world. The novelty in this point of Vitoria's is exactly in this perspective—not only "sub specie urbis" or "status," but "sub specie orbis," that is to say, of the community of all the earth's peoples: "totus orbis."[21] Overcoming the Au-

---

18. "Sermo intellectus est nuntius, et in hunc solum usum datum Aristoteles tradit, quo uno homo ceteris animalibus antecedit, qui extra hominum societatem nullus foret. Atque adeo etiam, si fieri posset, si sapientia esset sine sermone, ingrata et insociabilis esset ipsa sapientia" (Vitoria, *De potestate civile*, n. 4, p. 155).

19. "Patet ergo fontem et originem civitatum rerumque publicarum non inventum esse hominum, neque inter artificiata numerandum, sed tanquam a natura profectum, quae ad mortalium tutelam et conservationem hanc rationem mortalibus suggessit" (ibid., n. 5, p. 157).

20. "Inter omnes societates societas civilis ea sit in qua commodius homines necessitatibus subveniant, sequitur communitatem esse naturalissimam communicationem naturae convenientissimam" (ibid., n. 4, p. 156).

21. See "totus orbis" used in speaking of war: "Cum una respublica sit pars totius orbis et maxime christiana provincia pars totius reipublicae, si bellum utile sit uni provinciae, aut reipublicae, cum damno orbis aut christianitatis, puto eo ipso bellum esse iniustum" (Vitoria, *De potestate civile*, n. 13, p. 168).

gustinian idea of a theocratic Christianity, Vitoria's idea presents itself as the fundamental catholic principle of the new international relationships and permits the successive incorporation of the non-Christian states into the international community.

Ancient Greece sustained egalitarianism with the Sophists and cosmopolitanism with the Cynics and the Stoics, but these doctrines frequently contained elements of hostility to the *polis*. Even more, they were founded upon the Greek concept of man, which placed the ultimate dignity of man in knowledge and in reason. The uncultured peoples, the barbarians, did not have a right to be called "men." They were less than men and could be slaves. Only Christianity created the basis of universal history because the unity of history presupposes the unity of humanity advocated for the first time by Christ with His doctrine of the universal paternity of God. With St. Augustine (354–430) in the *City of God*, we have for the first time the idea of the international community, for Augustine presents the first theology of history. This is conceived as the community of peoples, saved by Christ and organized under the direction of the pope and emperor (the doctrine of the two swords), which Arquillière calls "political Augustinism."[22] Vitoria develops the Thomistic idea of the value of the first creation of man made in the image of God and of man's re-creation in Christ through grace. His Thomistic formation caused him to propose as the starting point and supreme principle of all his philosophy of law the Thomistic distinction of a double order in the world, natural and supernatural. This is the foundation of the clear distinction of the two powers, the spiritual and the temporal, which have two independent social structures and two orders of law: the order of natural law, which is the basis of civil society and of its political authority, and the order of divine law, which is proper to the Church and limited to the spiritual order.[23] Because of this Vitoria rejects the universal political jurisdiction of the pope and the emperor and incorporates the non-Christian nations in the universal community, recognizing in them a complete juridical subject *(personería)* in the measure that a minimum of political organization is presented.

In the ancient world, the city-state of the Greeks was the perfect and self-sufficient type of state. But in the Middle Ages, this type of political society was already considered too limited: St. Thomas transposes the

---

22. H. X. Arquillière, *L'augustinisme politique* (Paris, 1934).

23. In his work *De regno seu de regimine principum* (bk. 1, chaps. 14–15), St. Thomas Aquinas expounds masterfully on the necessity of a spiritual authority, distinct from the civil, within the human community. This fundamental argument of his is always used by Vitoria.

city-state of Aristotle into the kingdom or the nation.[24] Undoubtedly, with this dramatic entry of the peoples of America onto the horizon of the West, the latent problem of the relations of men as such, organized into non-Christian socio-political structures, had to establish itself for the first time, and urgently. This singular historical circumstance created the new consciousness of the value of man as man—the image of God—and of its cultural, social, juridical, and religious consequences. Vitoria knew how to give form to this new consciousness with a bold innovation that perfects the ideas of the city-state of Aristotle and the kingdom of St. Thomas: the idea of the world as a universal community of peoples, already organized by free people into free nations. Thus he proposes for the first time international law in modern terms, parting from the requirements of the social, cultural, and religious plurality of states.

Man is also a religious animal. For Vitoria, this is a natural and necessary dimension of the human being, by the sole fact of being created by God, which is a preamble or, as Kant would say, "the condition for the possibility" of revealed religion. Vitoria proves this affirmation historically: "Even though the gentiles might have false beliefs about God, one will always find in them, in some way, the notion of the existence of God, whether as one or as many, to whom they offer cult and religion."[25] This Vitorian principle, according to which "there are no atheistic peoples," a position confirmed by modern ethnology, is at the basis of the religious rights and liberty sustained by Vitoria. That is why Vitoria proposes a method of free choice for the conversion of the Indians: not by force, but "with provable and rational arguments and accompanied by manners both decent and observant of the law of nature, such as are themselves a great argument for the truth of the faith."[26]

With this, the typical wars of religion, so frequent in the Middle Ages, are condemned and a new law is proclaimed by the Salamancan

---

24. "Triplex est communitas: domus, sive familiae, civitas, et regni.... Communitas civitatis omnia continet quae ad vitam hominis sunt necessaria: unde est perfecta communitas quantum ad mere necessaria. Tertia communitas est regni, quae est communitas consummationis. Ubi enim esset timor hostium, non posset per se una civitas subsistere; ideo propter timorem hostium necessaria est communitas civitatum plurium, quae faciunt unum regnum" (*In Mat.*, chap. 12, 25 [Torino, 1951], n. 1011, p. 158). See also *De regimine principum*, bk. 1, chaps. 1, 4–15.

25. "Etiam si gentiles haberent falsas sententias de Deo, tamen semper hoc erat omnibus commune quod erat aliquis Deus, sive unus, sive plures, cui debebant cultum et religionem" (Vitoria, *De eo ad quod*, n. 4, p. 1337).

26. "Cum argumentis probabilibus et rationabilibus et cum vita honesta et secundum legem naturae studiosa, quae magnum est argumentum ad confirmandum veritatem" (*De Indis*, n. 13, p. 694).

magister: the law of modern international order, by which the peaceful cohabitation of peoples and of nations with different beliefs and religions is possible. In order to establish this principle, Vitoria only needs to turn to St. Thomas's precisely formulated thesis, according to which the pagans should in no way at all be compelled by any type of coercion, whether physical or moral, to convert in a forced and insincere way to the Catholic religion.[27] This was not only "the conclusion of the doctors as well as that of both canon and civil lawyers." This has always been Catholic doctrine, because the Church has always defended the freedom of belief as a reasonable and voluntary offering made to God, as it has done even since the Fourth Council of Toledo, when it opposed the abusive practice of Sisebutus, who compelled Jews to receive baptism.[28]

Finally, within Christianity, not only does man retain the dignity of the person but also exalts it. Vitoria presents one of the proofs in a singular text in which he expounds that the Church is at the service of man. "For him the natural parts in the body are for all the body; but in the Church, instead, each man is only for God and for himself, in this case the private good is not ordered to the good of all, at least in its principal and precise sense."[29]

We can therefore conclude that in the history of the progressive consciousness of the human person, his rights, and his duties, Francisco de Vitoria appears as the original philosopher of rights. He, in opposition to a historicist vision (be it of an Augustinian fideist or Ockhamistic-Rousseauistic positivist), proposed moral humanity from the perspective of the person as an individual substance in a rational nature *(individua substantia rationalis naturae)*, taking his inspiration from the best developments of thought in his time. His choice to follow St. Thomas led him to establish morals on the basis of the dignity of the human person, which has its origin in the first creation by God, who made man in His image and likeness. The rights and duties of each person arise from his or her nature, which one discovers in the progressive path of the reflection on human experience accrued in the history of peoples. These morals in their substance are common to all men and should be applied in both liberty and solidarity. They guide both the conduct of

---

27. Aquinas, *Summa theologiae* II-II, q. 10, a. 8.
28. Cf. Vitoria, *De Indis*, n. 15, pp. 695–96. As regards the Jews, see chapter 45 of the Council of Toledo, which says: "De iudaeis autem praecepit sancta synodus nemini deinceps ad credendum vim inferre; cui enim vult Deus miseretur et quem vult indurat."
29. "Pars naturalis est praecise propter totum in corpore. In Ecclesia singuli homines sunt propter Deum et propter se solum, nec bonum privatum ordinatur ad bonum totius, saltem praecise, nec principaliter" (Vitoria, *De potestate Ecclesiae*, in *Obras*, n. 5, p. 365).

states and governors as well as the flow of international relations. So in this world which passes, it orients men and peoples towards God, the beginning and the end of history and of every human person.

We hope that the message of Vitoria, the five hundredth anniversary of whose birth was commemorated in 1992, might be a beam of living light for the peoples of America and of the world in this decisive moment at the end of the millennium when its most transcendental event is being commemorated: the discovery of America, which is also the discovery of the natural sacredness of man as man, the image of God.

5 Bartolomé de Las Casas and Juan Ginés de Sepúlveda: Moral Theology versus Political Philosophy
EDUARDO ANDÚJAR

In 1550, the city of Valladolid was the site of a *disputatio* between the very well known Father Bartolomé de Las Casas and the lesser-known Doctor Juan Ginés de Sepúlveda, a discussion that has been studied in detail by numerous historians of ideas, among the most important of whom are Lewis Hanke, Angel Losada, Venancio Carro, John Phelan, Beltrán de Heredia, Marianne Mahn-Lot, and Vidal Abril-Castelló. All scholars agree that this was an event of the first magnitude in the history of Spanish imperial policies toward the Americas. The purpose of the debate, according to the summary prepared by Domingo de Soto, was "to investigate and constitute the forms and the laws so that our Catholic Faith can be preached and diffused in the New World that God has discovered for us, in order to better serve Him, and to examine by which method these people can become subjects to the Majesty of our Emperor without damaging their royal conscience, in accordance with Alexander's Bull."[1] In other words, procedures had to be instituted that would govern the proclamation of the Gospel to the inhabitants of the New World and the establishment of legitimate Spanish sovereignty over the newly discovered territories and its people.

It should be noted that the controversy was surrounded by rather special circumstances that are not usually associated with academic exercises. Notwithstanding the wealth of details available on the subject, quite often descriptions of the controversy give the impression that the two authors had a long and bitter debate face-to-face, following the university tradition. In fact, the two adversaries never met during the sessions. Each of them explained his point of view; there was no discussion either with the other speaker nor with the audience of theo-

---

1. Domingo de Soto, *Summarium*, in *Tratados de Fray Bartolomé de Las Casas* (México: F.C.E., 1965), 1:228–29.

logians, jurists, and crown counsellors. Sepúlveda spoke for three hours during the first session, which probably started August 1, 1550; Las Casas occupied the podium during the following five days, reading his *Argumentum Apologiae*. He interrupted the reading and Domingo de Soto wrote a *Summarium*, which is the only "official" document containing information on this session. The judges did not reach a final decision and a planned second series of sessions was postponed, first until January 1551 and then until April.[2] This whole process was surrounded by tactical maneuvers by the two adversaries that were intended to diminish the political effects of the opposing doctrinal position, or, more simply, as an answer or reaction to the actions of the other.

For example, Las Casas used all his political influence on Prince Felipe and the Council of Indias to obtain from the Council of Castilla a ban on the publication of Sepúlveda's book *Democrates Secundus*. Meanwhile, Sepúlveda was writing to the emperor, requesting permission to publish his work, which permission the emperor granted. Las Casas retaliated by using the influence of his acquaintances to have the imperial authorization revoked until the promulgation of a judgment by the Universities of Alcalá de Henares and Salamanca concerning the content of Sepúlveda's work. The judgment was negative. In reply, Sepúlveda demanded the condemnation of the opusculum *Aviso y Reglas para los Confesores*, written by Las Casas years before, and characterized by Sepúlveda as "un libelo infamatorio."[3] All these tactical maneuvers speak very clearly of an ideological debate destined to influence the political decisions of the royal power. The content of the debate may have been philosophical and theological, but its immediate objective was to establish the theoretical basis for the solution of a practical political problem.

Because the theme of the debate possesses special significance in the context of the predominantly pluralistic vision of our contemporary society, almost all scholars who have studied the case have taken one side or the other, with a majority in favor of Las Casas. The two characterizations that have emerged from the commentaries greatly influence the reading of the documents, so that it is now difficult to read Las Casas without seeing him as Liberator of the Oppressed, or to

---

2. Vicente Beltrán de Heredia, "Introducción Biográfica," in *Domingo de Soto y su Doctrina Jurídica*, by Venancio D. Carro (Madrid: Real Academia de Ciencias Morales y Políticas, 1943), 56–57.

3. Venancio D. Carro, *La Teología y los Teólogos-Juristas españoles ante la Conquista de América* (Salamanca: Biblioteca de Teólogos Españoles, 1951), 609. See also note 49.

read Sepúlveda other than as a bellicose and impenitent advocate of slavery.

Some of Las Casas's contemporaries were less than benevolent, treating him as "hypocritical and vain,"[4] as "dishonest and lacking charity."[5] In contrast, most of our contemporary scholars hold him in high esteem: "an honour not only to Spain and America, but also to the whole world," said Manuel Quintana;[6] for Pope Paul VI, he is a "specialist in humanity,"[7] and Marianne Mahn-Lot calls him "the Precursor of Human Rights."[8] In view of Las Casas's passionate discourse and his long and untiring work, it is not surprising that readers find his writings convincing. Lewis Hanke, while paying tribute to "the power and the persuasive force of Father de Las Casas," acknowledged that there was a danger that his own historical objectivity was endangered by Las Casas's rhetorical seductiveness.[9]

Sepúlveda, perhaps understandably so, did not meet the same fate as Las Casas. Manuel García Pelayo synthesized in one sentence the characterization of Sepúlveda that emerges from the major scholarly work in the first half of this century: "a staunch defender of the Indian's slavery; ... his doctrine is nothing else but the product of an arrogant and conceited nature."[10] This opinion might not be entirely fair, especially if we take into consideration the judgment of Diego de Covarrubias, who, even if he disagreed with some aspects of Sepúlveda's doctrine, considered him *"Vir quidam Graece et Latine apprime doctus, et omni genere scientiarum quoad humanam et divinam philosophiam insigniter eruditus."*[11] Covarrubias praised Sepúlveda's opinions and rec-

---

4. In a letter to the emperor, Bishop Marroquin wrote: "Yo sé que él ha de escrivir invinciones é imaginaciones que ni él las entiende ni entenderá en mi conciencia S.M., que todo su edificio e fundamento va fabricado sobre iproquesía i así lo mostro luego que le fue dada la mitra, rebozó la vana gloria, como si nunca oviera sido Frayle, i como si los negocios que ha traido entre las manos no pidieran más humildad i santidad para confirmar el zelo que había mostrado" (quoted in A. M. Fabié, *Vida y Escritos de Don Fray Bartolomé de Las Casas* [Madrid, 1881], 2:149).

5. Toribio Motolinía to Emperor Charles the Fifth, 2 January 1555, in *Proceso a la Leyenda Negra*, ed. Luciano Pereña (Salamanca: Universidad Pontificia de Salamanca, 1989), 28–36.

6. Quoted from Benno M. Biermann, *El Padre de Las Casas y su Apostolado* (Madrid: Fundación Universitaria Española, 1986), 9.

7. See Marianne Mahn-Lot, "Supplique adressée au Pape," in *Bartolomé de Las Casas. L'Évangile et la force* (Paris: Cerf, 1991), ii.

8. Marianne Mahn-Lot, introduction to *De l'unique manière d'évangéliser le monde entier*, by Bartolomé de Las Casas (Paris: Cerf, 1990), 12.

9. Lewis Hanke, *Bartolomé de Las Casas* (Buenos Aires: EUDEBA, 1968), xii.

10. Manuel García Pelayo, "Estudio Preliminar," in *Tratado sobre las Justas Causas de las Guerras contra los Indios*, by Juan Ginés de Sepúlveda (México: F.C.E., 1979), 1.

11. Diego de Covarrubias, *Variarum Resolutionum* IV, ch. 1, n. 2., quoted in Luciano Pereña, *Misión de España en América* (Madrid: C.S.I.C., 1956), 154.

ognized his authority on the fundamental themes of the American problematic.[12]

Marcel Bataillon points out that Sepúlveda "is one of the rare peninsular scholars mentioned in the *Ciceronianus*."[13] Erasmus characterizes him as an erudite man and a good Latinist.[14] One should also remember that Sepúlveda's work, the *Democrates Secundus*, was approved by Doctors Guevara and Moscoso from the Castilla Council and by Father Diego de Vitoria, the famous preacher, brother of the renowned Francisco de Vitoria, and one of the declared enemies of Erasmus and his followers in Spain, who stated: "I have read this work and I have not encountered anything that does not conform with the truth; but, on the contrary, I found many things worth reading; as a result, I not only recommend, but also admire, the work and its author."[15]

Finally, the one who best and most humorously summarized the role of both antagonists in our controversy is Venancio D. Carro, who called them "two noisy representatives of the two opposite trends that divided the allegiance of the Spanish people in the sixteenth century."[16] As this remark suggests, we should keep in mind the idea of an intellectual Spain divided in two, along the lines of the controversy's theme.

The essential step in the study of doctrines is the analysis of their constituent ideas. In the field of political ideas, however, the historical circumstances surrounding their birth and evolution are important additional factors to consider in order to determine their reach, importance, and pertinence. The controversy between Las Casas and Sepúlveda has an immediate historical setting that has been meticulously described by most of the authors who have researched this theme. It has also a wider politico-social context, which begins with the discovery of America and includes numerous events that give the controversy a special character, and it is this context that I wish to examine. First, however, I will review the background of the *disputatio*.

1492 was the year of the discovery of a new geographic region and a new race of mankind. This event marked a point of no return. America and Spain became subjects of an irreversible historical movement in which the protagonists' behavior was determined by their culture, their ideas, their previous experiences, their vices, and their virtues. Spain brought to this movement a decisive element that had no coun-

---

12. See Pereña, *Misión de España*, 154.
13. Marcel Bataillon, *Erasmo y España* (Madrid: F.C.E., 1986), 407.
14. See Marcelino Menéndez y Pelayo, *Historia de los Heterodoxos Españoles* (Buenos Aires: Librería Perlado Editores, 1945), 2:484.
15. See Sepúlveda, *Democrates Secundus*, A. Losada, ed. (Madrid: C.S.I.C., 1951), 125.
16. Carro, *La Teología*, 564.

terpart on the other side: a spiritual mission to preach the Gospel and a secular mission to introduce into the host society a new cultural vision.

It is very important to take into account the fact that the new journeys, the heroic explorations, the search for new horizons, the eagerness for adventures and wealth, were all the result of an irresistible impulse that could not have been restrained by any force or crown, even an imperial crown on which the sun never sets. Two trajectories, until now absolutely independent, blended irreversibly to generate a new entity. But all generation has a corresponding pole of corruption. Soon after the Spanish visitors had gotten over their initial surprise and enchantment, they began to feel urgent needs and interests, which were eventually and inevitably accompanied by their corresponding miseries. The Spanish crown was therefore confronted with the obligation to implement mechanisms to adapt community life to the particular and unknown conditions of the New World.

From the first moment, a firm decision was taken to establish bases and institutions for an efficient and protective colonization of the natives.[17] In the 1493 *Instrucciones* to Columbus, he is entrusted "by all ways and means to endeavor and work to attract the residents of the said islands and *terra firma* so that they will become converted to our Holy Catholic Faith . . . to seek and have the said Admiral to treat the said Indians very well and lovingly, without annoying them, encouraging much conversation and familiarity from one to the other, doing the best work possible."[18]

---

17. Ferdinand and Isabella's precepts for the treatment of Indians is expressed in the first clause of their instructions to Columbus: "First, when you are in the said Indies, God willing, you will try with all diligence to inspire and draw the natives of the said Indies to ways entirely of peace and tranquility and impress on them that they have to serve and be beneath our lordship and benign subjection, and above all that they be converted to our holy Catholic Faith, and that to them and to those who go to live in the said Indies be administered the Holy Sacraments by the clerks and friars who are or shall be there" (*Instructions* [1493]).

18. See Vicente D. Sierra, *El Sentido Misional de la Conquista de América* (Buenos Aires: Ediciones Dictio, 1980), 28. And concerning slavery: "Sepades que el Rey mi señor y yo, con celo que todas las personas que viven y están en las Islas, en Tierra firme del mar Océano, fuesen cristianos y se redujesen a nuestra santa fe católica, hovimos mandado por nuestra carta que persona, ni personas algunas, de las que por nuestro mandato fuesen a las dichas Islas e Tierra firme, no fuese osado de prender, ni cautivar a ninguna, ni alguna persona, ni personas de los indios de las dichas Islas, para los traer a estos mis reinos, ni para los llevar a otras partes algunas, ni les ficiesen otro ningún mal, ni daño en sus personas, ni en sus bienes, so ciertas penas, en la dicha nuestra carta contenidas, y aún por les hacer más merced, porque algunas personas hayan traído de las dichas Islas algunos de los dichos indios, se los mandamos tomar, e los mandamos poner e fueron puestos en libertad, y después de todo esto fecho por los más convencer y animar que fuesen cristianos e porque viviesen como hombres razonables, hovimos mandado que algunos de nuestros capitanes fuesen a las dichas Islas e Tierra firme del dicho Mar

In 1503, Isabel la Católica established the *Encomienda,* an institution that would evolve over the years and that would later be the target of Las Casas's most severe criticisms. However, in its original form this institution was dedicated to the protection and promotion of the natives, who were to be treated as free individuals and not as slaves. The 1512 *Leyes de Burgos* modernized the *Encomiendas* system so that "the holder is now at the same time guardian and company manager, and is responsible for the protection and the christianization of the natives."[19] In 1513, the so-called *Leyes de Valladolid* established standards for the protection of the natives at work, with, among other things, rules concerning hours of work, and a prohibition against labor by children fourteen years old and younger and pregnant women; it also required that persons hiring unmarried women must receive their parents' consent.[20]

On the other hand, and at the same time, the practice of mixed marriages would eventually create a racially mixed elite, many of whom were descendants of Indian chiefs on their mother's side, and this mixing of races influenced the social structure of the new communities. Within a political reality that was generally characterized by harsh conditions, sometimes extremely so, largely because of the situations of violence and injustice that I shall not describe in detail, coexistence, the fruit of the institutions established by the Spanish crown, was slowly finding its place.

Las Casas himself was a witness and actor in this process. In 1513, when he was almost thirty years old, he participated actively in the incursions against the natives of the island of Española and in other expeditions, obtaining an allotment *(Repartimiento)* of Indians in reward for his services. Father Las Casas always considered himself a good *encomendero* for treating his Indian employees humanely. We must assume, contrary to his affirmations in his *Brevísima Relación de la Destruición de las Indias* (1542), that his case was not unique. In that respect, Toribio Motolinía, a priest with a long experience in the New World, in his letter to the emperor dated January 2, 1555, rejects Las Casas's arbitrary generalizations about the colonizers' conduct.[21] In

---

Océano e enviamos con ellos algunos religiosos que les predicasen e adoctrinasen en las cosas de nuestra santa fe católica" *(Instructions* [1503]; see Carro, *La Teología,* 25–26).

19. Jean Dumont, *L'Heure de Dieu sur le Nouveau Monde* (Paris: Editions Fleurus, 1991), 12.

20. Ibid. The author indicates that the first law in France regulating working conditions for children less than fourteen years old, the Villeneuve-Bargemont-Gérando-Montalembert law of 22 March 1841, came more than three centuries after.

21. Toribio Motolinía to Emperor Charles the Fifth, in Pereña, *Proceso a la Leyenda Negra,* 28–36.

1537, the Bull *Sublimis Deus* was published, in which Pope Paul III reaffirmed the human nature of the natives and their rights to liberty and to the ownership of their properties.[22] Also noteworthy is the inexhaustible labor of the numerous missionaries who denounced abuses and requested justice.

At the same time as colonizing and evangelizing efforts were extended to the whole continent, contacts with other native cultures became more and more complex. According to some authors, two factors were involved: on the one hand, quite apart from the real abuses by the Spanish, the cultural traditions of many native peoples were bloody. On the other hand, it was accepted as a fact that the evangelization of this multitude "was not usually possible until this bloody tradition had been repressed or rendered ineffective by permanent and efficient control."[23] Examples were numerous. Intervention was, in these cases, the necessary shock that "permitted the natives to liberate themselves from the blood vertigo of their own traditions," and frequently became the point of departure for massive and passionate adhesion of the natives to the *Pax Hispanica*.[24] This key point of intersection between theory and practice is the central theme in the controversy between Las Casas and Sepúlveda. Past experiences set the terms of a political and moral dilemma that confronted the Spanish crown. This problem had to be solved, after a consideration of the concrete historical circumstances, and the solution, once adopted, could not be renounced.

Even if the theme of the debate in the assembly was the form of preaching that should be adopted in America, and the conditions that determined the legality of the Spanish dominion, both Sepúlveda and Las Casas concentrated their efforts on finding "whether it is right for His Majesty to fight these Indians before preaching the faith to them, in order to subject them to His Empire, so that it would be easier and more convenient to teach and enlighten them, using the evangelical

---

22. "We, therefore . . . who with all our zeal seek to attract the sheep of the Lord's flock who are commended to us and who wander outside the fold, considering that the said Indians, as true men, not only are capable of receiving the Christian faith, but, as we have learned, are eager to receive it; and wishing to provide appropriate remedies in this matter; by the present do decree and declare, with our apostolic authority, that the said Indians and all other peoples who may in the future come to the notice of the Christians, though they be outside the faith of Christ, must not be deprived of their liberty or ownership of their possessions; and moreover, that they can use, possess, and enjoy freely and lawfully their liberty and their dominion, nor must they be reduced to servitude" (quoted in "Las Casas on the Conquest of America," by Manuel M. Martínez, in *Bartolomé de Las Casas in History*, ed. Juan Friede and Benjamin Keen [DeKalb: Northern Illinois University Press, 1971], 316).

23. Dumont, *L'Heure de Dieu*, 18.

24. Ibid., 19.

doctrine to demonstrate their errors and the Christian truth."[25] To this query Doctor Sepúlveda answered in the affirmative, pointing out that this war was not only lawful but also the most expeditious method to attain the desired results. Las Casas answered negatively, arguing that the war is not the most expeditious method and that it is furthermore immoral, iniquitous, and contrary to the Christian religion.[26] Sepúlveda founded his position on four principal factors: (a) the seriousness of the natives' crimes, particularly their idolatry and their sins against nature; (b) the roughness of their talents, which makes them people destined to serve those who have more developed aptitudes; (c) the utility of the faith, given that submission facilitates preaching; and (d) the human sacrifices and the cannibalism practiced by the natives. I shall discuss in particular the second point, which may be said to establish the theoretical basis for the other three. It is important to note that the initial terms of the debate assume the possibility of preaching the Gospel and bringing the natives to the Catholic Faith, so that the goals of conversion and the preservation of the Faith are common reference points in the development of the themes of both our authors.

For Sepúlveda, the native's barbaric nature is evident from known facts, and this condition in the natives requires political submission prior to evangelization. This political submission is further justified by the assumption that their condition disposes them naturally to serve, a concept of Aristotelian origin. But the concept barbarian is not univocal. Las Casas responds by a distinction among various species of barbarians: the first includes those who differ from others with respect to some customs; the second includes those who do not have languages that can be expressed in characters and letters; the third species includes those with perverse customs, undeveloped talents, and brutal inclinations, who are like wild beasts, incapable of governing themselves. According to Las Casas, this last is the only species that can be considered *natura servi*.[27] And only to members of this species can Aristotle's opinion that it is lawful to conquer them by force of arms be applied.

Las Casas denies that the American Indian belongs to the third species, and in his replies to the subsequent objections of Sepúlveda, he insists on the excellent capacities of the natives. However, his use of Aristotle's theory here is purely instrumental; his only purpose in raising it is to answer Sepúlveda on supposedly common grounds. In his

25. Soto, Summarium, in *Tratados*, 1:228.
26. Ibid.
27. Ibid., 282.

Argumentum Apologiae, he proposes that "the said barbarians be attracted gently, in accordance with Christ's doctrine," and he suggests that Aristotle be dismissed on this point, "because we have in our favor Christ's mandate: love your neighbour as yourself; ... although he [Aristotle] was a great philosopher, study alone did not make him worthy of reaching God."[28] The priest and the theologian overcome the philosopher.

It is easy to see at this stage that the central point of the discussion has become partially a question of facts, that is, an evaluation of the behavior and the supposed or real capacities of the Indians. Sepúlveda reaffirms his conviction concerning the brutal nature of the natives, founding it on the opinion of many of those who came back to Spain and on Fernández Oviedo's *Historia General*. Later chroniclers also attested to the roughness of the natives and the bloodiness of many of their cultural traditions. Las Casas's position in regard to the matter was consistent with the image of general natural perfection which he had presented in the *Brevísima*: "God created all these peoples as simple in the extreme, without wickedness, and without duplicity. They are very obedient and very faithful... They are exceedingly humble, unspiteful, patient, pacific, and quiet; no people in the world are so completely free of lust, discontent, hatred, and vindictiveness.... God created them as most capable of receiving our Holy Catholic Faith and of being endowed with very virtuous customs."[29] The New World and its peoples appear in all of Las Casas's descriptions as the preferred work of God, preserved in a certain original excellence.

This condition of "natural perfection" that Las Casas saw in the natives' world was, furthermore, the exact antithesis of the condition of those bestial creatures, almost monsters, at the limits of the human, who, lacking the capacity to create forms of human coexistence, corresponded, according to him, to the classification "slave by nature."[30]

---

28. "Valeat Aristoteles! A Christo enim qui est Veritas Aeterna habemus: Diliges proximum tuum sicut teipsum, (Matthaei 22°).... Diversa fuit haec venatio [he refers to Judes Tadeus's pacific 'manhunt' in Mesopotamia] ab illa quam docuit Aristoteles qui nimirum licet magna philosophia polleret non tamen dignus fuit illa capi ut ad Deum per verae fidei cognitionem veniret" (*Argumentum Apologiae adversus Genesium Sepulvedam theologum cordubensem* [1550], in *Obras Completas* [Madrid: Alianza Editorial, 1988], vol. 9, ch. 3, fol. 21–22).

29. Bartolomé de Las Casas, *Brevísima Relación de la Destruición de las Indias*, in Pereña, *Proceso a la Leyenda Negra*, 19–20.

30. "Tertia barbarorum species propria ratione et stricte sumpto vocabulo est eorum hominum qui vel impio et pesimo ingenio vel ex infelicitate regionis quam incolunt sunt saevi, feroces, stolidi, stupidi, a ratione alieni, qui neque legibus vel iure gubernantur neque amicitiam colunt neque rempublicam aut civitatem politica ratione constitutam habent, immo carent principe, legibus et institutis; non ineunt certis ritibus matrimonia,

These creatures, according to Aristotle, should be few in number and exceptional; to affirm the contrary would be, as Anthony Pagden remarks, in Christian terms, to speak of a fault in the order of creation. In effect, "if there were a great number of these creatures separate from the natural light common to all people and therefore unable by nature to call upon and to love God, the intention of God would have failed *in actu*. For the Christian (and above all the Christian theologian), this situation would be literally unthinkable."[31] Accordingly, the large size of the native populations in the New World permits us, with absolute certainty, to exclude them from the Aristotelian condition of natural slave. Sepúlveda was therefore wrong in identifying them as such and proposing that because of their nature they should be subdued by force.

The demonstration, theological in nature, incorporates the American natives in the universal human community, which is founded not only on an ontological equality but also on the equality of men as God's children, ordained as equal in relation to an ultimate goal simultaneously as individuals and as members of nations. In these circumstances, conversion cannot be realized by other means than those established by the Divine Providence, that is, "the persuasion of the intelligence by means of reasonable arguments and a gentle pressure on the will."[32] This excludes in all cases the use of force and political subjection prior to evangelization.

Sepúlveda, on the other hand, is thinking at a different level, clearly secular, in spite of his references to the Bible and the Fathers of the Church. His characterization of the barbarians does not seem to be the same as that attributed to him by Las Casas, even though some of his expressions might be ambiguous. Las Casas seems to believe him to be more Aristotelian than he really was, at least on this particular point.

When in the eighth objection to Domingo de Soto's *Summarium* Se-

---

denique nullum habent humanum commercium: . . . Hi simpliciter et proprie sunt barbari quales fortassis erant incolentes provinciam quae Barbaria apellata fuit" (Las Casas, *Argumentum Apologiae*, fol. 16).

31. Anthony Pagden, *La Caída del Hombre Natural* (Madrid: Alianza Editorial, 1988), 187. Las Casas wrote later, ". . . la Providencia divina más singular cuidado se dice tener de las criaturas racionales que de todas las otras criaturas que no son a su semejanza, . . . Luego no parece que la Divina Providencia quiere permitir que la naturaleza yerre haciendo monstruos en la especie de tan excelentes criaturas, tanto si no mucho menos más raras veces que en las demás. De lo cual se sigue necesariamente ser imposible de toda imposibilidad que una nación toda sea inhábil o tan de poco y barbarísimo juicio . . ." (*Apologética Historia Sumaria* [1551], ed. Edmundo O'Gorman [México: Universidad Nacional Autónoma de México, 1967], vol. 1, ch. 48, 259–60).

32. Bartolomé de Las Casas, *De unico modo vocationis omnes gentes ad veram religionem*, ch. 5, n. 1.

púlveda tries to clarify his concept of barbarian, he does not use Aristotle, but St. Thomas's commentary on the *Politics* of the Philosopher. The concept of the barbarian characterizes a person who lacks good habits and virtues, and is degraded; he is not subhuman or a monster: "Barbarians are those who do not live in conformity to natural reason and who have bad mores that are publicly approved; this can happen because of a lack of religion, which makes men grow brutal, or because of bad customs and lack of good doctrine and punishment."[33] On the same point St. Thomas refers to conditions under which "people can become irrational and almost bestial."[34] St. Thomas's definition coincides with the one set forth by Sepúlveda in *Democrates Secundus:* "The philosophers call servitude dimness of mind and inhuman and barbarian customs."[35] Political dominion is for Sepúlveda the necessary consequence of this natural condition.

But this political dominion is not *servil* (tyrannical), but *heril* (paternalistic), protective, founded on mutual interest. In the case of the Indians, the proposed political subjection aims at the material and spiritual elevation of their existence: "It will always be just and conformable to natural law that such people will subject themselves to the power of princes and nations more educated and humane, the mercy of whose virtues and the prudence of whose laws will put aside the barbarism and lead the subject people to a more human life and the cultivation of virtues."[36] And this, if necessary, by the use of force.

What is this natural, degraded condition, according to Sepúlveda? I believe that the answer will be found in the theory of natural law to which Sepúlveda make reference in the first part of the *Democrates Secundus*.[37] Natural law is defined as *"participatio legis aeternae in creatura*

---

33. Juan Ginés de Sepúlveda, "Objeción Octava," in *Tratados*, 1:311. It seems rather clear that Sepúlveda does not agree with the way Domingo de Soto and Las Casas have interpreted his concept of barbarian. See also note 30 above.

34. Thomas Aquinas, *In I Politicorum*, lect. 1, n. 1.

35. "Philosophi tarditatem insitam, et mores inhumanos, ac barbaros nomine seruitutis appellant" (*Democrates Secundus*, I, 10, 450–52, p. 20).

36. ". . . scriptum est enim in libro Prouerbiorum, 'Qui stultus est, seruiet sapienti', et tales esse docent barbaras, et inhumanas gentes a uita ciuili et a mitioribus moribus ac virtutibus abhorrentes, quibus commodum esset, ac natura iustum, vt humaniorum, ac virtute praestantium principum, aut gentium imperio subijcerentur, ut horum virtute, legibus, atque prudentia, deposita feritate, in vitam humaniorem, mitiores mores, virtutum cultum redigerentur" (ibid., I, 11, 502–510, p. 22).

37. "Legem naturalem Philosophi eam esse definiunt, quae vbique habet eandem vim, non quia sic placuit, . . ." (ibid., I, 5, 219–20, p. 11). The doctrine of natural law is the underlying theme in the development of Sepúlveda's thesis. The abundance of references might force us to restrain our judgment on its so-called radical aristotelianism. Natural law is a doctrine which medieval Scholastics brought to the highest perfection and the influence of this tradition on Sepúlveda seems not only evident but very impor-

rationis compote."³⁸ According to this formulation, the rational being is part of a superior order that is regulated by eternal law. This order is the work of a universal legislator, and the place that each creature occupies in existence has in itself the character of law. Therefore, this eternal law is nothing else than the *"voluntas Dei quae ordinem naturalem conservari iubet, perturbari vetat."*³⁹ A person participates in eternal law through *recta ratio*, which inclines him toward duty and virtue; therefore, *recta ratio* and natural law are inseparably interrelated. This is the basis of Thomas's doctrine on natural law, which Sepúlveda made his.

St. Thomas distinguishes the first principles of natural law fron the secondary precepts, which are *"quasi quasdam proprias conclusiones propinquas primis principiis."*⁴⁰ The first principles are those that manifest the universality of natural law. Regarding the secondary precepts, Thomas affirms that their truth is not identical in all humans and that they are not known by all humans in the same way. This is due to the nature of practical action, which is essentially contingent. The diversity of cultures and the weight of social customs, as well as the influence of passions, bad habits, and poor natural dispositions, contribute to the complexity of moral judgment and error.⁴¹ They are obstacles to the knowledge of natural law. Furthermore, for St. Thomas, it is not impossible that in a given historical moment and at the level of the secondary precepts, the law could lose its vigor and, because of the obstacles indicated, be erased from the heart of man.⁴² The natural

---

tant. The triple reference to the Holy Scripture, to the Fathers of the Church, and to the Greek philosophers, so common in the argumentation of the medieval Scholastic, can be found throughout Sepúlveda's *Democrates Secundus*.

38. Concerning philosophers' definition of natural law, ". . . Theologi alijs verbis, sed eodem pertinentibus in hunc modum. Lex naturalis est Participatio legis aeternae in creatura rationis compote" (ibid., I, 5–5v, 221–22, p. 11). Saint Thomas's definition is "Lex naturalis nihil est quam participatio legis aeternae in rationali creatura" (*Summa theologiae* Ia-IIae, q. 91, a. 3, c.). At this particular point of his exposition, Sepúlveda uses not only Saint Thomas's definition of natural law but also part of the arguments included in q. 91, a. 2, c.

39. Sepúlveda, *Democrates Secundus*, I, 5v, 223–25, p. 11.

40. *Summa theologiae*, Ia-IIae, q. 94, a. 5, c.

41. Ibid., a. 4, c.

42. "Quantum vero ad alia praecepta secundaria, potest lex naturalis deleri de cordibus hominum, vel propter malas persuasiones, eo modo quo etiam in speculativis errores contingunt circa conclusiones necessarias; vel etiam propter pravas consuetudines et habitos corruptos; sicut apud quosdam non reputabantur latrocinia peccata, vel etiam vitia contra naturam, ut etiam Apostolus dicit, ad Rom. 1, 24 sqq" (ibid., a. 6, c.). Sepúlveda's thesis is the same. After defining the natural law and mentioning certain of its characteristics, he adds: ". . . nam hoc est rectae rationis lumen, quae lex naturalis intelligitur. Haec enim quid bonum sit, atque iustum, quid vicissim malum, et iniustum in bonis viris declarat, non Christianis solum, sed in cunctis, qui rectam naturam prauis moribus non corruperunt, atque eo magis, quo melior quisque est, et intelligentior" (*Democrates Secundus*, I, 5v, 235–40, p. 12).

condition of inferiority that Sepúlveda mentions does not refer to a subhuman creature, or a faulty product of nature (of a creator God, in theological terms), but to real human persons from whose heart natural law has been erased. In other words, intellectual errors of judgment concerning the end to be sought and defections of the will from the end, even when rightly conceived, could in the end lead men toward a state of clouded moral conscience. Sepúlveda's argument differs from that of Las Casas in that it is not affected by the large numbers of American natives that he deems to be living in a state of natural servitude. The barbaric customs of the New World natives, in Sepúlveda's eyes, constitute a case in point. These are men who possess nothing of science, do not know letters, and have no written laws; they have given themselves to the most infamous vices, they lack temperance, they are cannibals.[43] Their barbaric institutions are proof of their roughness, savagery, and innate servitude.[44]

Confronted by these facts, intervention is, for Sepúlveda, a human obligation. It implies a possibility of initiating in the natives a progression of moral conscience, and at the same time an elevation in the condition of their existence. This intervention can be made, said Sepúlveda, in a right, just, and merciful way, with some benefits to the Spanish crown, but a much more important one to the natives.[45] Even more, "if such an enterprise is given to men who are not only strong, but also just, moderate, and human, it could take place without cruelty or criminal behavior."[46]

Sepúlveda's perspective is philosophico-political, and it originates in a problem of the practical order. Effective evangelization, that is, conversion of the Indians *and preservation of the faith of the converted,* cannot be realized without the consolidation of an order in which, in Sepúl-

---

43. "Confer nunc cum horum virorum prudentia, ingenio, magnitudine animi, temperantia, humanitate, et religione humunculos illos, in quibus vix reperias humanitatis vestigia, qui non modo nullam habent doctrinam, sed ne litteris quidem vtuntur, aut nouerunt, nulla retinent rerum gestarum monumenta, praeter tenuem quandam, et obscuram nonnullarum rerum memoriam, picturis quibusdam consignatam, nullas leges scriptas, sed instituta quaedam, et mores barbaros. Nam de virtutibus si temperantiam, et mansuetudinem quaeras, quid ab eis sperare liceret, qui erant in omne genus intemperantiae, et nefarias libidines profusi, et non pauci vescebantur carnibus humanis, . . ." (*Democrates Secundus*, I, 18–18v, 858–68, p. 35).

44. ". . . qui nihil esse certum habeo, quod magis illorum hominum ruditatem, barbariem, et insitam Seruitutem declaret, quam publica ipsorum instituta, Sunt enim pleraque omnia seruilia, et barbara" (*Democrates Secundus*, I, 19v, 916–19, p. 37).

45. Ibid., I, 15, 692–95, p. 29.

46. "Cui officio, si viri non modo fortes, sed iusti, etiam moderati, et humani praeficiantur, facile res sine vllo scelere, aut crimine confici queat, et non nihil Hispanorum, vt dixi, sed multo magis pluribusque rationibus barbarorum commodis consulatur" (ibid., I, 15, 698–701, p. 29).

veda's terms, the less perfect will submit themselves to the more perfect. Such political dominion implies not only the partial or total abridgment of sovereignty, but also the *possibility* (a very important term) of using force as a means of subjection.

The obligation to intervene is, for Sepúlveda, even more evident when the society in question practices the sacrifice of innocents for ritual reasons or for cannibalism. Sepúlveda's position is simple, commonsensical, and founded on natural law: to help a friend or neighbor constitutes an obligation for all honest and human individuals. This obligation will be even greater if the person is exposed to mortal danger.[47] This is the situation of those who are taken to their deaths on the altars of the barbarians, unjustly and without fault of their own.[48] And Sepúlveda adds, "the one who could have and did not defend his neighbor from such offense is as much a culprit as the one who did it."[49] The obligation here, a duty toward one's neighbor and human society, is part of natural law.

The political dominion will seek to halt these acts and to create conditions favorable to preaching. The treatment of the natives by the Christians will provoke, according to Sepúlveda, "a return to spiritual health and to honesty of customs,"[50] or, in other words, a recuperation of the clouded moral conscience.

As with Sepúlveda, the terms of Las Casas's answer are determined by the context in which he chooses to frame the question. Las Casas denies the rightness of using force to save innocents for three reasons: (a) because of the principle of the lesser evil—the death of innocents is a lesser evil than war; (b) because of the divine precept—the negative precept not to kill is more restrictive and binding than the positive one to defend innocents; and (c) because of the invincible ignorance of the

---

47. "... proximo autem, siue socio, auxilium exemplo Samaritani viri probi, et humani, omnes homines, si facere id possint sine suo graui damno ferre iubentur, lege illa diuina, quam ex Ecclesiastico citaui, Mandauit deus vnicuique de proximo suo, atque eo magis, si quis iniuria ad necem abstrahatur, ..." (ibid., I, 32, 1564–70, pp. 61–62).

48. "Erue (inquit) eos, qui ducuntur ad mortem iniuste scilicet ac sine culpa, vt illi miseri homines, qui a barbaris istis ad impias aras mactabantur..." (ibid., 1571–73, p. 62).

49. "... qui enim non repellit a socio iniuriam, si potest, tam est in vitio, quam ille qui facit" (ibid., I, 32v, 1580–81, p. 62).

50. "... hujusmodi barbari, possunt, ... compelli ut Christianorum imperio subjiciantur, a magnis injuriis magnisque sceleribus prohibeantur, et justis, piis religiosisque monitis et consuetudine Christianorum resipiscant, ad sanitatem redeant morumque probitatem, et volentes sui commodi salutisque gratia veram Religionem accipiant" (ibid., p. 62; cf. cod. D [Menéndez y Pelayo edition]). See also *Democrates Secundus*, I, 20–20v, 951–58, pp. 38–39.

natives: they do not believe; therefore, they are not guilty; therefore, they must not be punished by war.[51]

The fourth argument, which is the longest one, and puzzling in a certain way, is developed on the basis of a series of biblical texts. Neither the immolation of innocent victims nor the cannibalism justifies the use of force. Such events are not frequent, affirms Las Casas (a very doubtful opinion, subject to discussion), and, more important, they are part of the native cultures' sacred ceremonies. These native customs, says Las Casas, have a religious origin. The offering of an innocent child's life expresses the greatest submission to God and gratitude toward Him. Las Casas uses the Holy Scriptures as proof, citing Abraham's decision to sacrifice his son as the model of submission to what is higher.[52] In the *Apologética Historia Sumaria* (1559), where the theme is developed *in extenso* and on the same basis, Las Casas states that in the case of native peoples, the sacrifice of innocents constitutes the highest form of gratitude to their gods and their way of responding to benefits received.[53] The areas in which the greatest and most frequent sacrifices are practiced correspond precisely, according to Las Casas, to the homelands of the people who are the most devout, religious, and intelligent, and who have the most noble and elevated concept of God and the greatest appreciation of what is due to Him.[54]

José Luis Abellán has pointed to the richness of these texts, which contain an anthropological doctrine well in advance of their time.[55] However, concerning the subject of the controversy, Las Casas's position can be characterized by a definitive withdrawal of the concept of a right and duty to intervene. The absence of coercion is an absolute principle independent of the particular circumstances of a situation.

Las Casas proposed an ethics based on evangelical grounds, and a project that is outlined in his book *De unico modo vocationis omnes gentes ad veram religionem*, without much concern about the real possibility of its being actualized. It is an ethics that involves peaceful conquest and an attempt by the Church to bring pressure to bear upon the consciences of the natives. It is for Las Casas the only legitimate method for the incorporation of the Indians into the Church and then into the empire.[56]

---

51. Domingo de Soto, *Summarium*, 275–79.
52. Ibid.
53. Las Casas, *Apologética Historia Sumaria*, vol. II, chs. 143 and 183–85.
54. Ibid.
55. José Luis Abellán, *Historia Crítica del Pensamiento Español* (Madrid: Espasa-Calpe S.A., 1979), 2:485.
56. See Vidal Abril-Castelló, "La bipolarización Sepúlveda-Las Casas y sus conse-

The major principle of this project is the certitude that there is an absolute incompatibility between violence and the Gospel. Las Casas rejects the use of force as a means of conversion—a position based on the teaching of Thomas Aquinas, and shared by the majority of theologians and philosophers—but he also rejects the use of force as a means of preparing the conditions of peace necessary to a missionary's work. According to Las Casas, operations of pacification or prevention are harmful to the work of preaching, because the presence of armed men predisposes the will and the intellect of the natives in a negative way.

The incompatibility between the Gospel and force is founded on Christ's mandate to the Apostles to go and teach all nations without exception and on the peaceful and persuasive example of Jesus's manner of teaching, which is a copy of the Divine Wisdom, which moves all creatures toward their natural and supernatural ends in a very delicate, soft manner.[57] *Affabilitas* has the power to domesticate the proud barbarian, to soften the fierce expression of enemies, and to tame the spirit made arrogant by victory, as Las Casas, following Valerio Maximo, affirms.[58]

Concerning the real possibilities of success, the position of Las Casas is affirmative and to some extent optimistic. However, a judgment concerning the real possibilities of success depended upon a recognition of two factors: that the process of colonization had been under way for half a century, and that the natives' authorities would have to permit the preaching, and, even more important, to accept within their communities the continued presence of the newly converted. These two important difficulties were among the reasons for the Valladolid Assembly.

The test of Las Casas's project, which he conceived as a model for the whole of America, was the experiment of *Vera Paz* (1544), which unfortunately ended in failure. The Lacandons, a warrior tribe that practiced human sacrifices, ended the experiment with the sacrifice of several newly converted sons and the martyrdom of two Dominicans.

Another practical difficulty with Las Casas's project should be noted. He advocated the separation of the Spanish and the native communities, which not only did not favor the formation of a new racial entity, but to some extent, and indirectly, nourished the conflicts between the two racial groups. For these reasons and the circumstances mentioned

---
cuencias: la revolución de la Duodécima Réplica," in *La Etica en la Conquista de América*, D. Ramos et al. (Madrid: C.S.I.C., 1984), 233.

57. Las Casas, *De unico modo*, ch. 5, n. 1.
58. Ibid., n. 2.

at the beginning of this paper, it remains an open question whether Las Casas's project was realistic. In any case we must take into account that the calling of the Valladolid Assembly points to the urgency of deciding upon the political means of solving a critical situation for the crown both in material and spiritual terms.

Sepúlveda proposed an ethics based on principles of natural right. His position drove him to formulate a project whose direction is exactly the opposite of Las Casas's. It is an ethics whose conclusions pointed to political pressure, and force if necessary, as a means of incorporating the Indians into the empire as a prior step to evangelization. Naturally, this course of action is, according to Sepúlveda, the most efficient and just for obtaining the objective pursued. It therefore arises from human necessity, and consequently, according to Sepúlveda, it is founded on the Law of Peoples.[59]

It should be noted that concerning military actions, Sepúlveda distinguishes between the removal of obstacles to preaching and the preaching itself.[60] Neither the faith nor the sacraments can be imposed.[61] Moreover, the use of force is limited by certain principles. The just use of force requires not only a right cause but a right intention; to start a war looking for the spoils of war is a sin.[62] To extend the actions beyond the limits of what is necessary is illicit.[63] The end of war

59. "Quid autem necessarium est, ad naturalem societatem tuendam, id justum esse lege naturae sapientes viri testantur. Ad summam quod necessitate humana fuerit inductum, id jure naturae niti philosophi declarant" (*Democrates Secundus*, p. 92; cf. cod. D [Menéndez y Pelayo edition]).

60. Sepúlveda, *Democrates Secundus*, I, 44v, 2194–201. Concerning the removal of obstacles, see I, 36v–38, 1825–92, pp. 72–74. In a letter to Francisco de Argote, Sepúlveda wrote: "... ut primum Barbaris moribus sublatis, humane et ex lege naturae vivere congatur, deinde praeparatis ad Christianam religionem excipiendam animis, in veri Dei cultum per apostolicam mansuetudinem piis blandisque verbis inducantur..." (quoted in Abril-Castelló, "La bipolarización," 278).

61. "Non possunt pagani ob solam infidelitatem puniri, nec cogi, ut christi fidem accipiant inuiti, Nam credere voluntatis est, vt ait Augustinus, quae cogi nequit, possunt tamen a flagitijs prohiberi" (*Democrates Secundus*, I, 31, 1514–17, p. 59). See also I, 33v–34, 1643–74.

62. "Bellum iustum, non modo iustas suscipiendi causas, sed legitimam etiam auctoritatem, et rectum gerentis animum desirat, rectamque gerendi rationem.... Magni ergo interest ad belli iustitiam, quo quisque animo bellum suscipiat, id est quem sibi finem belli gerendi proponat. Quod animaduertens noster Augustinus, militare (inquit) non est delictum sed propter praedam militare, peccatum est,..." (ibid., I, 6v, 274–76, p. 13, and 7, 312–16, p. 14). Concerning a war aimed at territorial conquest, even in the case of "vital necessity": "... istud enim latrocinari esset, non belligerare" (ibid., I, 8, 349–50, p. 16).

63. "Modum quoque dixi, vt caeteris scilicet in rebus, sic in bello gerendo tenendum esse, vt si fieri possit innocentibus non fiat iniuria, neue ad legatos, aduenas, aut clericos, et res sacras serpat maleficium, nec hostes plus iusto laedantur.... Itaque Augustinus idem alio in loco nocendi inquit cupiditas, vlciscendi crudelitas, impacatus, et implacabilis

is the establishment of peace.[64] The use of force with cruelty is iniquitous.[65]

It does not make sense to me to ask who won the controversy. Of course, one must not forget that, as in all processes of colonization, abuses were committed. However, laws are largely determined by the reality of existing conditions. These laws are thus, in a sense, natural laws.

Paradoxically, the solution to the controversy had been given some years earlier in the works of Francisco de Vitoria. Let me finish by quoting some short texts from the *Sócrates Español*, because they constitute something like an answer in advance to the dilemma that the crown faced in 1550:

> Spain's right to remain in the Indies with the intention of overseeing and governing the natives is acceptable only because of the need for change there, only on the condition that this reform and protection be carried out for the benefit and development of the native peoples.[66]

> The Kings of Spain can licitly take the Indians under their tutelage and protection while the latter exist in a state of dependence and underdevelopment, on the condition that their occupation and rule tend more to the good and utility of the Indians than to the benefit of the Spaniards, so that the Indians' situation might improve and not become worse than it was previously.[67]

> By reason of prescription and more than forty years of *bona fide* possession, the Spaniards have the right to remain in the Indies, and are even bound to

---

animus, ferocitas rebellandi, libido dominandi, et similia, haec sunt quae in bellis culpantur" (ibid., I, 7–7v, 318–21, pp. 14–15, and 7v, 323–26, p. 15).

64. "Finis autem iusti belli, est, vt in pace, et tranquilitate, iuste, et cum virtute uiuatur, substracta malis hominibus nocendi, et peccandi facultate, ad summam, vt hominum bono publico consulatur, . . ." (ibid., I, 7v, 328–31, p. 15).

65. "Igitur quoniam lex noua, et euangelica perfectior est, et mitior quam vetus et Mosaica, illa enim lex timoris erat, haec gratiae, mansuetudinis, et Charitatis, bella etiam mansuete, et clementer gerenda sunt, nec tam ad punitionem, quam ad emendationem improborum suscipienda" (ibid., I, 32v, 1593–98, p. 63). Consequently, the cases of cruelty and abuses in the Spanish intervention in America, have to be condemned and punished rigorously; "Si bellum igitur, sic, ut dixisti, geritur Leopolde, impie geritur, et flagitiose, et qui sic gerunt in eos pene, tamquam in latrones, et plagiarios animadvertendum censeo. Parum est enim aut nihil iusta facere, nisi eadem iuste faciamus. Quod iustum est (inquit deus) iuste persequeris" (ibid., I, 14v, 684–88, pp. 28–29). And concerning the political dominion in America, Sepúlveda affirms that the natives must be treated ". . . tanquam ministros, sed liberos quodam ex herili et paterno temperato imperio regendos, et pro ipsorum, et temporis conditione tractandos. Nam temporis progressu cum ijdem fuerint humaniores facti, et probitas morum, ac Religio Christiana cum imperio confirmata, liberius erunt, et liberaliusque tractandi ministri, et ut mancipia vero nulli unquam tractari debent, . . ." (ibid., II, 65, 901–6, p. 120; cf. cod. D [Menéndez y Pelayo edition]). See also 65–66v, 906–57, pp. 120–22 and note 87.

66. Quoted in *The Rights and Obligations of Indians and Spaniards in the New World*, ed. Luciano Pereña Vicente (Salamanca, 1992), 30.

67. Ibid.

do so, because of the need of these newly converted Christians to be defended from the persecution and repression of caciques.[68]

In addition, out of human solidarity and in defense of those innocent Indians who are still sacrificed to idols or are killed that their flesh might be eaten, the Spaniards cannot abandon the Indies until the necessary political and social changes will have been accomplished that will put an end to that regime of terror and repression.[69]

The King of Spain can licitly employ a certain moderate and gradual political coercion, including even the legal prohibition of idolatry and the destruction of idols, in order to get the Indians to abandon their religious rites. However, a policy of coercion and force, which requires the Indians to abandon their ancestral religion by violent means rather than by persuasion, would be intolerable and morally unacceptable.[70]

These are some of the principles stated by Vitoria, who combined theological science, philosophical reflection on human matters, and a Christian heart.

Historians are not unanimous concerning the effective importance of the Valladolid Assembly for the future of the relations between the colonies and the crown. Let us say, however, that the term *conquest* was abandoned, and even if the military interventions were not judged illicit in essence, a clear consciousness arose that the effects of military interventions were not always appropriate, and that they should in the future be exceptional.

Regarding the two parts of the controversy, Sepúlveda's position is more philosophically rich and nuanced than what has been suggested by some of his critics; in any case, it is far from a mere and crude rationalization attempting to justify conquest by force. Concerning Las Casas, by the, in a certain sense, avant-gardism of some of his theses, he was in fact one of the forefathers of a new way of understanding social and cultural relations between peoples. Armed with the letter and the force of the Scriptures, he was also and above all a voice that served to prevent men from falling asleep with a falsely satisfied conscience.

In the longer term, and in regard to the historical significance of the events, the controversy between Father de Las Casas and Doctor Sepúlveda must be considered to be the clearest instance of an imperial power openly questioning the legitimacy of its rights and the ethical basis of its political actions.

68. Ibid., 32.
69. Ibid.
70. Ibid., 36.

6 The Controversy between Las Casas and Sepúlveda at Valladolid
RAFAEL ALVIRA AND ALFREDO CRUZ

The famous Junta de Valladolid of 1550–51, at which a disputation was held between Bartolomé de Las Casas and Juan Ginés de Sepúlveda, was one of the many meetings of jurists and theologians summoned after 1504, usually by the king of Spain, with the aim of examining the justice of the conquest and civilization of America. From these great gatherings there emerged legislation which tended increasingly to protect the rights of the native Indians and to place more stringent conditions on the use of force. In Spanish legislation on America a continuous progression can be seen, albeit one which is not entirely free of moments of vacillation, towards the abandonment of armed conquest and the establishment of a peaceful system of expansion, which reaches its apogee in the famous Ordinances of 1573. The inspiration and moving force behind this progress are to be found not simply in these great conferences, but also in the myriad treatises, addresses, and debates of a theological, philosophical, and juridical nature in which the Spanish intellectuals of the day examined, with tremendous freedom of thought, the legitimacy and ethics of Spain's actions in the New World. This communal attempt, on both the theoretical and the practical plane, to submit the business of the nation to the demands of morality and law, which has come to be known as the *gran Requisitorio,* or "great interrogation," is perhaps the most distinctive feature of Spain as a colonizing nation.

Within the framework of this series of debates, and the strenuous attempt to rethink policies and attitudes, belongs the meeting between Las Casas and Sepúlveda at Valladolid in 1550, called at the emperor's request, which represents the focal point of their dispute. The antecedents of this debate and of their confrontation can be traced in the history of what happened to their previous works on this subject. Las Casas had battled tirelessly and succeeded in prohibiting the publication of Sepúlveda's *Democrates Alter*, which defended the legitimacy of war against the Indians. Sepúlveda in turn had denounced various theses included in Las Casas's *Avisos y reglas para los confesores*, in which he maintained that all the conquests made and territory gained in America were null and void; orders were consequently given for this work to be confiscated.

The purpose of the discussion was, however, not to examine either of these two works, but rather, as Domingo de Soto relates in his summary of the debate, to deal with the general question of how the faith could be preached in those lands, and in what way their peoples could remain subject to the authority of the king, "without harming his royal conscience, in accordance with Alexander's bull."[1] Nonetheless, as Soto himself points out, both orators concentrated on the specific question of the legitimacy of war against the Indians. This focus was far from a coincidence, as we shall see below. The legitimacy of war was a crucial issue, both for the royal validity of Spain's possible right to expand into the New World, and for the legitimate ownership of many of the properties acquired in the new continent, which required a just war as the basis for their existence and title.

Sepúlveda defended the existing subjugation of the Indians for the purposes of civilization and evangelization and reasoned that the war was a just one based on the following four reasons: the sins of the Indians against natural law (idolatry and human sacrifice), the Papal bull, the defense of the innocents among the Indians, and the doctrine of natural servitude. Las Casas, on the other hand, denied not only the expediency of this subjugation, but also the justice of the war and the validity of the above reasons.

The first two of these reasons correspond to a law which is religious or theocratic in kind; the second pair reflect a law whose basis is natural. The entire controversy was to oscillate between arguments of these two types. This was far from illogical. No positive laws existed which could justify dominion over the lands in question, and so such a justification was only to be found in laws based on something that was not the work of man: on religion or on nature. For this reason, both contenders were in agreement that the matter for discussion was a theological issue, and that the participants in the debate should be primarily theologians.[2]

Despite their accord on the subject of methodology, however, their positions were diametrically opposed. The reason for this, and its

---

1. *Aquí se contiene una disputa o controversia* . . . , in *Obras de Bartolomé de Las Casas*, vol. 5 (Madrid: Ediciones Atlas, 1958), 295.
2. Angel Losada, "Introducción" to *Demócrates Segundo*, by Juan Ginés de Sepúlveda (Madrid: C.S.I.C., 1984), xx.

underlying meaning, lies in the differences of personality, viewpoint, and background between the two men.

Sepúlveda was a secular priest, trained in Italy, whose outlook was Renaissance through and through. The context in which we should seek to understand his position *vis-à-vis* the war against the Indians is that represented in his previous works: *Cohortatio ad Carolum V* (1529), *De convenientia militaris disciplinae cum christiana religione dialogus que inscribitur Democrates* (1535), and *De appetenda gloria dialogus que inscribitur Gonsalus* (1541). These works contain a critique of the pacifist mentality which sees Christianity as being incompatible with military activities and took its inspiration from Luther's teachings, which had already come under fire from Sepúlveda in his work *De Fato et libero arbitrio*. Sepúlveda attacked this mentality by defending the compatibility between evangelical and political exigencies, between Christian virtues and military virtues, and between the yearning for eternal glory and the noble zeal for earthly fame and reputation.[3] Thus, when the question of war against the Indians was raised, Sepúlveda saw this problem as a case to which he could apply the doctrine that he had already developed and defended. He approached this concrete problem, how the Indians should be treated, from the general theory, from the doctrinal battle in which he himself was a protagonist.

Las Casas's perspective was exactly the opposite. Las Casas was first and foremost a man of action, a reformed *encomendero* converted into a missionary friar, who recoiled in horror from the injutices he had witnessed. For him, what matters is the concrete, practical problem which surrounds him. The theory comes later: it is a necessary doctrinal development, inspired by and shaped to the requirements set by that experience of repugnance in the face of these injustices. His mode of thinking thus becomes strategic, with his thoughts undergoing changes according to the needs of the moment while being primarily directed at debunking the arguments brought forward by his opponent at each stage of the controversy. This detracts from the coherence and unity of his ideas, which are consequently difficult to summarize. To Las Casas, the fate of the Indians is a live, even a burning issue, which he cannot handle in a stylized academic fashion. He thus not only argues back, but throws himself into outbursts of invective against Sepúlveda's ideas, branding them as "venomous poison," "scandalous and deadly teachings," "injurious and an impediment to the Gospel," and so on.[4]

3. Sepúlveda, *Demócrates Segundo*, 32.
4. Las Casas, *Aquí se contiene*, 338, 345.

For Sepúlveda, the appropriate way to consider and approach this issue is to start by clarifying the general theory, and then proceeding to the particular, practical case. Las Casas, perhaps unwittingly, is moving in the opposite direction, reaching and reflecting on the theory from the point of view of the practical problem. Both men set out from what was immediate to arrive at what was remote. Sepúlveda approached the issue from Europe; Las Casas, from America.

Sepúlveda was not insensitive to the acts of cruelty and injustice that were possibly being committed against the Indians. He refutes the false accusations which his detractors must have levied, and he harshly condemns these unfair allegations again and again,[5] even alerting the Crown to its responsibility to forestall them.[6] Nonetheless, on the one hand he strongly doubts that the abuses are as widespread as Las Casas maintains (many others, like Friar Toribio de Benavente, "Motolinía," also voiced doubts); but more fundamentally, on the other hand he stresses that the object of the exercise is to clarify the nature of this war, whether it is just or unjust, the answer to which is not to be found in the practical errors which any given individuals might make during the course of that war.[7] The first task is thus to determine the justice of this war in itself, which forms the contents of the thesis that he defends. The practical problem of waging this war in the optimum way, taking into account its peculiar circumstances, would come later; to confront this problem, it would be necessary to apply suitable measures, but only in light of the general principles involved could a sound judgment be achieved. For this reason, after a clinical exposition of what would theoretically be appropriate to do with the Indians according to strict justice, he recommends that Christian monarchs, taking into account the circumstances and the objective of this war, should act in practice as clemency and piety required, seeking the salvation of the peoples in question, rather than their punishment.[8] The purely peaceful and evangelical more of action proposed by Las Casas represented an ideal which could as such be desired by all. The problem lay in its potential practical viability, and there were reasons enough to place this in doubt. As always, it was the clash between the pure idea and the real possibilities which made juridical reflection both possible and necessary, as any type of conduct which fell short of the ideal might constitute either

---

5. Sepúlveda, *Proposiciones temerarias* . . . , quoted in J.A. Fernández Santamaría, *El Estado, la Guerra y la Paz. El pensamiento político español en el Renacimiento 1516–1559* (Madrid: Ediciones Akal, 1985), 171.
6. Sepúlveda, *Demócrates Segundo*, 29, 123, 124.
7. Ibid., 29.
8. Ibid., 43, 63, 118, 123.

a legitimate concession or an injustice, and this dilemma could only be solved in the light of theory.

Sepúlveda's intention and interest was thus as follows: to clarify what theory had to say about the possible justice of the war against the Indians. As far as the practice went, he himself recognized that reasons and circumstances might arise which made it more appropriate to look after the Indians in some way other than by ruling over them;[9] but it was essential to begin by clarifying whether the war, and the dominion which was its result, were in themselves just or not, quite aside from whether this was then put into practice in the most appropriate or desirable way.

Las Casas, on the other hand, subordinated theory to practice. For him, the only objective, and one in which he had a strong personal interest, was to put a stop, once and for all, to the maltreatment of the Indians. To this end, if necessary, he exaggerates facts, glosses over the Indians' shortcomings, distorts the words of authorities on the subject,[10] or puts on them an interpretation which is more than just personal.[11] What for Sepúlveda belongs to the realms of prudence, to Las Casas is a matter of what is just or unjust in itself. Sepúlveda, like so many others, was able to defend the justice of institutions while censuring their failures and abuses. Las Casas identified the two aspects, viewing the practical mistakes as being necessary and natural consequences of the institutions themselves, and thus condemned the latter without exception. This rigorous and sweeping censure was criticized by many other religious and missionaries, including some from his own order, who denounced the evils which occurred in practice without calling for the abolition of the institutions. This attitude colors, for example, the conclusions of the third Mexican Council (1585), and it can be said to have been the most widespread opinion.[12]

In order to put an end to all violence against the Indians, Las Casas

---

9. Ibid., 79.
10. Cf. Anthony Pagden, *La caída del hombre natural. El indio americano y los orígenes de la etnología comparativa* (Madrid: Alianza, 1988), 178 n.
11. See, for example, his evaluation of Jephthah's vow, where he quotes St. Augustine but not St. Thomas or Vitoria who censure it (*Aquí se contiene*, 337); his distorted summary of Sepúlveda's ideas (ibid., 347); or his interpretation of the gospel phrase "the workman is worthy of his hire" (*Tratado de las Doce Dudas*, prin. 5, cited in *Los postulados teológico-jurídicos de Bartolomé de Las Casas*, by V. Carro [Sevilla: Escuela de Estudios Hispano-Americanos, 1966], 69 n).
12. Cf. Jaime González, "La Junta de Valladolid convocada por el Emperador," in *La Ética en la Conquista de América*, ed. D. Ramos et al. Corpus Hispanorum de Pace, vol. 25 (Madrid: C.S.I.C., 1984), 205; and Vidal Abril-Castelló, "La bipolarización Sepúlveda-Las Casas y sus consecuencias: la revolución de la Duodécima Réplica," in Ramos et al., *La Ética*, 269, n. 101.

needed to show that, for one reason or another, all war against them was unjust. He therefore strives to refute any reasoning which, while limiting the uses of war, might leave open the possibility that war could in some cases be just. In this sense it is indicative that Las Casas, who for many reasons must have been acquainted with Vitoria's ideas, completely avoids quoting them, as Vitoria's doctrine of just titles would allow for this possibility. This same intention, to rule out all possibility that the war might be just, explains the meaning behind Las Casas's correction in the twelfth reply of what he says in the nineteenth proposition of his *Treinta proposiciones muy jurídicas*.[13]

In general, Las Casas proceeds by acknowledging that the pope and the monarchy had rights and powers over the Indies to an extent that Vitoria would have considered excessive; but he then sets such stringent requirements for the justice of the war that it becomes impossible to exercise these rights legitimately. He thus states various rights which are devoid of real content and effectiveness.[14] In the summary of the debate, Soto himself feels obliged to introduce a further nuance to what Las Casas was saying, when he points out that the right to preach to the Indians can be held and defended without its being necessary that the Indians should wish to listen to that preaching.[15]

Las Casas's attitude is revealed with particular clarity when he states that those who write like Sepúlveda are sinning gravely, as they are hindering the repentance of those who have committed injustices.[16] It appears even more sharply when, after bringing a battery of arguments to bear against his opponent's theories, he ends by stating that even in the hypothetical case that his opponent might be right, Sepúlveda should nonetheless keep silent because of the scandal he was causing and the encouragement he was giving to men of violent tendencies.[17] What was necessary, urgent, and of paramount importance for Las Casas was not the understanding of the general doctrine but rather the halting of concrete abuses, even at the expense of the profession of that doctrine, if necessary. For him, the situation in America is so dramatic and so all-inclusive that cold, academic speculation on the subject seems irresponsible, frivolous, and shocking. Over and above the details of the theory, what concerns him is the moral effect, the offering of pretexts and excuses, which this theory might have on the less well-intentioned. This is what seems to lead him to pass over the primitiveness and cruelty of many aspects of the Indian's lives in si-

13. Las Casas, *Aquí se contiene*, 342.
14. Cf. ibid., 302 and 342.
15. Ibid., 305.
16. Ibid., 343.
17. Ibid., 344.

lence, and to idealize their image in order to give not the slightest motive for an attitude of severity towards them.[18]

One could maintain that in this controversy, each protagonist contributed one of the necessary elements, the sum of which would in fact constitute the satisfactory response to the problem considered in its full breadth. Whereas Sepúlveda proves more solid and coherent as far as the theory is concerned, Las Casas demonstrates greater sensitivity and deeper knowledge of human frailty and its dangers. Each man has the edge in his own field: in theoretical reflection, the academic wins out; in moral preaching, the missionary. As in so many other disputes, the ideal solution seems to be the synthesis of the two opposing views. But neither of the protagonists was capable of reaching this conclusion, and the very dynamics of the controversy drove them to push their antagonism beyond what was strictly necessary. On this point it should be noted, however, that although Sepúlveda moderated his stance and softened his image of the Indian, for example in the last version of *Demócrates Segundo* and in his *Crónica Indiana*,[19] Las Casas entrenched himself even more deeply in his position, thereby losing many of his followers.[20] The willingness to synthesize, so lacking in the two protagonists, is the attitude which prevails in the actions taken by official bodies. The recognition, on the one hand, of the theoretical reasons for the justice of the American enterprise, together with the establishment, on the other hand, of strict practical restrictions in view of the grave dangers which might occur, forms the position which seems to inspire both the universities' refusal to publish the *Demócrates Segundo*[21] and the assembly's supposed final conclusion of the Valladolid meeting,[22] as well as the legislation on the Indies itself.[23]

In his struggle against Sepúlveda, Las Casas sometimes acts by refuting the former's theses. More often, however, he does not confront Sepúlveda's doctrine as a whole (he seems in some way to accept it), but concentrates his efforts on disproving its possible application to the American case, either by an idiosyncratic reinterpretation of the doctrine, or by bearing witness to the facts. This strategy, and often his

---

18. Ibid., 345.
19. Cf. Sepúlveda, *Demócrates Segundo*, 33 n.
20. Cf. Abril-Castelló, "La bipolarización," 269 n.
21. Cf. Losada, "Introducción," xvi.
22. Cf. Pedro Borges, *Quién era Bartolomé de Las Casas* (Madrid: Rialp, 1990), 223ff.; and González, "La Junta de Valladolid," 201.
23. Indian legislation gave more attention and care to the rights of the Indians than to those of the Spanish in the Indies. In the Law Code for the Indies there appears a whole section dedicated to "good treatment of the Indians."

apparent lack of initiative and originality in the debate,[24] mean that as far as principles are concerned, the two men are often closer than one might imagine from the heated nature of the controversy. For example, faced with the four reasons proposed by Sepúlveda to justify war against the Indians, Las Casas does not produce a radical and all-embracing rejection. Regarding the sins against natural law (human sacrifices and idolatry), his approach is to cast doubt upon whether human sacrifices were contrary to natural law,[25] and to recognize that it would be licit to eradicate idolatry as long as this did not involve scandal, grave dangers, or harm.[26] Like Sepúlveda he accepts the papal bull as the source of dominion over the Indies, with the difference that this right could only be exercised after the conversion of the peoples involved. Equally, he accepts the defense of the innocents as justification for the Indians' subjection; but while Sepúlveda sees this defense as an obligation which corresponds to all princes, by natural law and the *ius gentium*, for Las Casas this belongs only to the Church, by divine right.[27] To this, he adds that if this defense can only be carried out by warfare, it is better to "tolerate" the situation, as war would inevitably bring about worse evils than the death of the few innocents who might be sacrificed or eaten.[28] Finally, with regard to natural slavery, although he sometimes rejects this altogether, he more often takes greater pains to demonstrate that the Indians amply fulfill the conditions established by Aristotle for the good, human life, and to distinguish different types of barbarian, to only one of which—the man who lives *more ferarum*—the doctrine of slavery could be applied, this obviously not being the type to which the American Indians belong.[29]

The explanation for this basic affinity between the two polemicists and their ambiguities is that neither of them opted definitively to examine the problem strictly from the perspective of natural law, as had been the case with Vitoria. This approach led Vitoria boldly to reject the papal bull as the legitimate title deed for Spanish rule over the Indies. By contrast, Sepúlveda and Las Casas continued to accept the bull and to argue about its interpretation. The absence of a perspective from which the problem could be viewed, such as that of Vitoria, caused them to fall into numerous ambiguities, and obliged them to balance precariously between the dictates of nature and the requirements of faith. Regarding war in general, the hierarchy of civilization and barbarism, and other issues, Sepúlveda defended the autonomy and validity of nature

24. Cf. Carro, *Los postulados*, 133.
25. Las Casas, *Aquí se contiene*, 306, 307, and 334.
26. Ibid., 328.   27. Ibid., 302.
28. Ibid.   29. Ibid., 307.

as opposed to religion. But as far as the Indians' rights were concerned, he inclined towards theocratic positions: the Indians deserve to lose their property and to be punished by war because of their crimes against natural law, which are seen not merely as injustices against men, but chiefly as sins against God.[30] For his part, Las Casas adopts the natural law position with respect to the Indians' rights, defending the autonomy and validity of what is natural; but when he comes to the actions of the Spaniards in America, his stance is Augustinian and curialist, as we shall see below. Both men changed their style of argumentation to win what the other approach would make them lose. In fact, each of them won or lost, from our given perspective, in different areas: that of the freedom of the Indians, or the freedom of the Spaniards.

In Sepúlveda's case, this lack of unity could be explained by his Italian education and his Renaissance spirit. As he had been trained in Italy, it is highly likely that he was ignorant of the Scholastic philosophy of Salamanca and its endeavor to renew natural law and the law of peoples. As his turn of mind is profoundly Renaissance, the imbalance between the Christian and the pagan, the supernatural and the natural, so characteristic of the Renaissance, is apparent in him.

In Las Casas, this phenomenon is even more striking. As he was a Dominican, had lived in San Gregorio at Valladolid, and had known followers of Vitoria, he must have been acquainted with the latter's ideas. Regardless, as we indicated above, he avoids Vitoria's doctrine based on the concept of universal human society and the law of nations. This could be due to his desire to discard every possible means of justification, however restrictive, of the war against the Indians. Curiously, quite unlike Vitoria, Las Casas concentrates all rights and responsibilities in the Church. Against the reasons for a just war defended by Sepúlveda, the Dominican presents six cases in which *the Church* could wage war against the Indians. The last of these, the defense of the innocents, could justify the war, but not because this constituted an obligation of natural law for all men, but because the innocents were commended to the charge of *the Church* by divine law.[31] If this were an obligation under natural law, it could be performed without the need for a warrant from the pope, as Vitoria had argued, but if it were a responsibility which belonged exclusively to the Church, this warrant would indeed be necessary.

Las Casas thus turns the pope's authority into the sole source of Spanish rights within America, denying all other means, either by nat-

---

30. Sepúlveda, *Demócrates Segundo*, 60 and 88.
31. Las Casas, *Aquí se contiene*, 302.

ural law or law of peoples, such as the theory of legitimate titles put forward by Vitoria. But with this apparently theocratic approach, what he was really doing was shackling the Christians' possibilities for action concerning the Indians. First, he denied any right of a simply human kind which might arise immediately in men and rulers and which would therefore prove difficult to control. And secondly, by making the pope's authorization into the sole basis for Spanish rights over America, he managed to subordinate these rights completely to the only end which the pope might properly pursue, that of evangelization. If evangelization were the only motive for which the bull had been granted, the bull could only concede the right to act with a view to achieving that end. He then had to demonstrate that war was not an appropriate and beneficial procedure for converting the Indians, which naturally did not prove particularly difficult, and thus conclude that all war against them was illegitimate. While Vitoria's legitimate titles, and the law of peoples in general, yielded not only rights but also duties for Spaniards and Indians alike, the papal bull as interpreted by Las Casas was a source only of duties, and that, only for the Christians. As the king of Spain had no other source of rights in America than the pope's authority, he could only possess what this authority had and could give him. If the powers which the pope might hold over temporal matters were powers only over Christians, and only to the extent that the spiritual ends required this, so the king's powers were limited with respect to the Indians; he would only hold temporal power over them once they had been converted, and to the extent that this might be necessary for the preservation of the faith. Meanwhile the king, like the pope, possessed no other right than that of preaching, and everything should be subordinated and sacrificed to the needs of evangelization, even if this meant "giving one's life for this," as such a mission would constitute a divine precept for a Christian prince, and was moreover, in this particular case, a command from the pope.[32]

As we have seen, the king not only held the same powers and rights as the pope, and only those, but also held them in the same way that the pope did, that is, they were wholly founded in and integrally subordinated to the spiritual ends. Las Casas turned the duties and requirements of the Church into duties and requirements of the State,[33] making the Spanish and their monarchs into missionaries alone, and eliminating the legitimate aims and rights which might naturally be

---

32. Las Casas, *Tratado de las Doce Dudas*, prin. 5, cited in Carro, *Los postulados*, 9 n.
33. We use this term in its general sense of the organization of political society, bearing in mind that it is, strictly speaking, an anachronism to apply this to the sixteenth century.

theirs within the political sphere. In his *Principia quaedam*, he states clearly that all powers should be subordinated to the spiritual end, and that the concern for this end belonged exclusively to the pope.[34] His zeal for defending the Indians' natural rights, and for peaceful evangelization, led him to fall into Augustianian and curialist categories with respect to the Christians. All these characteristies of Las Casas's doctrine manifest the great distance between his ideas and those of Vitoria's, as well as the error therefore of situating the former—as many scholars presume—in the latter's school of thought.

From Las Casas's point of view, the issue at hand was a simple problem of a purely religious nature which affected only one party (the Indian) and which had one conclusive solution (radical and ideal). For Sepúlveda, however, the problem was complex and many-faceted: it was at once religious, political, and anthropological in nature; affected two different parties (Indians and Spaniards); and its solution would have to be pluralistic, balanced, and prudent, a solution which would necessarily involve running certain risks.

In Las Casas's eyes, America meant one kind of undertaking alone: evangelization. And this task should be carried out with a pure, evangelical spirit, with the heroic disposition of the missionary ready to die, if necessary, so that the Word of God is preached.[35] Faced by this spiritualistic idealism, Sepúlveda displays the prudent realism of a political thinker. In a venture undertaken by men, even one of an evangelical nature, it would not be appropriate to rely solely on extraordinary means; such a venture should take correct reasoning and human prudence as its basis, for the contrary would be to tempt God.[36]

Las Casas was an idealistic figure and, without doubt, a generous one, but he was too exacting, and he lacked the statesman's practical wisdom;[37] his mind fed more upon ideals than ideas. Such a man would never accept as legitimate a solution which was any less than the direct and complete application of the optimum. On the contrary, a less "celestial," more "earthly" spirit like Sepúlveda was well-able to accept that justice in this world might contain imperfections, and to recognize that it was not for the political order to demand or pursue absolute perfection.

Moreover, for Sepúlveda the task that arose from the discovery of the New World was manifold: to evangelize, but also to civilize. This

---

34. See Carro, *Los postulados*, 45.
35. Las Casas, *Aquí se contiene*, 346–47.
36. Sepúlveda, *Demócrates Segundo*, 68.
37. His failures in the practical field bear witness to this. Cf. Josep-Ignasi Saranyana, "Sobre los orígenes del cristianismo en América. Historia doctrinal de una polémica," *Anuario de Historia de la Iglesia* 1 (1992): 282.

undertaking was envisaged in three phases: pacification, humanization, and Christianization. The first two were the most urgent and inescapable, and those which therefore allowed greater use of authority; whereas the third was the most perfect, but also the most voluntary. This gradation from the essential to the desirable, from what was to be imposed to what was to be suggested, is reflected in the very terms used by Sepúlveda: "to root out" their vices and customs, "to urge them pleasantly" in the direction of a more human life, and "to attract them gently" to the Christian faith.[38]

In the formulation of this threefold aim and its hierarchical ranking, the humanist sensibility, so unlike that of the missionary, is clearly visible. Civilization, as far as Las Casas was concerned, was implicit in evangelization, and was subordinated to the requirements and method of the latter. For Sepúlveda, civilization was an autonomous task which made demands of its own and justified different measures. The Christians' duty towards the Indians, and the benefit that the latter were to receive, was their conversion not only "into Christians and worshippers of the true God," but also "into human and civilized beings, in as far as this is possible for them."[39]

The appearance of these new races of men on the Europeans' horizon set a great challenge, that of integrating them into the world. But as the Europeans were Christians, *the* Christians, this integration was twofold: integration into human society and integration into the Church. An effort was made to incorporate them into the history of mankind, on the one hand, and the history of salvation, on the other. The former would open them up to their temporal destiny, human fullness; the latter, to their eschatological destiny, eternal life. The question lay in how these two integration processes should be ordered and combined. Las Casas placed integration into the Church before all else; this would take care of the whole task, including the humanizing element, and the other incorporation process would follow naturally as a simple consequence of the first. His experience led him to believe that incorporation into civilization might endanger assimilation into the Church, thus reducing the latter's importance and sphere of influence. Las Casas depicts the Indian as a man with a high degree of civilization whose sole defect was that he did not hold the Christian faith, and whose circumstances perhaps made him a little backward in the more liberal arts. In his *Apologética Historia*, the exaggerations of which are

---

38. Cf. Abril-Castelló, "La bipolarización," 256; Sepúlveda, *Demócrates Segundo*, 118; and Santamaría, *El Estado*, 221.
39. Sepúlveda, *Demócrates Segundo*, 63.

recognized by even his most fervent admirers, he frequently compares the Indians to the ancient Greeks and Romans, finding the Indians to be superior to both. Las Casas was nonetheless aware of the Indians' shortcomings, and on certain occasions, sometimes in an indirect manner, he acknowledges them. But when he does so, it is only to point out that these few vices, however serious they may seem, could easily be eliminated by preaching alone, for no race exists, "however barbaric and inhuman," that could not be led to a civilized life by means of exhortation and conviction.[40] It would be easy, then, to eliminate their unfortunate customs, and evangelization alone would suffice to perfect their humanization.

Sepúlveda's opinion was very different. He saw the Indian's situation as being primitive. The first and most pressing need was to integrate him into civilization, to humanize him, and only in this way could he then be converted to Christianity. His moral failings and savage state were consequences of his customs and institutions, all of which constituted an enormous obstacle for the faith. It was essential to remove this obstacle so that his reason could be liberated and the faith could enter.[41] While evangelization could only be carried out by means of peaceful preaching, the pacification and humanization which had to precede this stage, including the elimination of certain customs and institutions, could require and justify rule by force.[42] In contrast to Las Casas's optimism, Sepúlveda followed Aristotle in underlining the difficulty of changing people's habits and the influence and importance of institutions and customs.[43] The fact that these peoples had been capable of complying with such barbaric and inhuman laws and forms of behavior clearly demonstrated the corrupting force of a people's customs and authorities. And when such habits are inveterate, they constitute a second nature which it is difficult to modify. It was thus necessary to conquer them first, so as to replace their customs by other, more human ones, and thus to prepare them to receive the faith. A first imperative impulse was needed in order to make way for the exhortatory moment of the faith.

40. Cf. Las Casas, *Aquí se contiene*, 335; Silvio Zavala, *La filosofía política de la Conquista de América* (México: F.C.E., 1947), 92; and Lewis Hanke, *La lucha por la justicia en la conquista de América* (Madrid: Ediciones Istmo, 1988), 369.

41. Recognition of the need for this preliminary task also appears in the canons on education and promotion of the Indians at the Lima Synod of 1586.

42. This view was shared by others, including Motolinía himself, who considered it necessary to overcome them in order to remove their "abominations" (Ana de Zaballa, "Visión providencialista de la actividad política en la América española. Siglo XVI," *Anuario de Historia de la Iglesia* 1 [1992]: 292).

43. Cf. Sepúlveda, *Demócrates Segundo*, 73–74.

For Las Casas, humanizing the Indian was hardly necessary, and extremely easy to achieve. Within such a framework, the use of force seemed shocking, and its negative consequences all the more obvious. For Sepúlveda, there was a deep need for the Indian to be humanized, so that he could be integrated into the civilized world, and this would be very hard to bring about. If, to this, we add Sepúlveda's view that overcoming the Indians would prove fairly easy and would not require an inordinate use of force, we can see the context in which the positive, civilizing consequences of rule over the Indians stood out.

Once again, what underlies Sepúlveda's position is his own Renaissance preoccupation with the restoration of nature through, rather than opposed to, grace. Sepúlveda demands that we take into account the relevance of what corresponds to human nature, and the need to use the channels and faculties peculiar to this nature to bring it to its proper perfection. Natural perfection, and the means of achieving this, had not been abolished or substituted by Christian perfection and its means. Man, by virtue of his nature, is called to a specific fullness—civilization, *humanitas*—and in order to attain this, needs to draw on specific means (virtues, sciences, arts). Faith is not sufficient in itself, and its humanizing action is limited. Together with the dignity which comes of being the intended recipient of supernatural gifts, man possesses another type of dignity, arising out of the fact that he bears the values of human fullness. Both forms of dignity must be reflected in the order of human affairs; both forms of dignity should influence this order, and have consequences for it.

Las Casas's ideas appeared extremely spiritualistic in Sepúlveda's eyes. Faced with such unilateralism, he drew attention to the human sphere. Respect for this demanded that the degraded human condition of the Indians should be taken into account properly, something that Las Casas refused to take seriously when he sought the appropriate form that the relationship between Spaniards and Indians should take.

As one expert on this subject has accurately pointed out, Sepúlveda exemplifies the anxious awareness of the danger which lay in the destruction of the synthesis formerly achieved between grace and nature, Christian wisdom and pagan wisdom.[44] Against "ultramundane" views like those of Luther or Las Casas, Sepúlveda was struggling to conserve the possibility of embodying Christianity in this world, which meant taking on the things of the world in order then to raise them up with what was Christian. The truth of the natural sphere, natural order and criteria, were found plentifully in pagan wisdom. Christian revelation

44. Cf. Santamaría, *El Estado*, 187.

had not cancelled out this wisdom, which retained its validity in a general sense. Consequently, the Christian response to the problems of this world continued to require man to make a journey of recognition along paths which pagan wisdom had already travelled.

Christian truth and goodness could not be forms of truth and goodness which hardly touch this world, or which dictated standards for the world from the heights of Olympus with no heed to the specific nature of the affairs of the world. Such a Christianity would end up leaving the world defenseless, producing more confusion than clarity. Christian virtue must maintain within itself one feature which had also characterized pagan virtue: proving effective, that is, proving to be a genuine virtue, when confronted with the real and possible ways of this world. And this meant taking on the world, in other words, accepting its conditions, its requirements, and its demands.

All this leads up to the question of the appropriate way to apply the spirit of the gospel to the things of this world; to what extent human order could remain subject to the demands of the gospel. Could the command to "turn the other cheek" be applied literally to the relationships between countries? Could this be the appropriate response to disputes between nations? Would accepting a lower standard constitute a betrayal of the gospel or allegiance to the world?

The literal fulfillment of these demands might represent a form of perfection which was sublime and exacting, but it was only part of the life of the individual, and in no way within the limits of what could be asked. What was correct and applicable in the communal life of mankind and the nations of the world was somewhat less elevated, as this would have to take into account the nature of what was temporal and worldly, and therefore act with greater prudence and efficiency.

All this sheds light yet again on the differences in points of view between the two thinkers. Las Casas's viewpoint was moral, focusing on what was good and correct for the concrete person and his individual behavior. Sepúlveda's viewpoint was rather juridical, concerned with more general goods, with the business of institutions and societies.[45] While morality calls for an abundance of goodness, juridical thinking seeks only what is strictly just.

Regarding the problem of America, Sepúlveda's approach meant that there was no reason why the advent of Christian truth should override a difference which had been judiciously established by pagan wisdom, that between civilization and barbarism. This difference was still very real and was deeply rooted in the world of men; in no way was it

---

45. Cf. Sepúlveda, *Demócrates Segundo*, 91.

of only trivial importance when it came to the proper ordering of that world. On the contrary, the presence and value of this distinction implied that the correct order within a world which included civilized men and barbarians could only be a hierarchical order, in which the former ruled over the latter, as it was only natural that lower orders should be directed by their superiors.

For Sepúlveda, this difference belonged to the nature of human life, and it was thus perfectly legitimate to take it into account when recommending the way men should live. For Las Casas, this contrast was spurious, a product of the human will, and it would be wrong to take it into account. What separated the two men was not so much the facts as the way these were evaluated. At bottom, both were aware that a great cultural distance existed between Indians and Spaniards. But while Sepúlveda's humanist sensibility, attentive to the natural and the human aspects of the issue, brought out this distance and lent it importance, Las Casas's Christian sensibility, mindful of spiritual matters and salvation, reduced its importance, and required truly extreme situations, such as the case of the barbarians who lived *"more ferarum,"* to concede any importance to these differences.

Neither Las Casas nor Sepúlveda considered the Indian a barbarian because he was not a Christian.[46] For the former, the Indian was not a barbarian precisely because he was only a non-Christian; and for the latter, the Indian was a barbarian precisely because he was *not* only a non-Christian. This last argument had a connotation that Las Casas cannot have liked. Whereas paganism was a perfectly innocent misfortune, which could only inspire the desire to preach the gospel to the pagans, an inhuman way of life seemed like a mistake of a kind which was in some way culpable, which might suggest that measures of punishment or subjection could be warranted, as in fact was argued by Sepúlveda.

This had two consequences. First, Sepúlveda could assert that once the Indians had been converted this would not mean that they were then equal to the Spanish,[47] as faith was not the only factor which distinguished them. Second, he could consider it justifiable to subject the Indians in order to civilize them, which meant that the type of subjection applied would have to fulfill the mission which justified it, that is, it would have to be a form of civilizing guardianship. The means by which Sepúlveda proposed that the Indians should be ruled did not in

---

46. It is true that both thinkers held the idea that only a Christian society can become fully human, as in the last instance it becomes difficult to follow the natural law without the Christian faith.

47. Cf. Sepúlveda, *Demócrates Segundo*, 119.

any way constitute slavery as such, but rather a mixed regime, a blend of the lordly and the paternal, as he calls it, in which the subject would be considered free, would own property, and would have rights and freedoms that would grow as he became more civilized, so that he also reached a certain level of participation in government.[48]

The question raised by Sepúlveda's view was why the Indians, unlike other pagan peoples, had not discovered the natural law, the measure of what was human, but on the contrary, had degraded themselves to the point of reconciling themselves with inhuman laws. This could only be explained by an inability to direct themselves towards civilization and humanity. And this constituted the statute of natural servitude: naturally being destined to be incorporated into civilization, by means of another person's guidance. For a man of this kind, freedom gives rise to deviation and lack of moral direction, whereas obedience to a superior being, to a prudent and human guide, is beneficial, as this is what corresponds to his nature.

This conclusion could not have been reached without making two presuppositions. In the first place, those beings of rudimentary behavior were without any doubt men. The times in which fantasies about the possible existence of monsters and *similitudines hominis,* of which the ancients had spoken, were now over. Both Las Casas and Sepúlveda accepted and desired the baptism of the peoples in question, which implied the conviction that they were indeed men. Secondly, although the forms of human behavior were liable to a certain degree of variation, there were limits dictated by natural law.

In order to understand properly the controversy we are studying, we have to recognize that in neither of its protagonists do we find the suggestion of cultural relativism, so widespread in our own days; nor was either man an enlightened skeptic who would question whether civilization represented an elevation or a corruption of nature. In general terms, both were convinced of the value of civilization, insofar as this was development and a stylization of what was spontaneous and primitive, and agreed that the canons of civilized behavior essentially consisted of the European norms. The difference lay in the fact that Las Casas was disposed to interpret the requirements of civilization in a more relative way, and to question these canons more. In this way, the cultural distance between Indians and Christians is partially blurred, and the conclusions which Sepúlveda drew from this distance

---

48. Cf. ibid., 120ff. In this way, Sepúlveda expanded the forms of dominion considered by Aristotle by introducing this middle way which belonged, strictly speaking, to neither the political nor the domestic sphere.

are undermined. In any case, despite what has been said, it is necessary to emphasize that Las Casas's words were directed not so much towards throwing the models of civilization into doubt, but towards pointing out the flexibility and ease with which they could be acquired.[49] Rather than showing the forms of civilization in themselves to be relative, what he does is to render their possession relative, seeing this as being purely a question of time. The Indians were like all men "at the time when the earth was first populated."[50] As we have seen, the civilization which they lacked would easily be acquired, with the passing of time and the aid of evangelization.

Of Sepúlveda we could say that, in addition to not sharing Las Casas's optimism, as we have seen, he was characterized by greater ridigity in his concept of the norms of civilization. In circumstances such as this, in which an attempt was being made to integrate two different worlds into one, one could reproach Sepúlveda with not having been capable of relativizing sufficiently the institutions and measures of his own world in order to discover the forms which were necessary and common to both. It seems reasonable to think that as the cultural difference was so wide, he was unable to have recourse to any aspect of culture to adjust relations between the Indians and the Spanish. It was necessary to go back to what they genuinely did have in common, that is to say, to truly natural features which were free of all cultural connotations. They had to be understood as mere human beings, and the tendency to identify what was natural with one's own cultural forms had to be suppressed. There are grounds for considering that Sepúlveda was guilty of this to a greater degree, and Las Casas less so. We should, however, also ask whether this attempt really is possible: whether what is human can be understood and directed according to strictly natural criteria, quite detached from all cultural formalization. The limitations of Sepúlveda and Las Casas might perhaps only be a manifestation of the great difficulty, if not impossibility, inherent within such a perspective.

As has been indicated, Sepúlveda held up natural law as an absolute limit to the variations permissible among the different forms of human life. But when confronted with the fact that the Indians did not obey this law, he did not deduce that the law itself might not be so natural; he did not imagine that it could have been conceived according to cultural parameters. Natural law was the law which was accepted and

---

49. What Las Casas generally does to defend the Indians' culture is to compare their institutions with those of Europe and subject both to the same value judgments, thereby deducing their similarity and closeness.

50. Cited in Zavala, *La filosofía política*, 82.

lived out by all the *civilized* nations.[51] It was in the spontaneous consensus of these nations that natural law was to be recognized. Sepúlveda saw no difficulty in this, since he followed Aristotle, accepting as he did that, in the last instance, we find what is just in the just man. With Aristotle, he recognized that a certain moral quality was needed in the subject for him to know the measure of what was good. Sepúlveda was not a modern, and the law for him was not pure rationality, a formulation which was obvious in face of the spontaneous actions of nature.

While the Indians lived in isolation, undiscovered by the civilized world, they ruled themselves according to their own standards. In their barbaric world, their law, authorities, and regimes were legitimate and sufficient, as they conformed with the demands which that world made, as Aristotle had recognized with respect to the barbarians of his time.[52] But once the world was unified, and the Indians incorporated into the civilized world, their laws and institutions were no longer valid, as they did not respond to the higher requirements of their new context. This is what Sepúlveda was demonstrating. The formation of a single globe made up of Europeans and Indians meant suspending the Indian order and placing the Indian under the tutelage of the European. The Indian's position was to be that which corresponded to the Indian in his new world, that is, what was just and beneficial for him, as this was the appropriate way for him to integrate and to participate in the riches of civilization. It was when Europeans and Indians first came into contact that the dichotomy between civilization and barbarism appeared, and this showed that the two parties could only be unified by establishing a hierarchy. With such a difference between the two groups, union could only be achieved by subordination; this means would be advantageous for both, since every society is beneficial for its members when they all occupy their appropriate position.

One point which merits explanation is the meaning of the expression "by nature" within Sepúlveda's writings on slavery or natural servitude. Sepúlveda speaks of human beings who are incapable by nature of directing themselves, and so whose lot it naturally is to be ruled by others. As we know, Sepúlveda once more follows in Aristotle's footsteps on this subject; and in spite of the ambiguities and vacillations present in both Aristotle and Sepúlveda, we may conclude that in both philosophers, generally "by nature" means "by culture": habit, custom, education, and so on.[53]

51. Sepúlveda, *Demócrates Segundo*, 56.
52. See *Politics* 1285a.
53. It is true that in Aristotle as in Sepúlveda the issue of whether such a cultural

For Aristotle, the difference between slave and free man, between barbarian and civilized person, reflects the difference between two types of activity, *poiesis* and *praxis*, each of which constitutes a kind of life which is exclusive to and defines a type of man. But to pass from one kind of activity to another, from *poiesis* to *praxis*, is the proper and exclusive fruit of the *polis*. The *polis* is the condition that makes the life of *praxis* possible, that is, the life which consists of activities that are ends in themselves and which therefore make man perfect insofar as he is a man. Therefore, only men who participate in the *polis* enjoy the right conditions for attaining this type of life. Attaining this kind of life means managing to embody one's own essence or constitutional ontological principle, in the principle of operations *of this type*, that is, in strictly human *nature*. As we have seen, this process is rendered possible by the action of the *polis*, and is therefore a cultural process: human nature is the product of a socio-cultural genesis. Aristotle understood the concept of nature in a finalistic sense. Nature is the result of a process in which something which was only an ontological principle, or metaphysical essence, establishes itself as a principle of operations. The type of nature thus depends on the type of operations. In the case of man, the process that forms human nature requires the concurrence of a set of socio-cultural conditions—the *polis*—and if these conditions are not available, the process will be frustrated. Thus, whereas the metaphysical essence of man is universal among men, human nature in the strict sense might not be so, since this is subject to the restrictions imposed by the condition which make it possible, the *polis*. The consequence of this is the presence of men who are slaves by nature, that is, individuals whose metaphysical essence is human, but whose nature has not been formed under the appropriate conditions, in other words, within a "socio-cultural setting" appropriate for human persons. This nature thus suffers a shortfall in its humanity.

As we can see, Aristotle's concept of human nature was more ethical than metaphysical. Saying "by nature" was tantamount to saying "by character," and in the formation of the latter, the cultural framework played a key role. It is all the more difficult to discern whether reference is being made to nature or to culture when we realize that in Aristotle there exists no clear distinction, such as was to arise later, between the two concepts. In fact, as we have just observed, culture introduced itself into and operated within the constitution of what was natural. The

---

concept of nature is or is not exempt from metaphysical implications remains open. Probably this uncertainty is what is present in Sepúlveda's mind when considering whether the Indians would ever finally be able to reach or not the same level of civilization as the Europeans.

counterpart of this was that Aristotle viewed the cultural according to the categories of the natural, that is, he conferred on the cultural forms, which were the condition of the human—concretely on the *polis*—and consequently on the restrictions imposed by them, a fixed and definitive character proper to what is natural, thus losing all historical sense.[54]

It was first and foremost in this Aristotelian, ethico-cultural sense that Sepúlveda understood "servitude by nature"; and it may have been this sense which Las Casas failed to grasp. The latter seems to have understood it in a post-Aristotelian sense that proceeded from the contrast between nature and culture, that is, in a metaphysical sense. This is why he may on occasion react to this doctrine with expressions of horror, calling it "the most absurd, vain, scandalous and disturbing idea of which mankind is capable."[55]

Sepúlveda was, however, a Christian, and for this reason he could not be completely Aristotelian. In the concrete, he could not maintain the naturalist fixedness which Aristotle had attributed to the cultural ambit. The historical conscience was a genuinely Christian contribution. Culture belonged to history, and was therefore subject to change and progress. The cultural sphere, like the *polis*, could continue to be thought of as a condition which permitted the formation of human nature; but the concrete form of this condition, the possibilities which it might offer and the restrictions it might impose, were always provisional and could be superseded. For this reason, Sepúlveda conceived of the natural servitude of the Indians as being provisional, and dominion over them as a regime which would raise them up and further their development. The only doubt which persisted in his mind was whether the Indian's capacity for self-mastery and civilization was subject to any limit. But on this point only time could tell.

Despite the fact that his turn of mind was Christian, Sepúlveda continued to maintain the balance between the Christian and the pagan. Las Casas, on the other hand, was a "radically" Christian thinker. We can affirm that at the bottom of the dispute between the two men, what we find is a confrontation between two forces which had long been in conflict; and that this struggle, as a result of the circumstances (the discovery of America and the Renaissance), had here reached one of their most decisive moments. The forces of Christian metaphysical egalitarianism and pagan culturalist elitism thus impinged upon each

---

54. This topic has been lucidly dealt with by Higinio Marín in his doctoral dissertation, entitled "La antropología aristotélica como filosofía de la cultura" (University of Navarra, 1992), the reading of which has provided me with these enlightening insights.

55. Quoted in Hanke, *La lucha*, 368.

other, two tendencies which, without being identified strictly either with Christianity or with classical paganism, were reflected in both.

As we were able to observe above in the case of Aristotle, when considering the conception and ordaining of human realities, ancient thought paid more attention to the ethico-cultural differences than to the essential uniformity. What gained in importance was the different forms which the human could take on in practice, while the specific community, the common possession of one essence, lost significance. The unity of the human race was a reality which belonged to the metaphysical or biological plane, but these two dimensions yielded little that might indicate how men's lives should be ordered. *So historicized* nature gained in importance and served as a source of criteria, while *innate* nature was more or less relegated to silence.

Christianity, on the other hand, bore within it a tendency to the contrary, which was in some sense anticipated by stoicism. Christianity tended to underline and put into effect the metaphysical unity of mankind and consequently to relativize all diversity. Christianity had opened the world up to a new dimension, a supernatural one. Man's highest inheritance lay in this dimension, and man was the intended recipient of this wealth by virtue of his nature, not of his *historicized* nature but of his *innate* nature, what Aristotle would have called his essence or form. All men, simply because they were men, were called to salvation, and could therefore participate in and partake of the highest fullness. All this obviously helped to lend importance to the metaphysical dimension and its equality, and to rob the historico-cultural dimension and its diversity of their significance. What was highest and most perfect for man came to him through the first dimension, not the second. It was logical that the term "human nature" in its strongest sense (what man is and is called to be) should edge towards the metaphysical plane, to be identified in terms of essence and contrasted with the cultural aspects of the question.

As a result, the first and most important consideration regarding man was his metaphysical identity. And if the view we take from this is an egalitarian one, this equality will become the normative criterion and tendential objective for every other consideration and dimension of what is human. The equality and universality proper to the metaphysical plane were thus turned into an ideal model for the ordering of all the planes of human existence. If what belongs to the metaphysical dimension was what destined man for his highest vocation, it was this that had to be the only adequate basis for everything that was genuinely important for man. And everything which was based on this foundation would take on the egalitarian and universalist character of that foundation. It would be this tendency which would lead in modern times to the conversion of human nature, in its egalitarian and innate condition, into the home of political rights.

Christianity thus favored a certain aversion to accepting that human matters could be ordered on the basis of any foundation other than the metaphysical one. This tendency devalued all that was not essential, "accidentalizing the accident."[56] This naturally implied regarding all inequality with suspicion, as though it were a spurious addition or the result of some defect. In fact, the traditional teaching repeated by Las Casas spoke of an original state which was the home of equality. Inequality and servitude belonged to the later state, which, as a result of sin, was no longer ideal. Historical arguments are hereby added to the metaphysical concept. Anthropology turns into philosophy of history, and the philosophical idea into a historical ideal.

While Christianity invites us to think that culture is too inconsistent to legitimize the differences between men, ancient thought suggested that the essential and metaphysical were too distant and silent to serve as criteria for arranging human affairs. In short, what lay beneath the struggle between these two tendencies, and what, consequently, was being discussed in the debate between Sepúlveda and Las Casas, was the question which Aristotle had already posed: what human characteristics and qualities should form the basis on which legal, social, and political structures take shape?[57]

From what we have seen until now we may conclude—contrary to what has often been affirmed—that regarding the two positions that we have studied, that of Las Casas's is the most medieval one, whereas that of Sepúlveda's is the most akin to the Renaissance. And as regards the problem of the relationship between Indians and Spaniards, Christianity, and not Renaissance classicism, was that which provided the resources in order to formulate a solution in terms of equality.

56. So, for example, Las Casas asserted that "judgment on things should be given according to what they are *per se,* and not according to what they are *per accidens*" (cited in Carro, *Los postulados,* 42).
57. See *Politics* 1283a.

PART III

7 Domingo de Soto and the Iberian Roots of Galileo's Science

WILLIAM A. WALLACE

Visitors to the Dominican priory of San Esteban in Salamanca are much impressed by the sixteenth-century Escalera de Domingo de Soto, a stone stairway leading from the church garden to the cloister above it. Just as impressive is El Puente de Domingo de Soto, a plaza and a bridge that still connects the priory with Salamanca proper. Both were built in the late 1550s with proceeds from the sale of the many textbooks Soto had written. A philosopher and theologian of great renown, chaplain to Emperor Charles V and leading Dominican at the Council of Trent, Soto was as well known for his treatises *On Nature and Grace, On Right and Justice,* and *On the Cause of the Poor* as he was for his textbooks. Thus, were I to use Soto to celebrate Hispanic philosophy today, there is no dearth of materials from which I might draw. But since the focus here is on the Age of Discovery, I prefer to draw attention to a different facet of Soto's career, his role in a little known but very important discovery, that of the law of falling bodies.

Born at Segovia in 1494, Soto did his early studies in logic and natural philosophy under Thomas of Villanova at the University of Alcalá, earning the baccalaureate there in 1516. He then traveled north to the University of Paris to pursue higher studies in the College of Santa Barbara. There he studied under the Valencian, Juan de Celaya, under whose tutelage he became acquainted with the terminist physics then current in Paris. He completed the master's degree in arts and, while teaching in the arts faculty, began the study of theology. During this period he came under the influence of the Scottish nominalist John Major, who was then teaching at the College of Montaigu (along with two of Soto's fellow Segovians, Luis and Antonio Coronel), and the Spanish Thomist Francisco de Vitoria, who was lecturing at the Dominican priory of Saint-Jacques. In 1519, however, Soto's longing for Spain prompted his return to Alcalá, where he completed the course in theology under Pedro Ciruelo; immediately thereafter he was given the chair of philosophy at the College of San Ildefonso. Much impressed by Vitoria and upset by internal conflicts at the college, he resigned that post in 1524 and decided to enter the Dominican Order. He became a novice at the priory of San Pablo in Burgos, where he was professed on 23 July 1525.[1]

The nature of Soto's contribution to early modern science can be appreciated by drawing a contrast between him and the Catalan humanist, Juan Luis Vives, who was born in Valencia two years before Soto, in 1492. Vives was also at the University of Paris in the early sixteenth century, along with a goodly number of teachers and students from the Iberian peninsula. Both he and Soto followed the same course of instruction in logic and in physics at the university. They studied the same subject matters, but they did so to very different ends.

On the one hand, we have the well-known story of Vives, the humanist who never returned to Spain and who was so disenchanted with the instruction he received at Paris that he spent much of his later life attacking the decadent Scholasticism being taught in Belgium and in England.[2] On the other hand, we have the lesser-known story of Soto, actually a countertheme to that of Vives. Soto returned to Spain and there, through his teaching first at Alcalá, then at Burgos and Salamanca, laid important foundations on which Galileo Galilei would one day build his science. For the one, Vives, Paris was a disaster; for the other, Soto, it was the starting point for innovations that would prompt the great French historian of science, Pierre Duhem, to hail him as the "Scholastic precursor" of Galileo.[3] So we pose a question: what was the difference between Vives and Soto that made their lives diverge so markedly, such that historians would accentuate the anti-logic, anti-science stance of the one as contrasted to the pro-logic, pro-science stance of the other, and so evaluate the *fortuna* of Scholastic teaching at Paris in such radically different ways?

The question, so posed, is difficult to answer. But the key to the answer lies in the way logic was taught in the arts faculty at Paris, against which Vives directed many of his attacks. The basic text there was the *Summulae logicales* of Peter of Spain. This gave rise to the "summulist"

1. For a brief survey of Soto's life and works, see the entry written by W. A. Wallace in *Dictionary of Scientific Biography*, s.v., "Soto, Domingo de." The definitive account is Vicente Beltrán de Heredia, *Domingo de Soto, Estudio biográfico documentado* (Salamanca: Biblioteca de Teologos Españoles, 1960).

2. Juan Luis Vives, *In Pseudo-dialecticos*, ed. and trans. C. Fantazzi (Leiden: E. J. Brill, 1979).

3. Pierre Duhem, *Études sur Léonard de Vinci*, 3 vols. (Paris: Hermann et Fils, 1906–13), 3:263–583, esp. 555–62.

tradition, a series of textbooks used in the Parisian colleges to drill schoolboys in dialectical subtleties. These may have sharpened the memories and argumentative skills of youths, but they were ultimately to prove useless for serious work in philosophy and theology. A more humanistically inclined student such as Juan Luis Vives would easily have been repelled by the exercises to which he was subjected. The experience seems to have been so bad, in fact, that it diverted him from "the learning of the Schools" and caused him to focus instead on the *litterae humaniores* as the repository of true knowledge. So he turned to the new Renaissance movement, humanism, and devoted all of his energies to it.

Soto's reaction to the drilling associated with summulist teaching at Paris was quite different from that of Vives. Probably he realized that the *Summulae* were never intended to be the whole of logic; rather, they were simply a propaedeutic that would exercise students in abstract logical forms and so prepare them for the more difficult discipline of Aristotle's *Organon*, culminating in the material logic of the *Posterior Analytics*. The *Posterior Analytics* provided a methodology essential to scientific reasoning that would find its best exemplification in mathematics and in the science embodied in Aristotle's *Physics*. More persevering scholars like Soto could endure the summulist training and pass beyond it to do original work that would bear fruit in the Scientific Revolution of the seventeenth century. Two innovations were particularly important: the development of the demonstrative *regressus* found in the first book of the *Posterior Analytics*, and the search for new ratios of motions, including the *uniformiter difformis* relationship, that could be used to revise Aristotle's teaching on falling motion in the seventh book of the *Physics*. Both of these can be traced back to Soto, whose path in this respect differed markedly from that of Vives.

This essay, as its title indicates, is devoted to Soto's achievement and its sequel. But it is important to issue a *caveat* at the outset. The innovations to be discussed were not "writ large" in the intellectual history of the times and for that reason are not well known, even among historians of science. For the most part they do not appear in sixteenth-century texts but have to be dug out of manuscript sources. A surprising amount of this material is preserved in rare books and manuscripts produced at the time in Spain and Portugal. That explains the latter part of my title, "The Iberian Roots of Galileo's Science." And yet no great generalizations can be expected to emerge from this study. History, even the history of science, unfolds in capricious fashion and only in retrospect can any rationality be discerned in its unfolding.

SUMMULIST PROFESSORS AT PARIS

The easiest way to begin is to provide an overview of the summulist teachers at Paris in the early sixteenth century to show what their intellectual interests were and how these led them into more fruitful fields of scholarship than the teaching of schoolboy dialectics. Our focus will be on professors who went beyond formal logic to write commentaries on Aristotle's *Analytics*. These instructors we divide into two groups, the first including those whose later work was mainly in the field of mathematics, the second, those who produced commentaries on the physical works of Aristotle.

The summulists who studied the *Analytics* and whose main contributions were to mathematics were all Spaniards of distinction. They may be treated here in the order of their birth: Pedro Sanches Ciruelo (1470–1554), Juan Martínez Silíceo (1486–1557), and last but not least, Gaspar Lax (1487–1560). Ciruelo began his studies at Salamanca, then came to Paris in 1492 to complete his education. While pursuing courses in theology he supported himself by "the profession of the mathematical arts," as he later explained. While at Paris he published a treatise on practical arithmetic that went through many printings; this was accompanied by his revised and corrected editions of Thomas Bradwardine's treatises on speculative arithmetic and speculative geometry. About the same time Ciruelo produced an edition of the *Sphere* of Sacrobosco, along with the questions on it by Pierre d'Ailly; this was reprinted repeatedly and became the main source for instruction in astronomy at Paris. Returning to Spain in 1515 he taught at the University of Alcalá, where Soto was among his students and where he produced other textbooks, among which was a complete course in mathematics, both pure and applied, including optics and music.

Juan Martínez Silíceo began his studies in Valencia before going to Paris in 1507, where he studied physics under one of Vives's teachers, Jean Dullaert of Ghent. While at Paris he published an *Ars arithmetica* in 1513, then a treatise on the use of the astrolabe, and finally a complete course in logic, all before returning to Spain in 1517. Actually, he was called back to teach philosophy at Salamanca *secundum methodum parisiensem*, "following the Parisian method," which he did with distinction. Later he was named Archbishop of Toledo and raised to the rank of Cardinal in the Roman Church.

Finally there is Gaspar Lax, also Vives's teacher at Paris, who along with Dullaert, by Vives's own testimony, regretted the many years he had spent there teaching the trivialities of *Summulae* doctrine. Lax began his studies at Zaragoza, and returned there to teach mathematics and philosophy after a long career at Paris. A prolific writer, while at Paris he turned out so many tomes on terminist logic he became known as "the Prince of Parisian *sophistae*." But he also had serious interests in mathematics, publishing an *Arithmetica speculativa* based on Boethius and a formalistic treatise on ratios or *proportiones* that went beyond the earlier works of Euclid, Jordanus de Nemore, and Campanus of Navarre. His views on the ratios of motions are not found in that treatise, but they are expounded in a later work published at Zaragoza, his *Quaestiones phisicales* of 1527, wherein he recapitulates in systematic form the teachings of Thomas Bradwardine, William Heytesbury, and Richard Swineshead at Oxford and their terminist counterparts in fourteenth-century Paris. What is important about that work is the many times Lax uses terms such as *suppositio* and *uniformiter difformis*, terms that assume importance in our later discussion.

Expositors of the *Summulae* who turned their attention to the physical sciences include a number of those already mentioned: John Major (1467–1550), Jean Dullaert (1470–1513), Juan de Celaya (1490–1558), and Domingo de Soto (1495–1560). To these we would add the name of a Belgian Dominican, Peter Crokaert of Brussels (1465?–1514). Crokaert is significant for his adding Thomism to the nominalist and Scotist influences at Paris deriving from John Major. First studying under Major and then teaching nominalism at Major's college, the College of Montaigu, in 1503 Crokaert entered the Dominican Order in the priory of Saint-Jacques. There he converted to Thomism, embracing it so enthusiastically one would have thought he was a Thomist all his life. At Saint-Jacques he taught Francisco de Vitoria and also influenced Soto, who was Vitoria's friend and frequented Saint-Jacques at the time. Crokaert wrote commentaries on all of Aristotle's *Organon* as well as on the *Physics* and the *De anima*, and is particularly important for redirecting his Parisian contemporaries to the thought of St. Thomas Aquinas.

Dullaert had also studied under Major at Paris and there in turn taught Celaya, Silíceo, and Vives. An Augustinian friar, Dullaert published questions on the *Physics* and *De caelo* of Aristotle (1506, 1511, 1512), and was working on the *Analytics* and the *Meteorology* at his death in 1513; interestingly, Vives himself put the *Meteorology* into print in the following year, prefacing it with a brief biography of his teacher. Earlier Dullaert had revised and edited Jean Buridan's questions on the *Physics* and two of the physical works of another Augustinian, Paul of Venice. He also was preparing a general edition of the writings of St. Albert the Great, based on previously unedited manuscripts he himself had discovered, but unfortunately, this was never completed.

No less universal in his interests was Dullaert's disciple, Juan de Celaya. Born in Valencia around 1490, Celaya went to Paris in the early years of the sixteenth century, studied there under Lax and Dullaert, and completed the M.A. around 1509. As an arts master, Celaya numbered Soto among his students, as already mentioned. He also taught with the Portuguese mathematician Alvaro Thomaz and learned from him "calculatory" techniques. These techniques assume prominence in Celaya's questions on the *Physics* (1517), which not only summarize the teachings of the English Mertonians, the Paris terminists, and the Paduan *calculatores*, but also expose the teachings of Aristotle *secundum triplicem viam*, as he put it, "according to the threefold way of St. Thomas, the realists, and the nominalists." A prolific writer, Celaya also turned out commentaries on *De caelo* (1517), *De generatione* (1518), the *Posterior Analytics* (1521), and the *Ethics* (1523), all written in the same "threefold way." Following this last work, Celaya left Paris in 1524 and returned to Valencia, where he taught theology and was made rector *in perpetuo* of the university. In his later years he lost interest in nominalist teachings and devoted himself instead to the Aristotelian-Thomistic tradition.

Fortunate indeed was Soto in having had Celaya as his philosophy teacher at Paris. Soto's main teaching as a Dominican was at Salamanca, where he first taught in the *studium generale* at the priory of San Esteban. Then, during the academic year 1531–32, he substituted for Francisco de Vitoria, who held the "prime chair" of theology at the University of Salamanca. So successful was he that the next year he was elected to the "vesper chair" of theology, a post he held for sixteen years. It was at this time that he found his theology students to be poorly prepared in philosophy. Having already published a *Summulae* (1529), to this he now added a *Dialectica* that exposed all of the *Organon*, including the *Posterior Analytics* (1543), and a commentary and questionary on the *Physics* (1551), the last of which figures importantly in our account.

Note that all of the professors we have just surveyed may with justice be referred to as *summulistae*, for they all either taught or wrote expositions of the *Summulae* of Peter of Spain. Many of them did so to support themselves while continuing their studies at the University of Paris. Some, it is true, became so engrossed with formal logic that it dominated their interests for a considerable period. But note here a parallel in the present day, namely, the many philosophers, especially in England and the United States, who became so fascinated with mathematical logic, parts of which were adumbrated by the summulists, that they used it to spawn a new mode of philosophizing we now call "analytical philosophy." What is noteworthy about those we have discussed is that they were all scholars with broad intellectual interests who made significant contributions to sixteenth-century thought, contributions possibly more significant than those of their twentieth-century counterparts.

THE ENIGMA OF DOMINGO DE SOTO

A good illustration of such a contribution is associated with an expression used by *calculatores* in the summulist tradition, namely, *uniformiter difformis*, which translates into English as "uniformly difform." When applied to the velocity of motion, the sense of the expression would be that the velocity is "difform," that is, varying or of different form, but that it is doing so "uniformly" or in an unvarying way. To use the modern idiom, to say that a motion is "uniformly difform" is to say that it is uniformly accelerated, that is, that its velocity is changing and so the motion is accelerating, but that the change is regular and so the acceleration is uniform. Now historians of science commonly teach that Galileo Galilei was the first to discover the laws of falling bodies, among which is the fact that their motion, in free fall, is uniformly accelerated, in other words, that their motion is *uniformiter difformis* with respect to time. One can imagine therefore the surprise that attended Pierre Duhem's pronouncement in 1913, reasserted by Marshall Clagett in 1959, that Galileo was not really the first to discover this, for it was already known to Domingo de Soto, who stated it some eighty years before Galileo in his questions on Aristotle's *Physics*, published at Salamanca in 1551.[4] How did Soto come to make this remarkable statement, and when he did, why did he present it only in matter-of-fact fashion, as though everyone already knew it? These questions pose what has been referred to by Alexandre Koyré as "the enigma of Domingo de Soto."[5]

Almost twenty-five years ago I published an essay on that enigma.[6] I was able to verify then that Soto truly makes such a statement. After defining motion that is uniformly difform with respect to time, he notes that this motion is

---

4. For Duhem, see the previous note; Marshall Clagett, *The Science of Mechanics in the Middle Ages* (Madison: The University of Wisconsin Press, 1959), 555–56.
5. In Koyré's essay on "The Exact Sciences" in the second volume of René Taton's four-volume *History of Science*, entitled *The Beginnings of Modern Science*, trans. A. J. Pomerans (New York: Basic Books, 1964), 94–95.
6. W. A. Wallace, "The Enigma of Domingo de Soto: *Uniformiter difformis* and Falling Bodies in Late Medieval Physics," *Isis* 59 (1968): 384–401; reprinted and enlarged in W. A. Wallace, *Prelude to Galileo: Essays on Medieval and Sixteenth-Century Sources of Galileo's Thought* (Dordrecht-Boston: D. Reidel Publishing Co., 1981), 91–109.

properly found in objects that move naturally and in projectiles.... For when a heavy object falls through a homogeneous medium from a height, it moves with greater velocity at the end than at the beginning. The velocity of projectiles, on the other hand, is less at the end than at the beginning. And what is more, the first increases uniformly difformly, whereas the second decreases uniformly difformly.[7]

Soto goes on to explain that the falling body will cover the same distance during its fall as another body moving at half the velocity with uniform speed, which he calculates out to yield the correct distance of fall.

Here is not the place to review the details of my earlier essay. Suffice it to mention that Soto's use of the expression *uniformiter difformis* has to be set against the way it was used in the fourteenth century by the Oxford "calculators" of Bradwardine's school and Parisian terminists of Jean Buridan's school, in the fifteenth century by Paduans, and in the early sixteenth by his predecessors at Paris. Practically everyone prior to Soto who treated the expression did one of two things: either (1) they viewed it in a logical or imaginative way, without any reference to motions in the real world, or (2) they employed a "two-variable" schema when discussing it, with the result that they always tied uniform difformity with respect to time to uniform difformity with respect to space and never separated the two. Only two of Soto's predecessors, William Heytesbury and Juan de Celaya, used the one-variable schema, defining uniform difformity with respect to time alone, but neither of these thought to apply this definition to any motion in the real world. Domingo de Soto alone illustrated the definition with an example, and when so doing made the important statements cited above.

Why Soto supplied this particular example has puzzled scholars for a long time. My initial reply was that Soto was intent on combining his early training in the nominalist tradition with his later commitment to Thomism, and that this prompted his exemplification of this nominalist expression in the real world. This would accord well with Soto's own admission that he was "born among the nominalists and reared among the realists." Apparently he was proud of this dual intellectual heritage, for, when questioned about nominalist elements in his questions on the *Physics*, he protested that he would not remove them lest in taking out the weeds he might tear up the wheat. In his biography of Soto, Vicente Beltrán de Heredia notes that both Soto and Vitoria felt that some nominalist teachings were superior to those of their realist confreres, particularly in physics and in ethics, and resented attempts to impose any orthodoxy on them in this regard.[8]

7. Quoted in ibid., 400 (reprint, 106).
8. Beltrán, *Domingo de Soto*, 22.

A more difficult problem is whether Soto had empirical evidence for characterizing falling motion as uniformly accelerated. He provides none in his *Physics* questionary, and scholars have generally taken this to mean that he had none. But the question is far from settled. In this connection we should note that Soto had finished writing his commentary and questions on the *Physics* up to book VII, where the passages I have quoted are to be found, early in 1545, at which time he was called to the Council of Trent. To make them quickly available to students his texts were printed in an incomplete edition of 1545, which does not contain the passages about falling motion. But Soto returned from Trent in 1550 and then finished both texts, printed at Salamanca in 1551. While en route to or while present at Trent, in northern Italy, Soto could have become acquainted with experimental work being done there on laws of fall, and this would have buttressed his rejection of the traditional Aristotelian teaching.

Little is known about such experimental work, but what is known is suggestive. As early as 1544, it appears, tests were being performed to show that Aristotle was wrong in his claim that heavy bodies will fall to the ground at uniform speeds directly proportional to their weights. Benedetto Varchi, in his *Questioni sull'Alchimia* finished by that date, in a discussion of experimental evidence relating to the motion of heavy bodies, mentions the findings of Francesco Beato, a Dominican philosopher at Pisa, and Luca Ghini, a Bolognese physician and botanist, as contesting Aristotle's claim. Likewise, Giovanni Battista Bellasco of Brescia, in a work entitled *Il vero modo di scrivere in cifra* published in 1553, inquires why it is that a ball of iron and one of wood fall to the ground at the same time. In the same year Giovan Battista Benedetti published his *Resolutio omnium Euclidis problematum*, and a year later his *Demonstratio . . . contra Aristotelem,* in both of which he also attacks Aristotle's ratios of motions. Now Benedetti held in high regard another Spanish Dominican, Petrus Arches, who had told him that criticisms of Aristotle's dynamic laws were being discussed in Rome the summer before he prepared his *Demonstratio.* Evidence such as this implies that tests of Aristotle's laws of falling bodies were being performed in Italy in the early 1550s. The fact that Beato, Arches, and Soto were all Dominicans enhances the possibility that Soto learned of such experimentation during his travels through Italy to Trent. If so, it could have provided the background for the example he gave of uniformly accelerated motion upon his return to Salamanca.[9]

9. W. A. Wallace, "Science and Philosophy at the Collegio Romano in the Time of Benedetti," in *Cultura, Scienze e Techniche nella Venezia del Cinquecento* (Venice: Istituto Ve-

SOTO'S INFLUENCE ON GALILEO

A second enigma associated with the famous passage in Soto's *Physics* is whether or not the passage was known to Galileo and so could have influenced his formulation of the principle of uniform acceleration in free fall. Now Soto's *Physics*, both commentary and questions, became quite popular and went through nine editions in the second half of the sixteenth century, the penultimate of which was published at Venice in 1582, just as the young Galileo was beginning his study of the *Physics* at the University of Pisa. So it is not impossible that Soto's text was known to Galileo and, if so, could have been the direct source from which the latter took the law of falling bodies. Supporting this conjecture is Galileo's having mentioned Soto's *Physics* in one of his early notebooks. Pierre Duhem, whom I have mentioned earlier, seized on Galileo's use of *uniformiter difformis* in that context to claim for Soto the title of "Scholastic precursor of Galileo."

Now Duhem's thesis, what historians of science call the "continuity thesis," has claimed my attention for two decades. Over that time I have come to the conclusion that Duhem's original claim is unfounded, but that there are still good grounds for believing there was an influence of Soto on Galileo. My argument is not based directly on the Galileo manuscript cited by Duhem, but rather on the sources that lie behind that manuscript. We now know that these were Jesuit teaching notes Galileo appropriated for his own use while teaching or preparing to teach at the University of Pisa. Through a study of books and manuscripts written by Jesuits in the century following the publication of Soto's *uniformiter difformis* doctrine, mainly in Italy, Spain, and Portugal, we can make the case for an influence on Galileo that was indirect and mediated by Jesuits, many of whom either came from or worked on the Iberian peninsula.[10]

This new argument, like Duhem's, uses the *uniformiter difformis* doctrine deriving from Soto, but adds another link in the person of Franciscus Toletus, Soto's favorite student at Salamanca. After himself teaching in the arts faculty at Salamanca, and already a priest, Toletus entered the newly formed Society of Jesus at Toledo in 1558. In 1559 he was sent to Rome, while still a novice, to teach at the Collegio Ro-

---

neto di Scienze, Lettere ed Arti, 1987), 126; reprinted in W. A. Wallace, *Galileo, the Jesuits, and the Medieval Aristotle* (Hampshire: Variorum Publishing, 1991).

10. W. A. Wallace, "The Early Jesuits and the Heritage of Domingo de Soto," *History and Technology* 4 (1987): 301–20; reprinted in *Galileo, the Jesuits, and the Medieval Aristotle*, 1–20. See also W. A. Wallace, "Late Sixteenth-Century Portuguese Manuscripts Relating to Galileo's Early Notebooks," *Revista Portuguesa de Filosofia* 51 (1995): 677–98.

mano. There he wrote a series of philosophy textbooks that set the pattern for Jesuit teaching in philosophy over the next three decades. In brief, Toletus brought Soto's doctrine to Rome, and through his influence it was so widely propagated that it ultimately reached the ears of Galileo.

Precisely how this was done could easily be the subject for another lecture. Here we can simply note that the expression *uniformiter difformis* occurs not only in Toletus's writings but also in books of two Spanish Jesuits who taught philosophy in Rome, Benedictus Pererius from Valencia and Francisco Suárez from Granada. All three recognize the significance of that expression, and Toletus in particular remarks that terms like this "should be carefully considered in order to understand many matters that are met with in physics."[11] Toletus's advice, it seems, is quite apparent in the writings of Antonius Menu, who taught in Rome from 1577 to 1582 and frequently quoted the *Doctores Parisienses* in his lectures. Like Toletus he was acquainted with the calculatory tradition developed at Merton College in Oxford and then applied to physical problems by the Parisians. Menu in turn was succeeded by three other Jesuits, Paulus Vallius, Mutius Vitelleschi, and Ludovicus Rugerius, who taught natural philosophy at the Collegio Romano between 1585 and 1592 and who, like Menu, left fairly complete records of their lectures. All mention the works of Burley and Bradwardine, of Heytesbury and Swineshead, in their notes. Vitelleschi, for example, cites experimental evidence against Aristotle's exposition of the ratios of motions in book VII of the *Physics* and refers his students to Bradwardine's *De proportione motuum* for a better view. Rugerius likewise discerns difficulties with Aristotle's ratios and sends his students to Soto and Toletus for more satisfactory accounts of how the velocity of fall varies over the distance of fall.[12]

These three professors in particular are of interest because we can detect parallels in their lecture notes for practically the entire content of Galileo's notebook referred to above, providing excellent evidence that Galileo appropriated the material in the notebook from lectures such as theirs. Three other professors at the Collegio might also be mentioned in this regard. One is Christopher Clavius, the mathematician who taught the *Sphere* of Sacrobosco there from 1564 to 1595 and some of whose work is clearly reproduced in the notebook. An-

---

11. In his *Commentaria una cum quaestionibus in octo libros Physicorum* (1573), bk. 4, q. 12, cited by Christopher Lewis, *The Merton Tradition and Kinematics in Late Sixteenth and Early Seventeenth Century Italy* (Padua: Editrice Antenore, 1980), 86.
12. W. A. Wallace, *Galileo and His Sources: The Heritage of the Collegio Romano in Galileo's Science* (Princeton: Princeton University Press, 1984), 184–91.

other is Stefano del Bufalo, who taught the *Physics* in 1596–97 and makes good use of the *Calculatores* and the *Parisienses* in his lectures. Yet another is Andreas Eudaemon, who taught the same course in the following year. Eudaemon is of interest for having left in manuscript a treatise on the motion of projectiles which starts out with the interesting *suppositio* that "every natural agent acts *uniformiter difformiter* on a quantified subject when applied to it," and then goes on to show the many ways in which the related expression, *uniformiter difformis*, applies to the agent's effects.[13]

There is thus clear evidence of Soto's influence, mediated by Toletus, on lectures given at the Collegio Romano in the latter part of the sixteenth century. Similar evidence is available to show an influence in the lecture notes of Jesuits in Portugal, at Evora and Coimbra, some of which derives from teaching materials sent them by the Collegio Romano. In that connection I have examined sets of notes composed in 1570, 1582, 1587, and 1588 in these two *studia* by the Jesuits Juan Gomez de Braga, Luis de Cerqueira, Antonio del Castelbranco, and Manuel á Lima, respectively. Another set of notes written anonymously in 1580 apologizes for not discussing at length the velocity of motion and simply states that such "questions are treated more fully by Domingo de Soto and can be studied there. For this reason, and especially because of limitations of time, we will pass over them quickly." Cerqueira, lecturing in 1582, apparently took this reference to Soto seriously. After defining what is meant by uniformly difform motion, he writes:

Such a motion is said to be *uniformiter difformis* with respect to time, and it is found in heavy and light bodies when they move naturally, since the more they depart from their starting point the greater is the velocity with which they move.[14]

Manuel á Lima expands on this discussion in his lectures of 1588, writing:

... if one and the same stone were to descend from the middle of a tower and later from its top, it would descend much more swiftly at the end of the later motion than at the end of the earlier. For the longer the space that is traversed the greater is the impetus impressed by levity and gravity throughout the motion, since it is continually intensified until the object arrives at its natural place.[15]

From these citations, and I could give more, there is little doubt that

---

13. Wallace, "The Early Jesuits," 311 (reprint, 11).
14. Ibid., 313 (reprint, 13).
15. Ibid., 314 (reprint, 14).

Soto's teaching on falling motion was preserved among the Jesuits both in Rome and on the Iberian peninsula during the period under discussion.

But how, you wonder, could teachings such as this have influenced Galileo in arriving at the laws of free fall? The answer to that is most interesting, but it can be sketched here only briefly. It is now known that at the time he wrote the notebook cited by Duhem, around 1590, Galileo did not yet possess the correct law governing natural acceleration. In fact, even in 1604, when he was beginning his experiments on free fall at Padua, he was speculating that the speed of fall varies uniformly difformly with distance of fall, not with time of fall, as we now know it to do. The two—velocity increase with respect to time and velocity increase with respect to distance—are not the same, and this was recognized by the *Calculatores*, as we have already seen. Shortly after 1604, we also know, Galileo became aware of his mistake. How did he learn of the error? One possibility is the Jesuits who were then teaching in Padua, for they had a *studium* there until 1606, at which time they were expelled from the Republic of Venice. Two of those Jesuits, by an odd coincidence, just happened to be Paulus Vallius and Andreas Eudaemon. We also know from Jesuit correspondence that Eudaemon personally discussed problems like this with Galileo himself. So either he or Vallius could easily have informed Galileo of the correct formulation, namely, that speed of fall increases uniformly with time of fall and not with distance traversed. Shortly after that it appears that Galileo performed experiments at Padua that discriminated between the two possibilities and so arrived at the correct law.[16]

SUPPOSITIONES AND THE POSTERIOR ANALYTICS

Earlier I mentioned Aristotle's *Posterior Analytics* and its key role in bringing to completion the logic course at the University of Paris. Now I would like to return to logic and make a few remarks relating to *suppositio*, a term much used by Peter of Spain and the summulists at Paris. When Toletus began to teach logic at the Collegio Romano in 1559, apparently he patterned his course on the logic contained in Soto's *Dialectica* of 1543. He also took care to preface it with a slim volume, entitled "Introductio in dialecticam," in which he gave in summary form the entire contents of the *Summulae*. (Soto himself had put out a second

---

16. Wallace, *Galileo and His Sources*, 269–80; see also W. A. Wallace, *Galileo's Logic of Discovery and Proof: The Background, Content, and Use of His Appropriated Treatises on Aristotle's* Posterior Analytics (Dordrecht-Boston: Kluwer Academic Publishers, 1992), 268–73.

edition of his *Summulae* in 1539, an indication that he did not class it with his *Juvenilia* but saw it still as helpful to students.) One of the topics treated in the *Summulae* is the supposition of terms, that is, how meanings are to be assigned to terms depending on the context in which they occur. Much of this material was tedious and onerous to students, and elicited complaints such as those we have seen voiced by Vives against Dullaert and Lax.

Apart from the supposition of terms, however, there is another use of *suppositio* that pertains to the principles on which demonstrations or scientific proofs are based. This is the supposition of propositions, which is not the same as the supposition of terms. In his scientific writings Galileo himself frequently says that he is demonstrating *ex suppositione*, that is, "from a supposition," but scholars have had great difficulty understanding precisely what he could mean by that expression. In my attempts to understand it, and I have been working on this now for some years, I came across another of Galileo's Latin notebooks, different from the one referred to by Duhem. This one, written like the other in Galileo's own hand, is still preserved in manuscript in the National Library in Florence, where it bears the simple title *Dialettica*. Oddly enough, though composed in 1588 or 1589, as I have found, it was never transcribed and so was left out of Galileo's *Opere* when they were published at the beginning of this century.

In 1988, four hundred years after it was written, William F. Edwards and I published the Latin text of that manuscript, along with a preliminary account of the sources on which it was based.[17] The notebook turns out to be a questionary on the *Posterior Analytics* of Aristotle, and it gives all the answers one would wish to understand the demonstrations proposed by Galileo in his scientific writings. In it we can find what it means to demonstrate *ex suppositione*, and, if we reflect on Galileo's scientific findings with his telescope and experiments on motion, why he used that expression to characterize and validate much of his later work.

What do you suppose is the source on which the logical questions in that notebook are based? I have already stated that the first notebook was taken from the writings of Clavius and possibly from those of three other Jesuits—Vallius, Rugerius, and Vitelleschi—all of whom cover materials very similar to those found in Galileo's manuscript. For the second notebook the case is much more clearcut. It was appropriated directly from the logic course taught at the Collegio Romano in 1587–

---

17. Galileo Galilei, *Tractatio de praecognitionibus et praecognitis* and *Tractatio de demonstratione*, ed. W. F. Edwards and W. A. Wallace (Padua: Editrice Antenore, 1988).

88 by Paulus Vallius, who later published a complete version of the course in two folio volumes of seven hundred pages each. If we study Galileo's compositon with the aid of those volumes we can find all we need to know about the scientific methodology and epistemology that underlies his life's work. Furthermore, on the basis of the evidence supporting the identification of Vallius as the source behind Galileo's second notebook, we now have very good reason to believe that Vallius was also the source behind his first.

One of the key teachings in Galileo's notebook on logic is that on the demonstrative *regressus*, the process whereby in the physical sciences one can discern the cause of a phenomenon from the effects it produces, and then regress, or go back in the opposite direction from cause to effect, and so provide scientific demonstrations of the phenomenon being investigated. Historians have associated this *regressus* with two well-known Paduan Aristotelians, Agostino Nifo and Jacopo Zabarella. Additionally, a few remarks Galileo makes in his scientific writings have led some, such as Ernst Cassirer and John Hermann Randall, Jr., to claim that Galileo became acquainted with that methodology from his association with Aristotelian professors during his teaching days at Padua. Now we know that such could not be the case. The logical notebook was written at Pisa before Galileo moved to Padua, and it provided the methodology he was using long before he experimented with falling motion at Padua or made his discoveries with the telescope there, for which he quickly became famous. And its source was not the Paduans but the Jesuits, who first were taught the *regressus* by Franciscus Toletus in his *Logica* of 1572, basing his teaching on Soto's exposition of the *Posterior Analytics* given thirty years earlier at Salamanca.

This discovery is truly momentous, and it has led me to go back over all of Galileo's scientific writings to see the extent to which he used *suppositiones* and the demonstrative *regressus* in them. The complete results of that study will be found in my two volumes, *Galileo's Logical Treatises*, which provides an English translation of his logical questions along with commentary and notes, and *Galileo's Logic of Discovery and Proof*, which explains not only the context in which these questions must be located but also the way Galileo relied on their teaching throughout his scientific career.[18] The second volume, in particular, shows that despite Galileo's disagreements with the peripatetics over their teachings on motion and the heavens, he himself followed Aristotelian method-

18. W. A. Wallace, *Galileo's Logical Treatises. A Translation, with Notes and Commentary, of His Appropriated Latin Questions on Aristotle's* Posterior Analytics (Dordrecht-Boston: Kluwer Academic Publishers, 1992). See note 16 for the full citation for *Galileo's Logic of Discovery and Proof*.

ology when making his own discoveries. As he was to write to Fortunio Liceti, and this only sixteen months before his death, he may have disagreed with the Aristotelians in the universities on many matters, but in matters of logic he had been a peripatetic all his life![19]

Philosophers of science, to be sure, will find much to contest in this new thesis, for it implies revisionism of the most drastic sort. No longer can the "Father of Modern Science" be seen as breaking away from the learning of the schools and using radically new methods to make discoveries about nature and the universe. The methods he used were old, tried, and true. Especially in their combining mathematical with physical reasoning, they owe much to the fusion of nominalist and realist thought that began to appear almost a century earlier in the writings of Domingo de Soto.

What, then, can be said about Soto's influence on Galileo? Was the Pisan physicist actually influenced by the *uniformiter difformis* teaching I have been sketching out here? Can we see in Soto, as Pierre Duhem was tempted to see, Galileo's precursor in uncovering the law of falling bodies? Surely the case is not apodictic, the evidence far from overwhelming. And yet one would be quite rash to discount completely the materials I have presented. Particularly when we consider the notebook containing Galileo's physical questions in light of his newly available notebook containing the logical questions, we begin to discern elements of continuity that have been completely overlooked before that now require a complete reassessment of Galileo's intellectual heritage. Undoubtedly he owed a debt to the Jesuits from which he appropriated those notebooks. And they in turn owed a debt to those who preceded them, a debt, for the cases in which we have been interested, that extends all the way back to Domingo de Soto.

To summarize: the title of this essay is "Domingo de Soto and the Iberian Roots of Galileo's Science." The summulist tradition I have been sketching originated in England, was nourished in France, but it found its most enthusiastic proponents among the Spanish and Portuguese who studied at the University of Paris in the early decades of the sixteenth century. In a most unusual way it was transplanted to Rome by Spanish Jesuits, and there it took up new roots in the Society of Jesus. It also continued to flourish on the Iberian peninsula, especially among the Jesuits, although unfortunately it is not conspicuous

---

19. The letter was written on 14 September 1640. An English translation is given in W. A. Wallace, "Aristotle and Galileo: The Uses of ΥΠΟΘΕΣΙΣ *(Suppositio)* in Scientific Reasoning," in *Studies in Aristotle,* ed. D. J. O'Meara (Washington, D.C.: The Catholic University of America Press, 1981), 75; reprinted in Wallace, *Galileo, the Jesuits and the Medieval Aristotle.*

in the *Cursus philosophicus* that was edited by the Jesuit faculty at Coimbra, the famous *Conimbricenses*. One has thus to search in lecture notes, in manuscript sources, to discern its presence. But it was there nonetheless, especially among professors who taught the *Physics* and who later shared the same interests as Galileo. Once this is understood, considerably new light is cast on the twofold enigma of Domingo de Soto.

8 The Economic Teachings of Spanish Scholastics
JUAN ANTONIO WIDOW

I

It is quite common, nowadays, to judge the economies of different historical times according to univocal criteria. Current models are applied to conclude, simply, that the economic life of such and such a century was in this or that degree of backwardness with reference to our times. To measure according to standards of our times the degrees of "backwardness" or "progress" of humanity is a bad habit very strongly rooted in our contemporaries. And this is all the more serious because current economic criteria are applied to judge not only the economic life of past ages, but other, more fundamental aspects of their cultures as well.

Because of this, many of the studies made on the habits and criteria commanding economic life in times different from ours (I understand as ours those of the last two centuries), although academically worthy for their amassing of information, have not led to a very deep understanding either of their internal motivations or of their ends. They suffer, rather, from a lack of understanding. There is no wish to accept all that is involved in the fact that, in those times, judgment of human behavior took into account not only its concrete results, whether successful or ruinous, but also, and in a foremost way, its order or disorder in relation to the final end of human life. To value in practically an absolute manner the advantages and comforts that contemporary technology and economy put within our reach is something that distorts judgment about the value systems according to which the lives of our ancestors were organized. To apply moral criteria to economic behavior is now considered to be imposing an altogether alien frame to it and, therefore, doing violence to it, as it prevents the spontaneous development that distinguishes it. It is said that the ethical purposes of ancient censors of economic behavior could be very praiseworthy, but that they do not have nor can have any relation with the reality over which it has been wished to impose them.

To understand the economic teachings of Spanish theologians of the sixteenth and seventeenth centuries we must, therefore, take the intellectual viewpoint they had, according to which economic acts, because they are willful human acts, have a moral quality. That they do have it does not exclude, however, that the character of their specific object, the economic, should be considered according to its own nature—something that was never forgotten by those theologians. Thanks to the fact that they remembered it, they developed a wide and thorough knowledge of all the habits of the economy in their times.

II

In the sixteenth and seventeenth centuries, the assumptions on which economic life in both Spains—European and overseas—was based were the same that had been present for some centuries in all Christendom. Régine Pernoud writes:

> To understand the Middle Ages, it is necessary to imagine a society living in accordance with an absolutely different model, a society where the notion of salaried work, or even that of money, was absent or quite secondary. The foundations of human relations were the double notion of faithfulness on the one hand and protection on the other. He who pledged his loyalty to somebody else, expected safety in exchange. He did not commit his activity to a precise job, with set wages, he committed himself, or more exactly, his faithfulness, demanding in exchange livelihood and protection, in the whole sense of the word. This is the substance of the feudal link.[1]

That same historian adds that "as from the fourteenth century onwards, the bond will refer more to things than to people; it will be associated with the possession of some good, and will be the consequence of the basic obligations existing between the lord and the vassals, whose relations, from then on, will begin to resemble very much those between an owner and his tenants."[2]

The development of trade is what gives increasing importance to means of exchange and a greater complexity to economic life. This does not imply a change of the criteria used to judge and to order it. At least, they do not change significantly. There is a homogeneous evo-

---

1. Régine Pernoud, *Lumière du Moyen Age* (Paris: Bernard Grasset, 1981), 31.
2. Ibid., 34–35. She continues: "But through the period of the Middle Ages, the bonds are set between individuals. *Nihil est praeter individuum*, it was said. A taste for everything that is personal and precise is typical of the times, as is a horror for everything abstract and anonymous."

lution; Saint Thomas Aquinas already attends to some of the problems originating from that more complex economic activity. Writing in the first half of the fifteenth century, Saint Antonin and Saint Bernardin (the former in Florence and the latter in Siena, main trading centers in Italy and Europe) apply those same criteria to problems of a notoriously greater complexity, almost all of them arising from the increasingly essential function in the economy that money had been taking. The evolution is homogeneous because the feudal age's characteristic criteria are maintained: All human acts that somehow affect other human beings must be signaled by loyalty, that is, they must be just.

In Spain, the evolution is similar, with a large expansion in economic life brought about by the end of the *Reconquista,* following the seizure of Granada, and Spain's presence in America, which gives Spanish commerce a remarkable boost. These are the circumstances surrounding the theologians in Salamanca, Alcalá, or Coimbra who will occupy themselves with the problems posed by economic life. What must be acknowledged is that the basic criterion of feudal society persists: economic relations must be "good and loyal," in other words, there must exist protection from deception and fraud, particularly for the weak, the small consumer who often has no resources of his own to discern the quality of what is sold or the reasonableness of the price asked from him.[3]

III

This reality, that of an economy inseparable from the ends of human behavior, is the one Spanish theologians, from Francisco de Vitoria and Martin de Azpilcueta onwards, have in mind when they consider this subject and its practical connotations.

It is known that dominion over physical goods, which can be translated into the juridical institution of property, is the foundation on which the economic life pertaining to political society is based. Because of this, the notion one has about the nature of this dominion determines the global conception of economy.

"Nobody owns a thing unless it is in his power to use it: now then, among creatures, only man, because of free will, has this power." Domingo de Soto sums up in this way the doctrine about the dominion of

---

3. "'Good and loyal' economics are, in fact, only the application of Christian principles that permeate the entire community. They are occasionally found articulated in the works of the Church Fathers and are gathered in the *Summae* of the thirteenth-century Scholastics, led by St. Thomas" (Régine Pernoud, *Histoire de la Bourgoisie en France* [Paris: Ed. du Seuil, 1982], 1:92).

physical goods. "Which is corroborated," he adds, "by the way people talk, since it is not said of things that are naturally inclined toward their acts that they have dominion over those same acts, as fire is not called owner of his power to heat, because it is not capable of not heating; and we deny that the drunkard has dominion over his acts because he has no power over himself."[4]

If only he who has free will can have dominion, free will being the essential condition for its existence, we can infer here some of the attributes of dominion, which we must consider in order to understand the notion sustained by the theologians with whom we are concerned. Free will does not refer to the ends of behavior, but to the possible means of attaining them. An end is never chosen as such; if it has been chosen, it is as an alternative in order to attain another end. Consequently, the object of the dominion men have over physical goods is not that dominion itself. Dominion is not an absolute thing. The use of such goods can place obligations, as in fact it does, upon their owner. According to the modern concept of property, this would imply a restriction on it, unacceptable in itself because that concept assumes the autonomy, in its most rigorous sense, of the owner to dispose of what belongs to him.

The difference between the traditional notion of dominion and the modern concept of property takes root precisely in this. "The owner is he who has the capacity of free use," wrote Cardinal de Lugo.[5] The owner is he who determines the use of what is his. If there exists any obligation in relation to that use, it is the owner who must fulfill it. This does not lessen or restrict his condition as owner, but rather assumes it. One of the arguments theologians gave in favor of private property was that without it, it would not be possible to give alms: Vitoria writes that "vainly would the Lord advise, if everything were common, to give alms, because alms must be given from our own goods and not from those that are common."[6] And they insist on the obligation that those who own goods have of giving alms to the poor: "Nobody should ignore

---

4. Domingo de Soto, *Relección sobre el libro cuarto de las Sentencias acerca del dominio*, quoted in Restituto Sierra Bravo, *El pensamiento social y económico de la escolástica* (Madrid: C.S.I.C., 1975), 2:627.

5. Juan de Lugo, *De iustitia et iure*, vol. 1, disput. 6, lec. 1, quoted in Sierra, *El pensamiento*, 2:772.

6. Francisco de Vitoria, *Comentarios a la II-II de la Suma Teológica de Santo Tomás*, q. 66, a. 2. He adds: "en Math. 25 consta que en el juicio último se hará gran examen sobre las obras de misericordia, que no pueden cumplirse sin apropiación.... En cuanto a la comunidad de los Hechos de los Apóstoles digo que fue voluntaria, pero no sabemos cuánto duró. Únicamente se lee en las Sagradas Escrituras que tuvo lugar en Jerusalén, y que allí poco duró, y que se hacían colectas para los pobres, lo que no se realizaría si todas las cosas fueran comunes" (Spanish version quoted in Sierra, *El pensamiento*, 601).

that he has not received either body, or soul, or life, or money for his exclusive comfort and use, on the contrary, he is their dispenser and conscientious distributor, and for no other end has he received them from God."[7]

In this way, having dominion over physical goods always involves the responsibility related to the use given to those goods. It pertains to the owner's good discernment or discretion to give them a suitable use, which could be for no benefit of his own, but for that of others. This discernment, because it has in mind the end of such goods, which is no other than the satisfaction of the natural necessities of man, be they the owner's or those of others—human good as such—must be founded on the virtues leading us towards that same good, be it temperance in what concerns our own good, or justice and charity in what belongs to the good of others.

The dominion or ownership of external goods is, consequently, the essential assumption of the economic life pertaining to political society, in the sense that without dominion that economy could not exist, since, as Soto says, "if his will establishes the owner, by that same will anyone can renounce his dominion";[8] in other words, he can sell what is his for whatever purpose. But, besides the fact that dominion is the essential assumption of economic relations, because of its very existence, its nature determines the nature of those relations. In other words, selling, buying, or any other act of this kind are willful decisions of the individual, acts by which he freely disposes of his own inasmuch as it involves a relation of proportion to another's good. And if this good pertains to the other by right, as is the case in any exchange where there is no intention, in either party, of donating, such acts must necessarily have the quality of being just or unjust.

This is the basic premise from which the classical problems of economic life are set forth, those that have been discussed by the theologians and for which they have proposed criteria for resolutions. These are the questions of a fair price, fair interest, and fair wages. We will

---

7. Juan Luis Vives, *Del socorro de los pobres o de las necesidades de la Humanidad*, bk. 1, ch. 9. "De manera que ladrón es no el que merma la hacienda que ha de dejar al heredero, dando participación a los pobres, sino quien abusa inútilmente de su talento, o consume sus fuerzas, o deja enmohecer su ciencia, o derrocha el dinero o lo retiene con estéril tenacidad. Dirá alguno, y esto con ceñuda altanería: Hago esto de lo que es mío" (quoted in Sierra, *El pensamiento*, 535–36).

8. Domingo de Soto, *De iustitia et iure*, bk . 4, q. 5, a. 1: "Si ergo per voluntatem constituitur dominus, per eandem potest dominium ab se quodcumque abdicare" (Madrid: Ed. Instituto de Estudios Políticos, 1968), 2:309. Also: "Nihil aliud est dominium rei quam facultas et ius eadem uti, quocumque usu lege permisso: puta donandi, vendendi, consumendi, et quomodocumque alienandi" (ibid.).

briefly examine the way in which Spanish Scholastics have dealt with the first two.

IV

A price is just if, in the performance of an exchange, neither of the parties involved loses something of his own for the gain of the other party, which gain, obviously, is not measured based upon the exchanged good, but according to its exchange value in the market. In other words, it is a question of commercial exchanges not having as a consequence the enriching of some parties at the expense of impoverishing others; or that the benefit of one of them is not the result of depriving the other of his patrimony, which happens if the price paid for a good is manifestly higher or lower than what is usual and reasonable. This is what is called "reciprocity" in exchanges, the effectiveness of which is the essential condition of justice in pricing. One contemporary author who has been concerned with the economic doctrines of the Scholastics explains the notion in these terms: "It is my opinion that reciprocity in exchanges can be better understood from an accounting perspective. When we exchange money (an asset) for goods (another asset) the only thing appearing in our balance sheet in the first instance is a change in the composition of assets. The total asset is not altered and the situation is similar to that existing before the transaction."[9] The need of submitting to reciprocity in exchanges is founded, as Vitoria graphically notes, on the fact that "I am not obliged to provide any benefit or give pleasure to my neighbor, for nothing and with no reward, even if it costs me nothing and it does not involve any exertion for me. So that if he asks me to dance, I can tell him I do not want to, unless you give me a gold coin; and I can say the same of any other thing he asks me."[10]

Commercial exchange, then, requires, in order to be normal, the free will of the parties and the absence of a specific obligation to benefit another. The will of the parties engaging in the transaction and this lack of obligation constitute the true market freedom. Nevertheless, in making this freely willed transaction, the parties assume, by virtue of that same freedom, the mutual obligation of giving each other the equivalent of what has been received—in other words, they assume freely an obligation of mutual justice. This justice is damaged or pre-

---

9. Alejandro A. Chafuen, *Economía y ética* (Madrid: Rialp, 1991), 121.
10. Francisco de Vitoria, *Comentarios a la II-II de la Suma Teológica de Santo Tomás*, quoted in Chafuen, *Economía y ética*, 119.

vented through violence, fraud, or deception. The ease and frequency of use of these means in commerce generally brings about an attitude of mistrust towards merchants, to which Domingo de Soto refers when he writes, "It must be particularly noted that commerce, I do not know owing to which of its conditions, arouses a perpetual craving for profits over the remaining arts and offices. Because farmers and workers living from their jobs, feel satisfied; but traders, whether because they always have money in their hands, or because this profession is exposed to many risks from fate, burn with desire for profit. In this they resemble gamblers very much. And this lust for profit sucks their soul, fosters falsehood and weaves deceit."[11] Despite such remarks, Soto explains that "trading is not in itself intrinsically good, as is the virtue of charity, nor is it in itself intrinsically bad, as falsehood is, but, in itself, it is indifferent, as eating is, being able to be bad or good, depending on the end and the circumstances." On the other hand, he adds that "commerce is necessary to society."[12]

The concern of theologians and confessors over the need to respect the just price in exchanges is emphasized because of such circumstances. They point out clearly that an unjust price is in itself a deadly sin and it compels restitution. This does not imply the existence of a rigoristic and simplistic attitude in them—on the contrary, it is this same concern that moves them to investigate the causes that can influence the variations in exchange values and, for that same reason, in prices, so that moral judgment should always consider the circumstances and the real object of behavior.

Vitoria, Soto, and Molina repeat the same conscientious considerations over the factors that bring about the natural variations in prices. Molina, who lived and taught after the first two and in certain points amplifies their doctrine, writes:

It must be noted . . . that there are many circumstances that make the price of things fluctuate between rising and falling. Among them, for instance, is the scarcity of goods, because of a bad harvest or other such causes, that makes the just price rise. Abundance, however, makes it descend. The number of buyers who concur at the market, at times larger than at other times, and their greater desire of buying, also make it rise. Similarly, the greater need that many have of a particular good at a definite time, assuming the quantity to be the same, makes its price increase, as happens with horses, which have more value when war is forthcoming than in peacetime. In the same way, the lack of money in a particular place makes the price of the other goods descend, and the abundance of money makes the price rise. . . . The manner of the sale also has an

---

11. Soto, *De iustitia et iure*, bk. 4, q. 2, a. 2; ed. cit., 3:545.
12. Ibid., 544; "Negotiatio est simpliciter reipublicae necessaria."

influence and makes the price of goods vary. For instance, in the following cases it is usual to sell goods at a lesser price than that at which merchants sell: when something is sold at an auction or, in order to be sold, it is taken to an agent, or a street vendor, or to the women that in some places sell the goods of others; when a student sells his books or his furniture is sold after his death. However, provided that the price is what is usual in that kind of sale, it should not be judged unjust.[13]

The criterion that, in normal conditions, should be looked for so as to discern if prices are just or unjust is that of "the common estimate of people in each territory; and when in some territory or place it is usual to sell some good for a definite price, not existing in it fraud, monopoly, or other tricks or cheatings, that price must be assumed to be the measure or rule to judge the just price in that territory or place, provided that circumstances on which the price justly fluctuates to rise or fall do not change."[14] Domingo de Soto writes that, when "the republic does not impose a rate," that is, when there is not a price fixed by law, and when there are some of those particular circumstances that make the common estimate uncertain, it is necessary to appeal to the judgment of the wise.[15] Juan de Lugo asserts something seemingly contrary, when he says that "we must have in mind not only the valuation of wise men, but also that of the unwise, if in some place the latter are in a big enough number. This is the reason why Ethiopian crystal glass trinkets are exactly exchanged for gold, because generally these things are more valued in Abyssinia."[16] He does not deny, however, the need of appealing to the judgment of the wise man, nor does he pretend that the number of the unwise gives them the wisdom they do not have; he only affirms that the many can establish their opinion as the "common estimate."

"To ascertain the just value of merchandise," writes Domingo de Soto, "it is necessary to consider many things, which are reduced to three types. In the first place, one should consider the need of the

---

13. Luis de Molina, *De iustitia et iure*, disp. 348; in Luis de Molina, *La teoría del precio justo*, ed. Francisco Gómez Camacho (Madrid: Editora Nacional, 1981), 169–70.
14. Ibid., 169. "En otras cosas (cuyos precios no están determinados por ley) por útiles que sean a la vida, se entiende que el precio vulgarmente corriente entre los vendedores y compradores es el justo, y de ordinario lo suele ser cuando no hay fraude, ignorancia o monopolio, y por eso, en ellas no es necesario que la república ponga tasa, ni usa ponerla, porque la necesidad no aprieta a los compradores más que a los vendedores" (Pedro de Valencia, *Discurso sobre el precio del trigo la Rey Nuestro Señor*, quoted in Sierra, *El pensamiento*, 701). See Soto, *De iustitia et iure*, bk. 4, q. 2, a. 3.
15. "Cuando no está señalado el precio por la ley, no es necesario someterse al arbitrio de cualquier mercader, sino que es necesario recurrir al juicio de los prudentes, y de aquellos que tienen por oficio practicar la justicia" (Soto, *De iustitia et iure*, bk. 4, q. 2, a. 3).
16. Lugo, *De iustitia et iure*, disp. 26, lect. 4, quoted in Chafuen, *Economía y ética*, 111.

thing; after that, the abundance and the scarcity; and finally, the business toil, care, industry, and risks."[17] The first factor concerns the buyer: it is the degree of necessity and desire he has for the good; the second refers to the good itself; and the third pertains to the seller.

Lastly, we find enunciated by Francisco de Vitoria the principles one has to have in mind to decide upon the just price:

> One has to have in mind three principles. First, that excluding fraud and deceit, he who wants something gets no harm, particularly in worldly things. So, if things not necessary to human use are sold at much more than their value and the buyer receives them willingly and freely, then in this case nobody is obliged to make restitution, because no harm is done to him that wills *[volenti non fit injuria]*. The second principle is that in human exchanges it is not enough for commutative justice that they are *simpliciter* voluntary in relation to each party, it is necessary that nothing involuntary is mixed in them. . . . So, if somebody sold something either because he was afraid of punishment, or due to ignorance or violence, this contract, even if it is *simpliciter* voluntary in both parties, is, however, unjust, because it has something involuntary mixed in it. The third principle is that what is done because of necessity, even if it is *simpliciter* voluntary, is, notwithstanding, partly involuntary. Therefore, in this kind of exchange it is not enough that it is *simpliciter* voluntary, but it is required that no necessity or violence exist. Because somebody, forced by necessity, may *simpliciter* want to exchange something, and there exists, however, some violence because of necessity. Wherefore if, forced by it, he sells the thing cheap, the buyer would not buy it justly.[18]

V

In her book *Heloïse et Abelard*, Régine Pernoud quotes the following experience in the life of Guillaume le Marechal, who lived in the Plantagenet's court, in the twelfth century:

> One day, when Guillaume is riding with a squire, Eustace de Betrimont, a couple on horseback goes past them: a man and a woman; the man looks troubled, the woman cries and sighs. Guillaume looks at his companion questioningly, both of them spur their horses to overtake these people, who have impressed them as sad. They talk: it is, actually, a suspicious couple: a runaway monk with a woman he has abducted. Guillaume and his companion try to encourage them, they grieve with them over the *mal d'amour* that makes one do so many wrong things, they comfort the woman, so visibly anguished, as best they can; they are going to part when Guillaume asks: "Have you got, at least, something to live on?" Upon which the secularized monk puts him at ease; they have a

---

17. Soto, *De iustitia et iure*, bk. 4, q. 2, a. 3.: "Además ha de tenerse en cuenta si las mercancías mejoraron, o sufrieron deterioro al pasar frecuentemente por las manos de compradores y vendedores, y otras cosas parecidas a estas, que cada uno prudentísimamente puede averiguar."

18. Vitoria, *Comentarios a la II-II*, q. 77, a. 1, quoted in Sierra, *El pensamiento*, 607.

purse: forty-eight pounds that they intend to place at an interest; they will live of their income. Both gentlemen burst out in anger: "So you expect to live from usury! By God's power, that will not be done! Get the money, Eustace!" And they fiercely attack the secularized monk, taking away what he has, they send him and his companion to the devil, and return to the castle, where that night they tell the deed to their comrades, distributing among them the money they have taken from the monk.[19]

This episode shows, better than many explanations, what is behind the ancient condemnations against usury—to live from another's work, without a personal and fair agreement, is considered in the feudal society as the worst of crimes. There are other sins that deserve mercy, but not this one; in effect, it goes against the very principle on which that old society is founded, that of personal relations being based on loyalty. To profit from another's necessity is something that is directly contrary to that principle. Seen from a specifically economic perspective (though not "merely" economic, as this cannot be, for the economic consists in free relations between individuals), the loan with interest destroyed, moreover, the balance of an economy of stability—not of growth—based on the various kinds of dominion over land.

We have seen before that the principles of the feudal society persist as criteria for personal behavior in the following centuries, even though society is not entirely patterned according to them anymore. They persist, more than in other places, in sixteenth-century Spain. This does not mean, however, that condemnations against usury are repeated in the same way, or that in the sixteenth century, new circumstances—requiring a distinction in the subject being judged and, for that same reason, discrimination in judging—are not considered. In this century, the charging of interest and usury are no longer the same thing; in the thirteenth century, Saint Thomas already made the distinction, and in the fifteenth century, Antonin of Florence and Bernardin of Siena expand upon it, clearly establishing the difference between moneylending and capital, that is, between the moneylender and the investor. But, with the necessary stipulations, the condemnation of usury unequivocally remains. Domingo de Soto establishes, after specifying and considering what relates to usury, the two following conclusions: "First, usurious lending, that is, to receive an agreed-upon price for something loaned, is by its nature a mortal sin, because it is contrary to commutative justice. . . . The second conclusion, which comes as an extension of the first, [is that] the profit of usury compels restitution, even

---

19. Régine Pernoud, *Heloïse et Abelard* (Paris: Alban Michel, 1970), 63.

if this is not asked, because the moneylender does not acquire dominion over it in any way whatsoever."[20]

The same Domingo de Soto, who with such a final verdict on usury would, according to the judgment of many economists of our times, rule out the possibility of economic growth through the creation of new businesses, devotes the entire *quaestio sexta* in that same book of his treatise *De iustitia et iure* to the defense of the "partnership contract" *(contractus societatis)* by which one party contributes its labor and the other its capital in order to undertake a common business: "If he who contributes the money, also takes the risk, the contract is just and there is no suspicion of usury in it.... As trading is just, it doesn't matter if you trade with your money, or hand it over to another to trade with it in your name, provided it remains under your dominion. He who contributes his money into a society does not transfer its dominion but keeps it, so that he takes the risk, and therefore he can rightfully get the profit that pertains to his money *[ergo licite potest lucrum recipere quod pro illa pecuniae forte sibi contingerit]*."[21] However, "the contract is never just if one of the parties contributes the money in such a way that he does not risk anything, while the other is obliged to keep it undamaged whatever may happen. The reason is clear: this is not a society, but a veritable loan."[22] After establishing the difference between a loan and a capital investment, Soto justifies the insurance contract, by means of which he who invests capital guards against the risk of losing it, paying a certain amount of money to the one who takes up the risk. This is just "if it is done according to law and custom..., because both take risks, the owner of the ship of paying the price if the ship arrives safely, and the other, of paying for the merchandise if the ship is lost."[23]

The subject of usury is directly related to that of *lucrum cessans:* it poses the question of whether it is legitimate to charge him who has

---

20. Soto, *De iustitia et iure*, bk. 6, q. 1, a. 1: "Prima: Usuraria mutuatio, hoc est pretium usus mutuatae rei ex pacto suscipere, peccatus est genere suo mortale, iustitiae commutati-vae contrarium.... Secunda conclusio quae prioris appendix est. Usurarium lucrum obnoxium es restitutioni, etiam si non petat: quippe cuius dominium minime foenerator aquirat."

21. Ibid.

22. Ibid., a. 2; p. 577. In book 6, Soto comments on *Summa theologiae* II-II, q. 78, by Saint Thomas Aquinas, who in that place (a. 2, ad 5) establishes the same distinction: "Ille qui mutuat pecunium, transfert dominium pecuniae in eum cui mutuat. Unde ille cui pecunia mutuatur sub suo periculo tenet eam, et tenetur integre restituere. Unde non debet amplius exigere ille qui mutuavit. Sed illi qui committit pecuniam suam vel mercatori vel artifici per modum societatis cuiusdam, non transfert dominium pecuniae suae in illum, sed remanet eius; ita quod cum periculo ipsius mercator de ea negotiatur, vel artifex operatur; et ideo sic licite potest partem lucri inde provenientis expetere, tamquam de re sua."

23. Ibid., q. 7, a. 1; p. 579.

received a loan what the lender has not earned because he could not invest it in something profitable. The answer of the sixteenth- and seventeenth-century theologians is almost unanimous.[24] The charge is unjust, because in those cases, dominion is renounced and with it the risk, so that, if there are profits, these no longer belong to the lender. For the moneylender, profit, precisely because it is *cessans*, does not exist. This assertion requires, however, some complementary distinctions: if there is some kind of unwillingness in ceding the money to another, it is just to charge for the loss of profit, in proportion to this unwillingness. This situation is vividly described by Francisco de Vitoria:

> In order to demand something it is not enough that one fails to win at the start, when the loan is handed over, it is necessary to lose some profit all along.... So, if a merchant should prefer trading and his trading profit, and, notwithstanding, another begs him for his money until he gets it, then I say it is right for him to demand the usual profit. However, if afterwards he feels glad of having his money in the other's hands, thereby obtaining a profit every year, and he likes better this profit than trading, then it is not right for him to demand that profit.[25]

On the other hand, in many cases it becomes necessary to distinguish between *lucrum cessans* and *damnum emergens*—in fact, the existence of damage when someone is denied the use of his own money could be demonstrated; if so, it becomes just to charge for compensation. A valid criterion to determine the just amount of compensation is to make it always smaller than the probable *lucrum cessans*. Vitoria himself says

---

24. Chafuen (*Economía y ética*, 153–58) points out two exceptions to this unanimity, the view of Fray Luis de Alcalá (*Tractado en que a la clara se ponen y determinan las materias de los préstamos que se usan entre los que tractan y negocian: y de los logros y compras adelantadas y ventas al fiado* [Toledo, 1543]) and that of Fray Felipe de la Cruz, whose position is more strongly in favor of the justice of money-lending when charging the *lucrum cessans* (*Tratado único de interés sobre si se puede llevar dinero por prestallo* [Madrid, 1637]).

25. Vitoria, *Comentarios a la II-II*, q. 78, a. 2, quoted in Sierra, *El pensamiento*, 609. "Cuando al prestamista le viene algún daño o pérdida de lucro contra su voluntad, puede exigir éste justamente y sin peligro de usura" (Domingo de Soto, *De iustitia et iure*, bk. 6, q. 1, a. 3; p. 522). "Cuando alguno concede un préstamo contra su voluntad puede exigir legítimamente el interés del lucro que por esta causa y por el tiempo fijado para el préstamo cesa para él, pudiendo acordarlo en el contrato. Más aún, si fuere coaccionado a dar el préstamo, y aunque no interviniera pacto alguno, el que así le coacciona estará obligado a pagarle todo el lucro cesante.... Se prueba porque, quien así presta contra su voluntad, en realidad padece injustamente el daño de tal lucro y, por tanto, no sólo puede pactar sobre él, sino la persona que se lo causa injustamente está obligada a restituir aunque no hubiera sido pactado; lo mismo que el que roba a un mercader el dinero que éste tenía preparado para sus negocios no sólo tiene obligación de restituirle la misma cantidad de dinero, sino que también el lucro del que injustamente le privó al robarle el dinero" (Luis de Molina, *De iustitia et iure*, disp. 315, in *Tratado sobre los préstamos y la usura*, ed. Francisco Gómez Camacho [Madrid: Instituto de Cooperación Iberoamericana, 1989], 129).

that "if on account of the loan someone loses a profit, which he would have obtained because he was prepared to trade, and he asks for less than what he would have earned, then it is just. Many merchants do business in this way. They give the king one hundred thousand gold coins saying: we would get ten gold coins for every hundred, give us eight for every hundred."[26]

There has been a constant—and, in some cases, even deliberate— lack of understanding on the part of modern economists concerning the reasons why the Church, theologians, and rulers condemned the practice of usury so harshly, though often ineffectively. They have not wanted to accept that every economic behavior is morally identifiable as just or unjust.[27] But there has been no wish of seeing the specifically economic assumptions of such condemnation, either. This blindness has, however, had several remarkable exceptions, two of which should be mentioned: Werner Sombart and John Maynard Keynes. Sombart writes:

> The forbiddance of charging interest on the part of fifteenth- and sixteenth-century Catholic moralists, expressed in technical terms, means: *Do not prevent money from becoming capital.* The notion that *forbidding the charging of interest implies the strongest inducement towards developing a capitalistic spirit* seems, at first sight, a paradox. And yet, it becomes so obvious when a more thorough analysis of our sources of information is made that, to say it openly, I find it difficult to understand why it has not been seen before now.[28]

And Keynes, regardless of the interdiction he suffers from the part of the current economic experts, was also right when he wrote:

> I was brought up to believe that the attitude of the Medieval Church to the rate of interest was inherently absurd, and that the subtle discussions aimed at distinguishing the return on money-loans from the return to active investment were merely jesuitical attempts to find a practical escape from a foolish theory. But I now read these discussions as an honest intellectual effort to keep separate what the classical theory has inextricably confused together, namely, the rate of interest and the marginal efficiency of capital. For it now seems clear that the disquisitions of the schoolmen were directed towards the elucidation of a formula which should allow the schedule of the marginal efficiency of

---

26. Vitoria, *Comentarius a la II-II*, q. 78, a. 2.

27. See Friedrich von Hayek, *The Constitution of Liberty* (London: Routledge, 1960), 442n16: "See the interesting discussion in R. G. Collingwood, 'Economics as a Philosophical Science,' *Ethics*, vol. 37 (1926), who concludes (p. 174): 'A just price, a just wage, a just rate of interest, is a contradiction in terms. The question what a person ought to get in return for his goods and labor is a question absolutely devoid of meaning. The only valid questions are what he *can* get in return for his goals and labor, and whether he ought to sell them at all'" (emphasis by Collingwood).

28. Werner Sombart, *Der Bourgeois;* Spanish edition *El Burgués*, trans. María Pilar Lorenzo (Madrid: Alianza Editorial, 1972), 256 (emphasis by Sombart).

capital to be high, whilst using rules and custom and the moral law to keep down the rate of interest.[29]

These are two opinions that should, at least, suggest more caution to those who make assertions like this of Raymond de Roover: "The usury doctrine was the Achilles heel of scholastic economics. It involved the Schoolmen and their sixteenth-century and seventeenth-century successors in insuperable difficulties that contributed greatly to bringing their whole doctrine in disrepute."[30]

VI

In order to fully understand the economic doctrine of Spanish Scholastics, it is necessary to comprehend the essential role that the notion of free will has in it. We have already seen that the dominion man has over external goods is considered to be precisely the consequence of free will.[31] This is the reason why all those acts of his that tend to such goods—and thus all his economic acts—always have a moral quality, that is, they are voluntary or properly human acts.

This is the essential difference separating the Scholastic economic doctrine from the so called classic or modern economic science. The latter is based on the assumption, sometimes tacit, sometimes explicit,[32] that man has no free will; that, on the contrary, his freedom consists in the absence of an external end or obligation transcending the individual, that is, in his autonomy, *stricto sensu*. Economic conduct, in this context, is free only when it consists in the spontaneous reaction of an individual looking for his private benefit. For that same reason, when the individual is invited to act according to an end that transcends the sphere of individual good, that freedom is destroyed. The common interest cannot become the end of human action; to say that it has been achieved is only to apply that name to the general results of the free concurrence of private interests.[33]

---

29. John Maynard Keynes, *The General Theory of Employment, Interest and Money* (New York: Harcourt, Brace and Co., 1936), 351–52.

30. Raymond de Roover, s.v. "Economic Thought," in the *International Encyclopedia of Social Sciences* (New York: Macmillan and Free Press, 1968), 4:435. Reading these categorical disqualifications, one feels inclined to ask the same question Sombart asked: "Could it not be, perhaps, that almost none of the scholars that have investigated these sources had either enough economic knowledge or the capacity to reach the general concepts we so admired in Antonin or Bernard of Siena?"

31. See note 4. See also Domingo Báñez, *De iustitia et iure*, preamble to q. 62.

32. See John Stuart Mill, *On Liberty*, I; Ludwig von Mises, *Human Action, A Treatise on Economics IV*, 15, 6; von Hayek, *Constitution of Liberty*, I, 4 and 5 (Spanish ed., pp. 83–121).

33. To this corresponds Adam Smith's oft-quoted "invisible hand" thesis; see *An In-*

The study of what can be called the "economic phenomenon," its constants or laws and its complex variables, has developed since the eighteenth century along lines as broad as they were unpredictable for the sixteenth- and seventeenth-century masters. This is certainly due more to the proportional development of economic activity itself than to weaknesses suffered by the Scholastic science. It would be advisable, therefore, to try to understand the true dimension of the criteria they set forth concerning economic behavior, which was not ordained primarily to the possible success or failure in obtaining physical goods, but to the good of man, which, though it is not contrary to economic success, is not identical with it.

---

quiry into the Nature and Causes of the Wealth of Nations, IV, 2. This thesis has an essential relation with that developed in *The Theory of Moral Sentiments* concerning the nature of what is called morally good and evil.

9   Teresa of Avila and the Meaning of Mystical Theology
JEAN DE GROOT

The following remarks are intended to clarify and interpret Teresa of Avila's use of the term "mystical theology." In general, Teresa uses the term to refer to all the stages of infused contemplation: the prayer of quiet, the prayer of union, and rapture. For Teresa, the term thus refers not to discourse about infused contemplation but to her own experience with each of the stages of union with God. It is obvious to the most casual reader of Teresa that her account of mystical theology is a description of her own emotions, states of mind, and inner life. This feature of her writing makes Teresa seem very modern to us. She seems introspective and concerned with understanding herself. This impression of a modernity we share with Teresa is, I believe, misleading and is based on a misunderstanding of the significance of experience for Teresa. In fact, this misunderstanding contributes to an important modern confusion about mystical theology. Part of my task here is to address this modern confusion. Consequently, my investigation of Teresa's use of the term "mystical theology" will involve as well an investigation of the conception of experience that is involved in the meaning of mystical theology. Let me explain why this task is important and how it can lead to a valuable positive characterization of mystical theology.

There are two widely divergent methods of treating mystical theology today. One is theological and is itself often called "mystical theology." This sort of mystical theology is discourse about infused contemplation and about its relation to dogmatic theology. An example of an issue treated in this discourse is whether a human being's union with God could ever be completely unmediated.[1] The other contemporary approach to mystical theology originates in philosophy of religion and

---

1. On theological treatments of mysticism, see Bernard McGinn, *The Foundations of Mysticism* (New York: Crossroad, 1991), 1:266–91.

consists in analysis of mysticism as a kind of human experience. Of particular interest to philosophers of religion is the evaluation of the claims of mystical experience to be a source of knowledge. A prime concern in these analyses is the objectivity of mystical truth claims.[2] I say these two approaches are widely divergent because I believe there is an important gap in the range of contemporary treatments of the issue. What is lacking is a philosophical treatment of mystical theology in the terms in which it is presented by Teresa herself, terms not reducible to either of the two approaches I have just described. Let me be more specific about what I believe to be the limitation of existing contemporary philosophical treatments of writers like Teresa.

Symptomatic of the problem is that no present-day philosophical treatment would call its subject matter "mystical theology." What they examine is mystical experience, not mystical theology.[3] The most obvious stumbling block is the concept of experience. Taken in relation to the individual, there are two contemporary meanings of experience. One is the sense of the word as used in a sentence like "He is an experienced mechanic," or "She has had more experience performing in

---

2. See, e.g., James R. Price, III, "The Objectivity of Mystical Truth Claims," *The Thomist* 49 (1985): 81–98. He is responding to Steven Katz, "Language, Epistemology, and Mysticism," in *Mysticism and Philosophical Analysis*, ed. S. Katz (New York: Oxford University Press, 1978), 22–74.

3. As examples, consider three passages drawn from different philosophical treatments of mysticism, in which the authors describe their purposes. The first is from Walter Stace's book, *Mysticism and Philosophy* (Philadelphia: Lippincott Co., 1960): "The aim of this book is to investigate the question, What bearing, if any does what is called 'mystical experience' have upon the more important problems of philosophy? We start with a psychological fact the denial of which could only proceed from ignorance. Some human beings do occasionally have unusual experiences which come to be distinguished as 'mystical'. These are recorded, or at least referred to, in the literatures of most advanced peoples in all ages. But since the term 'mystical' is utterly vague, we must first examine the field empirically to determine what types and kinds of experience are called mystical, to specify and classify their main characteristics, to assign boundaries to the class, and to exclude irrelevant types" (5).

The second passage is from Steven Katz's "The 'Conservative' Character of Mystical Experience," in *Mysticism and Religious Traditions*, ed. Steven Katz (New York: Oxford University Press, 1983): "The question I tried to answer was: 'Why are mystical experiences the experiences they are?' And in order to begin to answer this query, I adopted as a working hypothesis the epistemic thesis that there are *no* pure (i.e., unmediated) experiences" (4).

The third passage comes from Nelson Pike's book *Mystic Union* (Ithaca: Cornell University Press, 1992): "If what makes a mystical tradition specifically *mystical* is its connection with mystical phenomena, those speaking from within the Christian mystical tradition would insist that the states of infused contemplation constitute the experiential underpinnings of the tradition as a whole.

"What is it to experience union with God? More precisely, what are the experiential or phenomenological features of the various experiences traditionally included in the union class?" (x).

public than her sister." The second meaning, the one relevant to concepts of mystical experience, is quite different. In this second sense, experience is what occurs or happens to an individual and is highly personal, even subjective. In this sense, a person's experience is recorded somehow by him but is recorded, quite likely, in a disordered or "stream-of-consciousness" fashion. At any rate, experience is what has not yet been thought about and interpreted.

If we turn to Teresa's use of the term *experiencia* and its relation to the various forms of the verb *experimentar* in her *Vida*, we find many instances of the first contemporary meaning of experience, as being practiced or accomplished in an area. We do not find the second contemporary meaning of experience, as what happens to a person and is recorded uninterpreted. The meaning of *experiencia* for Teresa that most nearly approaches this second modern sense is a contrast between what is known through living, acting, and undergoing action and what is known by reading books or being informed by others who have lived, acted, and undergone action.[4] In other words, Teresa does not use the term *experiencia* to refer to a personal inner life which she is interpreting.

Nevertheless, it is very easy to read many, many passages in Teresa's *Vida* as recording her experience as understood in the sense of subjective inner life. Let me present just one example. This passage comes from Teresa's first remarks about the third degree of prayer, the prayer of union. Here she treats of the sleep of the faculties. She writes:

> The faculties have only the ability to be occupied completely with God. It doesn't seem that any one of them dares to move, nor can we make them stir unless we strain to distract ourselves, but even then I don't think we could do so entirely. One utters many words here in praise of God without thinking them up, unless it is the Lord who thinks them up; at least the intellect is worth nothing here. The soul would desire to cry out praises, and it is beside itself—a delightful disquiet. Now the flowers are blossoming; they are beginning to spread their fragrance. The soul would desire here that everyone could see and understand its glory so as to praise God and that they would all help it to praise Him and share in its joy since it cannot bear so much joy. I think it is like what is said in the Gospels about the woman that wanted to call or did call in her neighbors. This joy it seems to me must have been what was felt in the admirable spirit of the royal prophet David when he played on the harp and sang the praises of God.[5]

---

4. For examples of this meaning of *experiencia*, see her *Vida*, in *Obras Completas*, ed. with notes by Luis Santullano, 10th ed. (Madrid: Aguilar, 1966), 61b, 62a, 71a, 89b, 96b, 100b, 108a, and 111b. For an English translation, see *The Book of Her Life*, trans. Kieran Kavanaugh and Otilio Rodrigues, vol. 1 of *The Collected Works of St. Teresa of Avila* (Washington, D.C.: ICS Publications, 1976), 110, 121–22, 128–29, 141, and 147.

5. Teresa, *Book of Her Life*, ch. 16, sec. 3, 148–49.

In this passage, Teresa describes a sort of paralysis of the normal functions of sense and intellect. She also describes joy, the desire to share her joy with others, and unpremeditated exclamations of praise. These surely are experiences that are part of some personal life of Teresa's that she is struggling to understand. However, to interpret this passage as relating Teresa's experience in this way would be a mistake. In her *Vida*, Teresa wrote with eloquence and scientific precision about her emotions, states of mind, and inner life.[6] Yet, if any Christian ever conformed to the Christian ideal of dying to the concerns of self in order to be reborn in a new image, it must be Teresa. She is someone who has "died to the self." We should see a paradox in this detailed discourse about her inner life written by a woman who has no interest in herself. This paradox should make us cautious about applying the term "experience" to what she calls "mystical theology." In particular, we should be cautious about regarding mystical theology as something personal.

The history of the term *mustikē theologia* is relevant to understanding this point about the personal in relation to mystical theology. The meaning of the term is rooted in the use of the word *mustikos* by the Church Fathers, Clement and Origen.[7] They used *mustikos* in its original meaning, "hidden," to refer, first, to the allegorical interpretation of the Scriptures and, by extension, to the meaning of the sacraments. This hidden meaning, which is Christ's life and work, is understood by them to be perennially present in Christian understanding and in the material execution of the sacraments, especially the Eucharist. It is important to note that, until Pseudo-Dionysius, the term *mustikos* was not used in relation to an individual's spiritual journey. Rather, it was associated with Christ's divinity, and particularly with his divinity in contrast with his humanity. The association of *mustikos* with divinity makes it reasonable to understand the hidden meaning of the Scriptures as being Christ's mission of divinizing Christian believers. For Clement, the hidden meaning of the Scriptures and sacraments belongs to the few who are made God-like through possessing this special knowledge

---

6. In evaluating Teresa's discourse about her mystical experiences, it is necessary to keep in mind why she wrote her *Vida:* because she was encouraged to do so by Father Garcia de Toledo and others, who wished a positive judgment to be rendered on her extraordinary spiritual life by the appropriate professionals (see the introduction to *The Book of Her Life*, 35–36n8). Teresa had received no real theological or philosophical training. This is part of the reason her accounts of mystical theology take the form they do.

7. My summary of the early Christian meaning of mystical theology owes much to the incisive treatment of the meaning of the term *mustikos* for Clement, Origen, and Pseudo-Dionysius, presented by Louis Bouyer in his *Histoire de la Spiritualité Chrétienne*, nouvelle éd. (Paris: Aubier, 1966), 1:485–503. See also McGinn, *Foundations of Mysticism*, 1:84–130.

(*gnôsis*). However, the possibility of divinization belongs to all Christians because all share the benefit of Christ's mediation. Because of the necessity of Christ's mediation to the divinization of the believer, contemplation and Christ's role as priest are closely allied in the early Christian connotations of the term *mustikos*.

This connotation belonging to *mustikos* of divinity and Christ's hidden mission of divinizing mankind is central to Pseudo-Dionysius's meaning of mystical theology, which involves the divinization of the individual through contemplation *(theôria)*.[8] However, mystical theology remained, for Pseudo-Dionysius, understanding of the Scriptures. This understanding was achieved, for him, through undergoing divine things *(paschein ta theia)*.

We must bring this original use of the term *mustikos*, as connoting divinization, to bear on Teresa's descriptions of the seemingly personal experiences of joy, unpremeditated exclamations of praise, and paralysis of the senses. With some qualifications, we could say that these details of Teresa's life were a mere husk for the life of God she was living.[9] Mystical theology is this life of God. The distinction between mystical theology and mystical experience is an important one, then. Mystical experience is only the natural outward manifestation of a supernatural life that eclipses in importance all natural personal experiences. The very terms in which modern investigation is couched obscure the question of what it is that requires philosophical clarification. Mystical theology and its relation to natural human experience is of greater significance and interest than what is called "mystical experience." Thus, there is a problem of reference involved in the very use of the term "mystical experience."

A better conception of mystical experience comes out of Pseudo-Dionysius's term "the undergoing of divine things," because this term allows us to see the experiences of the individual as effects of specific divine causes. Let us consider what conception of experience issues from understanding Teresa's descriptions of her interior life in light of acting and undergoing.

We would not want to deny that, in the passage quoted above, Teresa

---

8. On the etymological connection between *theos* and *theasthai* presumed by ancient writers, see *Dictionnaire de spiritualité ascétique et mystique, doctrine et histoire*, ed. Viller, Marcel, et al. (Paris: G. Beauchesne, 1937), vol. 2, pt. 1, 1717–18. The connection is made by Plato in *Cratylus* 293. On the similarity to the divine that the Eucharist imparts to those suitably prepared, see Pseudo-Dionysius, *The Ecclesiastical Hierarchy*, 428b.

9. The qualifications I have in mind would distinguish Teresa's strongly incarnationist mysticism from Pseudo-Dionysius's apophatic, and more ascetic, mysticism. Though she enjoyed the vision of God, Teresa's passionate love of Christ issued in a very active life of reform in Counter-Reformation Spain.

describes something we would call her experience, which she would recognize, too, as something having a unitary character and belonging to her. Let us call this something "experience$_2$." Let us, furthermore, be specific about this experience$_2$ being comprised of the emotions and states of mind she describes throughout her *Vida*. This experience$_2$ has a dual character for Teresa. On the one hand, the single events, vignettes, and emotional states that comprise it are signposts along the road toward union with God. They alert the practitioner of mystical theology to the state of union he has achieved, and also inform him of the relation of this state of union to the patterns of living and the emotions of ordinary life. This function of experience$_2$ is evident on every page of Teresa's *Vida*, so I will not pause to quote particular passages. In this function, experience$_2$ is a practical guide to spiritual life. On the other hand, Teresa takes this experience$_2$ as the only means of representing the life of Christ within her, a life which cannot be described directly in words. That there is no direct discourse about mystical theology is the central point universally agreed upon by all its practitioners. However, that Teresa regards her experience$_2$ as a *representation* of what cannot be expressed in words is not as evident as the role of her experience$_2$ in providing signposts of the spiritual life. Let me quote just one passage where this representational function of experience$_2$ is suggested. In this passage, Teresa describes how rapture may be intermittent, accompanied by the alternate fading and reassertion of the function of the faculties of the soul. Teresa writes:

> The soul is often absorbed or, to put it better, the Lord absorbs it in Himself suspending all the faculties for a while and then, afterward, holding only the will suspended. It seems to me that the activity of these other two faculties [memory and intellect] is like that of the little pointer on the sundial that never stops. But when the Sun of justice wants to, He makes the faculties stop. This suspension of the two faculties, I say, is brief. But since the loving impulse and elevation of the spirit was great, the will remains absorbed—even though these return to their noisy way—and, like the lord over all, causes those effects in the body.[10]

Here, Teresa makes explicit that the functions of the soul always follow or point to God in mystical theology, even when these functions are suspended. Furthermore, she indicates that any effects of mystical theology she is capable of describing are due to the will's being in God. As such, they represent God to the extent that an effect figures its cause.

---

10. Teresa, *Vida*, ch. 20, sec. 19 (*Book of Her Life*, 180). The effects to which she refers are the suspension of the functions of the soul and the lightness of body mentioned in sec. 18.

Let us explore what else is involved in regarding experience$_2$ as a representation of mystical theology.

Any representation, simply in order to be grasped, requires a contrast of opposites—light and dark, essential and inessential, positive and negative. The representation takes shape in the relation of these opposites. In the case of experience$_2$, the contrast is between the divine effects of mystical theology and the normal functions of the soul in ordinary life. A contrast to the ordinary life of the emotions is actually *required* to represent the life of God in the individual. This means that the representation, composed as it is of both ordinary and extraordinary, remains wholly of and within the natural world. It is difficult to separate Teresa's mystical theology from her experience$_2$, because her description of mystical theology is the description of a representation which belongs entirely to the natural realm. For this reason, Teresa's discourse itself can be confused with mystical theology. On the one hand, we know her writing is simply discourse about mystical theology. Yet, the discourse is the means by which the light and dark of the representation are made known. Accordingly, the discourse is, for us, more closely related to what she describes than a discourse about the natural world would be. The problem is allayed if we think of the representation which is experience$_2$ as a natural effect, like a diffraction pattern which represents the interference of light rays with one another. From this standpoint, Teresa's discourse can be seen as describing an objective phenomenon which has a cause. Thus, the representation of mystical theology is like a naturally generated representation. It requires understanding to be recognized, but it is not humanly created, like a representation in art or discourse.

However, representations have parts, or at least points of correspondence. To what in mystical theology do the parts of experience correspond? To answer this question, we would first have to give a general characterization of what is being represented by experience$_2$. In this connection, the very important chapter 22 of Teresa's *Vida* provides a guide. In chapter 22, she sets her own mystical theology apart from the preceding Pseudo-Dionysian tradition of mysticism with her insistence upon the importance, for the practitioner of mystical theology, of continually keeping in mind Christ's humanity. Knowing what we do about the origin of the term *mustikos*, we understand this emphasis on Christ's humanity to be an important development in the history of mystical theology. Judging on the basis of this chapter, the practitioner of mystical theology alternately imitates Christ's suffering and loves the Father as Christ Himself does. To this extent, Teresa's experience$_2$ is a representation not solely of the loving life of the Trinity, but also of

Christ's life and saving actions on earth. This is an important point to which I will return momentarily.

Both aspects of the dual character of experience$_2$ that I have cited—the parts that make it up being signposts and the character of the whole as a representation—suggest that experience$_2$ can be understood as a map. A map is a schematized representation. It is not as independent from what it represents as a picture is, because a map needs a key to have meaning. However, precisely insofar as it needs a key, it has a certain independence as an object that a picture rarely attains.[11] Experience$_2$ similarly cannot be separated from the life of Christ to which its parts, as signposts, point. Nevertheless, as a unitary natural phenomenon, it can be taken as an independent object by someone who does not have the key.

Based on its character as a map, we could also regard Teresa's experience$_2$ as being an allegory of Christ's life and person. It might seem that no life of a real individual like Teresa should be regarded as an allegory of anything, but rather as an instantiation. Surely, Teresa's experience gives one instance of a soul saved, not a story about Christ's saving actions. Teresa's own attitude to her experience is relevant here. She insisted that she underwent divine things, because God chose it. It was useful to Him and had nothing to do with her merit or suitability. She willingly assumed what is to us the oddly impersonal role of a "stage" for God's love. What is of special interest is the relation betweeen her role as stage and her life as a particular person being saved. As a stage, her life reiterates the Incarnation, but necessarily in a way different from the original Incarnation. In her, the life of Christ is now framed: it is both lived and consciously displayed at the same time. Furthermore, it is lived, not as Christ lived it, but in the way that what is acted upon becomes its agent, that is, in the way a lover of Christ is possessed by the One she loves and acts in accordance with His actions. Highlighting Teresa's role as exemplar brings into relief again the difference between mystical theology and the modern idea of personal experience.

I would like to address this difference in another way that exhibits and criticizes the very great limitations that the modern conception of mystical experience imposes on understanding mystical theology. To give a more precise account of how contemporary philosophical scholarship defines mystical experience, let me present the basic contours of a contemporary analysis in relation to a famous passage from

---

11. On the difference between a map and a picture, see Robert Sokolowski, *Husserlian Meditations* (Evanston: Northwestern University Press, 1974), 26.

Teresa's *Vida*, where she refers to mystical theology. The translation of this passage by Kavanaugh and Rodrigues uses the modern language of experience where no comparable words appear in Teresa's text. For this reason, I have modified their translation slightly in the direction of a more literal translation of the passage. Teresa writes:

> I sometimes had *[Tenía yo algunas veces]*, as I said, although very briefly, the beginning of what I will now speak about. It used to happen, when I represented Christ within me in order to place myself in His presence, or even while reading, that a feeling of the presence of God would come upon me unexpectedly *[venirme a deshora un sentimiento de la presencia de Dio]* so that I could in no way doubt He was within me or I totally immersed in Him. This did not occur after the manner of a vision. I believe they call it "mystical theology" *[creo lo llaman mística Teología]*. The soul is suspended in such a way that it seems to be completely outside itself. The will loves; the memory, it seems to me, is almost lost. For, as I say, the intellect does not work, but it is as though amazed by all it understands because God desires that it understand, with regard to the things His Majesty represents to it, that it understands nothing.[12]

The initial modern analysis of this passage that I will present is not drawn directly from any one writer but can be related to the positions of particular scholars to whom I will refer. Let us concentrate on her statement that "a feeling of the presence of God would come upon me unexpectedly so that I could in no way doubt He was within me or I totally immersed in Him." From a contemporary standpoint, this statement can be viewed first as reporting an experience ("a feeling . . . would come upon me unexpectedly"), and second as interpreting that experience ("God was within me and I totally immersed in Him"). The statement performs a third task as well; it claims the interpretation is veridical ("I could in no way doubt"). When her statement is analyzed in this way, Teresa will be regarded as subscribing to a *belief* that God was present to her. We will then naturally want to know how she justifies that belief. But we find that, although she describes her awareness as if it were a perception, she gives no cues from ordinary perception to justify her belief. Nor does she bolster her claim with any intellectual insights. Indeed, she says explicitly that, when she knew God was present, the intellect did not function. In other words, there are no objective standards by which another could judge whether her belief is true or not. Accordingly, we are tempted to say her belief is purely subjective.

If I had more space, I would explain how this analysis is at work in the points of view of Walter Stace, Steven Katz, and Nelson Pike.[13] In

---

12. Teresa, *Vida*, ch. 10, sec. 1, p. 86 (*Book of Her Life*, 105).
13. There are two ways in which the distinction between experience and interpretation is made. According to Walter Stace's understanding of mysticism, experience and

his recent book, *Mystic Union*, Nelson Pike has argued that Stace in particular confuses the two separate issues of the relation of experience and interpretation, and the claim that the interpretation is veridical.[14] Pike argues against the distinction between experience and interpretation in relation to mystical experience. He would, nevertheless, still regard a statement like Teresa's, that she could in no way doubt that God was present to her, as a belief requiring justification of some sort. Here, we are not dealing with a concept of belief that can be identified with religious faith. Rather, we are in the realm of the empiricist, where it is propositions that are the subjects of rational belief, based on the evidence that can be brought to bear in their favor.

If we see Teresa as subscribing to a belief that God was present to her, then it would seem that Teresa's failure to provide justification for her belief on the basis of perceptual or intellectual data available to any person is an issue of considerable importance. If the problem is the lack of positive evidence, then we would do well to note the one positive remark Teresa makes about her experience in the passage quoted. She says, "The will loves. . . ." Does loving have value as evidence justifying a belief? On the basis of the analysis presented above of Teresa's claim that God was present to her, we can only answer "no" to this question. On this analysis, loving is the wrong kind of thing to qualify as evidence. Love has too much interest in its object. It is too desirous, too needy, to serve as justification for a belief. But is it possible for a plausible account of Christian mysticism to omit the issue of loving in relation to an analysis of knowledge of God? More particularly, is it possible that Teresa's loving has something to do with why she could in no way doubt God being present to her?

I would like to explore this question in a way that reframes the de-

---

interpretation are separate occurrences, the interpretation being a judgment made about an experience which Stace believes is common to all religious traditions. On another view, however, that of Katz, experience cannot be separated from interpretation. Rather, experience is always mediated by expectations peculiar to the religious tradition to which the mystic belongs. Nevertheless, from Katz's explicitly Kantian viewpoint, experience and interpretation are separable enough for us to be able to the make the judgment that interpretation always mediates experience.

Pike believes that it is possible for the identification of an object of perception to be part of the perception of the object. When I see a familiar object, like a coffee-maker, I do not first see patches of color and then infer there is a coffee-maker where the patches are. The object is identified in the perception itself. Arguing by analogy to this case, he seeks to establish the possibility of theistic experience. By saying theistic experience is possible, he means that the identification of an experience as an experience of the presence of God has legitimacy as a genuine conscious state. Whether the claim contained in it is veridical—in Teresa's case, the claim that God, as Christians believe in him, was present to her at that time—is, for Pike, another question which he does not address.

14. Pike, *Mystic Union*, 94–107.

scription of mystical theology without including the presumption that Teresa has a *belief* that God is present to her. I will attempt this reorientation through considering a passage from Aristotle's *Eudemian Ethics,* which is similar in an important respect to Teresa's description quoted above. In this passage, Aristotle discusses the relation between loving and knowing that one loves. This relation should be, I believe, the model for the relation between Teresa's loving and her knowledge that God was in her and she totally immersed in Him. In *Eudemian Ethics* VII.4, Aristotle says:

By nature some grow up fond of loving *(philêtikoi),* others fond of being honored *(philotimoi).* The one who delights in loving rather than being loved is fond of loving; the other [the one who is fond of being loved] is rather fond of being honored. The one, then, who delights in being admired and loved is fond of superiority. But the one who delights in the pleasure in loving is fond of loving. For it is necessary that he love by acting. For being loved is an accident; it can escape one's notice that he is loved but not that he loves. So loving is more in accordance with love than being loved, and being loved is more in accordance with the object of love. A sign of this is the following: The lover would rather choose, if it is not possible for him to have both, to know rather than be known, as in the case of women who give up their children for adoption, and Antiphon's Andromachê. In fact, it seems that wishing to be known is for the sake of oneself, and to undergo some good rather than to do [some good], but knowing is for the sake of doing and loving. For which reason also we approve of those who persist in loving the dead. For they know but are not known.[15]

In this passage, Aristotle moves with little explanation from the language of loving to the language of knowing. The crucial statement for understanding the passage is his statement that it cannot escape the lover's notice that he loves. In interpreting the move from the language of loving to that of knowing, let us consider Aristotle's example of a mother who loves her child, whom she has given up for adoption. When he says that the lover would choose to know rather than be known, he means that if the mother cannot both love her child and also have her love returned by the child, then she would rather know that she loves than have her child know that he, the child, loves her. Aristotle is surely right to see the mother's case as somehow definitive of what love is. As definitive, the mother's preference is taken by Aristotle to be proof that love is most properly active loving. For the one who is just fond of being loved wants to have others know they love him. But it is interesting that this proof that love is an activity also has a bearing on determining when someone might be in error about a judgment that he loves. Based

---

15. Aristotle, *Eudemian Ethics,* 1239a27–b1. The translation is my own following the text of R. R. Waltzer and J. M. Mingay, *Ethica Eudemia* (Oxford: Clarendon Press, 1991).

on Aristotle's assessment of the *philotimos*, it would appear that the greatest source of error in judging that one loves is to mistake being loved for loving. The lover who loves without being loved in return will be in the best position not to err when he says to himself, "I love." The two cases of the mother who gives her child up for adoption and those who love the dead, are limiting cases, because the lovers in these cases will not be mistaking being loved for loving. Therefore, they will not err in thinking that they love. I will return momentarily to the function of these examples as normative cases. For the moment, let us concentrate on the connection between loving and knowing.

Aristotle believes that, because love is an activity *(to poiein* or *to energein)* of the one who loves, love would not be something one could experience without knowing it. Some sort of knowledge will always accompany the activity of loving, simply because a person cannot help noticing himself performing an activity. This does not mean that every person who believes he loves truly does love. Rather, it means that anyone who truly loves will know that he loves. But the possibility of error in making such a statement is still present, mainly for the one who deludes himself but also, in a different way, for the true lover.

Let us consider how a true lover could err about whether or not he loves. Take a *philêtikos*, a truly affectionate person, who loves and, knowing that he loves, utters the statement "I love." But suppose our *philêtikos* has a timorous and retiring character and someone challenges him about his statement. If our *philêtikos* modalizes his statement and says "I believe that I love," he makes an entirely different statement from his original "I love." He has now allowed within his field of consideration, if only peripherally, the reasons he might be in error. He is now close to asking, "Is what I call love really infatuation?" or "Will I stand by my loved one when he is in trouble?" The important point is that the statement "I believe that I love" presupposes the integrity of the statement "I love." It presupposes the veracity of the statement "I love" in the situations that conform to the norm for its use.[16] Aristotle has himself given us the normative examples for the statement "I love" in the cases of self-sacrificing love and loving the dead.

---

16. See Ludwig Wittgenstein, *On Certainty*, ed. G. E. M. Anscombe and G. H. von Wright (New York: Harper Torchbooks, 1969): "Doubting and non-doubting behavior: there is the first only if there is the second" (para. 354). What Wittgenstein says about using the word "know" can apply also to the word "believe": "'I know that that's a tree.' Why does it strike me as if I did not understand the sentence? though it is after all an extremely simple sentence of the most ordinary kind? It is as if I could not focus my mind on any meaning. Simply because I don't look for the focus where the meaning is. As soon as I think of an everyday use of the sentence instead of a philosophical one, its meaning becomes clear and ordinary" (para. 347).

The role of these normative examples is extremely important for understanding the nature of belief. An example may clarify what their role is. Let us suppose I am away from home when a thunderstorm hits my neighborhood. I call my neighbor and say, "I believe I left some windows open in my house." My neighbor takes for granted that my statement is about a factual situation, the windows being open or closed in my house, and she replies, "I will look out the front door and see." It is important, in this example, that it is my neighbor who is similar to Aristotle's lover and not I, who am away from home. The statement "The windows in my house are open" is a belief for me because I am not in a position to verify the statement. But my neighbor does not even bother to entertain the statement as a belief before she looks outside in the direction of my house. This is because, once she looks outside, she cannot fail to know whether the windows are open or not. The point is that people have beliefs about things which, in the proper normative situation, can be definitively affirmed or denied. My neighbor is in the situation normative for affirming or denying my belief. In Aristotle's analysis of loving and knowing that one loves, the mother who gives up her child for adoption and the husband who still loves his wife who has died define the situations that are normative for judging that one loves.

It is important to return to the quotation from Teresa's *Vida* to delineate the relevance to Teresa's case of Aristotle's views on the lover's knowledge. Aristotle's treatment of the lover and my own example are relevant to the issue of belief in analyzing Teresa's report of mystical theology. In noticing God's presence to her, Teresa is like Aristotle's lover, who cannot fail to notice that he loves, and my neighbor who, looking outside in the direction of my house, cannot fail to see whether the windows in my house are open or not. When she says, "I could in no way doubt He [God] was within me or I totally immersed in Him," what she can in no way doubt is involved in her knowledge of her own loving. Just as she knows she loves God, she also knows that God is present to her. When "believe" is understood in relation to the normative situations in which what is believed can be verified, then it is clear that Teresa does not have a *belief* that God is present to her.

This is not to say that she never had doubts. Teresa was no timid *philêtikê*, but for a long time, she had doubts pressed upon her by confessors and her well-placed patrons about whether her mystical theology was genuine. But these doubts presupposed that there are normative situations in which "God was in me and I totally immersed in Him" is uttered truthfully by lovers of God. The doubt was about whether Teresa was a reliable lover, one undeceived by herself or by others. In evaluating her claim of God's being within her, we should not ask how her belief that God is present can be justified through that belief being examined by others. We should rather evaluate her statement about God's presence in much the same way I would evaluate my neighbor's judgment about whether the windows in my house are open or not. We should ask whether Teresa is the sort of person in the proper circumstances to be a competent judge of such a thing.

I cannot now explore the issues implicated by the broad structural similarities among mystical theology, loving, and seeing that I have invoked to explore the issue of belief in relation to Teresa's claim. Two broad conclusions can be drawn, however, from what I have said about understanding Teresa's statement that she could in no way doubt God was present to her. First of all, Teresa's loving does constitute something like evidence that God was present to her, if it is the case that she is a normative example of a lover of God. What would be the criteria for a normative lover of God is not a question I have addressed. Secondly, if we want to understand *why* the loving of such a normative lover is evidence, we must take as a starting point the mutual involvement of the lover and the object of her love. On this last point, an important connection can be made between the two parts of my discussion. I have argued that what is usually called "mystical experience" is, in truth, only the natural effects of mystical theology and is best understood as a representation, a map of the effects of divine causes. Understood in this way, the lover of God undergoes divine action. However, on Aristotle's analysis, a person knows that he loves (and so, too, Teresa knows that God was present to her) because of the activity of loving in the human being who loves. We are thus presented with the juxtaposition of a human lover who, by his active loving, undergoes action. I would like to call this "the typical inversion of loving." For it is typical of loving that the lover, desiring to be one with the loved one, seeks to become like the other and thus becomes a patient for the loved one's agency. I would suggest, finally, that there can be no account of mystical theology as a kind of knowledge that does not take account of the inversion of agency and undergoing that is involved in loving. As Aristotle says in the *Eudemian Ethics*, it cannot escape one's notice that he loves. If that loving implicates the undergoing of divine things, this cannot escape the lover's notice either.

There is more that could be learned from the passage in the *Eudemian Ethics* that would enhance our understanding of mystical theology and its effects in the lover of God. For example, what sort of knowledge is the knowledge that one loves? It is not the sort to be treated like a universal concept and defined. The lover's knowledge, when expressed in a judgment, would not be a universal proposition: "Love is X having properties Y and Z." It would, rather, identify a particular: "This is love." The sort of knowledge involved in loving is a recognition. This recognition lies very close to the activity itself of loving. It is, we might say, very much involved in "living love."

In the ancient Neoplatonic tradition, living love is closely allied with living truth and living justice. The idea that neither truth nor justice could be defined was bonded to the insight that some truths are known only in the context of a particular life. That there are such truths was well-understood in the ancient tradition of *philosophia* as a way of life.[17] A similar insight, about the relation of truth and the particular life, is at work in the meaning of mystical theology. The contemporary interest in mystical experience perhaps involves a tacit acknowledgment of the relation between some kinds of truth and the particular life. However, to capitalize on this insight requires a conception of objectivity that can include the involvement of the lover or knower with the object of love or knowledge. Plato believed that love liberates a person from self-interest—gives him an objective viewpoint—insofar as the lover begins to live for a beauty outside himself that transcends his own interest. With such a conception did Plato initiate the main current of the tradition of *philosophia* as a way of life. The philosophical understanding of objectivity that is contained in this tradition should be the starting point for a similar understanding of mystical theology.

---

17. Pierre Hadot makes a distinction between forms of life and forms of discourse in the philosophical tradition of late antiquity, suggesting that the discourse that today constitutes the whole of philosophy was, in antiquity, spiritual exercises undertaken in the service of the way of life defined by the basic principles of a given philosophical school. See his *Exercices spirituels et la philosophie antique*, 1st ed. (Paris: Études Augustiniennes, 1981), esp. his chapter on Socrates, "La Figure de Socrate." See also his "Forms of Life and Forms of Discourse in Ancient Philosophy," the translation of his inaugural lecture to the chair of the History of Hellenistic and Roman Thought at the Collège de France, in *Critical Inquiry* 16 (Spring 1990): 483–505.

10 The Christian Mysticism of St. John of the Cross and the Metaphysics of Being

YVES FLOUCAT
Translated by Michele Herbst

The question of the relation between mystical experience and philosophy has been addressed often and in many ways. How can one not think, for example, of Henri Bergson, Jean Baruzi, Maurice Blondel or Jacques Maritain?[1] I, for my part, do not claim to bring something new to this debate. It seems relevant enough, however, to reflect again upon the doctrine of St. John of the Cross when the occasion arises.

A complete exposé of the problem, which would require much greater detail, cannot be found in the remarks which follow. One would likewise seek in vain to obtain here a more profound knowledge of the great Carmelite Doctor's work. My comments will be limited to the question of the correspondence between the two very different ways of Christian experience: the mystical union, as exposed by John of the Cross, and the rational study of the ontological mystery by metaphysical inquiry. Little by little we will discover that the connection cannot be misunderstood without profound errors occurring in our comprehension of Christian mysticism, on the one hand, and metaphysical knowledge, on the other. The more particular domain of theological knowledge will be addressed only indirectly, but it goes without saying that the relation between philosophy and mysticism concerns it greatly.

After having then compared the pathways proper to St. John's mystical contemplation and to the philosophy of being, I will attempt to isolate a few metaphysical consequences of such theological contemplation. The very witness of the history of western thought will then

---

1. Cf. J.-J. Coutagne and Y. Périco, eds., *Chant Nocturne, saint Jean de la Croix, Mystique et philosophie,* Texts of Maurice Blondel, Joannes Werhle, Jacques Paliard, Gaston Berger, Louis Lavelle, and Aimé Forest (Paris: Editions Universitaires, 1991). Strangely, Jacques Maritain, whose name is constantly evoked in this work, notably with regard to the text reproduced by Maurice Blondel, is nonetheless absent.

perhaps allow us to draw some conclusions about the consequences, for our understanding of the mind's vocation and its connection to being, that seem to have resulted from the seduction that a completely different spiritual experience, one essentially dedicated to immanence and the negation of all distinction, has held for a particularly vivid and preponderant current of our philosophical heritage.

I

How can we characterize the mystical experience according to St. John of the Cross? It would be futile to attempt it in a few words, so I will keep to a few points which clarify our ultimate goal.[2] Nothing would be more false than to seek in the mysticism of St. John the result of a metaphysical inquiry in which the intelligence would, by a dialectical ascent leading to a break from all discourse, arrive, as in Plotinus, at an identifying vision. Undoubtedly St. John of the Cross presents the mystical union as a science *(connaissance)*, and a supreme science, but one in which the surpassing of concepts is the fruit of a love which can only ascend from the heart of man because it comes from the intimacy of God. St. John of the Cross speaks of the sort of "wondrous and sublime knowledge of God, enfolded in divine love," which is promised to the contemplative (AC, II, 15, p. 122). "Knowledge of the benefits received by the union that only God can give, come only to the soul that attains to union with God, for they are themselves that union" (AC, II, 25, pp. 183–84). How does faith, which has an object of superhuman knowledge, not aspire to this surpassing of its conceptual mode of knowing? This "immediation" between God and the soul which solicits love can be realized in no notion, even if revealed by God himself. That which no knowledge can provide, even if perfectly clarified or supernatural, theological love can; for it is God, without distance and by himself, in the mystery of his intimacy, whom it attains. "Knowledge of God, because it is mediate," says St. Thomas, "is called obscure and will disappear in heaven," whereas "charity is attached to God without intermediary [even] in this life."[3] So it is that "in this life, God can be loved in himself and not known in himself."[4]

---

2. Throughout this essay, the works of St. John of the Cross are quoted from *The Complete Works of Saint John of the Cross, Doctor of the Church*, trans. and ed. E. Allison Peers, 3 vols. (Westminster: The Newman Press, 1964). The following abbreviations will be used in this essay: AC for *The Ascent of Mount Carmel* (vol. 1), DN for *The Dark Night of the Soul* (vol. 1), SC for *Spiritual Canticle* (vol. 2), and LF for *Living Flame of Love* (vol. 3).
3. Thomas Aquinas, *Summa theologiae* II-II, q. 27, a. 4, sed contra.
4. Ibid., I-II, q. 27, a. 2, obj. 2.

This communion of love and "the eyes of faith" (DN, I, 6, p. 345) are "the road along which the soul must travel to this union" (AC, I, 2, p. 19), the "wondrous means" (AC, II, 2, p. 65) which "alone are the proximate and proportionate means" (AC, II, 9, p. 93) preceding mystical wisdom. But faith is compared by St. John of the Cross to "midnight" (AC, II, 2, p. 65). Vivified by charity—carried by it even to the depths of this God to whom it adheres without seeing and in the very breath of the Spirit who, by his gifts, awakens love (Cf. SC, XXVII, pp. 132–36)—it is a "dark and loving knowledge" (AC, II, 24, p. 177). Moreover, the knowledge to which God leads the soul in whom he loves himself, and who is the fruit of love, is regarded by the holy Doctor as "a non-knower who knows [*un no saber sabiendo*]."[5]

Already the detachment from all values of sense and of spirit through the active and passive nights—this entrance, in communion with the Son of God, "into the thicket of the Cross, which is the road of life" (SC, XXXVI, pp. 159–60)—has caused a sort of transmutation of the whole human mode of acting in a truly human-divine manner perfectly ruled by the Holy Spirit and his gifts. The understanding, the memory, and the will have been plunged by God himself into the most radical nakedness according to faith, hope, and charity. It is important to correctly understand the sense of this interior void. As regards the understanding, it certainly raises questions about the mystic's attention to certain words and concepts by which the faith expresses itself, but not his attention to the unsurpassable and unique reality of the revealed Mystery which these terms designate. The Mystery remains, because the evidence of the face-to-face has not yet come; but the certitude of faith, in this obscurity, even if it is the ransom of an "excessive light,"[6] is all the stronger because love makes it penetrate "even to the heights of God" (AC, II, 1, p. 64) and gives it a "secret," "simple," "general," and "spiritual" wisdom (DN, II, 17, pp. 428–29) from the Trinitarian intimacy. That which faith offers to the eyes of the spirit without being able to present it in the clarity of evidence is now no longer an intuition, but an experience which is, according to the expression of St. John of the Cross, "by love and in faith" (AC, II, 29, p. 197), which procures from it some sort of sensory contact. Deprived of all conceptual use, faith enters into a connaturality of love in which, in the glowing fire of charity, it is by a "science most delectable," that

---

5. Cf. "I enter'd in—I knew not where," in St. John of the Cross, *Complete Works*, 2:425.
6. AC, II, 3, p. 67: "Hence it follows that, for the soul, this excessive light of faith which is given to its thick darkness, for it overwhelms greater things and does away with smaller things, even as the light of the sun overwhelms all other lights whatsoever, so that when it shines and disables our visual faculty they appear not to be lights at all."

of love, that the soul is henceforth inhabited.[7] Hence, in this "Divine betrothal between the soul and the Son of God" (DN, II, 24, p. 455) is given "the sublime mysteries of God and man" (CS, XXXVII, Exposition, p. 365) and the soul "is transformed in the flame of love, wherein Father, Son and Holy Spirit communicate Themselves to it" (LF, I, 1, p. 19).

That is how St. John of the Cross, as a practitioner of contemplation, presents the Christian mystical experience that is "perfect life in Christ" (LF, III, 2, p. 59). It is a Trinitarian contemplation of which faith is the principle, of which God himself is the author and of which the supraconceptual and human-divine mode is the very one which constitutes the theological essence of charity in a life which receives rhythm entirely from the gifts of the Spirit. It is hard to see what relationship can exist between such a wisdom that makes the soul live from the very depths of grace in raising it to a science surpassing every human manner of knowing and a philosophical or metaphysical knowledge.

II

What do I mean by "metaphysical"? I am not at all ignorant of the fact, and I will come back to it, that diverse philosophies exist, certain "metaphysical principles" about which Claude Tresmontant has just written an "essay of typology."[8] Here I will consider precisely the metaphysical as it can be developed within Christian wisdom where alone, it seems to me, it can take on its true dimensions. It is, then, unreservedly and fully a metaphysics of being and of spirit, the same as that in which, certainly according to the norms of his time, St. John of the Cross had been trained.

But this metaphysical wisdom is not first of all conceived as a spiritual experience. Certainly this is not absent from the philosophical process. How could it be otherwise, since it is with the entire soul that one philosophizes? And how can the one who claims to reflect upon the most profound significance of things not be shaken, more than anyone perhaps, by the discovery of that which represents the simple fact of existing, to be posited *extra nihil,* independent of its causes? And how can one not be transported by a religious sentiment when this mystery of being leads one to the Being who is only being and whose every existent

---

7. CS, XVIII, p. 103. See also DN, II, 18, p. 434: "Contemplation . . . is the science of love."
8. Claude Tresmontant, *Les métaphysiques principales* (Paris: O.E.I.L., 1989).

derives from this primary actuality which renders him purely and simply a subsistent being or, according to the expression of St. Thomas, an *esse habens*?

Still, the wisdom of philosophy, anterior to all experience regardless of its importance, as we shall see, in the very exercise of such a wisdom, is essentially an affair of intellectual knowledge and even, it must be said, rational, since the demonstration and explicit argumentation from first principles occupies a determinant position there. This knowledge is strictly of the natural order in that it reverts to the light of the intelligence to scrutinize the most profound mystery of nature, which is the mystery of being. It is eminently contemplative, since it does not properly belong to it to produce something or to direct the execution of an action, but simply to better understand what is being. It originates in an intellectual perception in which the existent liberates, in the eyes of the spirit, the primary actuality that makes it an existent being and to which all human knowledge ultimately refers. The abstraction, by which the spirit is raised to the consideration of diverse determinations of reality, is at its highest point of extension here. In so doing, it is no longer a world of objective essences which the intelligence discovers, but a world of subsistent beings, of beings which, each in its manner and in proportion to its essence, are invested with this radical energy by which they exist. Hence when the intelligence, in a judgment of existence to which is accorded all the spirit's attention, says to itself that this or that *is*, it is in some sense plunged into a mystery which surpasses it, because this mystery is intrinsic to everything without anything being able of itself to account for it. At the heart of the real, such a mystery intimately constitutes the irreducible diversity of beings at the same time as their most radical communion. It is this intuition of being in its act of existing which allows the intelligence to have a certain conception of what it is to be. It also allows the intelligence to discover little by little the transcendental, universal perfections coextensive to being, the notions of which it should expand so as to render its conception of being more precise.

Metaphysical knowledge will not have attained its most profound vocation, however, if it is not convinced of the incapacity of finite beings to fully account for their intelligibility. Nothing exists if not by the act of being which is proper to it but which it cannot give to itself. It is, moreover, such a state of ontological inadequacy that requires, as metaphysical justification, the primary causality of the pure Act of existing, the *Ipsum Esse subsistens*. Metaphysics is only then fully a knowledge, or a science in the Aristotelian sense, when it knows the One that the whole world calls God, *aliquam causam efficientem primam quam omnes Deum no-*

minant,[9] even if the absolute transcendence of such a primary Cause forces one to refine the concepts with which he designates perfection by subjecting them to the rigor of a radical negation of every finitude from which they have been extracted. Mystical intelligence has eyes of love, and metaphysical intelligence is captivated by the intelligible radiance of its abstract intuitions; but both are engrossed in a captivating glance *(pur regard)*.

III

The Christian mysticism, the great laws of which St. John of the Cross admirably exposes, and the metaphysics of being appear to us, then, as two irreducibly distinct and original ways of wisdom. It is, in fact, certainly a matter of wisdom, since in both ways the knowledge of the first Truth is at the heart of the process and, St. Thomas assures us, "the office of the wise man is to meditate on the truth, especially concerning the first principle."[10] It is, however, of a very different manner that the two arrive at this Truth, the source of all truth. Mystic wisdom, supposing our participation of grace in the divine life and the work of the Holy Spirit, is guided by charity, which establishes a narrow connaturality between the soul and the Trinitarian intimacy of its God. Metaphysical knowledge, the work of natural reason, is guided by its own conceptual seekings and the order of its arguments such that God is only attained indirectly as the primary Cause, no longer in himself, but according to the way of analogy. Undoubtedly such a philosophical elevation of the spirit develops a certain connaturality with its object, but it is an intellectual connaturality insofar as the reality is offered to the conceptual grasp.

Nevertheless, if this loving, "simple," and "general" wisdom, which "is not restricted to any particular object of the intellect or affection" (DN, II, 8, p. 396), and rational wisdom, which struggles with the multiplicity of the abstractive intelligibles, are both—each in its own clearly distinct domain—cognitions *(connaissances)* of God, theologies; then there should certainly be a correspondence between them. Both are essentially contemplative. The recollection of the metaphysician, discovering in the very apophatic negations of his theological discourse a reverse image of God's supereminence, cannot help but feel some affinity for *(symboliser avec)* the intimate recollection in which the soul,

---

9. Thomas Aquinas, *Summa theologiae* Ia, q. 2, a. 3.
10. St. Thomas Aquinas, *Summa contra gentiles* I, chap. 1.

united to God, communicates with him "in loving and affectionate fellowship" (SC, I, 1, p. 33).[11]

Moreover, it is throughout the whole of his philosophical discourse that the metaphysician knows this "concentrated mediation" of which Jacques Maritain speaks,[12] and which, if it is not the fruit of a union of love, if "it does not itself advance in the steps of love," "can nevertheless be united to a natural love of the contemplated object and to a heartfelt complacency in it, which colors it with an affective and experimental hue."[13] After all, it is to the most profound natural mystery, the mystery of being, that the metaphysical intelligence is awakened from the beginning, and that already suffices to cast the spirit into a contemplative meditation which echoes the "rare and delectable" contemplation that the mystical Doctor evokes (DN, II, 17, p. 429).

More generally, should there not be granted to the metaphysical force a dimension other than that of simply knowing? Certainly, it is this latter which specifies the philosophical enterprise; but if the truth attained is the good of the intellect *(bonum intellectus)*, how could the desire for being and for the Principle of all being, which then enters the intellect, be a thirst for the most perfect knowledge without the spirit being simultaneously surrendered by the vow of a more profound love? André Marc thus carefully emphasizes that "if the mind *[connaissance]* thus awakens the appetite *[désir]* without the latter eventually escaping outside of itself, it must be, sooner or later, capable of filling it. It is necessary, in this case, that the ideal of the understanding coincide with that of love, and that tending towards a being as it is in itself, which is proper to the will, is no different from tending towards that being as it is in the intellect."[14]

It is certainly the beatifying face-to-face encounter which, supernaturally, can alone fill such a natural hunger of the spirit. How, in fact, would this desire be satisfied in its most consubstantial hope of seeing God if this ontological generosity—which, even beyond that which essentially distinguishes knowledge and love, constitutes its unlimited opening to the real—were not thereby honored and even exalted? Aimé Forest once observed in this sense that "knowledge and love are alike in that they both express and exercise, according to diverse mo-

---

11. See also AC, II, 12, p. 10: "the most interior recollection wherein the soul is united with God."
12. Jacques Maritain, *Distinguer pour unir ou les degrés du savoir*, in J. and R. Maritain, *Oeuvres complètes*, vol. 4 (Fribourg: Ed. Universitaires; Paris: Ed. Saint-Paul, 1983), 743.
13. Ibid., 744.
14. André Marc, *La volonté et l'esprit*, vol. 2 of *Psychologie réflexive* (Paris: Desclée De Brouwer; Bruxelles: L'édition universelle, 1949), 69.

dalities, the same primitive disposition of the mind," which is an unlimited opening to all of reality.[15] The perfect harmony of intellectual possession and affective union is undoubtedly not to be found until, in glory, God shows us his face, rid of every veil. Then, the intellect will no longer know hunger or thirst and charity will find its perfection.[16] Hence St. John of the Cross can regard beatitude as the tenth step of the ladder of love (DN, II, 20, p. 441), the place of "the fullness and satisfaction" of love that the soul can desire (LF, I, 4, p. 126), all in knowing with St. Thomas that it is the understanding which "must be dark until the day when the clear vision of God dawns upon it in the life to come"(AC, II, 16, p. 129). Jacques Maritain, commenting on both doctors, writes that "in beatitude we shall be deified by intellection. But this very vision will be the crowning effect of love, the hand by which it will grasp its good, and in the delights of exultant love this vision will blossom."[17]

If it is towards such a pacification of the spirit in a perfect reconciliation of the energies of the intellect *(connaissance)* and will *(amour)* that the appetite of wisdom, which metaphysics combines, tends, one can readily see that the fullness of the mystical Christian experience already supernaturally echoes it by an unheard-of anticipation of the beatific vision. It is not that metaphysics would be unable to examine its object whereas unitive love would not in some way continue the relay. On the contrary, it is the very acuteness and adequation of its intellectual regard that nourishes a love to which only the supernatural intimacy of the divine friendship could respond superabundantly. And such a friendship, in rendering the soul like unto God himself, will be, in return, the principle and the place of a loving but secret knowledge, for the intellect will only find the foretaste of evidence still denied for a time. It follows that if to know and to love are indissociable, it is not in the same manner that the bond between them is experienced on the metaphysical and the mystical levels. If metaphysics knows for the sake of knowing, such knowledge is for the soul no less an increase in being, life, and love; if the wisdom of the saints abandons everything for love, and if, as St. John of the Cross says, this wisdom leaves the soul knowing "nothing but love" (SC, XVII, 4, p. 101), nevertheless, God, in and by this very union of charity, "goes on to show the soul the arrangements and dispositions of His Wisdom" (SC, XXVIII, 4–5, p. 138), revealing

---

15. Aimé Forest, "Connaissance et amour," in *Jacques Maritain, Son oeuvre philosophique*, Bibliothèque de la Revue thomiste (Paris: Desclée De Brouwer, 1948), 119.
16. Cf. Thomas Aquinas, *Summa theologiae* I-II, q. 4, a. 8, obj. 3: "Charity is perfected in beatitude."
17. Maritain, *Distinguer pour unir*, 842.

to the understanding "the high mysteries of the Incarnation of the Word" (SC, XXXVI, Exposition, p. 160). The natural wisdom and the supernatural wisdom of love, taking into account their essential difference of degree and the diversity of their paths, are both carried by a desire for the vision of God such that "the more the soul knows God, the more grows her desire and anguish to see Him" (SC, VI, Exposition, p. 212). In this sense, the wisdom of the saints and metaphysical knowledge are marked, in different manners certainly, by this imperfection of the whole of Christian wisdom, which, even at its mystical heights, remains irreversibly at the threshold of vision. "In one case, the soul possesses by the intellect a presence which does not satisfy its love; in the other, it possesses by the realism of love that which is not entirely revealed."[18]

We will be able to pursue, proceeding in this way, a study of the organic relations within Christian wisdom between the metaphysics of being and the mystical knowledge of divine intimacy. One will first of all permit us this question in a different, albeit appropriate, manner. It could be very clarifying, in fact, to emphasize, with the aid of a few particular points, certain metaphysical implications of the Christian mysticism according to St. John of the Cross. We will thus see better not only that the wisdom of the saints is not indifferent to the metaphysical process, but that it is not unimportant which metaphysics is attributed to it.

IV

In a very general way, first of all, one can see in the interior purification that the mystical union entails an unequaled confirmation of the metaphysical vocation of the spirit inasmuch as, if the "passions reign, they allow not the soul to remain in the tranquillity and peace which are necessary for the wisdom which, by natural or supernatural means, it is capable of receiving" (AC, III, 16, p. 245). In fact, metaphysics, whose object, being *qua* being, is abstract, requires a stripping of images in order to develop freely. In the visible, it is the invisible that it pursues and, ultimately, in the invisible, that which does not in any way exist in

---

18. Aimé Forest, *Consentement et création* (Paris: Aubier-Montaigne, 1943), 87–88. Cf. also Jacques Maritain, *Science et sagesse*, in *Oeuvres complètes*, vol. 6 (1984), 100: "If philosophy is knowledge of a natural order, this is a good reason not to be *satisfied* with it, and not to seek in it the ultimate appeasement of the spirit. By no knowledge, even the most supernatural, will the soul, however full, ever be satisfied; it will always be there as in a foreign land, *tanquam in aliena, in casulis habitando* (Heb 11). The more knowledge increases, the more the desire also."

matter. Metaphysics is indeed, as St. Thomas said, the most intellectual science, *maxime intellectualis*.[19] It tends toward knowledge of the things of God, and the mirror of analogy is thus indispensable to the weakness of an intellect turned towards the sensible and not immediately reconciled to the transcendental world. Its effort must consequently be great in order to free itself, not, certainly, from the indispensable conversion towards images, which is the condition of abstraction, nor from the elaborate imagination in the great myths of humanity, in whose contact the philosophical intellect has always been on the alert, but from that which Jacques Maritain has called the "impact solidifying the idea by the image" or again the "impact notionalizing the exercise of the intellect," which is an obstacle to the metaphysical intuition.[20] In this regard, the climate of the contemplation of the saints is incomparable. St. John of the Cross in no way misunderstands the importance of the imagination in the life of the human spirit and even, for beginners upon the path of contemplation and perfection, the provisional necessity of images,[21] but he also knows that these "bear no proportion to proximate means of union with God" (AC, II, 12, p. 104) and that the contemplative soul must be free so as to arrive at the divine union. This liberty of the wisdom of the saints, in the face of human impotence and of the wounds of sin, remains for the metaphysician an urgent invitation—despite the painful sentiment which it can have of being at a loss after the manner of this *spiritus vertiginis* which John of the Cross mentions as one of the most painful proofs of the mystical night of the senses (DN, I, 14, p. 372)—to an always greater transparency of his thought to the pure light of being.

An essential condition of this transparency is the posture which from its entrance the spirit intends to adopt. And from this point of view, the primary attitude of mystical wisdom such as St. John of the Cross describes and which, moreover, proceeds from the contemplative essence of the faith, is not indifferent to the fundamental disposition of the spirit in metaphysics. For the Doctor of Carmel, the "loving attentiveness upon God" is indispensable for the soul to reach the state of contemplation (cf. AC, II, 13, p. 109). This attitude should even be so familiar to the soul that, when the moment arises, it "must forget even

---

19. Thomas Aquinas, *In Met.*, proemium (Marietti ed., p. 1): "Unde scientia, quae de istis rebus considerat, maxime videtur esse intellectualis, et aliarum princeps sive domina."

20. Maritain, *Oeuvres complètes*, vol. 13 (1993), 782: "[l']*impact solidifiant l'idée par l'image*"; "[l']*impact notionalisant l'exercice de l'intelligence.*"

21. See, e.g., LF, III, 3, p. 159: "And in order that we may better understand the characteristics of beginners, we must know that the state and exercise of beginners is one of meditation and of the making of discursive exercises and acts with the imagination."

that loving advertence" "so that it may remain free for that which is then desired for it" (LF, III, 3, p. 70). This loving attention, in fact, frees the regard of all "proprietary attachment" to creatures and directs it to the singular beauty of God.

Undoubtedly the metaphysician, for his part, turns first of all toward creatures, where he is nourished by the transcendentals. Nonetheless, echoing the loving attention of the mystic, the upholding of his spirit will be an intellectual consent to being, that is to say, above all, an attention to finite being in which, alone, he will be able to discern a sign *(témoignage)* of the creative efficiency of Being which is only being. The loving realism of the mystic summons the intellectual realism of the philosopher. A metaphysician who wants to be faithful to this mystical inspiration of the Christian wisdom of St. John of the Cross will not be idealistic. This would, in fact, be a singular perversion of the doctrine of St. John, to interpret the freeing and the negation of all created determination which it advocates as an idealist conversion of the spirit towards the *a priori* conditions of thought. This would be to transform the loving disdain of the contemplative vis-à-vis all that is not the very object of his love into an ontological negation of the value of the created and to separate himself, for all that, from the teaching of St. John of the Cross. It is never for him a matter, in the Plotinian manner and by the magic of a pure intellectual dialectic, of making oneself oblivious to a world of shadows, but of freeing himself for this union of love by which God wants to make us the guest of His intimacy. After all, the properly ontological value of the created is recognized in contemplation, beyond the negation of all proprietary utilization. Has God not left in each of his creatures "some trace of Who He was; not only did He give them being out of nothing, but He even endowed them with innumerable graces and virtues, making them beauteous with marvelous orderliness and unfailing interdependence and doing this all through His wisdom whereby He created them, which is the Word, His Only-begotten Son" (SC, V, Exposition, p. 210)? We are familiar with the magnificent song that John of the Cross ascribes to the contemplative soul arriving at the height of union:

Mine are the heavens and mine is the earth; mine are the people, the righteous are mine and mine are the sinners; the angels are mine and the Mother of God, and all things are mine; and God Himself is mine and for me, for Christ is mine and all for me. What, then, dost thou ask for and seek, my soul? Thine is all this, and it is all for thee.[22]

---

22. St. John of the Cross, *Complete Works*, 3:222.

How, therefore, would the metaphysician, whose office it is, in his wholly intellectual manner, to examine creatures and to find in them "the testimony which in themselves they bear to the soul concerning the greatness and excellence of God" (SC, V, Exposition, p. 210), not begin to exercise his knowledge with a consent to being? Aimé Forest can regard this as "the preparation and the sign of the highest disposition of the religious soul," because being presents itself to us there as "grace and gift."[23] By this consent, every temptation to submit the real to our grasp is set aside in order better to attend to the diversity of the concrete, to being as *aliquid,* that is, to being in its uniqueness, and at the same time to the community of beings in their proportional and ever-irreducible relation to the act of existing. One can say in this sense that it is indeed to a realism of being and of its manifoldness or analogy that the Christian metaphysics of St. John of the Cross invites us. It does not at any moment claim an identifying vision of the One in which the apparent and illusory multiplicity of beings reabsorbs itself. On the contrary, the contemplative soul "has lofty experience of the knowledge of God, which shines forth in the harmony of creatures" (SC, XIV–XV, Exposition, p. 248), and it "is able to see a marvelous fitness and disposition of the wisdom of God in the diversities of all His creatures and works, all and each of which are endowed with a certain response to God, whereby each after its manner testifies to that which God is in it" (SC, XV, 4, p. 259). It is in this polyvalence of being, which the soul knows in the contemplative way and in relation to God as an "ocean of symbols" (St. Ephrem)—this universal analogy which, according to Baudelaire, inspires the poet—that the metaphysician, in "an active and attentive silence of the intellect,"[24] focuses his regard in order to make sense of it. And this is perfectly clear when the philosopher discovers that the finitude of participating beings is only fully justified by the pure "To be" *(l'Exister pur)* which is their creative, transcendental Cause.[25]

Is that to say, for all this, that a metaphysics which will not fully honor,

---

23. Forest, *Consentement et création,* 91.

24. Jacques Maritain, *Sept leçons sur l'être,* in *Oeuvres complètes,* 5:576. Cf. also: The intuition of being "is difficult in the sense that it is difficult to come to the point of intellectual purification in which this act is fulfilled in us; in which we have become sufficiently available, sufficiently vacant, to *listen* to what all things murmur and to *hear,* instead of coming up with responses" (576).

25. Aimé Forest, *La structure métaphysique du concret selon saint Thomas d'Aquin,* 2d ed. (Paris: Vrin, 1959), 128–29: "All Christian philosophy should indicate and try to interpret with precision, the infinite distance which separates the being of God from the being of creatures. The philosophical translation of this idea is the affirmation, on the one hand, of simplicity, and of multiplicity and composition, on the other."

in its very constitution as knowledge, this analogical nature of being, cannot be considered Christian? In posing such a question, one might think of Duns Scotus, who teaches the univocity of being without any less admitting within it the essential distinction of created and uncreated.[26] Certainly in this sense Scotist metaphysics can and should be considered Christian. Nonetheless, precisely that which is Christian in it—with the affirmation that revelation implies of the absolute transcendence of the uncreated over the created—resists, in a certain manner, such a project of grasping being as an objective unity beyond or on this side of the distinction of the *ens creatum* and of the *ens increatum*, and removes it in every state of cause to the monist temptation. That is so true that, as Gilson has shown, if for Duns Scotus "there must be a certain point of view according to which all that is, is, in the same sense and of the same manner,"[27] anterior to all determination, then such a univocity cannot be in any way that of genre. This does not exclude, certainly, the metaphysical analogy of being, but corresponds to its being grasped "upon another level, which defines the problem of the intellect's primary object"[28] such that the question of the possibility of metaphysics as coherent and unified knowledge is raised. This is the reason for which—regardless of this willingness to base metaphysical knowledge upon an objectively univocal and perfectly abstract apprehension of being which can be applied without distinction to God and to his creature, a willingness which, certainly, directs philosophical wis-

---

26. See, for instance, *Ordinatio* I, dist. 3, par. 1; and *Collatio* 24. Cf. *Sur la connaissance de Dieu et l'univocité de l'étant* (Paris: Presses Universitaires de France, 1988). In particular, see the remarkable introduction by Olivier Boulnois, "La destruction de l'analogie et l'instauration de la métaphysique," 11–81. One can also invoke Suárez and his project of establishing metaphysics, "abstraction made of the finite-infinite, created-uncreated difference, in other words, by the directing aim of being in its logical in-difference"; cf. Jean-François Courtine, *Suarez et le systéme de la métaphysique* (Paris: Presses Universitaires de France, 1990), 278.

27. Etienne Gilson, "Avicenne et le point de départ de Duns Scot," *Archives d'Histoire doctrinale et littéraire du Moyen Age* (1927); reprinted in *Pourquoi saint Thomas a critiqué saint Augustin suivi de Avicenne et le point de départ de Duns Scot* (Paris: Vrin, 1986), 151.

28. Ibid., 155. Gilson continues: "Even when he concedes the metaphysical analogy of being, Duns Scotus maintains in this that there exists a concept common to the ten categories, and more general than them. It is this concept which assures the unity of the object assigned to metaphysics. . . . It is the same concept that our intellect applies to God and which permits him to give a sense to this name; and it is it, finally that our intellect generates anteriorly to every other, so much that it constitutes its primary object." Cf. also Gilson, *Jean Duns Scot, Introduction à ses positions fondamentales* (Paris: Vrin, 1952), and *La philosophie au Moyen Age* (Paris: Payot, 1944), 593, where the Scotist concern is emphasized by assigning a unity of object to metaphysics and, therefore, by "not considering the notion of being only in its ultimate degree of abstraction, that in which it is applied in a single and only sense to all that is. It is that which one expresses in saying that being is 'univocal' for the metaphysician."

dom in ways other than the unreserved proclamation of the primacy of *esse* in the finite being and of the irreducible originality with which such *esse* is, in each instance, possessed and exercised—Christianity and the mysticism which constitutes the heart of it, are directed of themselves toward the fundamental analogicity of the *ens finitum*. Only a metaphysics of finite being as *habens esse*, respectful of the intimate diversification by which it is allowed to perceive the necessity of its transcendental Cause, can be called, in this sense, fully Christian and fully metaphysical.

Hence the distinction of created and uncreated, which is at the heart of St. John's mysticism because it is at the very center of the faith, is found on the properly metaphysical level. Even with the ontological value of creatures being honored, it remains that all their being, "compared with the infinite Being of God, is nothing" (AC, I, 4, p. 25), for "God is of another being than His creatures in that He is infinitely far from them all" (AC, III, 12, p. 233). It is beginning with such confirmation that the apophatism of the mystic and the apophatism of the metaphysician can be developed according to the diversity of their particular processes. Despite this seeming devaluation of creatures, this does not cease to be a conceptual and affirmative theology of the absolute, divine transcendence. When it rejects every created limitation of the names that it applies to God, this is not to pass beyond concepts, but to better relate what they signify to the uncreated supereminence. Mystical theology, as such, is not negative in the sense that it seeks to make the intellect surmount every distinction and every opposition between yes and no, to consequently substitute the dogmas of the faith and the understanding that one can obtain from them; it is negative because it goes beyond all communication by way of words to enter into the ineffable experience of that which faith, theology, and also metaphysics affirm and must not cease to affirm. The mystic's way of not knowing by love does not substitute itself for the theologian and metaphysician's way of knowing, but presupposes it. Both are inscribed in the fundamental recognition of the essential distinction between created and uncreated. The Christian mysticism of St. John of the Cross consequently calls, at the rational level, for the constitution of a metaphysics of creation in which the created is conceived as given to itself.[29]

---

29. Cf. Henri de Lubac, *Le Mystère du Surnaturel* (Paris: Aubier, 1965), 107–8.

V

Our examination of metaphysical consequences of St. John's mysticism could be extended in other directions. It suffices for our purpose to show how the Christian mysticism, whose way John of the Cross teaches, involves, on the natural level of the intellect, a very precise metaphysics. In this regard, the theological experience of the depths of God is, certainly, entirely free and unpossessed *(désappropriée)*; but it supposes a capable spirit, in complete fidelity to its connatural vocation, to elaborate it, and it supports, even powerfully, the intellect in such a project. It is fitting, moreover, not to forget that this philosophical elaboration cannot be made outside of the very movement of the theological understanding of faith, whose proper dynamism, normally and of itself, is totally free. Hence fully differentiated but vitally united to theology as to the mysticism of the saints, the metaphysics required by Christian wisdom is a wisdom of finite and participated being, of analogy and of creation; and it is not only a philosophy of spirit, because it recognizes, as fundamental to the natural and reciprocal bond between the spirit and being, the primacy of being over spirit. It is, finally, a wisdom of God himself, but attained through the mediation of the finite, a theology which the analogically participated actuality of the finite, which alone is directly perceived, leads of itself to the affirmation of the pure Act of being. Such a metaphysical realism of finite and created being is thus simultaneously a spiritual realism, because the metaphysician discerns, in the very substance of the spirit, "the homologue of this 'metaphysical movement' which orientates the finite existence towards its creative hearth" and which is a desire to see God: "natural prayer, primary awakening which translates a call unpresumptuously towards the creative prodigality of all being, offered to our certitude, not yet to our regard."[30]

One such philosophy, dedicated to the full development of its metaphysical virtualities and in harmony with the knowledge of faith, as with the mystical fruits of the theological life, is nothing other than Christian philosophy, the metaphysics immanent to Christianity which, without always being recognized as such—and, alas, we know it well in Christians themselves—nonetheless remains, whether one wills or not, at the heart of all the tensions and debates in the history of western philosophy. It has recently been remarked that an essential question lies at the base of these ruptures in metaphysical thought: "God first

---

30. P. Fontan, *Le fini et l'absolu: Itinéraires métaphysiques* (Paris: Téqui, 1991), 133.

known—or unknown in himself, if not in his 'effects',"[31] an alternative which "will weigh upon the developments of philosophic thought, often reduced to oscillating between pure and simple atheism and a sort of theology opening the human conscience towards the infinite, not by the mediation of the finite known only directly, but by an immediate and conscious relation, at least of denying the relation on behalf of an identity with God."[32] In fact, when the priority of finite being is not honored in the life of the spirit—think, for example, of Spinoza—by rejecting all distinction between created and uncreated, the idea of creation appears, at the limit, according to Fichte, as "the fundamental absolute error of all false metaphysics."[33] Therefore, when one spirit is directed toward materialism or idealism, depending on whether the universe appears as its proper representation or not, it is conceived in immediate connection with absolute and uncreated Being. And that can go so far as a pure and simple pursuit of identity, whether such a quest be more manifest, as seems to be the case for Heidegger, or more secret and transposed in a new logic, the constructive dialectic of a new ontology, as for Hegel.

As a matter of fact, a spiritual requirement may be perceived behind the philosophical process, one that is often indissociably interwoven with it. It is indeed different, it seems, from the Christian mysticism which we have seen in John of the Cross, even if it is manifested in a Christian deeply imbued with the theological life, even to its spiritual heights, as, for example, Meister Eckhart. This requirement should be ascribed to the mystic if one intends this term in the analogical sense of an absolute experience which has its completion in itself; but it does not at all concern, evidently, the supernatural mysticism of transcendence, of which John of the Cross shows us the perfect accomplishment in Christianity. This time it is the affair of a natural mysticism of immanence which no longer seeks proof of the intimacy of God inhabiting the soul by grace, but an absorption of the self in the act of existing or even—a variation of the same experience—a cosmic identification with the universality of being.[34] This mysticism, the form of which one in-

31. Ibid., 9.
32. Ibid., 83–84.
33. Fichte, *Die Anweisung zum seligen Leben* (Berlin, 1806) sixth lecture; cited by Tresmontant, *Les métaphysiques principales*, 191.
34. Jacques Maritain was the first to develop this idea of a natural mysticism of immanence. Cf. *Quatre essais sur l'esprit dans sa condition charnelle*, ch. 3, "L'expérience mystique naturelle et le vide," in *Oeuvres complètes*, 7:159–95. One such analogical conception of the mystical experience as "fruitful experience of an absolute" certainly supposes a whole metaphysics of the spirit and of its natural reflexive. It also implies that the theological distinctions of nature and of grace be recognized, since the experience of the self proceeds from the natural capacities of the spirit, whereas the experience of divine

vokes most typically in India, or even certain chief characteristics of the Rheno-Flemish spirituality, is no longer a transforming *way of union* in which it is a unity by intentional union of love which is pursued, but a *way of unity* by identity of substance in which, as in Jacob Boehme, the soul is identified with the Absolute which it is in the ground-without-ground *(Ungrund)* of its being.[35]

This way of identity is already found in Plotinus, when he requires a wise man to go beyond all rational discourse and even the intellectual intuition which still admits the distinction of subject and object, for a state in which "the Intellect, intellection and the intelligible are altogether one."[36] The soul then comes upon what must be called the experience of a "vision" which is an identifying contact, since it "sees by a kind of confusing and annulling the intellect which abides within it," "and, by seeing, acquired intellect and is one."[37] Certainly, Plotinus seems to recede at times before this "identity with the divine"[38] and

---

intimacy is rooted in the supernatural instruments of grace, of the theological virtues, and of the gifts of the Holy Spirit. The testimony to the fecundity of one such distinction can be found (which in no way excludes the frequency of the mixed cases—Meister Eckhart seems to construct a remarkable example) in the works of Louis Gardet on the Muslim mysticism, or of Olivier Lacombe on India. See, e.g., Gardet, *Expériences mystiques en terres non-chrétiennes* (Paris: Alsatia, 1953); Gardet and M. M. Anawati, *Mystique musulmane, Aspects et tendances, Expériences et techniques* (Paris: Vrin, 1976); Gardet, *La Mystique*, Que sais-je?, no. 694, 2d ed. (Paris: Presses Universitaires de France, 1981); Gardet and O. Lacombe, *L'expérience du Soi, Étude de mystique comparée* (Paris: Desclée De Brouwer, 1981); and Lacombe, *L'élan spirituel de l'hindouisme* (Paris: O.E.I.L., 1986). See the next note for references to certain works of Heinz R. Schmitz concerning the profound impact that the mysticism of immanence has had upon a certain tradition of German thought, of which Jacob Boehme represents an essential inspiration. Henri de Lubac, in *La postérité spirituelle de Joachim de Flore* (Paris/Namur: Lethielleux/Culture et Vérité, 1979), 1:218–25, refers at length to these studies of Schmitz, whose accuracy and profundity he knew to appreciate. The fundamental distinction between mysticism of immanence and mysticism of transcendence is also taken up by Michel Delahoutre in the entry "Mystique" in the *Dictionnaire des Religions*, ed. Paul Poupard (Paris: Presses Universitaires de France, 1984), 1164–65. See also Paul Poupard, *Les Religions*, Que sais-je? no. 9 (Paris: Presses Universitaires de France, 1987), which discusses Delahoutre's entry (15–16). For a similar treatment of this same theme, although less sound, see A. Baudart, s.v. "Mysticisme," in vol. 2 of *Les notions philosophiques, Dictionnaire, Encyclopédie philosophique universelle*, ed. Sylvain Auroux (Paris: Presses Universitaires de France, 1990), 1711–12.

35. On Jacob Boehme, see Heinz R. Schmitz (Ernst R. Korn), "Sur le premier 'Philosophicus Teutonicus' Jacob Boehme," *Revue Thomiste* 73 (1973): 47–62; "L'option de Boehme," *Revue Thomiste* 74 (1974): 35–81; "La visée de l'expérience boehmienne: faire de l'homme un ange," *Nova et Vetera* (1974): 252–87; "Un mémorial de l'*Ungrund*," *Revue Thomiste* 76 (1976): 5–21; "L'âme et l'*Ungrund*," *Revue Thomiste* 76 (1976): 208–42; and "Jacob Boehme et l'avènement d'un homme nouveau," *Revue Thomiste* 78 (1978): 5–31 and 561–617.

36. Plotinus, *Enneads*, trans. A. H. Armstrong, 7 vols. (Cambridge: Harvard University Press, 1988), V, 3, 15; 7:89. Translation slightly modified.

37. Ibid., VI, 7, 35; 7:197.

38. Ibid., IV, 8, 1; 4:397.

maintains a distinction between "seeing and that which has been seen," for he says it would be "audacious" to consider them as being resolved in an identity.[39] And meanwhile, with what force he evokes in other respects this "super-knowledge" or "super-conscience" in which one is "itself pure light—weightless, floating free, having become—but rather, being a god."[40] Consequently, one must not be deluded by signification that clothes the language of love which Plotinus is led to utilize. There is indeed, in the experience that he invokes, an intellectual not-knowing and no longer an affective not-knowing in the supernaturality of theological love which, after all, can only have access to the intimacy of the transcendent and creative God. The love of which Plotinus speaks is indeed this ontological love which is the very dynamism of being and of knowing, and which makes the soul aspire to be reunited to its own sources. That is to say that "this love is not adventitious, added to being and to understanding *[connaître]*, but constitutes them both. It is love simultaneously ontological and spiritual."[41]

Such a mysticism of unity is not always manifested in the pure state. Hence it is found, it seems, intimately involved with the undeniable testimony of a union to the depths of God in Meister Eckhart, who seeks the Deity beyond God and the abyss beyond the Deity. One of his most recent commentators, whose admiration extends even to seeing in his work, and in the thought of the One who expresses himself there, the accomplishment of medieval intellectualism,[42] describes his experience as an "unchallenged" *(non duelle)* seizure by which the soul "becomes again that which 'it had been eternally in God.'"[43]

The influence this novel idea had upon a whole movement of German thought is evident. Indissociably philosophical, theological, and spiritual, it "transposes or sharpens the ideal of philosophical life which, in the confines of the 13th and 14th centuries, seizes the University of Paris,"[44] and seeks, following Averroës, after a sort of "natural and cosmic ecstasy."[45] In fact, whatever the diversity of the systemati-

---

39. Ibid., VI, 9, 10; 7:341.
40. Ibid., VI, 9, 9; 7:339. The preceding citations from the *Enneads* have been drawn from Olivier Lacombe's important study of Plotinus, which appears as chapter 1 in Gardet and Lacombe, *L'expérience du Soi*, 51–84.
41. Lacombe, in Gardet and Lacombe, *L'expérience du Soi*, 71. A sensibly different interpretation of the Plotinian process and of its mystical dimension is found in Henri Crouzel, *Origène et Plotin, Comparaisons doctrinales*, "Croire et Savoir" (Paris: Téqui, 1992).
42. Cf. A. De Libera, *Penser au Moyen Age* (Paris: Seuil, 1991), 347.
43. Ibid., 330. See, by the same author, *Introduction à la mystique rhénane, d'Albert le Grand à Maître Eckhart* (Paris: O.E.I.L., 1984). See also E. Zum Brunn and A. De Libera, *Maître Eckhart, Métaphysique du Verbe et théologie négative* (Paris: Beauchesne, 1984).
44. De Libera, *Penser au Moyen Age*, 334.
45. Ibid., 387. Cf. also F.-X. Putallaz, *La connaissance de soi au XIIIe siècle: De Matthieu*

zations in the philosophies concerned may be, it seems that several major aspects of the most distinguished forms of modern thought symbolize an experience of immanence or bring us back there. One may think, for example, of the idealist decision, invoked by Lachelier, of "suspending the spirit in the void,"[46] or of the "mystical" and "mystifying" heritage of the Hegelian dialectic assumed by Marx and his materialism.[47]

In reality, it is the emergence of a whole metaphysical structure that seems to have permitted the attraction exercised by the mysticism of immanence, when this is transformed in a form of thought *(Denkform)*. And, we repeat, whatever be the diversity of the converging currents and the multiformity of doctrines that go so far as to render themselves at times totally irreconcilable, some even claiming to be in accord with authentic Christianity, this metaphysical armature bears certain fundamental positions strictly opposed to those that we have discerned in Christian metaphysics. After all, it could have been otherwise. Even if Indian metaphysics tend in themselves towards monistic forms of expression, they [still] raise the question of being. "What is it to be *[sat]*?" was the question of Çankara which nonetheless resulted in an absolute

---

d'Aquasparta à Thierry de Freiberg (Paris: Vrin, 1991), 305: "It is at the height of medieval neo-Platonism that Thierry of Freiberg will be involved in the most daring ways, which curiously announce Nicholas of Cusa or, further still, the German thought of the modern era." On Thierry of Freiberg, cf. A. De Libera, *Introduction à la mystique rhénane*, 163–229.

46. It is certainly out of the question to render an account of the Cartesian *cogito*, reread or not by Husserl, as purely and simply referring to an experience of the self. Does he not invoke it, however, in some distant fashion and echo it in some way? In a recent study, in any case, Jean-Yves Lacoste shows the dissonance between the *cogito* understood as an experience of the nudity of the self and the denuding of St. John. "The denuding of St. John *dismisses* in advance the me of all that will *institute* the Cartesian experience of self, as sure and certain possession of self " (Jean-Yves Lacoste, "De la certitude au dénouement—Descartes et Jean de la Croix," *Nouvelle Revue Théologique* 113 [1991]: 534).

47. Cf. Heinz R. Schmitz, *Progrès social et Révolution: L'illusion dialectique* (Fribourg: Ed. Universitaires, 1983), 76–77: "But, for lack of submitting to the criticism the dialectical scheme itself, Marx, for his part, falls into this mystification for which he so much criticizes Hegel. Certainly, there is a fundamental difference between the 'Hegelian mysticism' and the 'Marxist mystification' of which we speak. The experience of Hegel is, in effect, a sort of evasion beyond the world to attain the absolute spirit at the same time that it is a re-production or re-creation of the world according to the movement of this same spirit, whereas the thought of Marx is entirely immersed in the social and economical; and, if one can speak of mystification, this is in the very manner that Marx regards the sociopolitical reality, that is to say, through a form of mystical, or rather mystifying, thought: dialectics. Its sign is what Marx considers not in the concrete of rich *men* and poor *men*, nor in the antagonism between those who live in abundance and those who are in need and the just struggle of these latter to have their share of this world's goods. Rather, he creates *abstractions* made especially to respond to the laws of dialectical movement."

nondualism. The cultural context of the west is indeed different. Profoundly impregnated by the Christian faith which in some way aggravates the tensions, it cannot see itself giving birth to some metaphysics of the One or of the Identity[48] that would not be tempted to constitute the radical and ontological negation of all determination in a denial of being as natural grace and in an indefectible will to do violence to nature, to the real itself. These philosophies thus detest contemplation and are conceived first of all as the spirit's confrontation with itself in a *praxis*. Just as if, for them, *omnis determinatio est negatio*, how can these doctrines of negativity, of void and of denial, identify themselves as bound to a primary grasp of the concrete as finite and always singular being? How would they not reject all mediation and, ultimately, all opening beyond their autosufficiency, on behalf of the exaltation of an original and fundamental immediacy in which all that is distinct and determined vanishes? How, consequently, could they free this mystery of analogy which is at the foundation of things and can in no way return from it to a fundamental univocity? How would they sustain to the end this radical distinction between the created and the uncreated which is an essential characteristic of Judeo-Christian metaphysics and not suffer the influence of an angelist temptation to refuse the human condition? Whereas the "Christian paradox of man" is constituted by "this sort of swaying walk *[dehanchement]*, this mysterious limp, which is not only that of sin, but first of all and most radically that of a creature made from nothing, who, strangely, touches God," because it naturally desires to see Him,[49] they open upon a neopaganism in which nature seeks the divine in itself in order to exhaust the energies of its achievement. In fact, these "metaphysics," in their search for "a unique, exhaustive, perfect intuition," manifest a "structure of thought," "total and unitary, so as not to say totalitarian."[50] They are, in the last analysis, antimetaphysics and would not lead to anything other than destitution, in the spirits, of every ideal of an intellectual penetration of the mystery of that which is. They constitute, one could say, a *"philosophy of subjectivity or of magic mirrors"* which is moved by an implacable hatred of human reason at the same time as by a mad hatred of being.[51]

48. On the metaphysics of the One or of the Identity, see the always suggestive reflections—even when one should not follow them in all their aspects—of Claude Tresmontant, *Les métaphysiques principales*, 163–200 and 248–50.
49. De Lubac, *Le Mystère du Surnaturel*, 149.
50. A. de Muralt, *La métaphysique du phénomène, Les origines médiévales et l'élaboration de la pensée phénoménologique* (Paris: Vrin, 1985), 195.
51. Schmitz, "L'option de Boehme," 64. The author opposes this *"philosophy of subjectivity or of magic mirrors"* to the *"philosophy of intelligibility or of the greedy look toward things"*: "The philosophy of intelligibility is a philosophy of being and by the same a

Such is then the true play of the history of philosophies in the western world. It is, in fact, first of all, of mystical and theological nature. The persistent difficulty of admitting the fundamental difference between the mysticism of grace and of transcendence, the way of which St. John of the Cross retraces, and the natural mysticism of immanence as the experience of the self, seem to me indicative of a dangerous blinding in which we accommodate ourselves and behind which resides a refusal of the very nature of our spirit and of its metaphysical vocation, which is the consent to be. Etienne Gilson concluded his *Christian Philosophy, An Introduction* by writing: "Let us restore theology as it was when it fulfilled the perfection of essence, for Christian philosophy is doomed to die the moment it separates itself from it."[52] One could add more radically still: "Give us, beyond all temptation of confusion, the purity of Christian mysticism, for it is in organic union with it and in respect for distinctions of level that theological knowledge takes shape and metaphysical knowledge takes its full measure." Have we forgotten that "the soul lives where it loves rather than where it breathes" (SC, XI, 2, p. 233)? If it is carried away to God according to charity, will it not also be with its intelligence? And intelligence, when it pursues its work of rational investigation in a human manner, does it not take from it a lucidity of the Mystery of faith, making it believable, as in its natural meditation upon the mystery of being? The cultural fecundity of Christian wisdom is, in any case, at this price. It is at the service of such a wisdom that a St. Thomas Aquinas or a St. John of the Cross have put their particular genius. They remain, for us and before us, apostles of the time to come.

---

philosophy of the spirit. In respecting being it also respects what is proper to the human spirit. If the philosophy of subjectivity (or of magic mirrors) addresses itself so violently against the philosophy of intelligibility (or of the greedy look toward things), that is because the first is moved by an implacable hatred of human reason and at the same time by a mad hatred of being. Here we are before a visceral resentment against all that which is, a resentment that Nietzsche exalts as one 'instinctive hatred against all reality, *Instinkt-Hass gegen jede Realität.*'"

52. Trans. Armand Maurer, Etienne Gilson Series, no. 17 (Toronto: Pontifical Institute of Mediaeval Studies, 1993), 134.

11   The Problem of God's Foreknowledge and Human Free Action in Spanish Philosophy
MIRKO SKARICA

The problem of divine foreknowledge regarding our future free acts originates undoubtedly in a theological question. It is a truth of the Faith that God knows beforehand what we shall do in the future. Christ tells Peter that he will betray Him three times. He does not express a conjecture as though saying that it is most probable that he will deny Him, nor does He say it as a logical truth in the sense that one of the alternatives in the future is that he will deny Him. Christ simply tells Peter that he will deny Him and he is stating a fact.[1] Furthermore, this problem has a theological importance insofar as our eternal destiny is at stake. In His eternal, infallible wisdom God knows beforehand everything that we shall do regarding our salvation or damnation. Now, it is also a matter of the Faith that God's foreknowledge of our future acts does not annul their freedom. The question we are dealing with in this exposition arises from confronting these two data; that is, how does God know a future act, hence not yet existing, and which depends on a decision of a free human will?

It is at this point that philosophy comes to the aid of theology. The Faith does not say anything on the matter, and the question becomes a challenge to human reason, which will have to show that there is no opposition between divine foreknowledge and the freedom of a future human act, as there is none between a truth of the Faith and rational truth. Historically, philosophical aid to theology on this point has been provided by Aristotle in his famous question regarding human foreknowledge of free future contingents. The Philosopher's views regarding the subject as stated in chapter 9 of his *De Interpretatione* have been a required point of reference throughout the centuries

---

1. Matt. 26:34; Mark 14:30; Luke 22:34; and John 13:38.

in the discussions of countless Christian theologians, and of course in the discussion of the philosophers with whom we shall deal with in this article.

As regards the present article, I shall focus on the problem of divine foreknowledge and human free acts just as it was debated by some of the Spanish thinkers in the centuries following the discovery of America, that is, in the sixteenth and seventeenth centuries. But in the spirit of the present volume, my exposition will include the discussion of a Spanish American thinker, the Chilean Franciscan Alonso Briceño. This discussion will help us realize that, as regards the cultural and the religious, America and Spain were parts of the same unit.

As an introduction to the theme, it is convenient to remember that the problem posed here attracted the minds of philosophers at the dawn of Christianity, giving rise to different positions, so that it became a must in discussions and teachings throughout the centuries; even more, in certain periods of history it became a burning topic, as is the case of the centuries under study, owing to the emergence of Luthero-Calvinist theories. Nowadays it has once more attracted the attention of some thinkers, not so much because of a theological but because of a logico-gnoseological interest. Thus attention has turned on the one hand to Aristotle's texts on the matter and on the other hand to the problem posed by theologians of past centuries, including the Spaniards Luis de Molina and Suárez. I cannot help mentioning here William Lane Craig's 1988 book, *The Problem of Divine Foreknowledge and Future Contingents from Aristotle to Suárez*, as an excellent contribution to the present debate of the theme.[2]

In the centuries prior to the sixteenth century, the debate on the divine foreknowledge of future contingents was held internally among the followers of the Catholic tradition, the main interlocutors being Thomas Aquinas, John Duns Scotus, and William of Ockham. But in the sixteenth century this debate was stirred up by Catholic theologians who sought new arguments to oppose the Luthero-Calvinist dogma. Some of them ended up by following it, as is the case with Michael de Bay in Louvain, whose doctrine culminates in the work of Cornelius Jansen in France. Others tried to remain faithful to the traditional doctrine, not without attempting innovations, as is the case of the Jesuit Lessius, who proceeded to refute Michael de Bay in Louvain itself. In Spain this agitation occurs in Salamanca and materializes in the defense

---

2. Leiden: E. J. Brill, 1988. This book contains a valuable bibliography of primary and secondary sources regarding the authors under discussion, with a brief evaluation of each of the secondary sources.

of the traditional doctrine made by Domingo Báñez, who updated the theses of Thomas Aquinas, while still following them rigorously, as he considered them the only means for such a defense, so much so that he accused innovators, if not of wanting to reconcile Catholic tradition with Luthero-Calvinist dogma, at least of wanting to reconcile Thomas Aquinas with Scotus.[3] Thus ensues the historic dispute between Báñez and Molina upon the appearance of the latter's book in 1588, *Concordia Liberii Arbitrii cum Gratia Donis, Divina Praesciencia, Providentia, Praedestinatione et Reprobatione.* In America this stir does not go unperceived, so that Alonso Briceño not only turns against the innovations of the Jesuits Molina and Suárez, but also against the statements of the Thomists, including Báñez himself. In my exposition I shall deal with a fundamental question of this discussion, and it is how does God know future free acts. Does He know them determinately? I shall discuss the key points of the differing solutions given by Báñez, Molina, Suárez, and Briceño.

Domingo Báñez (1528–1604) is an excellent commentator on the doctrines of Thomas Aquinas. He does not introduce any variations, except that he accepts Cajetan's interpretation that God knows free future contingents through ideas.[4] In this regard he will not disagree with Molina or Suárez or others who follow such a view reaching back to St. Bonaventure. For a good understanding both of the solution given by Báñez, as well as that of his master Thomas Aquinas regarding divine foreknowledge of free future contingents, it is necessary to go back to the latter's *Expositio Libri Peryermenias.*[5] There, in accordance with Aristotle it is stated that knowledge of the future in the case of human knowledge regarding the future is possible obviously insofar as the future is known in its causes, but not in itself, for it does not yet exist.[6] But this knowledge of the future in its causes with "determinate" truth is properly restricted to what is determined in its causes, so that it cannot happen otherwise, therefore it happens necessarily and not

---

3. Cf. *Dictionaire de Théologie Catholique,* s.v. "Molinisme."
4. Cf. *Scholastica Commentaria in Primam Partem Angelici Doctoris S. Thomae,* vol. 1 (Duaci, 1614). With regard to future contingents including the free, he holds there in q. 14, a. 13, con. 4, p. 207b: "Praeterea probatur Deus cognoscit futura contingentia per rationes ipsorum, quae sunt in Deo, idest per ideas proprias que sunt in Deo futurorum contingentium, sed idea repraesentat certo, et infallibiliter per modum exemplaris et efficientis, ut dicitur q. sc. XV, art. 3, ergo per ideam tanquam per causam habet Deus infallibilem cognitionem futuri contingentis. Maior asseritur a D. Tho. in hoc art. et explicatur a Caiet. dub. 2 huius articuli."
5. Thomas Aquinas, *Expositio Libri Peryermenias,* in *Opera Omnia,* vol. 1-1; 2d ed. (Paris: J. Vrin, 1989).
6. Cf. *Expositio,* I 14, 401–403: "futura autem non cognoscit in se ipsis, quia nondum sunt, set cognoscere ea potest in causis suis."

contingently.⁷ As regards the knowledge with determinate truth of future contingents, it is only possible in the case where in its cause it is more determinated to one outcome than to another, as for example, when the doctor states a determinately true statement about somebody who convalesces that he will get well, even though something which the doctor ignores may happen to hinder his healing;⁸ or in the case of somebody who has decided to leave announcing his departure, although something unforeseen may happen to hinder it.⁹ But this happens in human knowledge of future contingents. As regards God, He does not know future contingents in a human mode, which is within a temporal order, but in his own way, that is, out of time "as if standing at the summit of eternity, which is laid out as a whole at the same time."¹⁰ Therefore, God sees the whole duration of time "in a single simple intuition,"¹¹ so that He sees the future not in its cause but in itself: "in the same way that the human eye sees Socrates sitting down, in itself, not in its cause."¹² Thus Thomas's thesis is that God sees what is in the future for us in its real presence in eternity; so as regards God, more than foreknowledge, it is knowledge present in eternity.

The problem that seems to arise from this solution is that what God knows in itself as happening in eternity must necessarily happen, for God knows with a determinate truth.¹³ The above thesis is, however, complemented by the following one, that the divine will must be understood "out of the order of beings, as a certain cause that overflows all beings and their differences."¹⁴ Thus contingency in things has its ori-

---

7. St. Thomas distinguishes three modes wherein something future has being in its cause, in virtue of which something true may be asserted regarding the future contingent; that is, when the future act is to be necessarily executed by its cause, and when the future is determined in its cause, although its execution may be hindered. In the latter case the future may be asserted with determinate truth although not with absolute certainty as in the first case. (Cf. ibid., 13, 252ff.)

8. Ibid., 13, 183–87: "De eo enim quod est magis determinatum ad unam partem possumus determinate uerum dicere quod hoc erit uel non erit, sicut medicus de conualescente uere dicit : 'Iste sanabitur', licet forte ex aliquo accidente eius sanitas impediatur."

9. Ibid., 188–92: "Unde et Philosophus dicit in II De generatione quod futurus quis incedere, non incedet: de eo enim qui habet propositum determinatum ad incedendum, uere potest dici quod ipse incedet, licet per aliquod accidens impediatur eius incessus."

10. Ibid., I 14, 415f.: "quasi in arce eternitatis constitutus."
11. Ibid., 417f.: "secundum unum et simplicem eius intuitum."
12. Ibid., 425f.: "sicut oculus humanus uidet Sortem sedere in se ipso, non in causa sua."
13. Ibid., 359–62: "non enim potest eius scientia falli et ita ea que ipse scit, uidetur quod necesse sit euenire."
14. Ibid., 439–41: "ut extra ordinem entium existens, uelut causa quedam profundens totum ens et omnes eius differencias."

gin in the divine will just as necessity does.[15] Both the contingent and the necessary depend on the divine will as on their first cause "which transcends the order of necessity and contingency."[16] For the contingent, God has ordained causes that operate contingently, that is, causes that may fail.[17] In this way, the divine will is infallible, including regarding those effects that are contingent.[18] Thus God knows with determinate truth our free future contingent acts through a knowledge of vision. One must bear in mind that a determinate truth is due to the conformity of knowledge with that which is known, something that is perfectly fulfilled in the case of divine knowledge.

With regard to this doctrine of St. Thomas, Báñez makes the following observation, that there are two points "that present great difficulty and upon which not all Theologians agree." The first point is that everything existing, including that which is a future contingent, is already present in God's eternity; the second, that God knows the future contingent in itself, with certain and infallible knowledge owing to that same presence.[19] To ameliorate this difficulty in part, Báñez points out that the presence of the future contingent in God's eternity is not affirmed in order to found the certainty and infallibility of God's knowledge, but rather so that the future contingent can be an adequate object of the divine knowledge.[20] He adds that knowledge of the future contingent in itself does not exclude knowledge in its causes, which is also certain and infallible in God. Therefore, according to Báñez, if God did not know the future contingent in itself, including that dependent on a free will, but only in its causes, even then His knowledge would be certain and infallible.[21] The reason for this is that all determination of second causes is subject to the determination of the divine knowledge and will, "for God knows all created causes in His essence

15. Ibid., 441ff.
16. Ibid., 453f.: "que transcendit ordinem necessitatis et contingencie."
17. Ibid., 447ff.
18. Ibid., 459ff.
19. Báñez, *Scholastica Commentaria*, q. 14, a. 13, p. 206a: "Notandum tertio, quod duo inter alia docet D. Th. quae magnam prae se ferunt difficultatem, et in quibus non conveniunt omnes Theologi. Primum est. Omnia, quae sunt, vel fuerunt, vel aliquando erunt, sunt iam Deo praesentia in eius aeternitate.... Secundum est. Infallibilitas, et certitudo divinae cognitionis circa futura contingentia pensatur ex eo, quod Deus cognoscit ipsa futura contingentia in semetipsis, et extra suas causas, quatenus sunt illi praesentia in aeternitate."
20. Ibid., 207a: "ut futura contingentia sint obiectum divinae cognitionis, necessaria conditionis est, quod repraesententur Deo tanquam illi praesentia in aeternitate."
21. Ibid. "Itaque etiamsi Deus non cognosceret futura contingentia, tanquam praesentia in sua aeternitate, sed solum in causis ipsorum, eius cognitio esset certa, et infallibilis."

as He is the first cause of the being, power and determination of every cause."[22]

Báñez, following St. Thomas, holds that God knows the future as well the past and the present by a knowledge of vision, which differs from the knowledge of simple intelligence by which God knows what does not have being in any time whatsoever. The knowledge of vision presupposes a determination on the part of the divine will, differing from the knowledge of simple intelligence. In the latter God knows the possible which as such is undetermined regarding being or not being, and so does not presuppose any intervention of the divine will.[23]

The rejection of this explanation is the origin of the solution proposed by the Jesuit Luis de Molina (1536–1600), whose work *Concordia* deviates, according to Báñez, not only from the teachings of Aquinas, but also from Catholic orthodoxy. I shall not go into the details of the accusations made by Báñez and Molina's counterreplies, nor of Molina's accusations against Báñez and the Dominican Thomists.[24] Rather I shall move directly to the exposition of Molina's thought on the question to which we have limited this essay.[25] Molina questions the doctrine of Thomas Aquinas we have briefly delineated. Along the way he mentions that it is inspired by Boethius's *Consolatio Philosophiae*.[26] He not only disagrees with the above-mentioned theses, but goes on to ask himself whether Thomas Aquinas himself would not accept another solution, that is, a form of certain and immutable knowledge of future contingents other than through their real presence in eternity.[27] More-

22. Ibid. "Praeterea probatur Deus cognoscit futura contingentia in suis causis particularibus, quatenus ipsae causae particulares subijciuntur determinationi, et dispositoni divinae scientiae, et voluntatis quae est prima causa, sed causae particulares futurorum contingentium quatenus subijciuntur determinationi divinae scientiae, et voluntatis sunt determinatae, et completae, et non impeditae ad producendum suos effectus contingentes.... Nam Deus cognoscit omnes causas creatas per suam essentiam, prout est prima causa dans esse, et virtutem et determinationem omnibus causis."

23. Ibid., a. 9, p. 204b.

24. For an excellent account of this exchange, see *Dictionaire de Théologie Catholique*, s.v. "Molinisme."

25. Luis de Molina, *Concordia* (Paris: Lethielleux, 1876), q. 14, a. 13, d. 41: "Utrum ideo res futurae contingentes certo a Deo cognoscantur, quia ei sunt praesentes secundum suam existentiam: indeque contingentia earum cum divina praescientia recte concilietur."

26. Ibid., p. 286: "Divus Thomas, hoc loco, vestigiis Boetii quinto de Consolatione prosa ultima insistens, partem affirmantem amplectitur, quae sequentibus fundamentis, licet non eodem ordine ab eo propositis, innititur." Cf. d. 48, p. 282.

27. Ibid., 288: "Verum ut circa hanc rem totam dicam quod sentio, in primis rationibus paulo ante adductis nihil obstantibus, affirmare non ausim D. Thomam, quem in omnibus patronum potius quam adversarium habere percipio, credidisse, ex solo capite praesentiae rerum secundum esse existentiae Deum cognoscere certo futura contingentia; quin potius, ut credo, si ea de re consuleretur, contrariam sententiam affirmaret."

over, he maintains that such a solution in no way helps to prove the certainty of the divine knowledge of future contingents, nor to reconcile contingency and God's knowledge of it.[28] Thus, he deems it necessary to find another solution or explanation.

The point that is unacceptable in the Thomist solution is, as Molina sees it, that it requires a double existence of the contingent, a temporal existence and an eternal one, something that Molina judges to be senseless, especially as regards future contingents, for these by definition do not yet exist in time.[29] Thus Molina considers that Thomas's solution is simply contrary to contingency and contrary to free will. It is contrary to contingency for if the future existed previously in eternity, it cannot help but exist in time just as it exists in eternity, thus becoming necessary; it is contrary to free will because what has been done in eternity cannot but be done in the same way in time. If, in order to save contingency and free will, it is maintained that things need not necessarily happen as they do in eternity, this would be against God's certain and immutable foreknowledge, for it would be merely conjectural.[30]

Having stated his reasons for rejecting the Thomist solution, Molina attempts another explanation. The problem lies in how God knows future free contingents otherwise than by their real presence in eternity. Molina finds a solution by distinguishing in God a type of intermediate knowledge between what he terms "natural knowledge" and "free knowledge" in God, that is, a type of knowledge that he simply calls

---

28. Ibid., 292f.: "Quare propositio illa: Ex aeternitate omnia coexistunt Deo, aut sunt praesentia Deo secundum suas existentias extra suas causas; in sensu disputatione praecedente explicato, nihil, ut credo, conducit, vel ad ostendendam certitudinem presentiae divinae de futuris contingentibus, vel ad conciliandam contingentiam rerum cum divina praesentia."

29. Báñez (*Scholastic Commentary*, p. 208b) alludes to some of the followers of St. Thomas who erroneously distinguish a double mode of presence of the contingent, one in eternity, "secundum modum essendi, quem habent in divina essentia, in qua sunt virtualiter, et eminenter," and the other in its own temporal existence. But Molina refers to the thesis that holds, as does Báñez, that it is the same existence of the contingent which on the one hand is present in God's eternity, and on the other, is future in time. Existence in eternity would be prior to existence in time. Cf. *Concordia*, p. 292: "Arbitror nihilominus, neque esse concedendum res, quae in tempore fiunt, prius existere in aeternitate, quam existant in tempore, aut prius praesentes esse in aeternitate secundum suas existentias, quam in tempore sint re ipsa praesentes." Cf. p. 294: ". . . quia talis temporis pars nondum secundum se et absolute existit."

30. *Concordia*, p. 294: "Etenim neque liberum arbitrium, neque ceterae causae efficere possent in futurum, quin ipsae eaedem causae idem, eodemque modo, eademque actione in tempore futuro efficerent, quod jam in aeternitate effecerunt; vel si possent aliud efficere, non tanta profecto firmitate esset jam modo in aeternitate, quin possit non esse; atque adeo ex tali rerum existentia in aeternitate provenire non posset certitudo divinae scientiae circa ea, quae contingenter in tempore evenient."

"middle knowledge" *(scientia media)*, and through which God knows man's future free acts.[31]

We shall try to understand this middle knowledge by comparing it with the other two types of knowledge. Through natural knowledge God knows through ideas, prior to any determination of His divine free will, everything that may be the object of His cause as first cause or any of the second causes. Through this knowledge God knows both the necessary and the contingent. Thus God knows everything that He can do and how it is to be done in case He should do it as regards to its existence or such and such an end. It is a knowledge of something merely potential, as it is prior to any determination of His free will. Now, this knowledge of the contingents obtained by natural knowledge is, on the one hand, indeterminate, insofar as the contingent is known indistinctly with regard to being or not being; on the other hand, it is a knowledge of the necessary, that is, of what is necessarily convenient to the contingent in its potential state.

Through free knowledge, which comes after the free determination of His will, God knows absolutely and determinately what will be and what will not be in a particular time. But this unconditioned, divine knowledge has for its object the world that He has freely decided to create. Consequently, it is equally a knowledge of the necessary.

In between these two types of knowledge, natural knowledge and free knowledge, is the middle knowledge, through which God knows what any free cause will do if it is put in a particular set of determinate circumstances, being capable of acting otherwise.[32] It is the knowledge of what is known as *futuribile*. This middle knowledge is distinguishable from free knowledge, for it is prior to any free act of the divine will, so that what God knows through this knowledge does not depend on His power, but it is also distinguishable from natural knowledge insofar as its content may be determinately one or another depending on what human free will may determine when put in a given set of circumstances. For the same reasons it may be said that middle knowledge partakes of certain conditions of both natural and free knowledge. It shares the condition of natural knowledge insofar as it is prior to any act of the divine free will, and the latter has no power to change what

---

31. Ibid., d. 52, p. 317: "Triplicem scientiam oportet distinguamus in Deo, nisi periculose in concilianda libertate arbitrii nostri et contingentia rerum cum divina praescientia hallucinari velimus. Unam mere naturalem. . . . Aliam mere liberam. . . . Tertiam denique mediam scientiam, qua ex altissima et inscrutabili comprehensione cujusque liberi arbitrii in sua essentia intuitus est, quid pro sua innata libertate, si in hoc, vel illo, vel etiam infinitis rerum ordinibus collocaretur, acturum esset, cum tamen posset, si vellet, facere re reipsa oppositum . . ."

32. Ibid.

it knows; and it shares the condition of free knowledge insofar as it knows toward which of the possible opposites the human being will determinately incline himself if placed in any given set of circumstances, being capable of choosing either of the opposites.[33] Thus God knows in His divine essence what somebody will do if put in a given set of circumstances, even if it never occurs in the future. Molina confirms this, for example, with the Gospel (Matt. 11:21) when Christ says that if he had performed in Tyre and Sidon the miracles he had performed in Corozain and Bethsaida, they would have long since done penance in sackcloth and ashes. With this and some other examples from the Old Testament, Molina tries to confirm that God knew even possible future contingents which never became actual in time.[34] This is another proof for him that it is not necessary to apply to the real presence in eternity, because what will never occur, but it is hypothetically feasible that it may occur, cannot have real presence in eternity. In this way Molina thinks he can reconcile free will and divine foreknowledge, saving not only the character of being free, but also its being contingent and future, as is the human free act with regard to divine knowledge. Thus, this solution conceives of a divine knowledge of what a free will will do, without falling into a fatalistic position, for God only knows what such a free will by its own innate freedom will do if put in a certain set of circumstances. This knowledge does not determine free will. Besides, it conceives in man a free will that will determine itself to do or not to do something in certain circumstances, without, however, limiting God's will, as He knows how a free will is going to act in determined circumstances, and He knows it before any determination of his own divine will, so he has power to create or not to create such a free will or to create or not to create the definite set of circumstances in which it will determine itself to act if put in such circumstances.

The solution defended by Molina was welcomed and defended by another Jesuit, Francisco Suárez (1548–1617), although the latter would rather speak of a conditioned knowledge *(scientia conditionata)* instead of middle knowledge *(scientia media)* in the case of divine knowledge of future contingents. He expounds his position in two of his

---

33. Ibid., p. 318.
34. Cf. ibid., d. 49, p. 289: "quoniam ex Scripturis sanctis constat Deum optimum maximum habere certam cognitionem aliquorum futurorum contingentium, quae ex libero arbitrio humano pendent; quae tamen nec fuerunt, nec erunt unquam in rerum naturam, ac proinde nec existunt in aeternitate: ergo non ex eo solo capite, quod futura contingentia extra suas cusas in aeternitate existant, Deus certo illa cognoscit." Here Molina, apart from Matt. 11:21, refers to 1 Kings 21 (1 Sam. 23:10–12) and Wis. 4:11–14 as examples of something revealed as future, but which never occurred, and something that would have happened had it not been hindered by God.

works, the *Tractatus de Gratia Dei*, Second Prolegomenon,[35] and the Second Opuscule of *De Scientia quam Deus habet de Futuris Contingentibus*.[36] According to Suárez, middle or conditioned knowledge is the only way to reconcile the freedom of future free acts with God's foreknowledge and free determination.[37] Furthermore, he considers that whoever has accepted divine foreknowledge of future free contingents has implicitly accepted middle knowledge at least as regards the essence of the matter, if not the words.[38] For Suárez it is a question of an intermediate knowledge between what was usually called "knowledge of simple intelligence" *(scientia simplicis intelligentiae)* and "knowledge of vision" *(scientia visionis)*, for in certain aspects it coincides with the two types of knowledge but in other it differs from both. The reasons put forth by Suárez are similar to those of Molina when distinguishing middle knowledge from natural knowledge and free knowledge. Thus, divine knowledge of future free acts conforms itself with the knowledge of simple intelligence, insofar as it is prior to God's free determination, but it also conforms itself with the knowledge of vision in that it falls on an object following a free determination because of its futurity.[39] Suárez, on the other hand, sees no difficulty in conceiving middle knowledge as natural to God in a broad sense, as God knows everything through a knowledge that is connatural, and in this sense, both knowledge of simple intelligence and of vision as well as middle knowledge are types of natural knowledge, taken in a broad sense.[40]

Although Suárez follows Molina, he differs from him in his argument when dealing with the problem of how God knows future contingents, looking instead for the reason why God knows about them. Thus he focuses his discussion on the question whether such future acts are knowable in themselves, or, what is the same for him, whether

---

35. "Prolegomenum Secundum," in *Opera omnia*, ed. C. Berton (Paris: L. Vivès, 1857), vol. 7.

36. "Opusculum secundum," in *Opera omnia* (1858), vol. 11.

37. Cf. *Tertia Pars Summae Theologiae Doctoris Sancti Thomae Aquinatis*, in *Opera omnia* (1860), vol. 17, q. 1, a. 3.

38. "Opusculum," bk. II, ch. III, n. 4, p. 353: "Solum, propter difficultatem in principio tactam, orta est inter modernos scriptores dissensio de modo loquendi, potius quam de re.... Solum ergo videtur nova haec scientia quoad nomen, nam res ipsa satis antiqua est; hoc autem non est magnum inconveniens, saepe enim invenientur nova nomina ad res melius explicandas."

39. Ibid.

40. Ibid.: "nam si scientia naturalis vocetur ea quam Deus ex se, suaque naturali perfectione habet, non est dubium quin Deus haec omnia sciat per connaturalem sibi scientiam, quo nomine tam scientia visionis quam scientia simplicis intelligentiae, et scientia media (si est) comprehendi potest; nam Deus non habet scientiam adventitiam et extraneam, sed quidquid scit, ex intrinseca et naturali perfectione et comprehensione scit."

they are determinately true.[41] And this is precisely the point where his differences with Molina are made manifest, for the latter considers that the future contingent cannot, by nature, be determinately true, due to its indifference with regard to its existing or not, and therefore, one cannot even ask if they are knowable with determinate truth. In accordance with this, Molina asserts that God knows what a free creature will do only by virtue of his eminent comprehension of the root of contingency, and not by virtue of a conformity of his cognizing potency with this root.[42] But according to Suárez something is cognizable only if it is determinately true. As he sees it, what is true is determinately true, because what is indeterminately true is simply not true. So divine knowledge of the contingent future, contrary to what Molina sustains, must be determinately true, if God knows it.[43]

Suárez's argument for his thesis that God knows future contingents with determinate truth is based on the following principles, which he often repeats: (1) if it is possible to know future contingents, God must be able to know them due to his utmost perfection; it may only be admitted that God does not know what is not knowable for it entails no imperfection in Him not to know what is unknowable; (2) if propositions about free future contingents are knowable, then it must be possible to know them in accordance with the principle of reciprocity between knowability and knowledge; (3) if such propositions are true, then they are knowable, for truth is in itself knowable, being the proper object of knowledge.[44] Now, since it is proper of the infinitude of divine potency to be omnipotent, it is therefore proper of the infinitude of His knowledge to know everything that is knowable, that is, all that is true, and only what is true. It only remains to explain in what sense the

---

41. Ibid., bk. I, ch. II, n. 1, p. 296: "non dubitatum de potestate ex parte Dei, sed de possibilitate ex parte rei, de qua quaestio est, . . . ita in praesenti, ad examinandum an haec futura contingentia cadant sub scientiam Dei, ex parte ipsorum inquirendum est, an talia sint ut cognosci possint. Nam, si ipsa habent fundamentum cognoscibilitatis, ut sic dicam, quod es veritatis, non effugient scientiam Dei, quae infinita est, et perfectissima qaue excogitari potest."

42. Cf. Molina, *Concordia*, q. 14, a. 13, d. 52, p. 322: "Verumtamen contingentia futura ex natura rei esse determinate vera, et cum Aristotelis doctrina communique Doctorum sententia, et cum natura ipsa contingentium pugnat, quippe quae eo ipso ex ipsamet eorum natura indifferentia sunt, ut eorum unumquodque sit, vel non sit, ut ad cap. ultimum primi de interpretatione ostendimus." Cf. p. 323: "ad haec namque cognoscenda non satis est adaequatio potentiae cognoscentis cum radice contingentiae ipsorum, seu comprehensio talis radicis; sed necessaria est altissima et eminentissima comprehensio hujusce radicis, qualis est in solo Deo comparatione liberi arbitrii suarum omnium creaturarum." Suárez rejects the doctrine of God's most eminent comprehension of the undeterminated; cf. "Opusculum," bk. I, ch. VIII, n. 5.

43. Cf. "Opusculum," bk. I, ch. II, nn. 6ff.

44. Ibid., bk. II, ch. V, nn. 2ff.

knowledge of a free future contingent is true, determinately true. We have stated that Molina says that the free future contingent is by definition indeterminately true. To maintain this, he bases his argument on what he takes as the common doctrine taken from Aristotle, that is, that propositions regarding free future contingents are indeterminately true inasmuch as one cannot know previously which of the disjuncts the free agent will choose when it acts.[45] Suárez believes that Aristotle erred on this point, and that his error has been the cause of some mistaken doctrines regarding divine foreknowledge of free future contingent acts.[46] The mistake arises, says Suárez, when considering that knowledge which is determinately true is opposed to contingency and freedom, and so it is maintained that free future contingent propositions are indeterminately true.[47] Suárez defends the determinate truth of such propositions on both theological and rational grounds. From the theological point of view it must be admitted that what God reveals as future, for example, "Peter will sin," is determinately true, and he knows it to be so, for as already established, God can know only what is determinately true. From the merely rational point of view, free future contingent propositions cannot but be determinately true, for if they are not, they would all be false, which is absurd. For example, if "Peter will sin" cannot be determinately true, it is simply false, as its contradictory, "Peter will not sin," must also be false; and it is absurd to maintain that the whole disjunctive proposition, "Peter will sin or will not sin," is false. Suárez contends that, in short, the error is due to a failing in understanding what a free future contingent proposition means. When one says, for example, "Peter will sin," it does not mean that Peter is indifferent to the act of sinning, but that one states that he will determinately sin. Moreover, Suárez maintains that it is the truth of a future-tense proposition which makes a disjunctive proposition of the type "Peter will sin or will not sin" true, for it is true in case one of the disjuncts is determinately true, and the other determinately false. The question hangs on the fact that man does not know which is true, but God does.[48]

At this point the difficulty lies in explaining how a proposition can be true when it affirms something that, being in the future, does not yet exist. The difficulty is comprehensible if one understands that truth

45. See note 42.
46. Cf. "Opusculum," bk. I, ch. II, n. 2, p. 296: "Fundamentum hujus erroris videtur posuisse Aristoteles, 1 de Interpretatione, cap. 8, ubi negat propositiones de futuro contingenti habere determinatam veritatem, donec ponantur in esse."
47. Ibid., ch. II, nn. 2ff. Suárez rejects Aristotle's supposed reasons (ch. II, n. 12).
48. Ibid., ch. II, nn. 7–9.

is the conformity between knower and known. As we have seen, it was precisely the non-existence of the future that led Molina to pronounce himself in favor of an eminent and unlimited comprehension of the root of contingency.[49] Suárez rejects the type of explanation given by Molina, for God appears as doing something that is not feasible, that is, knowing something that is not in itself knowable, that is, what is indeterminately true.[50] Therefore, Suárez maintains that there is determinate truth in propositions in the future tense, and so there is adequacy. According to Suárez, the key lies in explaining what the future formally consists in. In his own words, that something is formally in the future consists in a certain transition of the being which it has in its cause to the being it will at some time have, that is, a certain tendency of the being in potency to being in act, which tendency is understood to be in the thing itself and not in the cause. The adequacy or conformity of a true future-tense proposition is with the tendency to the transition from being in potency to being in act.[51] For Suárez, only such a way of understanding the future form is compatible with contingency and freedom.[52]

This way of understanding the future form reconciles the determinate truth of a future-tense proposition with contingency because it deals with the determination of the effect and not of the cause; for it does not mean that the cause will act contingently because it will not act determinately, but it says it will act contingently because it will act in a way in which it might not have acted. What is meant by a future-tense proposition is that such a cause will determine itself some time in the future to such an effect, even though at present it is indifferent with regard to it.[53] In this sense, Suárez thinks free contingent future-tense propositions are not hypothetical, but categorical. One asserts something of a thing but hypothetically or conditionally, which, however, is not necessary.[54] Thus, God knows by intuition *sub conditione* the tendency toward a determinate being in the cause actually present to Him, although it is free.[55]

---

49. See note 42.
50. Cf. "Opusculum," bk. I, ch. VIII, n. 5.
51. Cf. "Prolegomenum," ch. VII, n. 7. Cf. also "Opusculum," bk. I, ch. VIII, n. 8.
52. Cf. "Prolegomenum," ch. VII, n. 25, p. 96: "Forma autem illa a qua illud esse possibile in causa denominatur futurum, non est causa ipsa, vel determinatio ejus, . . . nam hoc est tollere contingentiam effectuum, et libertatem causarum secundarum."
53. Cf. "Opusculum," bk. I, ch. II, n. 12, p. 300: "Solum ergo significatur, quod talis causa aliquando determinanda sit ad tale effectum, etiamsi nunc illa causa sit indifferens."
54. Cf. ibid., bk. II, ch. V, n. 10.
55. Cf. "Prolegomenum," ch. VII, n. 21.

Through the exposition of these statements I have tried to show the nucleus of a discussion that stirred theologians of peninsular Spain, especially in the sixteenth century and mainly between the Dominican followers of Thomas Aquinas and the innovating Jesuits. I hope it will be of interest to show how this stir was received within the confines of the new boundaries that Spain acquired with the discovery of America. In fact, I shall here present the case of a Chilean theologian, Alonso Briceño, who, as a follower of John Duns Scotus, opposed the views not only of the followers of Thomas Aquinas but also of the Jesuits, including Molina and Suárez.

Alonso Briceño was born of Spanish parents in Santiago de Chile in 1587. He passed on to Lima in 1603, where he took the habit of St. Francis when he was 18 years old and made his profession approximately a year later. In Lima he taught for fifteen years. The fruit of his teaching are three volumes on theological and philosophical questions. His fame as a follower of Duns Scotus's doctrines won him the appellations of Second Scotus *(Alter Scotus)* and Little Scotus *(Scotulus)*. His intellectual fame led to his election as bishop of the bishopric of Nicaragua in 1644, whose seat he acceded in 1646. In 1649 he was transferred to the episcopal see of Caracas. He died in Trujillo (Venezuela) in 1669.[56]

His published work amounts to more than 1300 pages in two-column folios. It is divided into two volumes entitled *Celebriores Controversias in Primum Sententiarum Ioannis Scoti*. The first volume was published in Madrid in 1638 and the second in 1642.[57] A third volume, according to Briceños's own words, was ready for publication, but as yet remains unpublished.[58] I have no information regarding the fate of the manuscript.

The first volume contains ten controversies, the second, only two long

---

56. Cf. W. Hanisch, *En Torno a la Filosofía en Chile (1594–1810)* (Santiago: Universidad Católica de Chile, 1963), 24–30.

57. *Prima Pars Celebriorum Controversiarum in Primum Sententiarum Ioannis Scoti* (Madrid: Ex Typographia Regia, 1638); and *Partis Primae Celebriorum Controversiarum in Primum Sententiarum Ioannis Scoti Tomus Alter* (Madrid: Ex Typographia Regia, 1639). On the last page of the second volume appears 1642. In this regard, see the explanation in the following note.

58. On the last page of the second volume there is the following clarification: "Ad Capitulum Generale Ordinis Minorum Romae celebratum Vocatus; deinde in Hispania Capitulo Generali Ordinis Cisterciensis interesse Iussus cum Reverendissimo Episcopo Gaditano Authoritate Apostolica eiusdem Capituli Praeside ex propositione Regis Catholici, alijsque gravibus negotijs interceptus, et distractus, Opus antea finire non valui; quare nunc primo prodit anno 1642. Tertius vero Tomus de Voluntate et Potentia Dei, de Praedestinatione, et Trinitate complectens caeteras Controversias ad Primum Sententiarum attinentes extat praelo paratus, qui brevi (dante Deo) lucem videbit."

controversies, the eleventh and twelfth. The eleventh controversy deals with *De Scientia Dei* and its main issue is, according to Briceño, the foreknowledge of the conditioned contingent which *theologi recentes* use to reconcile created freedom with the efficacy of divine help.[59] This controversy is divided into three distinctions. The first distinction deals with "De Scientia Dei in se et prout refertur ad objecta non contingentia" in two articles, to which is added an appendix with two articles dealing with "De actualitate attributi voluntatis divinae et objecto formali illius." The second distinction concerns "De Scientia Dei respectu futurorum contingentium absolutorum" in seven articles. The third distinction speaks about "De scientia futurorum contingentium conditionatorum" in five articles.

In the present exposition I shall limit myself to some points related to the theme under discussion, which can be found in article 4 of the second distinction, where Briceño asks himself "An futura contingentia cognoscantur a Deo in se ipsis, seu in determinata veritate illorum," in direct conflict with the Jesuits, especially Suárez, and with some Franciscan Scotists who deviate, according to Briceño, from master Scotus's doctrine.

Briceño begins by accusing the Jesuit Vásquez of being the first to introduce the doctrine that holds that God foreknows future contingents because he knows them with determinate truth. What further disturbs him is that Vásquez should hold that such a doctrine was found in Scotus himself; according to Briceño, "It will be evident from the very text that Vásquez cites in his favor that he either did not interpret Scotus seriously or that he did not understand Scotus."[60] Further on, and after showing the difference in the statement of the problem between Vásquez and Scotus, he displays his astonishment at Vásquez's quoting Scotus in his favor with strong words: "unless he is in a delirium or wants to blind us in plain daylight."[61] Briceño justifies his indignation toward Vásquez by pointing out that he is the one whom most of the Jesuits follow, especially Suárez, on the thesis in question.[62] Regarding the thesis itself he rightly points out that the discrepancy with

---

59. *Tomus Alter*, p. 1: "Praesens vero controversia, quae celebrem locum sibi vendicat in Theologia, praecipue ob conditionatorum praescientiam, a qua recentes Theologi conciliationem libertatis creatae; et efficacitatis Superni auxilij depromere satagunt; tripartita erit."

60. Ibid., 170a: "Sed potius evidenter constabit ex ipso texto, quem pro se citat Vasquez, vel Scotum serio non versasse, vel Scotum non precepisse ..."

61. Ibid., 175b: "... est cur miremur, quod Vasquez a se stare Scotum pronuntiet, eo apparatu verborum, nisi vel ipse allucinetur, vel nos in media luce caecutire velit."

62. Ibid., 170b: "Vazquium comitantur universi Jesuitae Authores; Soarius *Opuscul. 2. de scientia futurorum contingentium*, lib. I, cap. 8 ..." Cf. 173b, 10.

the Jesuits is greater with Molina than with the rest of them, as Scotus also admits foreknowledge of the contingent future with determinate truth.[63] In this regard Briceño notes that it is common tradition among the theologians, from which Scotus does not deviate, that the contingent is knowable by God with determinate truth, which is in accordance with faith. Briceño then specifies that the difference arises rather with regard to the origin of determinate truth, whether it arises from the intrinsic conformity of the proposition and the object, independent of the previous absolute decision of the divine will, or from outside, that is, from the absolute decree of the divine will.[64] Briceño is obviously in favor of the latter, in accordance with his master's doctrine. His answer in this dispute is based on Scotus's work, distinction 39 of the first book of *Sentences I*, q. 1, a. 2, n. 23, where Scotus tries to explain the certainty of divine knowledge regarding contingents. Scotus's thesis may be summarized as follows. The basis of the divine knowledge of future contingent propositions lies in the knowledge God has of His own will to choose one of the determinable opposites of the contingent. According to Scotus, in a first instant God knows all future contingents in an act of cognition prior to any determination of His will, so that at this instant God's knowledge is neutral with regard to which opposite will be determined by His will; in a second instant, by the absolute determination of His will, the contingent passes from undetermined being to determined being. Therefore, God does not know the contingent with determinate truth prior to the free determination of his will.[65] And here originates the difference in the statement of the problem with the Jesuits that follow Vásquez. Briceño goes on to explain that the adequacy or conformity with the contingent object is not essential to divine knowledge: "Because such is the way in which God foreknows that Peter will freely behave in a certain way that He could not know it, had He not determined to reduce such an object to futurity; therefore the conformity with that certain object undergoing such an objective change is not of the essence of divine knowledge, since such a determination could have been discarded had the object been discarded by God's assent if He had determined otherwise regarding the futurity or non-

---

63. Cf. ibid., 175a, 15: "Quare in hoc Vasquez; et Soarez cum schola Scoti nullatenus pugnant, quae complexis de futuro contingenti determinatam veritatem, ob praeeuntem divinae voluntatis determinationem, adscribit; sed cum Molina, qui futura a Deo determinate praesciri asseverabit ob infiniti luminis divini pernicitatem supercomprehendentem conatus voluntatis creatae, esto quod futuris nulla determinata veritas inesset; quod inconsulte traditum est, et ab omnibus Iesuitis authoribus improbatur."
64. Cf. ibid., 175a.
65. Cf. ibid., 175a, 16.

futurity of the object."⁶⁶ Nor is the conformity with the contingent object that is necessary by hypothesis essential to created judgment, thinks Briceño:

> That conformity of created judgment with the object necessary by hypothesis is not of the essence of judgment; for while remaining the same judgment such conformity may be withdrawn, as well the contingent object; hence it may happen that the created judgment may fail if the object having changed the assent and judgment regarding the object does not vary. Therefore it is not of the essence of judgment that the object should behave in such a way (as is expressed), even if it be of the essence of true judgment, for although it is of the essence of created judgment that it should apply to the object and compare itself with it by a transcendental disposition; it is not, however, of the essence of the assent that the object behave in the way expressed in the judgment; with the result that while the same assent as regards the substance remains, the object having changed, the accident of judgment, which is truth, might be destroyed even though the substance of the act remains.⁶⁷

Hence, for the above reasons, there is no problem for Briceño, in accordance with Scotus, that God has a neutral or indeterminate foreknowledge of the contingent future, prior to the free determination of His will; and that knowledge with determinate truth should be in virtue of the free determination of His divine will. Moreover, for Briceño the transition of possible being to the actual being of a *futuribile* is only feasible for God, after the free determination of His will, for the following reason:

> Every future being insofar as it implies futurity is not a being in itself, that is, it is not raised out of the mere whole of possibles to the series of future beings in virtue of its essence; therefore it is changed to determined futurity by the first cause. But this objective change must not be expected from the first cause, as having the attribute of knowledge which precedes free determination; for such knowledge is certainly a necessary predicate, so that the change to futurity cannot be made unless it becomes simply necessary and withdrawing freedom;

---

66. Ibid., 176a: "Quia sicut ita Deus praescit, Petrum taliter se libere habiturum, quod potuit tale obiectum non praescire, si Deus non decrevisset tale obiectum ad futuritionem contrahere; ita conformitas ad tale obiectum sub tali immutatione obiectiva, non est de quidditate scientiae Dei: siquidem tolli posset illa sicuitas, ablato obiecto pro nutu Dei aliter praestituente circa obiecti futuritionem, aut non futuritionem."

67. Ibid., p. 176b: "Ideo tamen conformitas illa iudicij creati cum obiecto necessario ex hypothesi, non est de essentia iudicij; quia perstante eodem iudicio, potest tolli talis conformitas sicut et obiectum contingens; unde et provenit, ut iudicium creatum falli queat, si mutato obiecto, non varietur assensus, et iudicium circa obiectum. Non est igitur obiectum taliter se habens de essentia iudicij, ut veri; quia licet sit de essentia iudicij creati extendi, et comparari ad obiectum per transcendentalem habitudinem; sed non est de quidditate assensus, quod obiectum taliter se habeat; qualiter per iudicium exprimitur; quo fit, ut perstante eodem assensu quoad substantiam, et mutato obiecto, destrui queat accidens iudicij quod est veritas, manente substantia actus."

therefore such objective change must issue from the essentially free form, which is the efficacious and absolute volition of God.[68]

I hope that this exposition may have somewhat clarified one of the key problems regarding divine foreknowledge and free human action in Spanish philosophy in the centuries after the Discovery of America. Furthermore, I hope that the exposition of part of the thought of Alonso Briceño may arouse an interest in the study of Spanish American authors of the colonial period, the works of whom still lie untouched and ignored in innumerable libraries on the continent discovered by Columbus, and thus help to extend the knowledge of the richness of Spanish thought in all its extension, including Spanish American thought. This will surely help in coming to understand fully the work that followed the Discovery, whose fifth century the present volume celebrates.

68. Ibid., p. 184b: "Omne ens futurum, quam importat futuritionem, non est ens a se, seu a sua quidditativa ratione non extrahitur a mera collectione possibilium ad seriem futurorum; igitur immutatur ad determinatam futuritionem a prima causa. Sed haec obiectiva mutatio peti non debet a prima causa, ut subest attributo scientiae antevertentis liberum decretum; cum talis scientia sit praedicatum omnino necessarium, a quo trahi nequeat mutatio ad futuritionem, quae non sit simpliciter necessaria, et tollens libertatem; igitur talis obiectiva mutatio ad fore hauriri debet a forma essentialiter libera; qualis est efficax et absoluta Dei volitio."

PART IV

12   Suárez and a Salamancan Thomist: A Tale of a Text
NORMAN WELLS

The position of Francisco Zumel, a Salamancan Thomist of the sixteenth century (d. 1607), on the status of the essences of creatures prior to their creation is deserving of consideration on a number of counts.[1] First, it will help to reveal and spell out various facets of the problem of eternal essences and their attendant eternal truths abroad at this time. Second, it can afford historical clarification to some of Francisco Suárez's cryptic allusions to certain of his anonymous adversaries among the Salamancan Thomists on these issues of eternal essences with their eternal truths, their relation to the essence and existence problem, and the question of their distinction.[2] Important among his cryptic allusions on these issues is Suárez's striking reference to certain unnamed *moderni theologi*.[3] Finally, since Suárez's text has, in turn, bulked large in considerable research dealing with the also unnamed adversary of Descartes' position on the eternal truths,[4] the spelling out

---

1. See Francisco Zumel, *In Primam D. Thomae Partem Commentaria* (Venetiis, 1597–1601), I, q. 10, a. 3, 155b–159b, where this question is discussed: "An essentia rerum fuerint ab aeterno antequam a Deo producerentur?" (155b). In his introductory remarks, Zumel restates the question in a number of different ways: "Num essentiae sint ab aeterno? . . . Num rerum quidditates antequam a Deo in tempore producerentur, habuerint aliquod esse? Eadem quaestio est si interroges, Utrum haec enuntiabilia complexa hominem esse animal; equum esse hinnibilem, sint aliquid reale ab aeterno extra divinum intellectum?" For Zumel as a Thomist, see L. A. Kennedy, *A Catalogue of Thomists 1270–1900* (Houston: Center for Thomistic Studies, 1987), 122. For biographical details on Zumel, see *Enciclopedia Universal Ilustrada Europeo-Americana* (Madrid: Espasa-Calpe, 1930–33), vol. 70, cols. 1516–19; and *Dictionnaire de Théologie catholique* (Paris: Letouzey et Ané, 1937), vol. 13, cols. 2010–11 and 4440–41.
2. See the introduction to my translation of Suárez's 31st Disputation, *On The Essence of Finite Being As Such, On the Existence of That Essence and Their Distinction* (Milwaukee: Marquette University Press, 1938), 8–9. For Zumel's discussion "De Distinctione inter esse et essentiam," see op. cit., *In Sum Theol.*, I, q. 3, a. 4, 91a–95b.
3. Francisco Suárez, *Disputationes Metaphysicae* (hereafter DM), d. 31, s. 12, n. 39, in *Opera Omnia*, ed. Louis Vivès (Paris, 1856–77), 26:294. See text in note 71 below.
4. Étienne Gilson, early on in *La liberté chez Descartes et la théologie* (Paris: J. Vrin, 1982),

201

of Zumel's position can serve as a fruitful occasion to reopen the issue of Descartes' anonymous adversary.

I

Zumel introduces his treatment of the problem of the status of the essences of creatures prior to their creation with a brief historical account. Albert the Great is cited as embracing a position which accords an *esse intellectuale* to the essences of creatures prior to their creation. This is accompanied with a *caveat* of John Capreolus, for Albert's position is declared to be neither safe nor certain because it acknowledges that there is something eternal *et non a Deo*.[5]

34–75, and quite unwittingly, I suspect, has added further perplexity to the initial puzzlement over Descartes' adversary, one which has taken on a life of its own in the literature on this matter. (See G. Rodis-Lewis, "Quelques compléments sur la creation vérités éternelles," in *Étienne Gilson et Nous: La philosophie et son histoire* [Paris: J. Vrin, 1980], 73–77. Also see J.-L. Marion, *Sur le théologie blanche de Descartes* [Paris: P.U.F., 1981], 27–69). For Gilson had surmised that Descartes may well have had no particular adversary in mind, or if he did have someone in mind, it could not be "quelque philosophe de l'école" because Gilson, perhaps unduly influenced by a judgment of Suárez ("Nec potuit in mentem alicujus Doctoris Catholici venire, quod essentia creaturae ex se, et absque efficientia libera Dei, sit aliqua vera res, aliquod verum esse reale habens distinctum ab esse Dei . . ."; DM, d. 31, s. 2, n. 3; 26:230), acknowledged that no Catholic teacher, no more than Descartes himself, could or would have claimed that some truths could exist if God did not exist. Ironically, this disclaimer of Gilson's has been responsible for diverting attention from Gilson's own citation and use of two pertinent texts of Suárez (see p. 49 for the text cited in my note 83 below and p. 48 for the other text noted at the end of this note) which embody the "adversary language" of Descartes' *Letters to Mersenne* in May and April of 1630 and which have become the dominant focus of much of the recent contemporary scholarship on the issue of Descartes' adversary (see Rodis-Lewis, "Quelques compléments," 73–75, criticizing P. Garin and the late T. J. Cronin. The work of S. Landucci is referred to in G. Rodis-Lewis, *Idées et vérités éternelles chez Descartes et ses successeurs* [Paris: J.Vrin, 1985], 9nn11–12). Though Gilson had cited these very texts and had even emphasized that Descartes was explicitly opposed to the positions delineated, and to the language used in the two critical texts of Suárez, he failed to judge, and refrained from designating, Suárez to be Descartes' adversary! Later on, aware of the work of Garin, and in possession of a pertinent text of Duns Scotus, Gilson will call for a reconsideration of his initial research on Descartes' adversary and will insist that there has been someone who has maintained: "Si Deus non esset, nihilominus istae veritates essent verae"! However, Gilson still refrained from citing anyone in particular. It is my contention that neither of the two key texts can be attributed to Suarez. The first belongs to Zumel (see notes 50, 83, and 84 below); the second is to be found in Soncinas, and, closer to home among the Salamancan Thomists, in Soto (see note 42 below). This latter material is material for a tale about another text! For Soncinas as the source for Suárez's citation, DM, d. 31, s. 12, n. 45; 26:297: "Unde si per impossibile nulla esset talis causa, nihilominus illa enuntiatio vera esset . . ."; see my article, "Descartes and the Scholastics Briefly Revisited," *The New Scholasticism* 35 (1961): 172–90, esp. 188–90.

5. Zumel, *In I Sum. Theol.*, q. 10, a. 3, 155b: "In hac quaestione varias video Antiquorum sententias. Nam Albertus Magnus c. de substantia docet quod esse intellectuale, quo sunt genera et species, sunt aeterna secundum suam naturam. Capreo., in 2 dist. 2,

Henry of Ghent's position is next cited, wherein Henry distinguishes an *esse essentiae* and an *esse existentiae,* insisting that God produces the latter as an efficient cause while producing the former as an exemplary cause. This exemplary causality confers what is also characterized as an *esse intelligibile* or *esse quidditativum* upon the essences of creatures in virtue of which they are termed "eternal."[6] It is worth noting that Zumel does not here sustain the same charge laid against Albert the Great to the effect that the essences of creatures are *non a Deo*. As forthcoming from an exemplary cause, these essences may not be properly created as befits an effect of an efficient cause, but they are certainly *a Deo*.

While Zumel is explicit in indicating that Henry's perspective is also embraced by others *(cum aliis distinguit),* he is clearly less than explicit in naming them. That is, he could have noted, but refrained from doing so, that the self-same Capreolus, of whose critical comments he has just made use, is one of those who espouses Henry's twofold causality at the source, first of essence and its *esse essentiae,* and then of *esse existentiae*.[7] In light of Suárez's frequent attempts to highlight disagreements among the Thomists, Salamancan and otherwise, the reticence of Zumel to cite Capreolus explicitly in this place and on this score is significant.[8]

Scotus is next cited as following a position similar to Henry inasmuch

---

q. 1, dicit quod haec sententia Alberti non est satis secura, nec certa eo quod constituit aliquid esse aeternum secundum naturam in speciebus, et in essentiis atque generibus, et in essentiis atque generibus rerum et non a Deo." For the texts of Albert and Capreolus, see my article, "Capreolus on Essence and Existence," *The Modern Schoolman* 38 (1960): 1–24, esp. 20–23.

6. Zumel, *In I Sum. Theol.,* q. 10, a. 3, 155b: "Henricus Gandensis cum aliis distinguit duplex esse; essentiae et existentiae. Et quantum ad esse existentiae inquit, quod Deus est causa effectiva rerum: at vero quantum ad esse essentiae, ait, quod quidditates rerum sunt a Deo tanquam a causa exemplari. Quoniam Deus per suum intelligere tribuit esse intelligibile, et esse quidditativum essentiis; secundum quam rationem, rerum essentiae dicunt aeternae." See Henry of Ghent, *Quodlibeta* (Paris: Jacobus Badius Ascensius, 1518), I, q. 9, fol. 6v–7r; J. Paulus, *Henri de Gand* (Paris: J. Vrin, 1938), 67–135.

7. See note 70 below and Wells, "Capreolus," 21–23.

8. See the text of Suárez in note 70 below. Zumel could have mentioned, but didn't, most of the Salamancan Thomists. See L. A. Kennedy, "Thomism at the University of Salamanca in the Sixteenth Century," *Tommaso D'Aquino nella Storia del Pensiero,* Atti del Congresso Internazionale, 1974 (Napoli, 1976), 2:254–58, esp. 257–58: "This doctrine that the essence has a reality in its own right and is not created, was held by most late medieval and Renaissance Thomists, including the leaders among them, Capreolus and Cajetan. It was held also at Salamanca by Francisco de Vitoria, Domingo de Soto, Mancio del Cuerpo de Cristo, Bartolomé de Medina, Domingo Bañez, and Pedro de Ledesma." By the same author, see "La doctrina de la existencia en la Universidad de Salamanca durante el siglo XVI," *Archivo Teológico Granadino* 35 (1972): 5–71; and "Peter of Ledesma and the Distinction between Essence and Existence," *The Modern Schoolman* 46 (1968): 25–38.

as he is alleged to have taught that the essences of creatures are eternal and perpetual *extra Deum,* in virtue of a certain *esse diminutum,*[9] all of which will be the subject-matter of Zumel's fourth conclusion.[10]

Zumel's historical account also confronts his anonymous contemporaries, affording him the opportunity to lament the fact that, from the mouths of young boys, one hears the refrain that the essences of creatures are eternal and perpetual *extra intellectum divinum.*[11] Seven arguments are catalogued in support of those who claim that essences are eternal *extra intellectum divinum.*[12] In turn, these are countered by one single argument in opposition, embodied in a classical text of Thomas Aquinas from *De Potentia,* q. 3, a. 5 ad 2, the very text cited by Capreolus as safer and purportedly more certain, to the effect that Aquinas is understood to claim, not only that *esse existentiae* is forthcoming from God, but that *esse essentiae* is equally so forthcoming. In keeping with Aquinas's position, all quiddities, prior to their creation, are *nihil.* Moreover, in the divine intellect such essences are nothing else than *Dei essentia creatrix.*[13]

---

9. Zumel, *In I Sum. Theol.,* q. 10, a. 3, 155b–156a: "Scotus quid simile voluit dicere in I, d.35, q. unica ubi docuit quod rerum essentiae sunt aeternae et perpetuae extra deum, in quodam esse diminuto. Deus in primo signo suae aeternitatis cognovit essentiam et substantiam sine ordine ad creaturas: in secundo autem signo cognovit suam essentiam quatenus imitabile et participabilis a creaturis: atque sic suam cognovit essentiam, prout in ea continentur ideae omnium crearurarum; et consequenter ex hoc Deus habuit cognoscere omnes rerum essentiae et quidditates in se ipsis ab aeterno. Quod si dicas, Quomodo Deus potuit cognoscere essentias et quidditates in se ipsis, cum istae essentiae non fuerint ab aeterno productae? Respondet Scotus, quod Deus cognoscendo universas creaturas futuras, eas produxit antequam in tempore crearentur in quodam esse diminuto, et in quodam esse cognito extra Deum. Quod sane esse non est purum ens rationis neque est tantum esse, sicut illud, quod habuerunt postea in tempore; quod fuit esse reale firmum, et perfectum: sed illud esse est tantum atque tale, quod fundare potest relationem producentis ad productum. Haec est Scoti imaginatio, quae a solo ipso excogitata est: et impugnabitur a nobis inferius." For the origin and significance of the term *esse diminutum* in this text, see A. Maurer, *"Ens Diminutum:* a Note on its Origins and Meaning," *Mediaeval Studies* 12 (1950): 216–22.

10. Zumel, *In I Sum. Theol.,* q. 10, a. 3, 158b–159a.

11. Ibid., 156a: "Verum quoniam quotidie versatur in ore etiam infantium et puerorum, rerum essentias esse aeternas et perpetuas, en argumenta, quibus suadetur rerum essentias esse aliquid reale ab aeterno, extra intellectum divinum."

12. Ibid., 156a–b. They end with Zumel's remark: "Haec argumenta sunt ob quae misere lapsi sunt quicunque existimarunt rerum essentias esse aeternas et ob quae parvuli ignoranter gratulant."

13. Ibid., 156b: "Sanctus Th. de potentia, q.3, a.5 ad 2 dicit quod essentiae rerum non sunt aeternae extra Deum. Inquit enim ex eo quod quidditas et essentia dicit aliquid esse, et non esse rationis, non solum producitur a Deo quantum ad esse existentiae sed etiam quantum ad esse essentiae: et ita omnes quidditates sunt nihil, antequam producantur: in intellectu autem divino nihil aliud sunt, quam ipsa Dei essentia creatrix." Báñez (contrary to L. A. Kennedy's text cited in note 8 above) agrees here with Zumel that the essences of creatures are created, along with their existence. See *Scholastica Commen-*

Before considering Zumel's resolution of this question of eternal essences, it is important to sample and savor three of the seven arguments cited on behalf of essences which are eternal *extra intellectum divinum*. It is still more important, in order to do justice to Suárez's relation to Zumel, to recognize the prevailing linkage between eternal essences, their eternal, necessary, essential truths, and the view that *scientia* deals only with eternal essences and the necessary, essential truths attending them, but in no way dealing with existential, contingent truths.[14]

The second of the seven arguments insists that the essential proposition, *Homo est animal rationale*, is perpetually true according to the opinion of St. Augustine. Since truth, in Augustine's Christian Platonic perspective, is an attribute of Being, then what is signified by a perpetually true, essential truth is an eternal being.[15] The third argument makes the point that *scientia* deals with what is eternal and perpetual and with what is necessary. But only the essences of things are necessary. Hence, the essences of things are eternal.[16] The fourth argument expands on the status of *scientia* by pointing out that *scientia* is really related (involving real dependence on its part) to its object (for the relation of a being *[ens]* to a nonbeing *[non entis]* is not a real relation), even if that object does not actually exist. Therefore, before they exist actually, things enjoy *esse quidditativum et essentiale reale*. And that *scientia* is really dependent upon its object is manifest by the fact that *scientia* is really dependent upon necessary truths, such as *Homo est animal rationale*, as upon a measure, whether any man exists or not.[17] In lieu of an immediate resolution of what he terms a *quaestio difficilis*, Zumel

---

taria in Primam Partem Summae Theologiae S. Thomae Aquinatis, ed. Urbano (Madrid, 1934), I, q. 10, a. 3, 227, and in an earlier printed edition (Salamanca, 1584), I, q. 44, a. 1, col. 646, where he embraces the position of Sylvester of Ferrara and Soncinas and claims "... ex hoc sequitur quod Deus non causat connexionem praedicati essentialis cum subjecto neque formaliter neque fundamentaliter..."

14. See notes 70 and 75 below.
15. Zumel, *In I Sum. Theol.*, q. 10, a. 3, 156a: "Secundo, sic disputo. Haec propositio, Homo est animal rationale, est perpetuae veritatis secundum sententiam D.Aug. Sed veritas est passio entis: ergo eius significatum est aliquod ens aeternum. Ostendo consequentiam. Quoniam ab eo quod res est vel non est, propositio dicitur vera vel falsa: ergo si illa propositio est perpetuae veritatis, sequitur quod res significata est perpetua et aeterna."
16. Ibid.: "Tertio. Scientia est de aeternis et perpetuis et de his, quae aliter se habere non possunt: sed solum rerum essentiae se aliter habere non possunt: ergo rerum essentiae sunt aeternae."
17. Ibid.: "Quarto. Scientia refertur realiter ad suum objectum, etiam si objectum non habeat existentiam: ergo res antequam sint habent aliquod esse quidditativum et essentiale reale. Patet consequentia. Quia entis ad non ens non est relatio realis. Antecedens probatur. Nam hoc complexum, hominem esse animal rationale, eodem modo mensurat scientiam; sive existat, sive non existat."

prefaces his four critical conclusions with four "observations."[18] It is fitting, then, to heed first what is to be observed.

Zumel's first observation, an unstated, critical confrontation of Henry of Ghent's and Capreolus's positions on the exemplary causality of essences and their *esse essentiae*, not unlike Suárez's critique of the same tradition, acknowledges that the essences of things, prior to their creation, were *in intellectu Dei per ideas*, in keeping with the classical Divine Artisan perspective.[19] As a consequence, Zumel, with Aquinas's text from the *de Potentia* in mind, along with Capreolus's interpretation, also acknowledges that, when it was said above that the essences of things, prior to their creation, are *nihil*, this must be understood as distinguished from *ens in actu*, but not from *ens in se*. That is, since no *ens in actu* is at issue, no question of actual causality, efficient or exemplary, as found in Henry of Ghent and Capreolus, is at issue. But what is *nihil* in the sense of "what is not actual" *(ens non actu)* is not to be taken as what is not *ens in se*. For what is not *ens in actu* is still *ens in se* either *in intellectu divino* and/or *in potentia activa Dei*.[20] Herein, we are in the presence of a distinction between "what is real" and "what is actual," made famous by Suárez,[21] which finally finds its way, through the German *Schulmetaphysik*, to Kant and his equally famous distinction between *Realität* and *Wirklichkeit*.[22] What is possible may not be "actual" but it is still "real" when contrasted with the impossible *ens fictitium* to be mentioned below.[23]

---

18. Ibid., 156b: "Quaestio haec difficilis, apetienda est a nobis."

19. Ibid.: "Ad quam intelligendam observa primo, quod antequam Deus mundum crearet, rerum essentiae erant in intellectu Dei per ideas, non secus atque in artifice res artificose, antequam producantur: quae non alter sunt quam in idea ipsius artificis."

20. Ibid.: "Cum ergo dicitur, Rerum essentiae antequam producantur, sunt nihil, accipitur (nihil) prout distinguitur contra ens, quod dicit actum existentiae: non tamen accipitur (nihil) prout distinguitur contra ens in se, quod vel in intellectu divino, vel in potentia activa Dei; in qua sunt omnes essentiae, antequam producantur." For all of his criticisms of Capreolus on the issue of the uncreated essences of creatures, Zumel here adopts a position which is terminologically not unlike Capreolus's distinction between two kinds of *nihil* and which has been directly criticized by Suárez. For Capreolus on the two kinds of nothing, see his *Defensiones Theologiae Divi Thomae Aquinatis*, 7 vols., ed. Paban-Pègues (Turin: Alfred Cattier, 1900), *In II Sent.*, d. 1, q. 2, a. 3, ad quartum argumentum Aureoli contra quartum conclusionem; 3:73a, or Wells, "Capreolus," 22n44. For Suárez's critique of Capreolus on this issue, see DM, d. 31, s. 2, nn. 3–4; 26:229–30; and my article "Suárez on the Eternal Truths Pt. I," *The Modern Schoolman* 58 (1981): 73–104, esp. n. 35.

21. See DM, d. 31, s. 2, n. 10; 26:232, for Suárez's citation of Cajetan. For Zumel's citation of the same text of Cajetan, see note 29 below.

22. See H. Siegfried, "Kant's 'Spanish Bank Account': *Realität* and *Wirklichkeit*," in *Interpreting Kant*, ed. M. Gram (Iowa City: University of Iowa Press, 1982), 115–32; "Kant's Thesis about Being Anticipated by Suarez?" *Proceedings of the Third International Kant Congress* (Dordrecht: Reidel, 1970), 510–20.

23. See further remarks on *ens fictitium* in notes 29 and 32 below.

Zumel's next observation spells out the three ways only in which the essences of things can have *esse*. They can have an *esse in intellectu*, in the fashion that all things have *esse ab aeterno in intellectu divino*, prior to their actual, extramental existence. They can have *esse in suis causis*, again prior to their actual, extramental existence, in terms of secondary causes (for example, *in potentia materiae et in virtute activa Solis*, after the fashion of the oft-mentioned rose-in-winter) or in terms of their primary cause (for example, *in potentia activa Dei*). Finally, these essences may have *esse in seipsis extra suas causas* wherein what was a real possible, enjoying an intramental, intracausal *esse*, becomes actual and dependent upon an actual, efficient cause.[24]

Zumel indicates that these points are acknowledged by all parties to the dispute in order to stress that the whole controversy focuses on the question of whether the essences of things in themselves and *extra Deum* have enjoyed some *esse aeternum*.[25] In making this second observation, one must not lose sight of the fact that Zumel reinforces his previous point that no causality, efficient or exemplary, is at issue. For there is no cause involved in the case of *esse in intellectu divino* nor with regard to *esse in potentia activa Dei*. With this granted, both Henry of Ghent and Capreolus must disavow their eternal, exemplary causality of essences with their *esse essentiae* or embrace the untenable consequences of an *esse aeternum extra Deum* on the part of the essences of things.[26]

Zumel's third observation constitutes a clarification of his initial formulations of the question under discussion. He had noted at the outset that the problem of the eternal essences *extra Deum* could be reformulated in terms of *enuntiabilia complexa*, such as *homo est animal* or *equus est hinnibilis*, asking whether they are something real *ab aeterno extra Deum*. This is the eternal-truth facet of the eternal-essence problem. His clarification is to the effect that, for an essential or *per se* proposition, wherein the predicate is identified with the subject, the actual existence of that subject is not required and consequently no existential import is at issue for the truth of such propositions. Such propositions

---

24. Zumel, *In I Sum. Theol.*, q. 10, a. 3, 156b: "Secundo observa, quod rerum essentiae tribus modis possunt habere esse. Primo, in intellectu: secundo, in suis causis: tertio, in se ipsis extra suas causas. In intellectu quidem divino omnia habuerunt procul dubio esse ab aeterno: in suis autem causis res dicuntur esse, sicut rosa antequam producatur, est in potentia materiae et in virtute activa Solis: sic etiam universae res et essentiae fuerunt in potentia activa Dei." See note 55 below for reference to the rose-in-winter.

25. Ibid.: "At vero cum haec sint certissima in omni opinione, controversia solum est, utrum essentiae rerum in se ipsis et extra Deum, habuerint aliquod esse aeternum? Et praeter hos tres modos essendi, non est imaginabilis aliquis modus, quo res possunt esse: sive quantum ad esse essentiae, sive quantum ad esse existentiae."

26. See notes 6 and 7 above.

are accordingly perpetually true *(perpetuae veritatis)* whether there is anything existing or not, for any proposition of the sort wherein an immutable and necessary connection is acknowledged cannot be falsified, even by God.[27] Adding here to his already extensive vocabulary of *esse*, Zumel makes it quite explicit that what is at issue at this point is neither *esse essentiale quidditativum* nor *esse existentiae*, but *esse* which signifies the truth of a proposition or a predicational connection. Such a connection properly exists only *in intellectu* because the intellect produces such a connection between the subject and predicates in question.[28] Zumel's fourth observation spells out the relationship of *esse existentiae* to *esse essentiae*.[29]

Zumel's first conclusion denies any essences outside the divine intellect and outside God's active power *ab aeterno* as repugnant to right reason. Nor do the essences signified by the above-mentioned "complex enuntiables," like *Homo est animal rationale* or *Rosa est flos*, enjoy any *esse essentiae quidditativum* nor any *esse existentiae ab aeterno*. Furthermore, this is the Catholic conclusion since the Catholic faith believes that nothing other than God is eternal. When things are created, the essences of those things are equally created or concreated.[30] Hence the essences

---

27. Zumel, *In I Sum. Theol.*, q. 10, a. 3, 156b: "Tertio observa, quod actualis existentia subjecti non requiritur ad veritatem propositionis per se loquendo, quando praedicatum concipitur ratione subjecti. Tunc enim propositio est perpetuae veritatis, sive re existente sive non existente: quia talis propositio non potest a Deo falsificari. Illa autem vocatur propositio perpetuae veritatis, quae dicit necessariam habitudinem terminorum et immutabilem."

28. Ibid., 156b–57a: "Ex his, quae dicimus, colligitur quod triplex est esse. Aliud est esse essentiale et quidditativum, aliud esse existentiae, aliud vero quod significat veritatem propositionis et connexionem: quae connexio fundamentaliter est in re, formaliter autem intellectu."

29. Ibid., 157a: "Quarto observa, quod esse existentiae duo facit respectu essentiae. Primum est, constituere esse essentiae in actu, quod antea erat in potentia: unde homo antequam existat, est in potentia objectiva ens quidem potentiale, non actuale. Secundum, quod efficit esse existentiae est quod essentias sint ens creatum. Nam antequam existat, est ens creabile, et non creatum: nam creatio terminatur ad quidditatem sub existentia. Unde ens reale prima divisione partitur in ens increatum quod habet esse per suam essentiam: et in ens creatum, quod habet esse non per essentiam, sed per existentiam, quae est accidentalis essentiae. Cajetanus c. 4 de ente et essentia q. 6 advertit quod est memoriae commendandum, ens reale bifariam usurpari. Uno modo, ut distinguitur contra ens fictitium et fabricatum ab intellectu; itaque quidquid non est fictitium aut fabricatum ab intellectu ens reale vocari potest. Alio modo sumitur, ut distinguitur contra non existens."

30. Ibid.: "Quibus ita praelibatis et constitutis, est prima conclusio. Essentiae rerum extra divinum intellectum et extra potentiam activam Dei secundum se non sunt aeternae et oppositum repugnat rectae rationi. Itaque essentiae rerum quae significantur per illa complexa enuntiabilis, Homo est animal rationale, Rosa est flos, non sunt ab aeterno; neque quantum ad esse existentiae, neque quantum esse essentiae quidditativum. Haec est Catholica conclusio. Quoniam fides Catholica praeter Deum nihil confitetur aeter-

of things have been *ab aeterno* only *in intellectu Dei* and/or *in potentia activa Dei*, but never, in any way, *extra Deum*.[31] Zumel acknowledges this to be the conclusion of Aquinas, Harvey Nedellec, and Soncinas, claiming, in an obvious but unstated rejection of Henry of Ghent and Capreolus, that, prior to creation, things were *in potentia* with respect both to *esse essentiae* and to *esse existentiae*.[32] No less than seven proofs of this first conclusion are offered, from deploring the pagan Platonism of eternal essences *extra Deum*[33] to noting that, given such eternal essences, if acknowledged to be unproduced as indicated against Albert the Great, something independent of God would then be granted.[34] Further, if such eternal essences are claimed to be produced (but not created), as is the case with Henry of Ghent and Capreolus, in the instance of their position on exemplary causality, then *creatio ex nihilo* is rendered impossible in spite of Capreolus's distinction between two "kinds" of *nihil*.[35] Moreover, given such eternal essences, God could not annihilate them, which flies in the face of divine omnipotence.[36] Finally, drawing out the implications of his third observation, Zumel confronts

---

num, et universa acceperunt Deo opifice initio temporis; et creatis rebus creatae sunt rerum essentiae: ut creato homine creata est hominis essentia, aut concreata..."

31. Ibid.: "... solum ergo rerum essentiae et quidditates in intellectu Dei, vel in potentia activa Dei, fuerunt ab aeterno, extra Deo vero nusquam ullo modo."

32. Ibid.: "Hanc conclusionem tenet D.Th. in hoc art. ad 3. et de potentia q. 3. art. 5 ad 2 et Herbeus quodl. 11, q. 1 qui affirmat quod res antequam fierent per creationem, erant in potentia quantum ad utrunque esse, essentiae et existentiae. Sicut contrario modo, chimaera non est in potentia, nec quantum ad esse essentiae, nec quantum esse existentiae: quia habet repugnantiam suae possibilitatis, Et idem placitum sequitur Paulus Soncinas 9 Met. q. 4." See Suárez on Harvey and Soncinas in note 70 below.

33. Zumel, *In I Sum. Theol.*, q. 10, a. 3, 157a: "Haec conclusio probatur primo: Quia si rerum essentiae sunt aeternae secundum aliquod esse extra Deum, Sequitur quod est defendenda sententia Platonis de ideis." See Descartes' *Letter to Mersenne* in note 94 below referring to the danger of the paganization of Christian thought on this issue!

34. Zumel, *In I Sum. Theol.*, q. 10, a. 3, 157b: "Aut rerum essentiae, quas contrarii auctores dicunt esse ab aeterno, sunt a Deo productae, aut nullo modo productae: Si dicas quod nullo modo: sequitur, quod est aliquid extra Deum ab aeterno, quod nullo modo dependet a Deo. Patet consequentia. Quia quod nullo modo est productum a Deo, nullo modo pendet a Deo."

35. Ibid.: "Si dicas quod istae essentiae sunt ab aeterno productae a Deo sequitur quod istae essentiae habent existentia ab aeterno. Ostendo sequelam. Quoniam omnes actiones causae efficientis et productivae, terminatur ad aliquid existens singulare ut nos fuse disputavimus I Met. q. 2. Quinto: quia sequeretur quod Deus non possit creare aliquid ex nihilo. Nam creare aliquid ex nihilo est producere totum ens ut ens est, nullo praesupposito subjecto: sed in quacunque divina providentia semper supponitur essentia et quidditas producendae, juxta oppositum sententiam; quae quidditas est principalior entitas in qualibet creatura: igitur cum haec essentia sit praesupposita, sequitur quod nihil creatur."

36. Ibid.: "Postremo: Si rerum sunt ab aeterno: ergo potuit Deus ab aeterno annihilare huiusmodi essentias non enim, sed modo potest annihilare essentias et existentias rerum; alias non esset omnipotens: ergo id ipsum potuit ab aeterno praestare."

the ongoing attempts of his adversaries to argue from the eternal truth of essential propositions to eternal essences. His point is that this is not a convincing argument on behalf of essences *ab aeterno* because such truths are eternal with essences annihilated.[37] In bringing his first conclusion to term, Zumel wants to know why his denial of eternal essences should cause any difficulty in view of the fact that God alone exists *ab aeterno* and Thomas Aquinas has stated that essence without existence is *nihil*.[38]

Zumel's second conclusion expresses his dissatisfaction with those who disclaim that the essences of things are eternal as to existence *(quantum ad esse existentiae)*, yet who nevertheless insist that they are eternal as to the connection of predicate with subject, just as the connection of *Homo est animal rationale, Quatuor et tria sunt septem*, and the like are *ab aeterno*.[39]

Zumel is convinced that such a rejection of eternal essences accompanied by an insistence upon eternal connections is not only insufficiently probable on its own merits, but it has proved to be personally unsatisfactory, since he was once an advocate of such a view.[40]

His adversaries here have claimed that, with no man prior to the creation of the world, *Homo est animal rationale* was true. Firmly spelling out the basis for his ultimate disenchantment, Zumel counters that, from the fact that a thing is or is not, a thing is called true or false. So, if no thing *(nulla res)* was extant, prior to creation, there was no prop-

---

37. Ibid.: "Tum sic, Annihilatis huiusmodi essentiis, adhuc rerum essentiae essent possibiles: similiter illae propositiones, Homo est animal rationale, Quodlibet est vel non est; eodem modo essent verae, sicut quando erant rerum essentiae vel existentiae: ergo si tota ratio quare constituuntur ab aeterno rerum a contrariis auctoribus est, quia illae propositiones sunt sempiternae veritatis, cum eodem modo se habeant illae propositiones facta annihilatione, sicut antea; sequitur quod huiusmodi ratio non est convincens ad constituendam essentias ab aeterno." See Suárez on this, DM, d. 31, s. 2, n. 3; 26:230.

38. Zumel, *In I Sum. Theol.*, q. 10, a. 3, 157b: "Profecto, solus Deus existit ab aeterno, et S. Th. de potentia q. 3 a. 5 ad 2 dicit quod essentia sine existentia nihil est: cur ergo difficile videtur, quod rerum essentiae non sunt ab aeterno?"

39. Ibid.: "Secunda conclusio. Non est satis probabile dicere quod rerum essentiae, quamvis non sunt aeternae quantum ad existentiam, nihilominus sunt aeternae in hoc sensu, scilicet quantum ad connexionem praedicati cum subjecto: ita ut connexiones illae sint ab aeterno, Homo est animal rationale, Quatuor et tria sunt septem." Zumel is here taking issue with the position of Sylvester of Ferrara and Soncinas which has been embraced by Báñez among the Salamancan Thomists (see note 13 above). Suárez refers to this tradition, agrees with it as it insists that the essences of creatures are created, but joins Zumel here in criticizing their *connexio aeterna praedicati cum subjecto;* see DM, d. 31, s. 12, n. 44; 26:295. See also my article "Suárez and the Eternal Truths Pt. II," *The Modern Schoolman* 58 (1981): 159–74. There is the barest hint of this in Mersenne; see P. Dear, *Mersenne and the Learning of the Schools* (Ithaca: Cornell University Press, 1988), 52–61.

40. Zumel, *In I Sum. Theol.*, q. 10, a. 3, 157b: "Quamvis aliquando cum versaret cum Philosophis, placitum hoc de aeternitate quantum ad connexionem praedicati cum subjecto: arriserit: modo tamen, satis mihi non probatur."

osition, neither vocal nor written, save for a mental one *in intellectu Dei*. The proposition in question, *Homo est animal rationale*, then, is not true.[41] Moreover, and in a most striking fashion, Zumel follows up his rejection of eternal connections, save *in intellectu Dei*, by seeming to controvert his very contention that essential connections are eternal in the divine mind. For he asserts that, if one were to say (as he himself apparently just did) that these propositions were eternally true in the eternal mind of God, *hoc nihil est*. His reason for this rather blunt rejoinder is expressed by an interrogatory: Were not contingent truths similarly eternal *in intellectu Dei*? Given the nature of the divine mind, not only are the essences with their essential truths eternal therein, but so, too, are contingent and/or existential truths eternal therein.[42]

Without saying so, in any obvious fashion, Zumel is confronting an ongoing problem in the Henry of Ghent/Capreolus tradition—the persistent failure to acknowledge the consequences of the fact that God knows not only the essences of things but their *esse* as well, *ab aeterno*.[43]

---

41. Ibid.: "Quoniam nullo homine existente ante saecula condita haec erat vera, Homo est animal rationale, ut dicunt authores contrariae sententiae: sed ab eo quod res est vel non est, propositio dicitur vera, vel falsa: ergo si ante condita saecula nulla res erat, nulla etiam erat propositio vocalis, vel scripta; sed tantum mentalis in intellectu Dei: ergo neque illa erat vera, Homo est animal rationale."

42. Ibid.: "Si vero dicas, propositiones illas esse aeternae veritatis in mente aeterna Dei; hoc nihil est. Non etiam hac consideratione contingentia, quae Deo ordinante futura erant, vera similiter; ut Adam erat creandus, et peccaturus, etc? Igitur secundum rationem divinae mentis non solum dicuntur aeternae rerum essentiae, verum et contingentes veritates apud divinam mentem erunt aeternae." See what appears to be a *reportatio* of Soto in Kennedy, "La doctrina de la existencia," 26–27: "Et probo quod essentia non habet causam quod sit essentia vel conveniat rei cuius est essentia. Nec Deus fecit illud quia non est factibile, quia, si per impossibile non esset Deus, esset verum dicere 'Homo est animal rationale'. . . . Sed arguitur: ante creationem mundi non erant essentiae nisi in intellectu divino, vel in virtute divina ut in sua causa; sed isto modo etiam erant existentiae. Ergo non est magis perpetua essentia quam existentia." Soto's reply to this *sed arguitur* must be related to Suárez in notes 69–84 below.

43. See the text of Capreolus wherein he grants that God eternally knows existence as well as essence, yet fails to insist on the eternity of existential truths while highlighting only the eternity of essential truths, *Def. Theol., In I Sent.*, d. 8, q. 1, a. 2, arg. 6 ad 1; 1:330: "Sed conceditur quod tam essentiam quam ipsum ejus esse, Deus aeternaliter intellexit; ac per hoc, quodlibet eorum fuit in Deo aeternaliter, ut intellectum in intelligente. Ex quo provenit quod aeternaliter rosa est rosa, rosa est essentia; sed non aeternaliter fuit, nec aeternaliter exsistebat." Zumel remarks on Cajetan's position as follows: "Caiet. 1.p. q. 14 art. 13 quamvis asseuerat rerum essentias esse aeternas secundum se: affirmat tamen quod respectu aeternitatis divinae, rerum essentiae et existentiae fuerunt praesentes in eadem aeternitate Dei. . . . Hic modus loquendi Caiet. alio tendit: nam praesenti instituto parum, aut nihil conducit. Profecto, quia si rerum essentiae aeternae dicuntur ob eam causam, quia aeternitate continentur praesentes: eodem pacto existentiae dicerentur aeternae, et omnia futura contingentia. Nam isthaec(sic) omnia in aeternitate contenta, ab aeterno praesentia sunt Deo in se" (*In I Sum. Theol.*, q. 10, a. 3, 156a). See the position of Francisco Araújo in my article "Francisco Araujo, O.P., On the Eternal Truths," in *Graceful Reason: Essays in Ancient and Medieval Philosophy Presented to Joseph*

Considerable care, then, is called for in order to recognize that Zumel's purpose here is not to disavow the eternal truth of essential propositions *in intellectu Dei*, but to criticize the failure of his adversaries to recognize the eternal truth of contingent propositions *in intellectu Dei*. He is, however, unyielding, up to this point, in his rejection of any eternal truths *extra intellectum divinum*.[44]

In keeping, then, with that ongoing rejection of his adversaries' position on eternal essences, however modified, Zumel continues to reaffirm that, since there were neither three nor four, prior to creation there was no seven. *Quatuor et tria sunt septem*, then, is not perpetually true.[45] Further, not unlike Suárez, Zumel states that, if essences are eternal as to the connection of predicates with subject, then one must heed that a connection obtains between connected terms. But there are no such connected terms extant *ab aeterno*, in keeping with his adversaries explicit disavowal of eternal essences. Hence, there can be no connections *ab aeterno*.[46] Still further, that connection of subject and predicate was either a real, extramental connection or a mental, intellectual one. It wasn't real, for there was nothing *extra Deum*. It was, then, mental and intellectual. No other mind than the mind of God, however, is *ab aeterno*, nor is there any other understanding *ab aeterno*, not only of essential truths, such as *Homo est animal rationale*, but of contingent truths as well.[47] Prior to their creation, things were *in potentia* and not only as to their essences but as to their essential connections, such as

---

Owens, C.S.S.R., ed. L. P. Gerson (Toronto: Pontifical Institute of Mediaeval Studies, 1983), 401–17.

44. See Zumel's *tertia conclusio* in note 50 below where it remains to be seen whether the move to accommodate the *modus loquendi Dialectici* is meant to reject what has gone before.

45. Zumel, *In I Sum. Theol.*, q. 10, a. 3, 157b–58a: "Antequam Deus visibilia saecula constitueret, neque erant quatuor, neque erant tria: ergo non est perpetuae veritatis illa, Quatuor et tria sunt septem."

46. Ibid., 158a: "Tertio, si verum est quod rerum essentiae sunt aeternae, quantum ad connexiones praedicati cum subjecto, sic argumentor: connexio est connexorum: sed ab aeterno nulla extabant, quae connecterentur: ergo ab aeterno non potuit esse ista connexio."

47. Ibid.: "Quarto: Ista connexio praedicati ad subjectum, cum dicitur, Homo est animal rationale; aut erat realis, aut mentalis, aut intellectualis. Realis non erat: quia tunc nihil erat extra Deum: ergo erat mentalis, et intellectualis: at tunc nulla mens aut intellectus fuit, nisi divinus, qui non solum intelligebat hominem esse animal rationale, verum et contingentia omnia: ergo, etc. Quinto sic disputo: Istae connexiones, quae a contrariis auctoribus defenduntur ut essentias rerum velint esse aeternas, vel erant ab aeterno aliquid, aut nihil: Si aliquid: ergo praeter Deum aliquid est aeternum; et ita non essent essentiae a Deo creatae: quod est alienum a fide. Si autem erant nihil: ergo non aeternae, Et confirmatur. Quoniam ista connexio aut est praedicati cum subjecto; et tunc non erant praedicata, neque subjecta; quia nihil erat creatum aut erat rei cum re, ut animalis rationalis cum homine?"

Homo est animal rationale. For Zumel, if the copula expresses the truth of a proposition, as noted above, then *Homo est animal rationale* is not *ab aeterno*, save *in intellectu Dei*. For truth is in an intellect and there is no eternal intellect save that of the deity.[48]

While there is very little in Zumel's first two conclusions with which Francisco Suárez can disagree, except to remove Scotus from the shadow of Henry of Ghent's perspective,[49] the somewhat startling formulations found in Zumel's third conclusion are another matter, as will become clear. Opening on a cautionary note, Zumel acknowledges that his third conclusion is probable and that he is reluctant to reject the teaching of the contemporary *Dialectici* and to preclude their common mode of teaching and discussing. Such an accommodation to the contemporary *modus loquendi Dialecticorum* apparently involves no capitulation to the perspective of the contemporary metaphysicians previously rejected, even though his language appears to go beyond his prior insistence upon the eternal essences with their eternal, essential truths only within an eternal intellect. For Zumel now contends that, though the essences and quiddities are not eternal *secundum se*, nevertheless, essential propositions, wherein subjects neither can be nor be understood without the predicates of those propositions, are perpetually true, just as he has maintained all along. However, his next concessions to the contemporary *modus loquendi*, which will bestir Suárez's critical responses, allow that such essential propositions are true in virtue of an intrinsic truth *(veritate quidem intrinseca)* such that they are true *ab aeterno* intrinsically and not true eternally merely because they happen to be *in intellectu aeterno Dei*.[50] It is just such a formulation as this that will cause Suárez and then Descartes, in turn, as we will see, to make the point that such truths are not eternally true because God eternally

---

48. Ibid.: "Sed neque hoc (istae connexiones quae a contrariis auctoribus defenduntur) potest esse verum, quia tunc neque homo erat, neque animal erat, neque rationale: ergo sicut ab aeterno res tantum erant in potentia, ita tantum habuerunt essentiam in potentia: ergo connexio, Homo est animal rationale; actu non erat, sed potestate, sicut caetera omnia. Ex qua doctrina satis liquet quod si verbum (est) dicat veritatem propositionis, in hac propositione, Homo est animal, tunc hominem esse animal, non est ab aeterno, nisi in intellectu Dei. Probatur, quia verum est in intellectu: sed ab aeterno non est alius intellectus nisi divinus: ergo."

49. See DM, d. 31, s. 2, nn. 1–2; 26:229; and d. 31, s. 3, n. 2; 26:233.

50. Zumel, *In I Sum.Theol.*, q. 10, a. 3, 158a: "Tertia Conclusio probabilis (ne doctrinam et communem loquendi modum huius aetatis rejiciamus, et Dialectici praecludamus viam loquendi et disputandi) sit, quod quamvis rerum essentiae et quidditates aeternae non sint secundum se, caeterum propositiones, in quibus praedicatum concipitur in ratione subjecti, quando subjectum nec potest esse, nec potest intelligi sine praedicato illius propositionis; sunt perpetuae veritatis, veritate quidem intrinseca: et non solum dicuntur verae ab aeterno, eo quod inveniuntur in intellectu aeterno Dei."

knows them; God knows them eternally because they are eternally true.[51]

Recalling his previous point about contingent truths as true *ab aeterno in intellectu Dei*, Zumel reaffirms that the contingent proposition, *Antichristus erit*, is true *ab aeterno*, but, in contrast to necessary essential truths, it is not so in virtue of an intrinsic truth since the predicate belongs contingently to the subject. Any eternally true, contingent proposition is eternal because, *Deo ita disponente, ut Antichristus futurus est*, such propositions are then perpetually true *in aeterna mente Dei*.[52] A further contrast indicates that contingent truths involve a copula which joins subject and predicate, but always in relation to some temporal difference, while Zumel maintains that the necessary, essential truths are propositions in which the verb is "absolved from time," as the Logicians say.[53]

Zumel establishes his third, and alleged to be *probabilis*, conclusion with three "persuasive" considerations, prefaced once more by two observations.[54] In his first suasive offering, Zumel repeats his previous point against his adversaries on the existential import of necessary, essential propositions. *Existentia rei ad extra* is not required for their truth and intelligibility since we can have an admittedly genuine *scientia* of nonexistents, such as of the aforementioned rose-in-winter.[55] Further-

---

51. For Suárez, see note 84 below. For Descartes, see note 94 below.
52. Zumel, *In I Sum. Theol.*, q. 10, a. 3, 158a: "Volo dicere quod haec propositio Antichristus erit, ab aeterno est vera. Quae sane non est vera intrinseca veritate, eo quod praedicatum contingenter convenit subjecto: sed quoniam Deo ita disponente, ut Antichristus sit futurus, illa perpetuo fuit in aeterna mente Dei."
53. Ibid.: "Reliquae vero propositiones perpetuae veritatis, veritate intrinseca dicunt aeternae veritatis, praeterquam quod sunt verae in intellectu Dei: quia praedicatum dicit habitudinem necessariam ad subjectum ex natura terminorum, et ex natura rei. Quare in his propositionibus, verbum absolvitur a tempore, ut dicant Dialectici: quia non unit in ordine ad aliquam temporis differentiam. Hanc conclusionem tenet D. Thom. de veritate q. 1 art. 5 ad 11 et Henricus Quodlib. 10 q. 3 et Herbeus Quodlib. 3 q. 1 et Soncinas, 9 Met. quaest. 5, Albertus Magnus lib, de Causis cap. 8 et in Postpraedicamentis cap. 9."
54. Ibid., 158a–b: "Antequam hanc assertionem propugnemus, observare oportet quod esse aliquid significatum, nihil ponit reale: sicut esse visum non dicit ens reale, sed ens rationis. Quare ad veritatem propositionis significantis aliquid, sufficit quod extrema sint in aliquo esse apprehenso ab intellectu, per se loquendo. Observa etiam quod esse, tribus modis accipitur. Uno modo quatenus dicit actum essendi, sive existentiam. Alio modo accipitur esse, quatenus dicit esse essentiale et quidditativum: et sic locuti sunt Philosophi quando dixerunt quod definitio indicat esse rei. Tertio, accipitur esse pro veritate propositionis: et in hoc sensu ista propositio. Homo est animal rationale, dicitur habere esse perpetuum et aeternum, ac proinde non requiritur quod eius extrema existant. Quoniam nec esse accipitur pro essentia neque pro existentia: sed solum pro veritate propositionis, sicut iam diximus. Unde sequitur quod rerum essentiae antequam existant aliquatenus vocari possunt entia, si sumatur ens reale, quatenus distinguitur contra ens fictitium."
55. Ibid., 158b: "His iam positis persuadetur conclusio, primo: Nam si existentia rei

more, Zumel notes explicitly that classical texts, which Suárez will use polemically against the *moderni theologi*, afford confirmation for his espousal of propositions like *Rosa est flos* as necessary, even with no roses actually existing.[56] For his second suasive argument, Zumel indicates, again, that the truth of *Homo est animal rationale* depends upon *existentia rei* or does not. If not, his point is granted that, in the absence of any actually existing men, such propositions are true. Anyone who insists that truth does depend upon *existentia rei* must face the fact that *existentia* (in contrast to *essentia*) is that by which something is constituted as contingent *(quo contingenter se habere)* and/or that by which a thing can be otherwise *(potest aliter se habere)*. How, then, can such a contingent *existentia* be the cause of such an immutable, necessary truth?[57] Zumel, then, reaffirms that it is plainly the case that, though the essences of things are not endowed with any *esse extra Deum*, still, those essential propositions *(propositiones enuntians essentias)* are perpetually true.[58] Finally, in his third suasive support for his third conclusion, again not unlike a similar gambit on Suárez's part, Zumel emphasizes the fact that a conditional proposition of the sort *Si Socrates currit, Socrates movetur*, or *Si Petrus est homo, est animal rationale*, posits nothing in existence and is thus true *ab aeterno*, whether anything exists or not.[59]

In evaluating Zumel's perspective herein, it is important to note at the outset that, contrary to what I will take to be Suárez's somewhat tendentious and polemical use of Zumel's texts, there is no evidence of

---

ad extra requiritur ad veritatem propositionis, sequitur quod nihil est scibile, nisi quando existit. Patet consequentia. Quia nihil est scibile, nisi verum: sed consequens est falsum, quia de non existentibus habemus scientiam, ut de rosa hyeme."

56. Ibid.: "Et propterea Divus Aug. 2 de Libero arbi. cap. 8 et 4 super Gen. ad literam cap. 7 inquit, quod tam necessaria est huiusmodi propositio, Rosa est flos, etiam rosa non existente, quod nihil potest extra Deum ipsum esse aut magis verum, aut magis necessarium."

57. Ibid.: "Secundo persuadetur: Quoniam haec propositio, homo est animal rationale, vel pendet quantum ad suam veritatem ab existentia rei, aut non? Si dicas quod non pendet a rei existentia: habeo intentum, quod seclusa existentia creaturarum illa est vera, Homo est animal rationale. Si vero dicas veritatem illius propositionis pendere ab existentia rei. Contra: Nam illud, per quod res potest aliter se habere, et quo contingenter se habet, et non potest esse causa alicuius veritatis immutabilis, et necessariae: sed existentia rei est id, per quod res se habet contingenter et mutabiliter: ergo veritas huius propositionis, Homo est animal rationale, non pendet ab existentia ipsius rei."

58. Ibid.: "Et ita constat plane, quod licet rerum essentiae non habeant aliquod esse extra Deum: verum propositiones, quae enuntians essentias, sunt perpetuae veritatis."

59. Ibid.: "Tertio persuadetur: Quoniam conditionalis nihil ponit in esse: ergo haec consequentia est bona seclusa omni existentia rei. Si Socrates currit, Socrates movetur, Si Petrus est homo, est animal rationale. Sed qua ratione istae consequentiae sint bonae et verae rebus non existentibus, sequitur quod ab aeterno rebus non existentibus fuerunt bonae et verae: sed huiusmodi consequentiae bonae fuerunt ab aeterno in virtute istarum propositionum, Currere est moveri; Homo est animal rationale: ergo tales propositiones sunt verae ab aeterno, et perpetuae veritatis."

any disenchantment on Zumel's part with Thomas Aquinas's position on the eternal truths as eternally so in an eternal intellect. Nor is there any disavowal of St. Augustine's position on the eternal truth of necessary, essential propositions in the absence of existing things, again contrary to Suárez's account.[60] What I trust we have come to see is that, when Zumel states, in his second conclusion, that a proposition such as *Homo est animal rationale* is not eternally true and, in response to any attempt to insist that such eternal truths are so in the eternal mind of God, responds *hoc nihil est*, he is not rejecting Thomas Aquinas's position. He is rejecting, however, the position of Capreolus and his followers in the Thomist tradition who, following Henry of Ghent, have tried to sequester the eternal, essential truths based upon an eternal *esse essentiae* forthcoming from God by way of an exemplary causality by claiming an intramental eternity, *in intellectu aeterno Dei*, at the same time that they fail to acknowledge the intramental eternity of contingent truths. But as we have seen, Zumel is equally disenchanted with the likes of Sylvester of Ferrara, Soncinas, and Báñez who have criticized the Henry of Ghent/Capreolus perspective on the issue of eternal, uncreated essences, opting instead for eternal connections between subject and predicate. They, too, fail to acknowledge the eternity of existential truths.

II

There is no question that Suárez is well aware of the Henry of Ghent/Capreolus tradition espousing the exemplary causality of eternal essences endowed with *esse essentiae*, attended by necessary, essential, eternal truths, as well as the efficient causality of *esse existentiae*. He has confronted it head-on in section 2 of his 31st Disputation and criticized it in a negative fashion not unlike that of Zumel.[61] Moreover, while allowing his adversaries to challenge (but not in any serious fashion, in Suárez's eyes) his solution to the status of the essences of creatures prior to creation, Suárez not only recapitulates the Henry of Ghent/Capreolus perspective with arguments reminiscent of those listed by Zumel, but, in responding to these arguments, also reaffirms his rejection in a fashion not unlike that of Zumel.[62]

In addition to this recorded dissatisfaction with the shortcomings of the Henry of Ghent/Capreolus perspective, Suárez is very much aware

60. See note 56 above and note 73 below.
61. DM, d. 31, s. 2; 26:229–32.
62. Ibid., n. 6; 26:230: "Contra hanc tamen veritatem objiciuntur nonnulla quae parvi momenti; sed ut omnibus satisfaciam, indicabo illa."

of the ongoing attitudes of the Salamancan *Thomistae* in the matter of essences, their eternal, necessary truth, and existence and its distinction from essence in creatures (especially the advocacy of a Scotist solution to this issue by some Salamancan *Thomistae*) and their separability.[63] As his discussion in section 12 of his 31st Disputation amply manifests, Suárez is aware that the separability of essence and existence, a fundamental indicator to the *Thomistae* of the real distinction between the essence and the existence of creatures, had caused a good deal of vexation among the Salamancan *Thomistae*.[64] As a very convincing case in point, even though Suárez is persistently reluctant to cite the names and sources of his contemporary adversaries in keeping with the ongoing practice, it is clear that he is aware of Zumel's very statement on this issue of the separability of essence from existence when he cites the position of Zumel, along with Zumel's own qualifying adverb, *forte*, that God can conserve a created essence outside its causes and *extra nihil*, without any existence.[65] There should be little doubt, then, that Suárez knows Zumel's text.

On the occasion, then, of confronting the issue of the separability of essence and existence, given his denial of any real distinction between an actual essence and its actual existence and his affirming of their real

63. Ibid., s. 1, n. 11; 26:227: "Secunda sententia est, esse creatum distingui quidem ex natura rei, seu (ut alii loquuntur) formaliter, ab essentia cujus est esse, et non esse propriam entitatem omnino realiter distinctam ab entitate essentiae, sed modum ejus. Haec opinio tribuitur Scot. in 3, dist. 6, quaest.1; et Henric., Quodl. 1, q. 9 et 10; de quorum sententia postea dicam. Eamdem opinionem tenuit Soto, I Phys., quaest. 2, et in 4 Sent., dist. 10, quaest. 2; et nonnulli moderni eam sequuntur." For the puzzlement of some of the Salamancan Thomists, such as Vitoria, Soto, and Cano, on this issue, see Zumel, *In I Sum. Theol.*, q. 3, a. 4, 91b–92a: "Secunda opinio est Scoti 3 d. 6 q. 1 asserentis, quod quamvis esse et essentia non sunt duae realitates, sed una et eadem res in genere rei; nihilominus distinguitur ex natura rei. . . . Secundo docet Scotus, quod esse et essentia distinguuntur realiter modaliter, tanquam intrinsecus modus rei. . . . Haec sententia est probabilis, et plurimi crediderunt esse sententiam D. Tho. Ita docuit Magister Vitoria, Soto, et Cano." For more on this, see Kennedy, "La doctrina de la existencia," 5–71; and my article, "Suárez, Historian and Critic of the Modal Distinction between Essence and Existence," *The New Scholasticism* 36 (1962): 419–44. On the issue of separability, see the following note.

64. DM, d. 31, s. 12, nn. 1–37; 26:283–94.

65. Ibid., n. 1; 26:283: "Ultimo potest quis excogitare essentiam creatam ita separari a propria existentia, ut sine illa et sine alia, quae munus ejus suppleat, in rerum natura conservetur, et hoc etiam modo (quod mirabile est) dicunt quidam moderni expositores, 1 p. quaest. 3 art. 4 (licet sub particula *forte*), posse Deum conservare essentiam creatam extra suas causas, absque ulla existentia." See Zumel, *In I Sum. Theol.*, q. 3, a. 4, 95a: "Sic dico quod est necessaria et intrinseca dependencia essentiae ab existentia: quare non valet, Distinguuntur realiter: ergo potest unum sine altero conservari. Dico secundo quod forte Deus potest conservare essentiam sine existentia formali reali superaddita essentiae, per manutenentiam Dei. In quo casu illa essentia esset in rerum natura extra nihil, prout nihil distinguitur contra ens, quod dicit actum existendi: non tamen illa essentia esset in genere existentium formaliter proprie."

identity, with merely a logical or conceptual distinction,[66] Suárez has to acknowledge the consequences of his position on that identity of actual essence and actual existence. That is, Suárez has to grant, and does so, that when actual existence ceases, so too does any actual essence.[67] With these actual essences reduced to the status of *nihil*, as he stated at the outset of section 2,[68] Suárez is now no longer in the initially enviable position of leveling devastating criticisms at the shortcomings of his adversaries. Rather, he is now quite plainly vulnerable to the counterattacks of those adversaries in the Henry of Ghent/Capreolus tradition who, as noted above, espouse the cause of *scientia* as dealing with eternal essences and their eternal, necessary truths. In their eyes, smarting from Suárez's initial critique, the position of the *Doctor Eximius* undermines the very possibility of any genuine *scientia:* the *scientia* of *nihil* is no *scientia*.[69] Suárez's victory over his Salamancan adversaries, then, is at best Pyrrhic. It is this very thrust, forthcoming from the Henry of Ghent/Capreolus tradition against him, with which Zumel has had to contend.

It is clear, then, that Suárez is aware of the rejection of the Henry of Ghent/Capreolus tradition, not only on the part of Soncinas and others among the *Thomistae* noted in section 2 of the 31st Disputation, but also on the part of some of the Salamancan *Thomistae*, such as Zumel.[70] For, when he reopens the issue of the eternal truths in a more definitive way than in his abbreviated response in section 2, rather than a direct confrontation of what he can only appreciate as an obvious *reductio ad absurdum* of the alleged consequences of his own position, Suárez deftly turns his adversaries' argument back upon those among the Salaman-

66. DM, d. 31, s. 1, n. 13; 26:228; and d. 31, s. 6, nn. 13–24; 26:246–50.
67. Ibid., s. 12, nn. 34–37; 26:293–94.
68. Ibid., s. 2, n. 1; 26:229: "Principio statuendum est, essentiam creaturae, seu creaturam de se, et priusquam a Deo fiat, nullum habere in se verum esse reale, et in hoc sensu praeciso esse existentiae, essentiam non esse rem aliquam, sed omnino esse nihil."
69. Ibid., s. 12, n. 38; 26:294: "Occurrit tamen statim trita difficultas superius tacta, sectione 1, prima ratione primae opinionis. Quia si, ablata existentia, perit essentia, ergo propositiones illa in quibus praedicata essentialia de re praedicantur non sunt necessariae, neque perpetuae veritatis; consequens autem est falsum, et contra omnium philosophorum sententiam. Quia alias omnes veritates circa creaturas essent contingentes, unde non posset de creaturis esse scientia, quia haec solum est de veritatibus necessariis. Sequela probatur, quia si, ablata existentia, essentia nihil est, ergo nec est substantia, neque accidens, et consequenter neque corpus, neque anima, neque alia hujusmodi; ergo nullum essentiale attributum potest de illa jure praedicari."
70. DM, s. 2, n. 2; 26:229: "Cujus sententiam (Henricus) impugnant etiam Thomistae, ut patet ex Hervaeo, Quodl. 11, q. 1; et Soncinat. 9 Metaph., q. 4; et recentioribus D. Thom. expositoribus, 1 part., q. 10, articulo tertio, q. 46, art. 1. Quanquam a sententia et modo loquendi Henrici non multum discrepit Capreolus, in 2, dist. 1, quaest. 2, art. 3, ad quartum argumentum Aureoli contra quartam conclusionem . . ." See Zumel in note 32 above.

can *Thomistae*, whence it comes, by choosing to chronicle the position of certain *moderni theologi*, one of whom is Francisco Zumel.[71] What better way to bring his adversaries up short, especially on behalf of an opportunity for salutary reflection on their part, and especially, too, when their critical *reductio ad absurdum* is off the mark. It is not the first time, in the course of this disputation, that Suárez attempts deliberately to focus on certain anomalies in the perspective of his opponents in order to silence or redirect their suspected hypercritical, if not hypocritical, tendencies against his position. Rather than being victimized by what amounts to a misinterpretation of his perspective, Suárez wishes his adversaries among the Salamancan *Thomistae* to become more sensitive to the doctrinal unanimity of their own school and then, especially in the case of the *moderni theologi*, to the internal consistency of their perspective.

In light of the above analysis of Zumel texts, it is difficult to deny that Suárez, in adverting to the response of the *moderni theologi* to the charge that genuine *scientia* is threatened by any denial of any actual eternal essence, is referring to Zumel's rejection of the actual, eternal essence of the Henry of Ghent/Capreolus tradition. The justice of Suárez's recapitulation, however, is another matter.

Suárez is certainly aware of Zumel's second conclusion, because he alludes to its content. Suárez is also aware of Zumel's disenchantment with the metaphysicians of his day who wish to disclaim actual, eternal essences at the same time that they embrace a metaphysics of the eternal, essential truths. But while Suárez, for his own purposes, chooses to emphasize, not only Zumel's opposition to contemporary, but to ancient metaphysicians as well, by making it appear that, for Zumel, essential propositions become true at that time when things come to be, not unlike contingent truths, he fails to acknowledge that Zumel is opposed to a metaphysics of the eternal truths as *extra intellectum divinum*.[72] Further, Suárez also chooses to place Zumel in opposition as well to the Patristic tradition represented by St. Augustine,[73] but again

---

71. DM, d. 31, s. 12, n. 39; 26:294: "Propter hanc difficultatem [cited in n. 69 above], quidam moderni Theologi concedunt has propositiones creaturarum non esse perpetuae veritatis, sed tunc incipere verae esse cum res fiunt, et veritatem amittere cum res pereant, quia (ut Aristoteles dixit), *ab eo quod res est, vel non est, propositio vera vel falsa est.*" For Zumel on this, see note 41 above.

72. See notes 30, 46, and 50 above.

73. DM, d. 31, s. 12, n. 39; 26:294: "Verumtamen haec sententia (modernorum theologorum) non solum modernis philosophis, sed etiam antiquis contraria est, imo et Patribus Ecclesiae; dicit enim Augustinus, 2 de Libero arbitrio, c. 8 . . . et in eodem sensu dicit lib. 4 Geneseos ad litter., c. 7. . . . Similiter Anselmus. in dialogo de Veritate, cap. 14, ex professo comtendit, veritatm harum enuntiationum esse perpetuum, neque destrui, etiamsi res ipsae destruantur."

fails to recognize that Zumel has explicitly embraced the Augustinian perspective which insists upon eternal truths in the absence of any extant things.[74]

Suárez is also apprised, because he chronicles it, of Zumel's further dissatisfaction with any attempt to locate the eternity of essential truths within the eternity of the divine intellect, while failing to acknowledge at the same time that contingent truths as well are eternal *in aeterno intellectu Dei,* the long-standing shortcoming of Capreolus, Henry of Ghent, and their followers.[75] However, even though Zumel's texts contain no indication whatsoever that he is, in any fashion, contradicting any position explicitly espoused by Thomas Aquinas, Suárez is not of a mind to report this in any explicit fashion. Rather, he goes out of his way to document carefully wherein the *moderni theologi* take issue with a number of Aquinas's explicit texts. What better way to rebuke and rebuff his adversaries, the *Thomistae,* than to highlight an alleged disagreement with the texts of their master, especially when those adversaries have saddled Suárez with a misinterpretation of his own position and its untenable consequences. In doing so, Suárez is oblivious to the very significance of the contention of the *moderni theologi* which he has chronicled, to the effect that both essential, necessary truths as well as existential truths are eternal *in intellectu divino*—a salutary advance over Capreolus's position and a clear acknowledgment of what amounts to an orthodox position.[76]

The same tactical intention to embarrass his adversaries is sustained and extended to the substance of Zumel's third conclusion wherein he addressed the differences, *intra divinum intellectum,* between the eternal, essential truths and the eternal, contingent truths. In addressing the same issue himself, however, Suárez uses it to emphasize an internal inconsistency between Zumel's second conclusion, in the abbreviated, self-serving version found in Suárez's account, and Zumel's third conclusion. He does this by pointing out, as Zumel did, that the essential truths are *in intellectu divino* such that they cannot not be in it and are accordingly necessary *sine suppositione*.[77] The contingent truths, while

---

74. See note 56 above.
75. DM, d. 31, s. 12, n. 40; 26:294–95: "Nec satis est, si quis respondeat cum D. Thom. 1 p., quaest. 10, art. 3, ad 3, q. 16, art. 7, ad 1 et quaest. 1 de veritate, art. 5, ad 11, et art. 6, ad 2 et 3, destructa creaturarum existentia, has enuntiationes esse veras, non in se, sed in intellectu divino. Quia hac modo non solum hujusmodi enuntiationes, in quibus attributa essentialia praedicantur, sed omnes etiam accidentales seu contingentes, quae verae sunt, habent veritatem perpetuam in intellectu divino."
76. See notes 42 and 43 above. See also A. Maurer, "St. Thomas and Eternal Truth," *Mediaeval Studies* 32 (1970): 91–107, esp. 106.
77. DM, d. 31, s. 12, n. 40; 26:295: "Quod si dicas esse differentiam, quia, licet omnes

always *in intellectu divino*, are there only on the supposition they would be at some time.[78] As Zumel had noted above, the former truths involve no temporal considerations, while the latter obviously do.[79] In view of this, Suárez can only remark that such a distinction *in intellectu divino* between the essential and the existential truths cannot fail to add to the alleged shortcomings of the *moderni theologi*.[80] For, as noted, Suárez had reported their position in such a way as to saddle them with the conclusion that essential propositions are no different than existential ones in that each begins to be true at the time when things come to be—a position contrary to both ancient and contemporary metaphysicians as well as to Augustine and Anselm. In light of the fact, then, that essential truths for Zumel involve no temporal consideration, Suárez wonders how Zumel can have it both ways and reconcile the fact that, in the one instance, essential propositions are true because such-and-such a subject will be at some point in time and, in the other instance, essential propositions are true regardless of whether such-and-such a subject will be at some future time.

Suárez believes he has to remind Zumel that, consistent with Zumel's own third conclusion, even if God had not ordained anything to come to be in time, He would know the eternal, essential truths for what they are, necessary, atemporal and true absolutely, in abstraction from any temporal consideration, altogether unlike contingent truths.[81] Again, Suárez wants it recognized that Zumel cannot have it both ways, with eternal, necessary, atemporal, true essential propositions strikingly different from contingent truths in the instance of his third conclusion, while, in the case of his second conclusion, essential propositions, given

---

sint perpetuo in intellectu divino, non tamen cum eadem necessitate; nam illae veritates, in quibus praedicatum essentiale tribuitur subjecto, ita sunt in intellecto divino, ut non potuerint non esse in illo, unde sunt simpliciter necessaria, et absque ulla suppositione; . . ." This characterization, "et absque ulla suppositione," of the necessary, essential truths cannot be understood to apply to Suárez's own position. Suárez himself has repeatedly insisted on the conditional necessity of the essential truths in DM; see d. 31, s. 2, n. 8; 26:231; and d. 31, s. 12, n. 45; 26:297. See my article "Suárez on the Eternal Truths Pt. I," 80, esp. n. 65.

78. DM, d. 31, s. 12, n. 40; 26:295: ". . . at vero aliae contingentes, licet semper fuerint in divino intellectu, non tamen cum absoluta necessitate, sed solum ex suppositione quod in aliquo tempore futurae essent; . . ."

79. See notes 52 and 53 above.

80. DM, d. 31, s. 12, n. 40; 26:245: ". . . si hoc (inquam) dicatur, inde magis confirmatur et augetur difficultas contra praecedentem sententiam, . . ."

81. Ibid.: ". . . tum quia etiam si Deus statuisset ut nil in tempore fieret, nihilominus cognosceret illas esse veras; tum etiam quia non solum sunt verae ab aeterno, quatenus de futuro enuntiari possunt in ordine ad tempus, sed simpliciter et abstrahendo ab omni differentia temporis, et in utroque valde differunt a veritatibus contingentibus, quae solum in ordine ad existentiam pro aliqua differentia temporis veritatem habent."

Suárez's deficient description, are on a par with contingent propositions in that the former, as the latter, have truth only in relation to some temporal instant.

Finally, Suárez takes further steps to remind Zumel that, in light of his third conclusion, he had insisted on the intrinsic eternal truth of essential propositions such that these essential truths are true *ab aeterno* intrinsically and not true only because they happen to be *in intellectu aeterno Dei*.[82] To Suárez's reading, this can only mean one thing for Zumel's perspective, and Suárez says as much—that such truths are not true because they are known by God, but rather, they are known because they are true. Otherwise, Suárez contends, no reason could be given why God would know them necessarily to be true, as He does. For if their truth derived from God Himself, as it does for the eternal, contingent truths in Zumel's third conclusion, it would do so voluntarily, in terms of the divine will, and not necessarily.[83] Further, in the instance of the eternal, essential truths, it is not the divine practical, but the divine speculative intellect that is at issue. This latter presupposes the truth of its object and does not produce it. So Suárez dutifully chronicles the conclusion, previously and strikingly embraced by Zumel, that the essential truths are not only true *ab aeterno* as they are *in intellectu divino*, but are true *ab aeterno secundum se* and prescinding from the eternity of the divine intellect.[84]

When Zumel's text is brought to bear upon Suárez's consideration of the *moderni theologi*, it must be seen that, far from espousing Suárez's own position in any manifest fashion, Suárez is rendering an historical account, however just it may or may not be, of the perspective abroad in Zumel. Suárez's chronicle, of course, is also deliberately critical as well, but the criticisms have to do with the internal consistency of Zumel's perspective. So, in light of this extended analysis of Zumel's position, to claim outright that the criticisms derive from Suárez's own perspective is, I fear, to beg the question. In short, Suárez's own po-

---

82. See Zumel's position in note 48 above.

83. DM, d. 31, s. 12, n. 40; 26:295: "Rursus neque illae enuntiationes sunt verae quia cognoscuntur a Deo sed potius ideo cognoscuntur, quia verae sunt, alioqui nulla reddi posset ratio, cur Deus necessario cognosceret illas esse veras; nam si ab ipso Deo provenerit earum veritas, id fieret media voluntate Dei, unde non ex necessitate proveniret, sed voluntarie."

84. Ibid.: "Item, quia respectu harum enuntiationum comparatur intellectus divinus ut mere speculativus, non ut operativus; intellectus autem supponit veritatem sui objecti, non facit; igitur hujusmodi enuntiationes, quae dicuntur esse in primo, imo etiam quae sunt in secundo modo dicendi per se, habent perpetuam veritatem, non solum ut sunt in divino intellectu, sed etiam secundum se, ac praescindendo ab illo."

sition cannot be derived from his text dealing with the *moderni theologi*, but must be sought elsewhere.[85]

III

It remains to be seen how all this late Scholastic give-and-take involves Descartes. I think it is safe to say that it is rather unlikely that Descartes would be directly aware of the puzzling facets in the position of Francisco Zumel. On the other hand, it is equally unlikely that Descartes was ignorant of Francisco Suárez and his *Disputationes Metaphysicae*.[86] Further, Descartes could in no way be unaware of a vigorous, ongoing tradition maintaining in his day a doctrine of eternal, uncreated essences endowed with eternal truths expressed in necessary, essential propositions. Indeed, a late Scholastic metaphysician, Martin Meurisse (d. 1644), chronicles the revival of the doctrine of Henry of Ghent at the University of Paris around the end of the sixteenth and the beginning of the seventeenth centuries. Its exponents claim that an essence is still real *ab aeterno* in the absence of existence. Such essences only become actual when they begin to *exist* in a temporal fashion.[87]

In addition, this very doctrine is espoused by Arnauld as he raises issues about Descartes' *Meditations* in the Fourth Objections.[88] Caterus, in the First Objections, embraces a doctrine of uncaused, eternal, essential truths, which he erroneously takes to be what Descartes is defending in his remarks, in the Fifth Meditation, on "the immutable and eternal essence of a triangle."[89] In turn, it is this very text which Gassendi interprets in the same fashion, unaware of Descartes' insistence (in his *Letters to Mersenne* in the 1630s) upon created eternal truths and

---

85. It seems to me that the analyses of Marion (*Sur le théologie blanche de Descartes*, 43–69) must be completely overhauled in light of the above texts of Zumel.

86. See T. J. Cronin, "Eternal Truths in the Thought of Suarez and Descartes," *The Modern Schoolman* 38 (1961): 272: "These very texts which Descartes cites are found in the *Disputationes Metaphysicae* of Suarez, a work which Descartes certainly had at hand when he was replying to the objections of Arnauld. If, in truth, the *Disputationes* are the source of the doctrine of the eternal truths which Descartes opposed, then as early as April–May of 1630 Descartes either had the *Disputationes* in his possession or else knew its doctrine so thoroughly that he could cite it almost *verbatim*."

87. M. Meurisse, *Rerum Metaphysicarum libri tres ad mentem Doctoris Subtilis* (Paris, 1623), I, q. 15, 173: "Haec sententia (Henrici) abhinc aliquot annis revixit apud alios, alioquin doctos et subtiles, in Universitate Parisiensi, qui existimantes realitatem essentiae non peti ab existentia; sed essentiam esse realem seclusa existentia; consequenter docuerunt essentias reales ab aeterno, licet tantum in tempore coeperint existere."

88. *Oeuvres de Descartes*, ed. C. Adam and P. Tannery (Paris: J. Vrin, 1969), *Obj. 4ae*, 7:212.5–13.4.

89. Ibid., *Obj. 1ae*, 7:93.8–16, esp. 14.

created eternal essences.⁹⁰ Nor should the philosophers and theologians of the Sorbonne, in the Sixth Objections, especially in light of Meurisse's remark about the revival of Henry of Ghent's position at the University of Paris, be overlooked.⁹¹

In further addition to this evidence internal to Descartes' systematic *opera*, there is Mersenne's position, which has to be reconstructed because his letters to Descartes have been lost.⁹² It would appear that Mersenne, while never claiming any independence from God on the part of the eternal essential truths, contrary to the claims of J.-L. Marion and a long-standing charge against Henry of Ghent made by Suárez, embraces the position of Henry of Ghent on the creative, exemplary causality of essence *ab aeterno* in contrast to the creative efficient causality of existence.⁹³ Just as Suárez before him, Descartes will reject these uncreated, but not uncaused, eternal essences and their attendant uncreated, eternal truths.⁹⁴ Moreover, while rejecting these actual, eternal essences of Henry of Ghent and his disciples, Descartes will extend his negative criticisms a step further to reject the uncaused and uncreated *essentia realis* and/or the *non nihil* of Suárez and many other Scholastics.⁹⁵ The God of Descartes is the actual creative, efficient

---

90. Ibid., *Obj. 5ae*, 7:312–21.
91. Ibid., *Obj. 6ae*, 7:417–18.
92. See P. Dear, *Mersenne and the Learning of the Schools*, 55.
93. P. Dear (ibid., 58) refers to a text of Mersenne which considers the divine essence as an infinite sun, the source of an infinite multiplicity of rays, one of which is eternal truth. Descartes is critical of this metaphor in one of his replies to Mersenne, 5 May 1630: ". . . or cette essence n'est autre chose que ces verités eternelles lesquel ie ne conçoy point émaner de Dieu comme les rayons du Soleil; . . ." (*Correspondance* [Paris: J. Vrin, 1969], I, 152, 4–6). In saying as much, Descartes is rejecting the exemplary causality of essence embraced by Henry of Ghent, Capreolus, and their followers, and, as Suárez, reducing it to God's creative efficient causality. See DM, d. 31, s. 6, n. 17; 26:247. For Dear's critique of Marion, see *Mersenne*, 58–61. For Suárez on Henry of Ghent, see DM, d. 31, s. 2, n. 2; 26:229.
94. *Letter to Mersenne*, 15 April 1630: "Mais ie ne laisseray pas de toucher en ma Physique plusieurs questions metaphysiques et particulierement celle-cy: Que les verités mathematiques lesquelles vous nommés eternelles, ont esté establies de Dieu et en dependent entierement, aussy bien que tout le reste des creatures. C'est en effait parler de Dieu comme d'une Juppiter ou Saturne et l'assuiettir au Stix et aus destinees, que de dire que ces verités sont independantes de luy" (*Correspondance*, I, 145, 5–13). In another early letter to Mersenne, 27 May 1630 (ibid., I, 152, 1–5), Descartes will insist: "Car il est certain qu'il est aussi bien Autheur de l'essence comme de l'existence des creatures: or cette essence n'est autre chose que veritez eternelles, . . ."
95. *Letter to Mersenne*, 6 May 1630 (*Correspondance*, I, 149, 21–150, 4): "Pour les veritez eternelles, ie dis derechef que *sunt tantum verae aut possibiles, quia Deus illas veras aut possibiles cognoscit, non autem contra veras a Deo cognosci quasi independenter ab illo sint verae*. Et si les hommes entendoient bien sens de leurs paroles, ils ne pourroient iamais dire sans blaspheme, que la verité de quelque chose precede la connoissance que Dieu en a, car en Dieu ce n'est qu'un de vouloir et de connoistre; de sorte que *ex hoc ipso quod aliquid velit, ideo cognoscit, et ideo tantum talis res est vera*. Il ne faut donc pas dire que *Si Deus non*

cause of both real, intramental essence (such as the intramental essence of "the immutable and eternal triangle") and extramental, actual essences.[96] For Descartes, prior to their creation, the essences of creatures are only extrinsically possible. They are possible only because God can create them.[97] However, with all this said and understood, the question of whether Descartes read the text of Suárez on the *moderni theologi* as expressing Suárez's personal position must be addressed. It appears to have been read that way in Suárez's own day in at least one instance.[98] We may never know if Descartes did, in fact, understand Suárez's text in this fashion. If he did, so be it, but that is scarcely any reason to acknowledge the historical accuracy of Descartes' judgment in light of the above analysis of Zumel's position.

Moreover, in light of that same evidence, the judgment of those Cartesian scholars who insist that Descartes was aware of Suárez's text on the *moderni theologi* and that he took it to be Suárez's own position, describing and rejecting it in his early correspondence with Mersenne, must be given rigorous reconsideration. There no longer appears to be any sound basis for accepting the historical accuracy of these claims by the Cartesian commentators dealing with this issue. The text in question is not a statement of Suárez's position, but his critical account of an adversary's position, that of the *moderni theologi,* one of whom is Francisco Zumel.

---

esset, nihilominus istae veritates essent verae; car l'existence de Dieu est la premiere et la plus eternelle de toutes les veritez qui peuuent estre, et la seule d'où procedent toutes les autres."

96. *Principia Philosophiae,* pt. 1, art. 24; 8:14: "Jam vero, quia Deus solus omnium quae sunt aut esse possunt vera est causa." See my article, "Objective Reality of Ideas in Descartes, Caterus and Suarez," *Journal of the History of Philosophy* (1990): 33–61, esp. 54–61.

97. See my article, "Descartes' Uncreated Eternal Truths," *The New Scholasticism* 56 (1982): 185–99, esp. 191–92nn22–23.

98. See Wells, "Francisco Araujo," 409n43 and 410n49.

13 Suárez, Nominalism, and Modes
STEPHEN MENN

I. INTRODUCTION: VARIETIES OF SCHOLASTIC REALISM

In trying to understand the Scholasticism of the Spanish and Portuguese "golden age," a first step is to distinguish the different schools, roughly corresponding to the different religious orders: if we first recognize the basic issues between the schools, we can then try to work out their histories. I will look at these schools to the extent that their differences emerge in metaphysics and in the theory of the categories. My main aim will be to elucidate the metaphysical program of what I will call "liberal Jesuit Scholasticism," and of its most important works, Fonseca's *Commentary and Questions on Aristotle's Metaphysics* (vol. 1, 1577; vol. 2, 1589; vols. 3–4 posthumously, 1604 and 1612) and Suárez's *Metaphysical Disputations* (1597). I will take my clue from Chauvin's *Philosophical Lexicon*, which says that "whatever the Peripatetics [i.e., the realists] explain by vulgar modes and vain dodges, the nominalists explain by connotations."[1] And indeed, while the nominalists reject the theory of modes, Fonseca invokes this theory on some occasions, and Suárez very systematically, to solve problems in their defense of realism against nominalism. The theory of modes is characteristic of Jesuit philosophy, and I will use it as a way to understand the differences between

---

1. Chauvin says more fully, "Whatever the Peripatetics explain by vulgar modes and vain dodges, the nominalists explain by connotations, so that while the *res* always remains entitatively the same, it really changes only extrinsically and connotatively" (Etienne Chauvin, *Lexicon Philosophicum*, 2d ed. [1713], s.v. "modus"). On Fonseca's chronology, see Joaquim Ferreira Gomes, "Pedro da Fonseca, sixteenth-century Portuguese philosopher," in *International Philosophical Quarterly* 6 (1966). The principal sixteenth-century sources I will cite are Soto's *In Porphyrii Isagogen, Aristotelis Categorias librosque de Demonstratione Commentaria* (1587; reprint, Frankfurt: Minerva, 1967); Fonseca's *Commentaria in Libros Metaphysicorum Aristotelis Stagiritae*, 4 vols. (1615; reprinted in 2 vols. (Hildesheim: Georg Olms, 1964); and Suárez's *Disputationes Metaphysicae* (hereafter DM), in his *Opera Omnia* (Paris, 1866), vols. 25–26 (reprinted in 2 vols., Hildesheim: Georg Olms, 1965). I will cite these, not by page numbers, but by books, chapters, disputations, questions, sections, and paragraphs as appropriate.

realism and nominalism, and between "liberal" Jesuit and "conservative" Dominican varieties of realism; this will lead me to a reconstruction of both the philosophical agenda and the formal structure of Suárez's *Disputations*.

The pioneer of what I am calling liberal Jesuit Scholasticism was a Dominican, Domingo de Soto; but Soto was an atypical Dominican, and his main influence was on the Jesuits, Toletus, then Fonseca and the *Conimbricenses*, then Molina and Suárez.[2] Among the Dominicans, by contrast, the authority of Cajetan and other standard commentaries on St. Thomas had imposed a conservative Thomist orthodoxy. Soto and Fonseca and Suárez are also Thomists in some sense. Unequivocally, they are realists. Soto says that "no one who is versed in Aristotle can deny universals *in rebus*"; when the nominalists do deny this, and conclude that the object of a science is only its mental propositions, Fonseca says that they are "showing themselves unworthy of the chorus of philosophers."[3] Even when Soto or Fonseca or Suárez agree with the

2. Soto was a pioneer, but no more: his treatments of the questions I will discuss are not nearly as thorough and satisfying as those of his successors, and on the crucial issue of whether there are distinctions intermediate between the real and the rational, he contradicts himself outright, as Suárez correctly protests (see note 10 below). I am not sure how far the ideas I cite from Soto are original to him: Soto studied at Paris and was part of a movement (including also Crockaert and Vitoria) turning away from the nominalism of their teachers (John Mair) toward Thomism (as Soto says, *In Isagogen, De Universalibus*, q. 1, "we were born among nominalists and raised among realists"); study of Crockaert and Vitoria might give a fuller context for Soto. In any case, Soto's background made him a less sectarian Thomist than he might otherwise have been. What I am calling the "liberalism" of the Jesuits, though characteristic of the Society for its first half-century or so, caused much controversy, and the Jesuits seem to have been told to retreat to a safer Thomism, especially on the burning issues of grace and predestination, but not only there. But the earlier Jesuit approach to philosophy and theology was faithful to the spirit of the Society, using its *libertas philosophandi* to reconstruct traditional teaching, serving the *utilitas* of the Church and preserving the peace of the faith, conforming with traditional authorities and drawing on whatever was serviceable in their teaching, but for the same reason avoiding the encumbrances of old sectarian quarrels.

3. "In reality, no one who is versed in Aristotle can deny universals *in rebus*. Whence Burley, who was a nominalist in his *Summulae*, and Paul of Venice, the eminent disciple of Gregory of Rimini, after they read [= lectured on?] Aristotle, could not *not* assert universals in the fashion of the realists. And Paul calls the contrary opinion, not that of the nominalists, but that of the Ockhamists, who he says are Heracliteans and Epicureans" (Soto, *In Isagogen, De Universalibus*, q. 1). (I know of no other evidence that Burley was ever a nominalist; the reference to Paul of Venice is probably to his *Isagoge* commentary, which I have not seen, and it is hard to assess without context: it might be a denunciation of nominalism, or an attempt to distinguish "true" nominalism from Ockham's position.) "Heracliteans" and "Epicureans" are old insults for the nominalists, traceable ultimately to Albert the Great ("Heracliteans" because the nominalists, being ignorant of any universals beyond the sensible things, deny that there is anything *in re* meeting the conditions for an object of science); on this see Zenon Kaluza, *Les querelles doctrinales à Paris* (Bergamo, 1988). Fonseca, at *In Met.* V, ch. 28, q. 2, s. 1, gives an account of nominalism as he understands it, connecting the old *nominales* mentioned by Albert

nominalists on some issue, they regard the nominalists as not-quite-respectable; they can say that the *sententia communis* of philosophers and theologians is that P, and yet that the nominalists believe not-P.[4] Within the *via realium*, although our philosophers are happy to reconcile Thomas and Scotus when they can (Soto says that Thomas and Scotus differ hardly at all on universals), they are far from the Scotism of the Franciscans. They are much readier to disagree with Scotus than with Thomas, and sometimes go to great lengths to save Thomas for their own position.[5] But our philosophers are separated from traditional Thomism by their acceptance of the authority of the Paris condemnation of 1277; thus they accept the voluntarist axiom that God can produce any creature in separation from any really distinct creature, and they use this axiom freely to derive consequences about existence and identity. Cajetan, by contrast, explicitly rejects this axiom;[6] and

---

and Thomas (i.e., Abelard) to the revived nominalism of Ockham, and explaining the connection with Heraclitus and Epicurus. Fonseca takes it as definitive of *Nominales* that "they think all sciences are concerned not with universal things (for they think there are none) but with common names for things" (s. 1); they thus "show themselves unworthy of the chorus of philosophers" (s. 2; cf. Cicero, *De Finibus*, I, 26, ejecting Epicurus from the chorus of philosophers). Soto and Fonseca give the same (false) account of why Ockham is called *venerabilis inceptor*, as the reviver and quasi-founder of the *via nominalium*.

4. Fonseca, at *In Met.* V, ch. 7, q. 5, s. 3, citing Avicenna's opinion that concrete accidental terms signify substances primarily and accidents only secondarily, says that this is "rightly rejected by almost everyone" (he cites no exceptions); Soto, on the same issue, speaks more frankly of "Avicenna . . . quem Nominales sequuntur" *(In Categorias*, ch. 5, q. 2). Suárez, after noting that the nominalists say quantity "is not a *res* distinct from material substance and qualities" (DM, ch. 40, s. 2, n. 2), says "contraria sententia est communis Theologorum et philosophorum" (n. 7).

5. On the question of universals, there are only two *viae*, the realist and the nominalist; "nor do I think it is necessary to distinguish *three* ways here, as a certain nominalist, our fellow-citizen, has recently done, since here and perhaps elsewhere we will see how little difference there is between St. Thomas and Scotus" (Soto, *In Isagogen, De Universalibus*, q. 1; William Wallace has identified this nominalist as Juan de Celaya, who wrote commentaries on Aristotle *secundum triplicem viam*, giving the Thomist, Scotist, and nominalist views). But none of our philosophers follow the distinctively Scotist positions on the transcendentals, on the six minor categories as extrinsically advening relations, and so on; only Fonseca makes a liberal use of the Scotist formal distinction, and even he does not go as far as Scotus. The most flagrant "saving" of Thomas is Luis de Molina's argument *(Concordia*, d. 49, n. 7) that Thomas cannot have thought the *scientia visionis* worked simply by the presence of things to God, since this has impious consequences, which a saint like Thomas could not have believed. But Fonseca complains *(In Met.* IV, ch. 2, q. 4, s. 3) about Soto and Vitoria dragging an unwilling Thomas into their own opinion positing a modal distinction between essence and existence—the view Fonseca himself supports. Fonseca is the most willing of our philosophers to distance himself from Thomas, and he is happiest aligning himself, as here, with the "Reales Scholastici"; Suárez works much harder at aligning himself with Thomas, and has much less sympathy with Scotus.

6. Cajetan, *Commentary on Being and Essence*, trans. Lottie H. Kendzierski and Francis C. Wade (Milwaukee: Marquette University Press, 1964), 190–91. Trombeta had

when his Scotist opponent cites another axiom from the condemnation of 1277, Cajetan replies (i) that since the condemnation was directed against the Averroists, it is unfair to use it against Thomas; (ii) that insofar as the condemnation affects Thomism, it was revoked when Thomas was made a saint; and (iii) that anyhow, the pope has endorsed Thomism, and the Scotists have a lot of nerve to use the authority of the Bishop of Paris against the authority of the Bishop of Rome.[7] When the Jesuits break with this reactionary brand of Thomism, and accept the voluntarist principles of 1277, they find it harder to refute nominalist arguments that draw on voluntarist principles. As we will see, they accept some particular nominalist theses, while continuing to defend realism against nominalism. In seeing this, we can see better what nominalism was, and how it was connected with voluntarism; and we can see how the Jesuits' attempt to be voluntarists without being nominalists led them to develop the theory of modes.

The conflict between *reales* and *nominales* had been basic to Scholasticism since the fourteenth century. The two sides knew full well who they were; but it can be difficult, among the many particular polemics, for us to recognize the defining theses of the two *viae*. (Even when a thinker *tells* us which issues were defining, we should be suspicious: he may be stating the issue in a way that favors his own side.) Although the *viae* had implications for metaphysics (and for physics and theology), they are originally schools of logic or (as we would say) semantics: the basic issues concern the signification of terms and the truth-

---

actually cited a much weaker form of this axiom, namely that "any absolute [i.e., non-relative] thing which is distinct and prior to another absolute thing can exist without that other without contradiction," (185); but even this (along with several other voluntarist axioms, all fairly weak, that Trombeta had invoked) is too strong for Cajetan. We will come back to this particular issue in section III below. By contrast, Soto (*In Isagogen, De Proprio*, q. 2), criticizing "Thomistas . . . inter quos est egregius Cajetanus" who deny that a *proprium* can be separated from its subject, says "God can supernaturally separate the accident, risibility, from its subject, and conserve either without the other; nor have I ever been able to doubt this proposition: for if they are distinct *res*, and neither is of the intrinsic quiddity of the other, then without doubt God can conserve one without the other." Báñez, in his commentary on St. Thomas's *Summa Theologiae*, I, q. 3, a. 4, Báñez's q. 2, considers and rejects the general axiom that of any two really distinct things [i.e., creatures] God can conserve either without the other; Báñez complains that this would imply the absurd conclusion that matter could exist without any form (which is what Trombeta had been trying to prove; Soto of course accepts this conclusion).

7. Cajetan, *Commentary*, 201–202 (replying to an objection at pp. 197–98): the immediate issue here is whether God can produce several intelligences in the same species without matter. St. Thomas maintains the (condemned) thesis that God cannot do this, since signate matter is the only principle of individuation within a species. The articles of the condemnation of 1277 are most readily accessible, in English translation, in *Medieval Political Philosophy*, ed. Ralph Lerner and Muhsin Mahdi (Ithaca: Cornell University Press, 1972), 337–54 (the articles relevant here are on p. 341).

conditions of propositions, not real universals or any other question of "ontological commitment." Ockham does claim that every being is an individual substance or individual quality; but the realist Suárez agrees that every being is really identical with some individual substance or individual quality or individual continuous quantity. This small difference in ontological commitment cannot be what makes the difference between the two *viae*.

Ontological commitment does come in, but as a consequence of semantics. A famous piece of nominalist propaganda puts the issue in a biased but effective way: "the realists are those who contend that things *[res]* are multiplied according to the multiplicity of the terms," whereas "those doctors are called nominalists, who do not multiply the things *[res]* principally signified by terms according to the multiplicity of the terms."[8] Against what they see as an absurd multiplication of *res*, the nominalists propose the radically simplifying theory that in any true judgment of the form "A is B," "A" and "B" must signify the same thing: this implies that a universal term ("man") or a concrete accidental term ("white") will signify not a universal or accidental being, but just the individual substances of which it is truly predicated. All Scholastic realists reject this nominalist theory of signification and predication: the realists say that in the sentence "A is B," the term "B" signifies, not the thing which is B, but the B-ness through which it is B: so "man" signifies humanity, and "white" signifies whiteness.[9] But

---

8. This is from the manifesto of the Parisian nominalist doctors of 1474, printed in Franz Ehrle, *Der Sentenzenkommentar Peters von Candia* (Münster, 1925), 322 (where I translate "signified," Ehrle prints "signatas"; perhaps we should read "significatas"—this is probably just a question of an ambiguous abbreviation). The doctors are echoing Ockham's remark that one source of the realist doctrine of relations is "[the tendency] to multiply beings according to the multiplicity of the terms, and [to assume that] any term has a *quid rei*, which however is erroneous and leads away from the truth most of all" (*Summa Logicae*, I, 51)—to assume that the term "X" has a *quid rei* is to assume that there is an account of X, and not simply an account of what the term "X" means and how sentences including it are to be expounded. It is a polemical exaggeration to say that the realists multiply *res* according to the multiplicity of the terms; the nominalist doctors go on to illustrate by claiming that "the realists say that the divine wisdom is divided [i.e., really distinguished] from divinity" (Ehrle, p. 322): this is false, and amounts to accusing the realists of heresy (the doctors also try to blame the realists for the Bohemian schism; p. 324). The doctors also suggest that the realists, through impatience or logical incompetence, fail to study the *proprietates terminorum*, and that this ignorance accounts for the realists' distinctive doctrine; this too is a slander. The doctors are being careful in speaking of things *principally* signified by terms, since for Ockham, although in a true sentence "A is B" (if the terms have, as usual, personal supposition), A and B must *principally* signify the same thing, they may have diverse *secondary* significations.

9. The realist view is thus that "white" signifies the same thing as "whiteness," differing only in *modus significandi*. This traditional doctrine is defended by Fonseca (*In Met.* V, ch. 7, q. 5, s. 3), and taken as obvious by Suárez (DM, d. 39, s. 1, n. 12). (There is an

this semantics need not commit the realists to "multiply *res* according to the multiplicity of the terms," as the nominalist caricature suggests. Indeed, almost all scholastic realists think that the common nature signified by a universal term (such as humanity) is not another *res* really distinct from its individuals, but is distinguished from them only in some lesser way. The Jesuits, however, make a further and more drastic ontological reduction, when they deny that the ten categories are nonoverlapping classes of *res*. While they must admit beings in each accidental category for the terms in the category to signify, they think that all accidents in the last seven categories are really identical with some substance or quantity or quality, and distinguished at most formally or modally.

The Jesuits were forced to this position, against more traditional realist views, by voluntarist arguments. Given the principles of 1277, a real distinction between a substance and an accident, or between two accidents, implies that either can exist without the other at least by God's power; and Ockham had exploited this principle to produce compelling arguments, in many cases, to show that the realist view of the categories would lead to absurdities. In many cases the Jesuits are forced by Ockham's arguments to admit that some kind of accident cannot be really distinct from substances or from some other kind of accidents; but they also have traditional arguments, based on realist semantic principles, to show that these different kinds of accidents must be more than rationally distinct. In defending a voluntarist and yet realist account of accidents, they are led to develop a theory of intermediate distinctions (against the Thomist thesis that all distinctions are either real or rational);[10] in particular, they are led to develop the theory of modes.

---

interesting discussion in Soto, *In Categorias*, ch. 5, q. 2: commenting on a passage [*Categories* 3b19] that said, in older Latin versions, that "white" signifies *solam qualitatem*, Soto points out that the Greek says rather *solum quale;* the text "is therefore not efficacious at proving that 'white' signifies only whiteness, although it is constantly being cited for this purpose, even by philosophers of better repute." Soto adds that this realist conclusion is true anyway, but is not at issue here. Suárez says the same, in his *Index in Metaphysicam*, VII.1.] Let me add, as a warning against reductionist readings of the realist-nominalist controversy, that the question whether "white" signifies whiteness has nothing to do with universals: if Socrates is white through a whiteness, it is an *individual* whiteness (universal whiteness is just the species whose individuals are individual whitenesses). Nor is it a question about whether there are abstract objects, i.e., objects named by abstract terms like "whiteness": the nominalists, like the realists, believe that there is a real accident of whiteness which is the formal cause of Socrates' being white, although the nominalists don't think this is necessarily entailed by the fact that "white" is a concrete accidental term.

10. Soto comes down on both sides of this issue (as Suárez complains; DM, d. 7, s. 1, n. 9): at *In Isagogen, De Universalibus*, q. 3, he rejects intermediate distinctions, and says

II. SCOTUS, OCKHAM, AND THE JESUITS ON RELATIONS OF UNION

To illustrate the difference between a classical realist position, the radical nominalist position, and the Jesuit restatement of realism, I will focus on one typical and highly controversial issue, the status of relations. The most important examples will not be *predicamental* relations (items in the *category* of relation), but *transcendental* relations of union.[11]

The *locus classicus* defending the reality of (some) relations, and their real distinction from absolute (non-relative) things, is Scotus's *Opus Oxoniense*, bk. II, d. 1, q. 5 against Henry of Ghent, who had said that no relation is a *res* other than its foundation, Scotus argues "nothing is really identical with anything without which it can really exist without contradiction; but there are many relations without which their foundations can exist without contradiction; therefore there are many relations which are not really identical with their foundation." These relations contrast with "relations of essential dependence," such as the relation of "passive creation" which a creature bears to God as its creator: since it would imply a contradiction for Socrates to exist without his relation of passive creation, Scotus concludes that Socrates' passive creation is not an accident inhering in Socrates and really distinct from Socrates, but is really identical with Socrates himself (it is still *formally* distinct from Socrates, since Socrates is an absolute thing and his passive creation is a relative thing). As relations which must be really distinct from their foundations, Scotus includes many familiar predicamental relations, such as Socrates' color-similarity to Plato; but he draws his most compelling examples from transcendental relations of union, and especially the relation of *inherence*.

Scotus argues, in particular, that "the separation of the accidents from

---

that as there are "only two kinds of beings, namely *entia rationis* and real beings, therefore neither are there more distinctions than the real and the rational"; but at *In Categorias*, ch. 5, q. 1, he wavers, and apparently admits an intermediate distinction between nature and *suppositum*, and perhaps also between essence and existence, and at ch. 7, q. 2, he gives in and posits a *distinctio formalis ex natura rei* between a relation and its foundation (in both places Soto seems embarrassed, and tries to suggest that the dispute is mostly verbal). (According to Suárez [DM, d. 31, s. 1, n. 11], Soto posits a modal distinction between essence and existence at *In Physicam* II, q. 2, and *In Sententias* IV, d. 10, q. 2; see *Francis Suárez: On the Essence of Finite Being etc.*, ed. and trans. Norman Wells [Milwaukee: Marquette University Press, 1983], 55nn53–54, confirming these references and correcting a misprint in the standard edition of Suárez.) Fonseca and Suárez have well-developed theories of the kinds of intermediate distinctions, which will be discussed below.

11. An excellent reference on the scholastic theory of relations is Mark Henninger, *Relations: Medieval Theories 1250–1325* (Oxford: Oxford University Press, 1989).

their subject in the Eucharist" shows that the relation of inherence, which the accidents of the bread bear to the bread, must be something really distinct from these accidents. For "if the same quantity of the bread remains which previously existed, and if its inherence in the bread is really nothing other than the quantity itself, then the quantity is united to the bread (or informs it) just as really now as before." Since we can form the judgment "the quantity inheres in the bread," by realist semantics there is *some* relation of inherence, namely, whatever the predicate "inheres" signifies; the question is whether this predicate just signifies the quantity itself, or whether it signifies a further *res* added to the quantity. Scotus's argument is straightforward: if the inherence were just the quantity, then, when the bread becomes the body of Christ and the quantity subsists without the bread, the quantity would continue to exist and so the inherence would also continue to exist; so the quantity would continue to inhere in the bread, contrary to assumption. This argument holds more generally for a wide class of relations of union: if A and B can both exist without being united, or even if A can exist without being united to B, A's relation of union-to-B must be something really distinct from A:

> If A and B compose AB, and if the union of these parts to each other is nothing other than these absolute things A and B, then when A and B are really separated, all the reality which belonged to the united A and B will remain; therefore [absurdly] the separated A and B remain really united.

If A and B here are bodies physically united, then it is obvious that they can exist without being united, and the argument works without any theological assumptions. Theology is needed if A and B are united in a less concrete sense, like matter and form or substance and accident: the example of the Eucharist shows that accidents can exist without their substances,[12] and voluntarist principles tell us in general that *whenever* A and B are really distinct, God can preserve them both separately.

---

12. This is a very common application of the condemnation of 1277: see the text of the condemnation in Lerner and Mahdi, *Medieval Political Philosophy*, 353nn196–99. Earlier writers (including St. Thomas) did of course accept the principle that, as is shown in the Eucharist, God can make an accident exist without a substance, but they did not use this principle systematically to derive consequences about the nature of accidents. Scotus's example of a subsisting accident is quantity rather than quality, because according to the realists it is the quantity which subsists after consecration, and the other accidents inhere in the quantity (the nominalists deny quantities apart from substances and qualities, and say that the qualities subsist after consecration). Scotus also cites another standard theological example, the union of the human nature in Christ to the person of the Word: here a nature, apt to subsist by itself, supernaturally becomes present in another *suppositum*, just as the Eucharistic accidents, apt to inhere in other things, supernaturally subsist by themselves.

Scotus thinks we could deny that such relations of union are really distinct from the united things only if we "shamelessly" denied the principle that "things one of which can remain without the other are really distinct";[13] and if we denied this, Scotus says, we would have no way to prove *any* real distinction, be it between Socrates and his whiteness, or even between Socrates and a stone. But Scotus's argument leads to serious difficulty. As Scotus recognizes, there is a threat of infinite regress: "it is argued that if a relation were a thing other than the foundation, there would be an infinite regress of relations; for if this relation is a thing other than its foundation, then by parity of reasoning that 'otherness' (which is a relation) will be a thing other than its foundation, and *that* otherness from *its* foundation, and so to infinity; but this is absurd." (Instead of the relation of otherness, the argument could be formulated for a relation's relation of *inherence* in its foundation.) But Scotus answers that he can avoid this infinite regress, since a relation's relation to its foundation is a relation of essential dependence, like the creature's relation to God; and a relation of essential dependence must be really identical to its subject, since the subject cannot consistently exist without it. Since a relation "cannot exist without its foundation (or without itself) without contradiction ... it cannot (without contradiction) exist without its relation to its foundation ... and so that relation by which it is related to its foundation will be identical with [the original relation] itself."

But in stopping the regress by maintaining that a relation cannot exist without its foundation, Scotus contradicts the principle that, for any two really distinct created *res*, God can preserve either without the other. Scotus is trapped: he has used the voluntarist principle that God can preserve an accident without its subject to argue that an accident's inherence in its subject must be a new *res* added to the original accident; but, by the same principle, since the inherence is really distinct from the original accident, God can preserve it without the original accident, and so, by the same argument, the inherence's inherence must be really

---

13. Scotus makes clear that this is a restatement of the major premise of the main argument that some relations are really distinct from their foundations, namely, "nothing is really identical with anything without which it can really exist without contradiction." Scotus recognizes that we could also avoid concluding that relations of union are really distinct from the united things, by denying that these relations are *res* at all. So first Scotus shows that these relations are not merely *entia rationis*, and then, interestingly, he argues against a solution close to what the Jesuits will say, that "although relations are not formally *entia rationis* but something outside the intellect and not identical with the foundation, still they are not *res* other than the foundation, but only proper modes of the *res*"; for, says Scotus, "although a *modus rei* may not be a *res* other than that *res* of which it is a mode, nonetheless it is not *nulla res*, just as it is not *nullum ens*, since then it would be nothing" (all quotes from *Opus Oxoniense*, II, d. 1, q. 5).

distinct from it. If Scotus's argument succeeds in proving that all relations "without which their foundations can exist without contradiction" are *res* distinct from their foundations, then it will also prove that there are infinitely many really distinct inherences in any given white bread. For any Scholastic, this conclusion is absurd, and gives ground for supposing that there is something wrong in the original argument.

We might try to solve the problem by restricting the scope of the voluntarist principle that God can preserve any one *res* without any other.[14] But for many Scholastics of the fourteenth century and after, this proposition is axiomatic, and any pleading for exceptions would seem to put both the Eucharist and God's omnipotence in question. If Scotus's voluntarism is preserved, perhaps it is his realist semantics that should be abandoned.

This is how Ockham argues when, discussing the category of relation in the *Summa Logicae*, he considers Scotus's arguments for the reality and real distinctness of relations, shows that these arguments lead to absurdity, and offers his nominalist semantics as the only way out. On Ockham's semantics, concrete, accidental terms like "white" or "father" primarily signify the things of which they are truly predicated, namely, those substances which are white or fathers; but in each category Ockham examines what these concrete terms *secondarily* signify or "consignify." Thus "white" secondarily signifies whiteness, since "white" means "something having whiteness," and the sentence "some man is white" is to be expounded as "some man exists and whiteness is in him." So although Ockham's semantics does not *force* him to admit abstract accidental beings, it *allows* him to admit such beings as secondary significata of concrete accidental terms. But he denies that there are real relations: he denies that "father" means "something having paternity," and he thinks that any such analysis leads to absurdity. Ockham gives a series of positive arguments for his view, but he also makes his point by considering realist objections, some drawn from Scotus.

Ockham considers the realist objection from relations of union: "it seems impossible, without the relation *[respectus]* of union, to explain

---

14. Scotus himself apparently tries to solve the problem by restricting the voluntarist principle to saying that if A and B are really distinct creatures, God can preserve A without B *unless* there is a relation of essential dependence of A on B. But this seems dangerously arbitrary: why should the inherence have an essential dependence on the whiteness, if the whiteness does not have an essential dependence on its subject, the bread? This will not satisfy any voluntarist philosopher or theologian in the spirit of 1277. Another possible solution, which Scotus perhaps adopts, is to restrict the principle to asserting the separability of *absolute* (i.e., non-relative) beings; if inherence is essentially relative (although it is not a predicamental relation), then this would block the regress. Once again, the restriction seems dangerously arbitrary.

how form is united to matter, or one part to another part in a continuum, or an accident to its subject, or a spirit to a bodily nature" (*Summa Logicae*, I, 51, obj. 9).[15] Even Ockham himself in an earlier work had seemed to be persuaded by this argument, and he had said that "if any relations [*respectus*] are to be posited, they are these: the union of the human to the divine nature [in Christ], the union of matter to form and conversely, the union of accident to subject, the union of one part of a continuum to another."[16] But in *Summa Logicae*, I, 51, Ockham replies that this argument, if it proved anything, would prove an infinite regress:

15. Chapter I, 51, is missing in some manuscripts of the *Summa Logicae*, and its authenticity has been questioned (see Boehner's introduction to his edition of the *Summa Logicae*, [St. Bonaventure: Franciscan Institute Publications, 1951], 1:x–xi; Boehner thinks that it is not by Ockham, but that its content is truly Ockhamist). It is probably a later addition, but the natural assumption is that it is an addition by Ockham himself; it goes beyond other things Ockham says, and there are minor tensions between it and other parts of the *Summa Logicae* (and more serious tensions with other works), but it represents a natural outcome of Ockham's earlier views on relations (which had been developing progressively throughout his career; see the following note), and is plausibly taken as Ockham's last word on the subject, although it is possible that it is by a disciple.

16. *Ordinatio*, I, d. 30, q. 4. Ockham's theory of relations develops from a more to a less realistic position (as he himself tells us in *Summa Logicae*, I, 49). *Reportatio*, II, d. 1, q. 1, is the earliest and most realist text; followed (sequentially?) by *Ordinatio*, I, d. 30; *Quodlibet* VI; the body of the *Summa Logicae;* and *Summa Logicae*, I, 51. (The *Reportatio* text also takes a much more realist position on the theory of predication than Ockham's mature writings: it admits that Socrates himself can be a subject of predication, and is willing to say that under some circumstances the copula, or the quasi-copula *inest*, signifies a *respectus actualis inhaerentiae*.) In the *Ordinatio* text Ockham says that all the arguments for positing real *respectus* in special cases turn on the principle that "it is impossible for contradictories to be verified simultaneously of the same thing except by the local motion of something, or the passage of time, or the production or destruction of something"; this gives far fewer real relations than Scotus wants, and on much narrower grounds (in the *Reportatio* text, Ockham's position may be closer to Scotus's). In the *Summa Logicae*, Ockham apparently denies all real relations, although I am not sure exactly how he would reply to the *Ordinatio* arguments. Henninger *(Relations*, ch. 7) and Marilyn Adams *(William Ockham* [South Bend: University of Notre Dame Press, 1987], ch. 7) think that Ockham's (mature) view is that natural reason alone would incline us to deny all real relations, but that faith forces us to admit real relations at least in a few exceptional cases, such as the Trinitarian relations and the union of the divine and human natures in Christ. This is possible (the *Summa Logicae* officially says only what Aristotle's view was, and avoids saying whether it is true or compatible with Christianity), but I doubt it: once we recognize that Ockham's view of relations developed, there seems to be no reason for thinking that he admitted theological exceptions at the time of the *Summa Logicae*, although he certainly admitted these (and others) earlier; the arguments of the *Summa Logicae* are absolutely general, and explicitly address the objection from the union of the natures in Christ. I suspect that Ockham by this time held radical theological views, including the denial that the persons of the Trinity are constituted by relations, but felt that he was involved in enough controversies (notably on the Eucharist) without taking up the defense of these positions too. Certainly later Ockhamists, notably Pierre d'Ailly, do take up these radical theses. All this needs further exploration.

The argument about matter and form, subject and accident, whole and parts, and spirits united to bodies, does not prove that there is some relative thing intermediate between the things which are united. For the same question will remain with regard to this intermediate thing: how does it compose a unity with the thing in which it is posited? Either by itself, and then by the same reason we should have stopped with the first things-to-be-united; or by some other union, and then there is an infinite regress. For let it be posited that this intermediate thing is separated (by whatever power) from the things-to-be-united, and then let it be united to them, as an accident to its subject: how, from being a non-united thing, does it [the intermediate thing] become a united thing? By another intermediate thing? Then the original difficulty returns.

This crucial point is Ockham's argument against Scotus's proposal that the accident of union is united to its subject by itself. "For let it be posited that this intermediate thing is separated (by whatever power) from the things-to-be-united, and let it be united to them"; this thought-experiment shows that the first relation of union can exist without its union to its subject, and so, by Scotus's principles, that the second union must be really distinct from the first union. Scotus can resist only by denying that God *can* preserve the relation of union separately from the things it unites; and Ockham thinks we cannot deny this once we have said that the union is really distinct from the things it unites.[17]

But what is Ockham's alternative? Will he "shamelessly" deny that "things one of which can remain without the other are really distinct," and accept the consequence that there is no way to prove any real distinction, between Socrates and his whiteness or even between Socrates and a stone? No: Ockham accepts the principle, but he says it does not imply that, if A can exist without being B, A must be really distinct from its B-ness; for there may be no B-ness at all. Since some whiteness may be inhering in this bread, even if there is no inherence, it is wrong to start asking what inherence (or any other union) is, and whether it

---

17. Something like Ockham's argument may have been anticipated by Peter Aureole (cited by Suárez, DM, d. 16, s. 1, n. 2 and n. 7, from Capreolus, *Defensiones*, II, d. 18, q. 1). Aureole certainly did *not* intend the proposition that Suárez initially takes him to intend, that "no accident is a *res* really distinct from the entity of the substance, but only a mode" (as Suárez says, this is blatantly inconsistent with the subsistence of the Eucharistic accidents); he must have meant what Suárez later suspects, that "an accident, whether or not it is a *res* distinct from its subject, is not distinguished *in re* from its actualization or inherence in its subject," because although the accident inheres (and although it is not essential to it that it inhere), the accident does not inhere through any further accident of inherence (as Suárez says at the end of n. 2, Aureole's arguments apply equally to all kinds of union). Suárez briefly reports three arguments of Aureole's in n. 7, of which the first involves God's absolute power to separate, and the third involves an infinite regress of accidents of union, but the information here is too scarce to decide how close Aureole's argument was to Ockham's.

is the same as or distinct from the things it unites. We should first ask how the word "inhering" signifies, and whether its signification involves such a thing as an inherence. The word "inhering" primarily signifies whiteness (and anything else that happens to inhere), just as "white" primarily signifies whatever happens to be white; the question is whether "inhering" also consignifies an inherence, as "white" consignifies whiteness. Ockham denies it: "inhering in the bread" signifies the whiteness, and consignifies *that it inheres in the bread*, but the only *thing* it consignifies is the bread, no "inherence," just as "father" signifies each thing that is a father, and consignifies *that it has begotten a child*, where the only *thing* consignified is the child, without any relation of paternity or action of begetting.[18]

Ockham's solution to the problem of inherence, and of relations in general, is not open to a Scholastic semantic realist. The realist must agree that, since some things inhere, there must be inherences; but then Ockham's argument shows that the inherence of an accident cannot be a *res* distinct from the original accident, and Scotus's argument shows that the inherence cannot be a *res* identical with the original accident. Caught in this dilemma, many Scholastic realists conclude that inherence and other relations of union are not *things [res]* at all, but only *modes [modi]* or ways things are *[modi essendi]*; and they try to satisfy both Scotus's and Ockham's arguments with the thesis that the inherence of an accident is a mode of the accident, distinct from the accident *ex natura rei*, but not *really* distinct from it *ut res a re*. These realists, including the Jesuits, are thus led to develop a theory of intermediate distinctions quite different from the Scotist theory of the formal distinction; this modal distinction coexists with the formal distinction in Fonseca, but wholly replaces it in Suárez.

It is impossible to say who invented the Scholastic doctrine of modes. The Scholastics had been talking about modes from the beginning, in broader and narrower senses; but only gradually do they distinguish a class of modes, modes in the strict and proper sense, that are not *res* or *entia*. Thomas had defined quality as *modus substantiae*, but (as Suárez says) this is *modus* in an improper sense, since qualities are typically *res* in their own right. But the scholastics also cite other *modi* or *modi essendi*, such as those by which a being is determined as infinite or finite, as belonging to substance or some other category, or as subsisting by itself

---

18. In *Reportatio*, II, d. 1, q. 1, Ockham implies that all consignification is consignification of *things*, and uses this against the theory of inherence that I take him to be endorsing later in the *Summa Logicae;* the *Summa Logicae,* by contrast, seems to presuppose irreducible consignification *that*. But these issues are delicate, and need further exploration.

or being *in aliquo* or *ad aliquid*. These ways of being, unlike whiteness, are not plausibly interpreted as beings in some accidental category, attaching to and modifying some other already constituted being; it seems better to say that the being-a-quality of some whiteness is not itself a being, at least not a being *other than* the whiteness and added to the whiteness, but that it originally constitutes the whiteness as the kind of being that it is.

These *modi essendi* first arise in the realist theory of signification. Since "white," for the realists, signifies the same *res* as "whiteness," they explain why "white" and "whiteness" are not interchangeable by saying that the concrete and abstract terms have the same primary *significatum* but different *modi significandi*, so that, in particular, "white" signifies whiteness *as being in a subject*. This *modus significandi* of the concrete accidental term corresponds to a *modus essendi* of the *significatum*, namely, its *inesse* in its subject; thus Henry of Ghent distinguishes the *modus praedicamenti*, the way of being consignified by a categorical term, from the *res praedicamenti*, the thing primarily signified by the term. But what ontological status does this mode or way of being have? Scotus insists that it must be a *res*, and Ockham says that it is nothing at all; but for Fonseca and Suárez, it is a clear example of a mode which must exist *in natura rei*, and yet cannot be a *res*, neither the *res* of which it is a mode nor any other *res*.

Suárez argues that there are such modes by taking the example of a quantity inhering in a substance, in which we can distinguish "the entity of this quantity" from "the union or actual inherence of this quantity with the substance":

The first we call simply the *res* of quantity . . . which remains and is conserved even if the quantity is separated from its subject. . . . The second, that is, inherence, we call the *mode* of quantity . . . [not in the extended sense in which quality is called a mode of substance, or in the sense of the "modes" by which being is contracted to its highest genera] . . . but because it is something which affects [the quantity], and as it were ultimately determines its status and its *ratio* of existing, but which does not add to it any new proper entity, but only modifies a preexisting entity. . . . For if it were an entirely new entity, it could not be the actual union between the quantity and the subject, but rather it would itself require something by which to be united to the subject and the quantity, just as the quantity required this inherence by which to be united to the subject. But if the inherence does not require another union or inherence by which to be united or to inhere, this is because it does not itself add a proper entity which would inhere and be united: it is only a mode, which is *per se* a *ratio* of union and inherence. A sign of this is that this inherence has such a mode of being that it cannot exist, by any power, without being actually conjoined to that form whose inherence it is. Numerically *this* inherence can only affect or be united to numerically *this* form to which it is attached: this mode of affecting is never found in those forms or *res* which have proper entities of their own. (DM, d. 7, s. 1, nn. 17–18)

Suárez does not explicitly say why, if the inherence were "an entirely new entity," it would "require something by which to be united to the subject and the quantity": the reason is that if the inherence were a *res*, it would be something created by God, and God could by his absolute power conserve this *res* in existence by itself; and so again we could distinguish the *res* of the inherence from its mode of inhering in its subject. But since inherence is just a mode, it is not properly created by God; it exists, not because God makes it, but because it is *the way God makes the* res *to be*, and it cannot exist except as belonging to this *res* (and so it is really identical with its own inherence). Since God does make some *res* united to other *res*, he must also incidentally produce their modes of union; and these modes cannot be *res*, since they can neither be the same *res* as, nor another *res* than, the *res* to which they belong.

Although Suárez uses the language of *res et modus praedicamenti*, his conception of the mode of inherence is importantly different from the semantic conception. For Henry of Ghent, whiteness is an accident because it has the mode of existence of an accident, namely, being-in, the mode of existence consignified by the concrete accidental term "white." But for Suárez, since an accident can exist (supernaturally) without inhering in anything, *actual* inherence cannot be the mode of being which determines whiteness as an accident; Suárez says instead that the mode of being which constitutes an accident (as necessary-existence constitutes God, and contingent-existence constitutes a creature) is *aptitudinal* inherence, the *tendency* to exist in another thing. The distinction between actual and aptitudinal inherence is not new. But what is new is that Suárez's argument for modes properly-so-called (that is, modes which are not themselves *res* and are distinct *ex natura rei* from the *res* to which they belong) applies only to actual and not to aptitudinal inherence: the argument works only when the *res* can exist either with or without its mode, and an accident cannot exist without the *aptitudinal* inherence that makes it an accident, just as God cannot exist without necessary-existence, or a creature without contingent-existence.[19] In-

---

19. The distinction between actual and aptitudinal inherence, and the special modal status of actual inherence, are clearly described in Thomas of Strasbourg (Thomas ab Argentina, fl. 1345), *In Sententias* IV, d. 12, whose voluntarist realism in some ways anticipates the Jesuits. Fonseca agrees with Suárez that actual inherence is distinguished from its *res* by a greater distinction than is aptitudinal inherence, or any of the other modes by which being is contracted to its inferiors (*In Met.* V, ch. 6, q. 6, s. 2). But Fonseca denies that these latter modes are distinct *ex natura rei*, not by applying Suárez's criterion

deed, Suárez (innovating) makes it the essential sign of a modal distinction that A is distinguished from B as mode from *res* just when A cannot exist without B, and yet B can exist without A.[20]

So Suárez is the "shameless" person of Scotus's fears, who denies that "things one of which can remain without the other are really distinct": Suárez admits that if B can exist without A, then A and B must be distinct *ex natura rei*, but he denies that they must be really distinct *ut res a re* (which is what Scotus means to assert). Scotus says that if this principle is denied, there remains no way to prove any real distinction, be it between Socrates and his whiteness or even between Socrates and a stone; but Suárez answers that the sign of a *real* distinction is *mutual* separability, and that *non-mutual* separability is the sign of a merely *modal* distinction. Indeed, if we admit (on realist semantic grounds) that there are relations of union, then we must distinguish one-way from two-way separability, and we must reject either Scotus's principle that one-way separability entails real distinction, or the voluntarist principle that real distinction entails mutual separability, to avoid the absurdities that come from supposing that things and their relations of union are *mutually* separable. Ockham does believe both that one-way separability implies real distinction, and that real distinction implies mutual separability, but for him this shows that there are no relations of union; for Suárez, the fact that there are relations of union shows that there is an intermediate distinction, marked by one-way but not two-way separability.

To put Ockham's result positively, he has shown that sometimes a thing A can be contingently B (A = whiteness, B = inhering), even though there is no B-ness which can exist apart from A. Since Ockham thinks that any B-ness distinct from A would be able to exist apart from A, he concludes that in these cases "B" does not signify any B-ness (inherence), but primarily signifies A (the whiteness) and consignifies or connotes some proposition (that it inheres in some subject). Suárez, as a realist, accepts that if A is called B, there is some B-ness through which A is B; and he answers the voluntarist objections against realism by allowing that B-ness may be neither an *ens rationis* nor a *res* (either a *res* distinct from A, or A itself), because it is a *mode* of A modally distinct from A *ex natura rei*. This is what Chauvin meant by saying that

---

of one-way separability (which he rejects), but because "*being* is not some nature which is contracted by these modes to the *summa genera*, which are entirely simple and irresolvable into other entities" (since being is said of its different genera only analogically).

20. Suárez, DM, d. 7, s. 2, n. 6; restated d. 47, s. 2, n. 9, against Fonseca. In Section III, I will contrast Suárez with his predecessors, including Fonseca, on the modal distinction and on its connection with separability.

"whatever the Peripatetics [i.e., the realists] explain by vulgar modes and vain dodges, the nominalists explain by connotations, so that while the *res* always remains entitatively the same, it really changes only extrinsically and connotatively." While *some* changes (Socrates, who was white, becomes black) are explained by the production or destruction of some *res* in their subject, other changes (this whiteness, which had inhered in Socrates, begins to subsist by itself) are not; and while Suárez explains these changes by the production or destruction of a *mode* of the subject, Ockham will say that a term ("inheres") which previously signified the thing (the whiteness) ceases to signify that thing, because of an extrinsic change in what the term consignifies.

III. SUÁREZ AGAINST FONSECA: MODES

Suárez shares with Fonseca, and with other voluntarist realists, the modal solution to the problem of relations of union. But Suárez goes beyond Fonseca, and far beyond earlier thinkers, in the way he develops the theory of modes. Suárez is unique, in particular, in taking the modal account of relations of union as a model for solving many of the difficulties of the realist theory of the categories. Suárez maintains that figures (in the category of quality), and all beings in the categories of action, passion, where, when, and position, are modes rather than *res*. He is responding here to voluntarist arguments, brought by the nominalists to show that there are no *res* in these categories, and thereby also to undermine realist semantics; here, as with relations of union, Suárez argues that realism can be saved if the beings signified by terms in these categories are modes rather than *res*. In these cases we can draw an instructive contrast, not simply between conservative realists, the nominalists, and the Jesuits, but also between the earlier Jesuit tradition (culminating in Fonseca) on the one hand, and Suárez on the other; and this contrast will bring out not only Suárez's development of Fonseca's ideas, but also his deep divergence from Fonseca's understanding of modes. We can take the case of figures to illustrate the issues.

Figures are, according to Aristotle, the fourth species of the category of quality; but a figure cannot exist without some extension or continuous quantity which is shaped in that way. Except for the nominalists (who deny that there are quantities distinct from the quantified substances and qualities), the Scholastics all agree that a continuous quantity is the immediate subject of which a figure is predicated; but they disagree about how the figure is distinguished from the quantity. Suárez notes that the figure cannot exist without the quantity, although the quantity can exist without the figure; so he infers that the figure is a mode of the quantity. (The quantity cannot exist without *some* figure, but this too is characteristic of the modal distinction: God can make a quantity without any other *res*, but he must make it *somehow*, that is, with some mode, for instance, of subsistence or inherence.) Suárez's solution here answers a nominalist challenge. Ockham argues that figure-terms, unlike terms in the other species of quality, do not consignify any qualities other than the qualified substance. Ockham's main argument is that, since a substance can become straight or curved merely by the local motion of its parts, without any *res* being added, no *res* other than the substance is needed to make it straight or curved; but this argument presupposes the voluntarist principle that God *can* move the parts without also producing any new *res*. As Ockham says, "if, by his absolute power, God were to separate every accident, both absolute and relative, from a substance disposed along a straight line, and if the parts of the substance were conserved in the same disposition, then the substance would still be straight, as before." Ockham concludes that "straight" signifies only a substance and its parts disposed along a straight line, since it signifies no other *res;* Suárez concludes that, besides the substance and its parts, it also signifies a *mode* or *way* in which these parts are disposed in relation to one another.[21]

Suárez's understanding of figures as modes of quantity contrasts sharply with Cajetan's conservative realist position. Cajetan's Scotist opponent (in arguing that matter can exist without any form) had cited the principle that any (absolute) *res* can exist apart from any other (absolute) *res* that are posterior to it; but Cajetan rejects this principle, citing the counterexample that quantity is "prior to the category of quality, especially to the fourth species, and nevertheless there can be no continuous quantity without figure."[22] Cajetan assumes that figure and quantity must be really distinct, because they belong to different categories or genera of being; and this assumption enables him to refute even very mild voluntarist theses. So the Jesuits, as voluntarists, must reject the thesis that items in different categories are always really distinct. Toletus, in a short and unresolved *quaestio*, says that the different categories of accidents may not all be really distinct, citing as problem-cases the distinction of figure from quantity and the distinction of a relation from its foundation; and in both of these cases, Fonseca answers that the two terms are not really distinct *ut res a re*, but only formally distinct *ex natura rei*.

21. The Ockham quote is from *Quodlibet* VII, q. 2. Ockham gives the same main argument in *Summa Logicae* I, 55, but without explicitly referring to God's absolute power.
22. Cajetan, *Commentary*, 191.

What is surprising, though, is that although Soto and Toletus and Fonseca share Suárez's concern to reconcile realism and voluntarism, and see the difficulty of supposing that (for example) figures are really distinct from quantities, none of them adopt Suárez's solution of saying that figure is only a *mode* of quantity; nor are they willing to say that items in the six minor categories, or in any other category, can be modes (although Fonseca agrees with Suárez about the status of *transcendental* relations of union). All Jesuit thinkers before Suárez seem to assume that figures, and all other predicamental beings, must be *res:* if figure cannot be really distinct from quantity, then perhaps it is only rationally or formally distinct; but they avoid saying that it is *modally* distinct from quantity, because this would imply that it is only a mode, and not properly a *res*.[23]

If we can understand this divergence between Suárez and earlier Jesuit scholasticism, we will understand a great deal about the program of the *Disputations*. In what follows, I will contrast Suárez with Fonseca, who sums up the earlier Jesuit tradition. Of the many earlier authors whom Suárez discusses, Fonseca is the closest to Suárez, in his general approach to philosophy and on many particular questions. It is easy to miss this affinity, since Suárez cites Fonseca rather infrequently, and often to disagree; but by pursuing some crucial references, and comparing the projects of Fonseca's *Questions on the Metaphysics* and Suárez's *Disputations*, we can see that Fonseca was in fact a model for the whole *Disputations*. Even so, Suárez's disagreements with Fonseca are important and systematic. In almost every case, Fonseca posits some distinction which Suárez thinks is too great: either Fonseca says that A and B are *formally* (and more than modally) distinct, and Suárez thinks they are only *modally* distinct; or Fonseca says that A and B are either *modally* or *formally* distinct, and Suárez thinks they are only *rationally* distinct. Questions about distinctions are fundamental to Jesuit metaphysics, and Suárez follows Fonseca in placing a systematic discussion of the grades of distinctions early on in his metaphysics, to be used in particular questions later on (Suárez DM, d. 7; Fonseca, *In Met.* V, ch. 6, qq. 6–7). For both Fonseca and Suárez, the crucial question is whether intermediate distinctions are to be admitted (and of what kinds, and on

---

23. On the six minor categories (action, passion, where, when, position, and habit), Fonseca accepts what seems to have been the usual Thomist solution (rejected by Scotus, and apparently by Cajetan, as insufficiently realist) that they are *res* extrinsically denominating the *res* of which they are predicated. Suárez accepts this for habit, where it is plausible (and he takes action to be a *mode* existing in the patient and extrinsically denominating the agent); but beings in the categories of passion, where, when, and position are modes intrinsic to their *res*.

what grounds and by what signs); both Fonseca and Suárez offer innocent reinterpretations of the old twofold division of distinctions into real and rational (which, as Soto says [*In Isagogen, De Universalibus*, q. 3], was good enough for St. Thomas and for everyone before Scotus), but they both deplore the Dominican attempt to erect this crude division into a dogma. Suárez cites Fonseca as his model for his own solution to the question of intermediate distinctions (DM, d. 7, s. 1, n. 19), but he also makes clear that he has disagreements with Fonseca. Suárez rejects any formal distinction intermediate between the modal and the real (explicitly against Fonseca, DM, d. 47, s. 2, nn. 7–9; cf. DM, d. 7, s. 1, n. 16); he also rejects Fonseca's "potential" distinction (DM, d. 7, s. 1, n. 23; cf. Fonseca, *In Met.* V, ch. 6, q. 6, s. 2); less obviously but more importantly, there is a basic difference in the ways Fonseca and Suárez are conceiving of modes, which will lead them to different answers to particular metaphysical questions.

After giving his reasons for introducing "modes only modally distinct from *res*," Suárez tries to find authorities who have recognized such modes. He can find some passages from earlier writers recognizing that the modes of inherence and subsistence have a special ontological status, but only Fonseca gives a systematic discussion of modes as such: "finally Fonseca, *In Met.* V, ch. 6, q. 6, s. 2, expressly posits these modes" (DM, d. 7, s. 1, n. 19). As Suárez reports, Fonseca distinguishes three kinds of modes: those "which are entities *ex se* distinct from others, like whiteness and sweetness"; those "which are not only not distinct entities, but are not distinguished in any way *in re*, but only by reason, from the things whose modes they are said to be, like the modes by which being is contracted to its inferiors"; and finally "those modes which *we* properly and by a special title call *real modes*, about which he thinks the same as what *we* have explained"—and indeed, Fonseca is clearly Suárez's source both for this tripartition of modes, and for the crowning of the third kind, the "modes only modally distinct from *res*," as modes "properly and by a special title."[24] But Suárez immediately adds that, although Fonseca has described the three kinds of modes correctly, Fonseca's examples are wrong. In the first class (of modes which

24. Suárez is closely paraphrasing Fonseca's descriptions of the first two classes of modes, in the paragraph from *In Met.* V, ch. 6, q. 6, s. 2, marked in the margin "tria genera modorum essendi." Fonseca notes that modes of the first and second kinds are *formaliter entia*, in the first case distinct "*ex natura rei*, and frequently even *realiter*, from the things of which they are *modi essendi*," and in the second case really identical with, and only rationally distinct from, their *res*. About the third kind of modes, Fonseca says that "even though they are distinguished *ex natura rei*, apart from any operation of the intellect, from the things of which they are *modi essendi*, they are not themselves *formaliter entia*, unless *ens* is taken in the broadest sense for whatever is not nothing."

are themselves distinct *res*), Fonseca cites not only whiteness and sweetness but also figure; "but wrongly, since [figure] affects [quantity] as a mode, and not as a *res* entirely distinct from it." Even in the third class of modes proper, "about which he thinks the same as what *we* have explained," Fonseca still "posits some examples that we find dubious, such as the existence of created *res*, and the mode by which a *res* is called necessary or contingent, and complete or incomplete." Although Suárez dismisses these modes as only rationally distinct from their *res*, they are in fact the *only* examples, besides actual subsistence and actual inherence, that Fonseca had cited for the third class of modes. If so many of Fonseca's examples are wrong, it seems likely that he and Suárez have different conceptions of the modal distinction, and are using different principles to classify modes into their three classes.

One clue is Fonseca's preferred description of modes as *"modi essendi,"* ways of being: *"modus"* is just an abbreviation for this phrase. (In Suárez, *"modus essendi"* is rare and vestigial: the important description is *"modus rei"* = *quod distinguitur modaliter a re*.) For Fonseca, the modes properly so-called are *modi essendi*, which are not *formaliter entia*, ways things exist, which do not themselves exist: the paradigmatic *modus essendi* is the actual existence of a created *res*, and existence does not exist, any more than whiteness is white (*In Met.* IV, ch. 2, q. 4, s. 4). Suárez tries to agree that "however his examples may fare, Fonseca says most truly that this mode is not properly a *res* or *entitas*, unless we use '*ens*' broadly and most generally for whatever is not nothing," but Suárez is at a loss to find a sense of *"ens"* in which a mode is *not* an *ens*. The best Suárez can do is to say that an *ens* is "what is something *ex se* and *in se*, so that it does not require entirely intrinsically and essentially to be always attached to something else," or, even more lamely, "what cannot be united to something else except by means of some mode distinct from it *ex natura rei*"; Suárez says that the imperfection of a mode is best shown by its failure to meet these two conditions (DM, d. 7, s. 1, n. 19). For Suárez, *separability* is the key to *res* and modes, and must be used to interpret any ontological concepts; for Fonseca, modes and the modal distinction cannot be defined in terms of separability (some modes-proper belong to their *res* contingently, others necessarily; *In Met.* V, ch. 6, q. 6, s. 2), but must be explained through primitive ontological terms. Any proper *ens* is an existing essence: following (ultimately) Henry of Ghent, Fonseca supposes that any real being has both an *esse essentiae*, by which it is eternally endowed with its essential attributes, and an *esse existentiae*, by which it exists in actuality outside its causes. When X actually exists, it exists in some way, so it has some mode or modes of being (including existence itself as the *ultimus modus intrinsecus* which actualizes the others; *In Met.* IV, ch. 2, q. 4, s. 2); these modes are not themselves *formaliter entia*, because they add no further *esse essentiae* to the *esse essentiae* of X.[25] If the modes themselves had *esse essentiae*, they would require some further *modus essendi* to be constituted as actually existing (the essence must either inhere or subsist, and so on), and there would be an infinite regress. As a mode does not have its own *esse essentiae*, neither does it have its own *esse existentiae*, since existence is the act of an essence; if a mode "exists," it does so only through the *existentia* of its *res*.

For Fonseca, we need these ontological concepts to interpret the theory of distinctions: in particular, they show how to distinguish an at-least-formal (formal or real) from an at-most-modal (modal or rational) distinction. As a real distinction is between two *res*, a formal distinction is between two *entitates* in the same *res*, where an *entitas* is whatever has its own *esse essentiae* and *esse existentiae*. Thus Fonseca says that predicamental relations "are distinguished from their foundation by a formal distinction, so that they all have their own peculiar *esse*, both *essentiae* and *existentiae*, distinct from the *esse* of the foundation"; whereas, if they were only modally distinct from the foundation, they would not add "any entity, to which a peculiar existence would belong, but only a pure *modus essendi* of this foundation" (*In Met.* V, ch. 15, q. 2, s. 5). Suárez, citing this passage, can make no sense of the ontological criterion that Fonseca appeals to. "In the first place," he says, "I do not perceive this distinction intermediate between the real and the modal" (DM, d. 47, s. 2, n. 8). If X exists *in natura rei*, either it can exist by itself, and then it is a *res*, or it logically requires to be attached to some Y, and then it is a mode of Y. Likewise, if X and Y are distinct *in natura rei*, either each can exist without the other, and there is "a wholly proper and rigorous real distinction," or one can exist without the other, but not conversely, and the distinction is modal; "there is no other way beside these two, since if each extreme is inseparable *in re* from the other, it will be a distinction of reason, and not *ex natura rei*" (n. 9). If X can exist when Y does not exist (or vice versa), then obviously the *esse* of X is not the same as the *esse* of Y; but if X and Y are inseparable, then Suárez sees no ground for supposing that they have different *esse*'s, or

---

25. Fonseca gets into odd binds denying that these modes are *entia:* at *In Met.* V, ch. 8, q. 6, on what a *suppositum* adds to a nature, he admits that what is added is a mode, but refuses to say that it is a *purus essendi modus*, "which has the *ratio* not of an entity, but only of a *modus essendi*," since to complete a substance it must itself be something substantial; he allows it to be called a *modus essendi*, because it is so called "by good authors"—only "not *pure*, but entitative and even substantial" (s. 4). This seems to be just an *ad hoc* evasion.

are in any way distinct beyond the way we conceive and signify them. Nor does Suárez see why Fonseca says that modes are not entities with their own existence: "as a mode is distinguished *in re* from the *res* whose mode it is, so it has some *esse* of its own, equally and proportionally distinct from the *esse* of that *res*"; and "as it is something existing *in rebus*, so it can be said to have some entity," less perfect than that of a *res* only because it is not self-sufficient (n. 8).

By Suárez's criterion of separability, a being and its existence are only rationally distinct: so for him it makes no sense for X and Y to be united by having the same *esse:* if the *esse* of X is the *esse* of Y, then X = *esse*-of-X = *esse*-of-Y = Y. For Fonseca, since the *esse* of X is the mode completing X's nature, it makes sense for X and Y to be modally distinct and to be completed by the same *esse,* so that the mode has no *esse* of its own. (For Cajetan, who thinks *esse* is *really* distinct from the *ens,* even two *really* distinct *res* can be united by having the same *esse.* This is how Cajetan explains the union of form and matter, and it allows him to say that matter cannot exist without form, since it has no *esse* of its own and exists only through the form's *esse.*) Conversely, because Fonseca conceives of modes as *ways things are,* and finds it intuitively obvious that these are ontologically different from existing entities, he accepts *esse* as a mode, even though it fails Suárez's test of separability (although Fonseca too uses the test of separability to refute the Thomist claim that a thing's *esse* is *really* distinct from the thing; *In Met.* IV, ch. 2, q. 4, s. 2).

Fonseca's ontological conception of modes explains why he does not use them, as Suárez does, to solve the problems of the realist theory of the categories. Since, for Fonseca, modes have no *esse essentiae,* they have no genera and species of their own, but belong reductively to the genus of their *res,* in the same way that an incomplete being like a human hand or a human soul has no species of its own, but belongs reductively to the species "man." Since the categories are genera of being, it follows that modes do not belong to categories *per se,* but belong reductively to the category of their *res* (*In Met.* V, ch. 7, q. 4, s. 1–2; q. 9, s. 2).[26] This, finally, is why figure cannot be a mode of quantity: because a figure is a quality, it has an *esse essentiae* of its own, different from that of its quantity, which belongs to a different genus. Figure is thus at least *formally* distinct from quantity (and the usual voluntarist arguments show

26. In these texts Fonseca primarily discusses the status of *existentiae,* then adds other *modi essendi* as an afterthought. At *In Met.* V, ch. 7, q. 4, s. 1, he claims to have the agreement of "all scholastics of any repute who have treated these things in detail" that *existentiae* are not *per se* in categories, but reductively in the category of their *res;* he apparently just assumes that this agreement will generalize to other *modi essendi.*

that it cannot be *really* distinct); for the same reason, a relation must be formally distinct from its absolute foundation (just as, for Scotus, Socrates must be formally distinct from his passive creation, because, although they are inseparable and really identical, one is absolute and the other is relative).[27]

One of Suárez's deepest departures from Fonseca, and from the entire older realist tradition, comes in a passage whose serene exposition gives no hint that Suárez is promoting a controversial teaching. Suárez is considering the difficulty that the division of created being into substances and accidents seems not to be exhaustive, since modes are not included in either division (difficulty raised at DM, d. 32, s. 1, n. 3; answered at nn. 13–19). Suárez first rejects two easy answers, first, that modes should not be included in a division of created *beings*, since "as these modes do not have an entity and reality of their own, they cannot be called beings, but modes of beings"; or, second (amplifying rather than contradicting the first answer), that although modes are not *per se* in any substantial or accidental category, they may be placed reductively in the category of their *res*. Although Suárez does not hint that anyone has actually said this, this was the view of Fonseca, and (as Fonseca assumes, probably rightly) of the entire realist tradition before him. But Suárez says that this is clearly wrong, since figure and *ubi* are accidents: these are only modes (figure of quantity, *ubi* of quantity or substance or whatever is primarily located), but they are in their own categories *per se*, and are not reductively or in any other way in the same category as their *res*. So Suárez gives a new answer: a mode of X may be placed reductively in the same category as X if it pertains to the "constitution and completion" of X (as do the union of form and matter, the mode of subsistence, and the mode of existence if there were one), or if it contributes to X's exercising its formal effect on its subject (as does the mode of inherence). But if the mode (like figure or *ubi*) comes to modify an X already "constituted and complete," then the mode is an accident of X (or a new accident inhering ultimately in X's subject), and it belongs *per se* in some accidental category of its own. For Fonseca, of

---

27. Action and passion do not have different *esse essentiae*, but this is because they are the same thing considered first as belonging to the agent and then as belonging to the patient. Fonseca's liberality on the formal distinction is quasi-Scotistic: X and Y are formally distinct whenever either contains a *ratio formalis* that the other does not, so that (for instance) the generic nature of animal (in Socrates) is formally distinct from the specific nature of man (in Socrates). (But Fonseca often says that X and Y are formally distinct even when X can exist without Y, although not vice versa, as in the case of quantity and figure; for Scotus this would be grounds for a *real* distinction.) Suárez sees no ground for different *esse essentiae* here: the generic nature in X is nothing *in re* distinct from X, just X compared to one or another class of things.

course, there are no modes of this kind: a mode is a *modus essendi* constituting some *res* as an actually existing thing; once the thing exists in some determinate way, anything further that attaches to it must bear some new *esse essentiae*, whether inhering in the *res* (like figure) or attaching from without (like *ubi*). But for Suárez, as the inherence of a quantity is just how it exists in its subject, so its figure is how it exists in its spatial limits; if we like, we can say that these hownesses add new *esse essentiae* to quantity, but they do not add anything that could be conceived (or could actually exist) without the quantity, and so they are merely modes.[28]

IV. SUÁREZ AND FONSECA: METAPHYSICAL PROJECTS

Although Suárez maintains against Fonseca that modes can be in the categories *per se*, and so that they can be beings *per se*, Suárez does not advertise this as a major criticism of Fonseca; he seems to think of it as a necessary technical correction within the overall program of Jesuit metaphysics. Suárez's official statement on the object of metaphysics (in DM, d. 1, s. 1) closely follows Fonseca (*In Met.* IV, ch. 1, q. 1): not only does he accept the same right answer as Fonseca *(ens reale per se)*, he also rejects the same six wrong answers (God; God and the separate substances; all substances [said to be Buridan's view]; all predicamental being [excluding God, who is substance only transcendentally]; all real being, whether *per se* or *per accidens;* and all being, whether *reale* or *rationis*). Both for Fonseca and for Suárez, this *ens reale per se* includes, precisely, all predicamental being plus God; but the shared formula covers an important correction, since *ens reale per se*, for Fonseca, meant *res* (or at least "entities"), while for Suárez it means both *res* and modes.

It seems reasonable to see Suárez's *Disputations* as a more efficient and systematic execution of the project of Fonseca's *Questions on the Metaphysics,* while recognizing that this efficiency has a doctrinal component in pruning away Fonseca's multiplications of realities and of ways of being. As is often said, the *Disputations* is the first Scholastic *Summa* of metaphysics, not as part of theology (as in Thomas's *Summae* and innumerable commentaries on the *Sentences*), not just studying a particular problem (like Thomas's *De Ente et Essentia*), and not following

---

28. Figure is, as Fonseca says, "a quality resulting from the termination of a magnitude" *(In Met.* V, ch. 14, q. 2, s. 3), and a magnitude cannot be terminated without being terminated in some particular way, or be terminated in some particular way without having a figure; so nothing beyond the mode of termination is needed. Modes of termination (like figure and subsistence), along with modes of union, are the most frequently cited, because least disputable, kinds of modes properly-so-called.

the order of a standard text (like the expositions or questions on Aristotle's *Metaphysics* by Scotus, Fonseca, the Thomists Soncinas, Javellus and Dominic of Flanders, and the Averroist Nifo).[29] Instead, Suárez lays out in d. 1 his conception of what metaphysics is supposed to be, and then pursues it systematically, treating first being-in-general (d. 2), then its attributes (dd. 3–11), its causes (dd. 12–27) and its kinds (dd. 28–53: first, infinite and finite being, then, the categories as kinds of finite being; d. 54 is an appendix on *entia rationis*, not because they are properly treated in metaphysics but for lack of anywhere better to treat them), and covering all traditional metaphysical questions in their place. But Fonseca's *Questions on the Metaphysics* (disregarding his Greek text, Latin translation, and expositions of Aristotle) are a close precursor to Suárez.

The first thing that strikes us about Fonseca's book is the staggeringly disproportionate bulk of his commentary on *Metaphysics* V, five hundred and seventy-one double-columned pages in the Cologne edition, occupying a whole volume by itself. The disproportion may be in part because Fonseca never finished his questions: the questions stop at the end of *Metaphysics* IX.5, although text and translation and exposition continue through the end of XII, and text and translation alone all the way to the end of XIV.[30] Still, Fonseca deliberately decides to leave some chapters of Aristotle's text (including the whole of III) entirely unquestioned, and to treat others very densely, as they give him occasion

29. But note that the *Summa philosophiae naturalis* of Paul of Venice (d. 1429) contains a section on metaphysics, which might be called a *Summa metaphysicae*, although it is nowhere near as comprehensive and detailed as Suárez's or as any of the great *Quaestiones in Metaphysicam*. This work would repay further study; a Renaissance edition (Venice, 1503) has been reprinted (Hildesheim: Georg Olms, 1974).

30. Books XIII and XIV were traditionally not commented upon, and are excluded from Suárez's index to the *Metaphysics*. The circumstances surrounding the posthumous parts of Fonseca's work are to me obscure. It seems (if we trust Fonseca's dedicatory letter, dated Coimbra, 4 days before the Ides of July 1597) that vol. 3 *(Metaphysics* VI–IX) was ready in Fonseca's lifetime; why was it not published until 1604, five years after his death? The editors explain neither this nor why the questions do not continue to the end; indeed, though Christopher à Govea, the Provincial of the Jesuit province of Portugal, includes a note ordering publication (and giving the Society's endorsement), he never explicitly says that the author has died. Now Suárez, according to his biographers, moved to Coimbra in May 1597, two months before Fonseca wrote this dedicatory letter; it was also in 1597 (but I don't know in what month) that the *Disputations* were published. What did Suárez and Fonseca know of the state of each other's work in 1597? Was there a competitive rush to publication (fostered by rivalries either personal or national)? Could this be why Fonseca was ready to let the commentary on books VI–IX go to press with the second half of book IX unquestioned? Contrariwise, could the publication of Suárez's *Disputations* have made publication less urgent? Or was Fonseca just too busy? He certainly had a great deal of Jesuit business in his hands—which he complains about in the dedicatory letter—and he was an old man with only two more years to live.

for asking the questions he wants to ask. The commentary on book V is three times as long as the commentary on book I and more than twice as long as the commentary on book VII, although the texts are all roughly the same length, and although Fonseca's questions on book V are confined to chapters 1–8, 10, 13–15, and 28, leaving chapters 9, 11–12, 16–27, and 29–30 unquestioned (and the question on chapter 10 is unconnected with the subject of that chapter). What is so wonderful about these chapters of *Metaphysics* V?

Part of the attraction of *Metaphysics* V is that it has no argument at all: it simply raises a series of metaphysical topics, and allows the commentator to investigate them as he likes. Fonseca takes *Metaphysics* V, along with the first two chapters of *Metaphysics* IV, as his occasion to write what is in effect a systematic *Disputationes Metaphysicae*, following his own conception of the subject to be treated, and having almost no connection with Aristotle's text.[31] *Metaphysics* IV, says Fonseca, is prefatory, asking about the subject of metaphysics (being; IV.1), then about the parts and affections of this subject (the inferiors of which being is predicated, and its transcendental attributes; IV.2), and then about the principles of the science (noncontradiction; IV.3); but *Metaphysics* V begins the "treatment of the *res*" themselves, dealing in three parts first with the causes of being (V.1–5), then with being itself and its parts (V.6–15), and finally with its affections (V.16–30).[32] Against Averroes and Thomas, Fonseca insists that the book is not concerned with the meanings of names, but with the *res* themselves which are analogous, picking out their primary instances and showing how the other instances are subordinated to them; so Fonseca feels free to develop a systematic metaphysics. In his questions on the first of the three parts of the book, and especially on chapter 2 ("cause"), Fonseca gives a systematic treatise on the causes. In the chapters on being, substance,

---

31. By contrast, Fonseca's treatment of *Metaphysics* VII is much more reactive to particular issues raised by the text (e.g., problems of the generation of animals). The commentary on book VII is disappointing, in part, because Fonseca had already treated the big issues in IV and V.

32. Fonseca, in his Prooemia to *Metaphysics* IV and V, distinguishes the preliminary *constitutio* of the science of metaphysics (establishing its subject, etc.) from its *tractatio*, its actual scientific work. Actually, Fonseca thinks the *tractatio* begins in *Metaphysics* IV.4–8 with the *tractatio* of the first *propositional* principle of metaphysics (the principle of noncontradiction, as opposed to *entitative* principles or causes), but he shows little interest in these chapters and writes no questions on them. Fonseca explicitly follows St. Thomas in his threefold division of *Metaphysics* V, which is accurate enough, except that the part on the "affections" is too loosely connected to be brought effectively under a single scheme (Fonseca in fact ignores this part of the book). But when, in his Prooemium to *Metaphysics* V, Fonseca criticizes Averroes for saying that this book is about names, he is also implicitly criticizing Thomas.

quantity, quality, and relation (7–8, 13–15), he develops everything that would normally be done in a commentary on the *Categories* (Fonseca devotes chapter 7, "being," to the division of being into the categories; since Aristotle says nothing about the six minor categories, Fonseca crams them into chapter 15, "relation"). In chapter 28, "genus," he does everything that would be done in a commentary on the *Isagoge* (192 columns on less than a column of text!), and he skips all the rest of the third part of the book. In chapter 6, "unity," he discusses the principle of individuation, and then the grades of distinction. Fonseca does not deal with the concept of being under "being," or with transcendental unity under "unity," because he has already turned *Metaphysics* IV.2 into a treatise on being and the transcendentals (truth and goodness are not mentioned in the text, but Fonseca crams them in along with unity), as he has turned *Metaphysics* IV.1 into a disputation on the object of metaphysics, omitting all the rest of *Metaphysics* IV (but for a solitary question on IV.3). Fonseca interprets *Metaphysics* V as applying these general principles to the particular kinds of being, to individuality and universality as kinds of unity, and to distinction as the opposite of unity.

Fonseca's questions on *Metaphysics* IV–V are thus very unlike Aristotle, and very much like Suárez's *Disputations*. Fonseca's *Metaphysics* IV.1 on the object of metaphysics corresponds to Suárez's d. 1; Fonseca's treatise on being in *Metaphysics* IV.2 corresponds to Suárez's d. 2, and Fonseca's treatise on the transcendentals corresponds to Suárez's dd. 3–11, except that Suárez inserts after transcendental unity the treatises on individuation, universals, and distinctions from *Metaphysics* V. Suárez then gives a treatise on the causes (dd. 12–27), corresponding roughly to Fonseca on the first part of *Metaphysics* V (though much more elaborate, and containing some material that would have been treated elsewhere, notably a treatise on God as first efficient cause); then a treatise on the kinds of being (dd. 28–53), corresponding to Fonseca on the second part of *Metaphysics* V (Suárez has a discussion of God at the beginning, dd. 28–30, but after that he, like Fonseca, follows the order of categories, raising similar questions although in greater detail); Suárez has nothing corresponding to the third part of *Metaphysics* V, but Fonseca says nothing about it either.

The point is not that Suárez was just copying Fonseca. Suárez's treatment is much more thorough than Fonseca's, and Suárez was his own man. But I think it is undeniable that Suárez framed his *Disputations* on the model of the order of questions to be treated in a commentary on *Metaphysics* IV–V, and that Fonseca was Suárez's most important model for what such a commentary would be; although questions from elsewhere are treated, they are all inserted into the framework, not of *Metaphysics* IV–V, but of what a *Quaestiones in Metaphysicam* IV–V had become.[33] Suárez himself thinks that these texts of Aristotle cannot bear the weight that has been put on them, and he proposes to break up Fonseca's weird marriage of systematic disputations with a scholarly presentation of an irrelevant text. Suárez prefaces to his *Disputations* an *Index Locupletissimus in Metaphysicam Aristotelis*, listing questions on each chapter of Aristotle's text, and saying where in Suárez's *Disputations* each question will be treated: this index is a key converting Suárez's work into a *Quaestiones in Metaphysicam*, for the "many" who will want such a thing. Suárez himself thinks this is a bad idea.[34] Suárez's comments in this index are occasionally caustic, and frequently designed to show the irrelevance of Aristotle's text. In particular, Suárez cites Averroes' remark (which Fonseca had disparaged) that *Metaphysics* V is about words, and has not yet started treating *res*. "So it happens that this book too, if we looked to Aristotle's intention, would be counted among the preliminaries to presenting the real science of metaphysics; but if we consider the custom of the commentators, they are accustomed to treat in it the *res* themselves which pertain to the object of metaphysics, especially all the categories, and the causes of being *qua*

33. Charles Lohr, in his chapter ("Metaphysics") in the *Cambridge History of Renaissance Philosophy*, ed. Charles B. Schmitt and Quentin Skinner (Cambridge: Cambridge University Press, 1988), cites some other interesting Jesuit precedents for Suárez's work, but (if we see past the artificial commentary form) Suárez is much closer to Fonseca than to any of these other models. Lohr notes the concentration on *Metaphysics* V, but fails to see its importance: he thinks that this book is about "philosophical terminology," and that discussions of substances and accidents must come from *Metaphysics* VII or XII. The Jesuit concentration on *Metaphysics* IV–V, and neglect of the bulk of the *Metaphysics*, indicate not that the Jesuits lacked interest in metaphysics, but that Aristotle's *Metaphysics* was not an effective vehicle for the kind of metaphysical issues that the Jesuits (for the purposes of Scholastic realist philosophy and theology) found it important to address. (Note, for example, that the division of being into actuality and potentiality plays no structural role for Suárez [as it does for Aristotle], and that Fonseca omits it from his questions on *Metaphysics* V.7, discussing only the division of being into the categories).

34. Suárez stresses the importance of an appropriate method or order of inquiry, "which I could scarcely (or not even scarcely) have observed, if, after the custom of the commentators, I treated all questions as they arise, incidentally and almost randomly, in the text of the Philosopher" (prefatory *Ratio et Discursus Totius Operis, Ad Lectorem*, first page); "but since there will be very many who will desire to have this whole doctrine applied to the books of Aristotle, both so that they can perceive which principles of so great a philosopher it relies on, and so that its use for understanding Aristotle himself may be easier and more useful, I have tried to serve the reader in this matter too, by means of an index that we have worked out, by which (unless I am mistaken), if it is read carefully, everything which Aristotle treated in the books of the *Metaphysics* can be both comprehended and kept in the memory; and also all the questions which are customarily raised in the course of expounding those books may be present to hand" (ibid., second page).

being, in the knowledge of which a great part of this doctrine consists."[35] This is as much as to say that Fonseca's *Quaestiones* on this book are already a *Disputationes Metaphysicae secundum ordinem rerum:* Suárez can simply liberate these questions from their artificial commentary-form.

On each of the topics raised in this way, Fonseca and Suárez pursue the realist agenda, which is not at all the agenda of Aristotle's *Metaphysics*. Typically, the questions arise from predication. Being is predicated of its inferiors, existence and subsistence or inherence of essences, the transcendentals of all beings, universals of individuals, form of matter, accidents of substances, relations of their foundations, figure and *ubi* of quantity: in each case, the realist must ask whether the predicate is something real or an *ens rationis;* if real, whether it is intrinsic or extrinsic to the subject; if intrinsic, whether it is really, or formally, or modally, or only rationally distinct from the subject. Again, if one *res* is predicated of many inferiors, by what kind of sameness is it the *same res* for all? Unless the realist can answer all these questions, there seems no escape from the nominalist conclusion that *res* are not predicated of *res*, that subjects and predicates are words, that in evey true predication the subject and the predicate signify the same *res*, and that the project of realist metaphysics is founded on a mistake.

The dilemmas that plague realism are in many cases founded on voluntarist principles. It is characteristic of Jesuit Scholasticism to confront this challenge head on, and to accept the voluntarist refutations of many real distinctions that had been proposed. What is distinctive of Fonseca is that he recognizes the systematic importance of the theory of distinctions, and the need for intermediate distinctions to solve these problems. The Dominican Soto, who shares Fonseca's principles, denies intermediate distinctions, because two were enough for Thomas; then, under pressure of argument, Soto admits a formal distinction in one place, a modal distinction in another, without ever saying how such distinctions differ or what are the principles for reasoning about them

---

35. Suárez's introductory comments on book V. Cf. on IV.2: "Although Aristotle in this chapter does not so much dispute about unity, as say that it ought to be disputed, it is customary to treat here all questions that pertain to unity, and indeed also to the other attributes of being . . . some people also dispute here about *esse existentiae*, how it is related to *ens* or essence" (Fonseca does all these things). Similarly on V.28 (the chapter on genus), Suárez says that it is about not the reality, but the significations of the word "genus"; "but since one signification of 'genus' is that it signifies the first [Porphyrian] predicable, some writers contrive here a very broad disputation on the predicables [Fonseca's 192 columns!]"; Suárez refers to his discussion of universal unity, then says, "but the rest, which are proper to the dialecticians, we leave to them." Suárez says that *Metaphysics* IV.4–8 are "of no particular use, and give no occasion for asking any questions," and he suggests that Aristotle has invented his opponents *disputandi gratia*.

(Soto seems to think this is all needless subtlety). Fonseca, with Jesuit *libertas philosophandi*, and with a care for thoroughness and consistency, forges ahead and tries to elaborate and apply a theory of distinctions. The resulting theory is, like Fonseca's book itself, vast and disorderly, with five kinds of distinctions, no single scheme that generates them all, and no way to recognize them without appeal to vague ontological intuitions. What distinguishes Suárez is his clear vision of the whole metaphysical project, his thoroughness in seeing principles through to their conclusions, and his lack of mercy for vague ontological intuitions. Suárez sets out to clean up both the structure of Fonseca's book and the content of the theory of distinctions. As Soto had complained, "since metaphysical distinctions of this kind are both obscure and difficult to believe, we should not admit more of them into the schools than reason proves."[36] Reflecting on the dilemmas of realism, Suárez sees that the problem is separability, and that realism is doomed if it continues to assume that one-way separability implies real distinction, and that real distinction implies two-way separability. Suárez uses this reflection to present a single scheme of three kinds of distinctions, with a clear test for recognizing them, sufficient for answering all the challenges if applied without ontological scruples, and minimizing the multiplication of entities. The great *Metaphysical Disputations*, however much they may disguise themselves as a Scholastic encyclopedia, are a systematic and ruthless execution of this program.[37]

36. *In Isagogen, De Universalibus*, q. 3. Soto had said before (*De Universalibus*, q. 1) that the realists were obscure and the nominalists difficult to believe (on the same question of universal natures that he is here considering); he now combines both these compliments for the Scotists.

37. I would like to thank Fred Freddoso and Alison Laywine for comments on a draft of this paper, and an audience at The Catholic University of America for comments in oral discussion. My views on Scholastic realism and nominalism continue to be shaped by conversations with Calvin Normore, and will be developed further in our collaborative book, *Nominalism and Realism*.

14   Francisco Suárez on Democracy and International Law
CARLOS G. NOREÑA

The 1492 encounter of European and Native American cultures and nations inaugurated in Europe an era of intense reflection about the origins and nature of political authority and about the lawful relations among sovereign states. As one could expect, in Spain the initial debate centered upon the legitimacy of the conquest itself. There were philosophers and theologians who, like Matías Paz and Juan Ginés de Sepúlveda, justified the conquest on the ground that the American natives, as pagan and natural slaves, were incapable of private ownership and legitimate political authority. But the founder and leader of the Salamanca school, the Dominican Francisco de Vitoria, in his lectures *De Indis* (1538), taught that neither the pope nor the emperor had any jurisdiction over the American lands, that the American natives were rational and free human beings, that their nations were sovereign republics and their chiefs legitimate rulers. Statehood and political authority, Vitoria maintained, belonged to the order of nature rather than to the order of grace. The relations between the Spanish Crown and the Indian rulers were therefore basically the same as those among the emerging national states of Europe and subject to the same precepts of the *ius gentium*. Vitoria, however, also taught that Spaniards and Portuguese were justified in using force to protect their right to reside in America and to trade with its people. Furthermore, he proposed a theory of tutelage, which, in spite of its self-liquidating and humane character, did little to discourage the ongoing colonization of the Indies and echoed ethnocentric views of cultural superiority.[1]

---

1. On Vitoria, see Alberto A. García Menendez, *Francisco de Vitoria y el derecho internacional* (Hato Rey: Ediciones Antillas, 1986); and Antonio Truyol Serra, *The Principles of Political and International Law in the Work of Francisco de Vitoria*, anthology and introduction (Madrid: Ediciones Cultura Hispánica, 1946). James Brown Scott's *The Spanish Origin of International Law* (Oxford, 1934) is still a useful introduction to the subject.

Vitoria's political writings can be read in the English translation of Anthony Pagden

The process of thought which began with Francisco de Vitoria, Diego de Covarrubias, Bartolomé de Las Casas, and Domingo de Soto, among others, culminated in the generation of Juan de Mariana, Gabriel Vázquez, Luis de Molina, and, above all, Francisco Suárez. To them the American conquest was more or less a *fait accompli*. By the time Suárez was admitted to the Jesuit order in 1564, the viceroyalties of New Spain and Peru had been firmly established. In this sense, Suárez's thought represents Hispanic philosophy *at the end of*, rather than *in*, the Age of Discovery.[2]

Nevertheless, Suárez's thought was still deeply rooted in the historical events of 1492 and in Vitoria's and Las Casas's basically egalitarian view of humanity. But Suárez died in 1617 during the reign of Philip III, and his thought was significantly shaped by the events and the intellectual milieu of the Baroque age. Machiavelli's and Bodin's books were widely read in Spain. Religious persecutions in England, France, and the German lands raised vital questions about the limits of political authority and the right to rebellion. Relations between the Spanish crown and other European states were complicated by the increasing presence of the British and the French in the North American continent and by the devastating effects of piracy on the open seas upon the Spanish economy.[3]

Suárez's thought on the relations between rulers and their subjects and on the relations among sovereign states is for the most part contained in two typically exhaustive treatises written toward the end of his teaching career in Coimbra, *De Legibus* (1612) and *Defensio Fidei* (1613).[4] Suárez's political and moral philosophy are perfectly inte-

---

and Jeremy Lawrance (New York: Cambridge University Press, 1991). A Latin-Spanish edition is also available: *Relectio de Indis; o libertad de los Indios*, ed. by L. Pereña and J. M. Pérez Prendes (Madrid: C.S.I.C., 1967).

2. On Suárez's legal and political philosophy, see Camilo Barcia Trelles, "Francisco Suárez (1548–1617)," *Académie de droit international: recueil des cours* 43 (1933): 385–553; Georges Jarlot, "Les idées politiques de Suárez et le pouvoir absolu," *Archives de Philosophie* 18 (1949): 64–107; B. Romeyer, "La Théorie Suarézienne d'un état de nature pure," *Archives de philosophie* 18 (1949): 37–63; Josef Soder, *Francisco Suárez und das Volkerrecht; Gedanken zu Staat, Recht und internationalen Beziehungen* (Frankfurt am Main: Metzne, 1973); Luis Recasens Siches, *La filosofía del derecho en Francisco Suárez*, 2d ed. (Mexico: Jus, 1947); Ignacio Gomez Robledo, *El origen del poder político según Francisco Suárez* (Mexico: Jus, 1948); and Joaquin Carreras Artau, *Doctrinas de Francisco Suárez acerca del derecho de gentes y sus relaciones con el derecho natural* (Gerona: Carreras, 1921).

3. Quentin Skinner's *The Foundations of Modern Political Thought*, 2 vols. (Cambridge: Cambridge University Press, 1978), and José Antonio Maravall's *La Cultura del Barroco, Análisis de una estructura histórica* (Barcelona: Ariel, 1975) provide an excellent background to Vitoria's and Suárez's legal and political philosophy. See also J. W. Allen's *History of Political Thought in the Sixteenth Century* (London: Methuen, 1928) and John Lynch, *Spain under the Habsburgs*, 2 vols., 2d ed. (Oxford: Blackwell, 1981).

4. *De Legibus*, bilingual edition (Latin/Spanish) by L. Pereña (Madrid: C.S.I.C., In-

grated into his philosophy of law. The relations between individual citizens and the relations between different political communities are ordered and regulated by natural law and by the dictates of human positive law, a law which embodies the intrinsic rationality of natural law but adds to it the historically contingent specificity of human choices. The contrast with Machiavelli could not have been expressed in a stronger language. The law is a just, stable, and public rule by which the members of a community are compelled to act or to refrain from acting in a certain way (DL I.1.1 and 12.5). In its original sense, "law" applies to human positive law, a human "invention" that regulates human free choices in a political community. By analogy to it we can speak about "eternal" or "divine law," which is "the reason which rules the universe as it exists in the mind of God" (DL I.3.6). Eternal law or divine providence presupposes God's free decision to create a physical universe in which the moral behavior of rational and free creatures is ordered to an end and properly legislated. The reflection of eternal law "written" in the human mind *(scripta in mentibus)* is called "natural law," a law that includes all the moral precepts evidently discerned by human reason (DL II.12.1). It is also by analogy to this moral divine providence that we can metaphorically speak about the "laws" that determine the specific nature of irrational creatures (DL II.2.2). Divine revelation promulgates divine positive law to direct human beings to a supernatural order and to help human reason to recognize the precepts of natural law both *in foro externo* and in *foro interno* (DL I.3.15).

All this is basically medieval and scholastic. But Suárez's legal and political philosophy includes also some features which are either novel or controversial and which gave his thought a distinctive character. Following the Ockhamists Almain and Mair, Suárez reinstates the difference between law and right. The law is a "rule of honest behavior" (DL II.17.2). Right, in its "true, strict, and proper meaning," is a moral power which people have toward that which is their own or is due to them (DL, I.2.5; II.17.2). The language and grammar of human rights—a language vitally important to understanding the American political tradition and some of its shortcomings—express the implications of justice from the point of view of the person who benefits from that relationship. The implications of justice from the perspective of those who have to respect the rights of others are called "duties." This

---

stituto Francisco de Vitoria, 1971–81), vols. 11–17 and 21–22 . Henceforth: DL, book, chapter, paragraph. Some sections of DL in English translation can be found in *Selections from Three Works of Francisco Suárez, S.J.*, Classics of International Law (Oxford: Clarendon Press, 1944). *Defensio Fidei*, bilingual edition by E. Elorduy and L. Pereña (Madrid: C.S.I.C., 1965). Henceforth: DF, part, chapter, paragraph.

subjective view of right as something that individuals, and possibly nations, "have," represents a decisive advance beyond the Scholastic tradition of right as essentially "that which is fair." Suárez did not by himself invent the modern view of human persons and human collectivities as carriers of moral rights by which they are empowered in their relations to others, but he gave it a key role in the philosophy of law and in political philosophy. Suárez's concept of right was repeated almost verbatim by Hugo Grotius in his epoch-making *De Iure Belli ac Pacis* (I.1.iii).[5]

According to Suárez, the law not only makes clear what is intrinsically fitting to rational nature, but makes it obligatory. The objective and intrinsic rationality of the law is thus rooted in the intellect of the legislator, but its obligatory character is based upon the will of the legislator. The precepts of natural law not only indicate what is fitting to human nature, but also bind the human will to comply with the legislative will of the Creator. Law is not only *illuminativa* and *indicativa*, but also *motiva* and *prohibitiva* (DL I.4.10 and II.6). The law provides direction and motion; it is at the same time good and true; it implies right judgment and an efficacious will. The law, Suárez says, is "an act of a properly ordered will" (*actus voluntatis rectae;* DL I.5.20).

Here Suárez, as on many other occasions, chooses an eclectic path between the objectivists, who appeal to Saint Thomas's authority, and the voluntarists, who follow the Ockhamists (DL I.4 and 5). Plato's question in the *Euthyphro*, "Is what is pious loved by the gods because it is pious, or is it pious because it is loved by the gods?" was given a complex answer by Suárez: what God prescribes as good becomes a moral norm to free rational creatures not only because it expresses the necessary and objective rationality of God's infinite intelligence, but also because it promulgates the binding will of an infinitely superior Being. The malice of a forbidden action depends on God's decree, but the divine decree itself is eternally and necessarily anchored in God's essence and intelligence.

Suárez, therefore, is not an Ockhamist voluntarist, as he has been

---

5. The significance of Suárez's notion of subjective rights is properly emphasized by John Finnis in his *Natural Law and Natural Rights* (Oxford: Oxford University Press, 1980), 206–10. Finnis writes that "somewhere between the two men (Aquinas and Suárez) we have crossed the watershed" (207). On the Ockhamistic origin of the concept, see Skinner, *Foundations*, vol. 2, 121–23. Skinner also points out that Suárez's discussion of the people's "right to resist" is a direct application of his subjective theory of rights (176–78). See also Knud Haakonssen, "Hugo Grotius and the History of Political Thought," *Political Theory* 13 (1985): 239–65; and Hersch Lauterpacht, "The Grotian Tradition in International Law," *British Year Book of International Law* (1946): 1–53, on Suárez's impact upon Grotius.

unfairly characterized, but he is a voluntarist in a much more interesting manner. To Suárez, moral obligation is based upon the power of a will to coerce the power of another will. Originally, this power is invested in the infinite will of God. But Suárez was convinced that, as a norm *(Providentia ordinaria)*, God rules over His rational and free creatures through the agency of other rational and free creatures (DF III.1.8), neither directly nor with the assistance of angels. The only direct communication between God and his rational creatures is through the demands of their conscience. Conscience is the practical moral judgment which applies to each concrete case the general demands of natural law (DL II.5.15). However, the precepts of natural law do not embrace all the norms that are necessary to the moral life of the human community, but only those that are either true by definition *(per se nota ex terminis)* or are derived from those by a simple reasoning process *(aliquo discursu;* DL II.12). Furthermore, natural law sometimes enjoins a form of behavior, but sometimes merely allows it. Natural law, for instance, does not prescribe the establishment of private property, but permits it under some circumstances (DL II.4); it prescribes human freedom, but allows people to freely sell themselves as slaves (DL I.8.5); it permits nudity, but makes it imprudent after the loss of original innocence (DL II.14.7). The institution of private property, the prohibition of slavery, and the need for clothing became reasonable human choices given some historical facts which themselves are the consequences of other human choices (such as Adam's fall; ibid.). Furthermore, life in a political community requires much more concrete norms than the general principles of natural law. Natural law does not have a history, but the precepts of human positive law based upon it and applied to concrete circumstances have a rich and complex history.[6]

The limitations of natural law and the origins of a positive human legislative authority invested in the state—a term which Suárez introduced into the idiom of Scholastic philosophy—are thus closely related to each other in Suárez's mind. The central problem of his legal and political philosophy is precisely to investigate how the legislative will of God expressed in the necessary commands of natural law must be and are rendered more specific in the historically contingent commands of human positive law, a law which at the same time expresses the will of a human legislator and participates in God's legislative authority (DL II.4.8). Furthermore, it needs to be explained whence does the human

---

6. José Antonio Maravall makes this point with typical lucidity in his *Estado Moderno y Mentalidad Social*, 2 vols. (Madrid: Revista de Occidente, 1972), vol. 2, pt. 5, ch. 1.

will, either that of an individual or that of an assembly, derive its authority to bind the will and the conscience of other rational creatures who are, before any legitimate authority is properly instituted, free, equal, and subject only to their Creator's commands (DL III.1.1). This is then Suárez's basic voluntarism, this profoundly Jesuit and Baroque vision (an expression which Antonio Maravall[7] finds redundant) of moral life as the constantly unresolved and frequently antagonistic relationship between wills that command with authority and wills that (contrary to what the Anabaptists upheld) must obey in conscience (DF III.4). Part of this tense dialectic of authority and submission is played directly between God and the individual human conscience through the demands of natural law. But God has left ample room for human initiatives and choices to institute other relations of authority which are indispensable for humans to fulfill their social nature in a moral way.

In explaining those human choices and institutions, Suárez made significant advances in articulating the concept of "state of nature," the contractual theory of the state, and the principle of popular sovereignty. The phrase "state of nature" was, to the best of my knowledge, never used by Suárez, although it had been introduced into the philosophical idiom of the times by his fellow Jesuit Luis de Molina.[8] Suárez uses the expression *ex sola rei natura* (DL III.1.1) to signify the same thing, not a historical stage chronologically prior to the establishment of a political community, but rather a heuristic device which reveals the nature of human beings in abstraction from their acquired traits as citizens of a state. Like Rousseau much later, Suárez was anxious to explore the nature of an original agreement among equals which justified the political inequality between rulers and subjects without which the political body cannot come into being.

Suárez's notion of human equality differs in substantial respects from the Hobbesian emphasis on the equality of power. For Hobbes (who in the opinion of most scholars was very familiar with Suárez's work), humans are equal in the twofold sense that even the weakest represents a threat to the strongest and that everybody considers himself as wise as the rest.[9] Suárez considers all humans equal because they all share the same specific traits given to them by their Creator. One of these traits is that even before the establishment of a political society, human beings are fully aware of the dictates of natural law and are

---

7. Maravall, introduction to *La Cultura del Barroco*.
8. Luis de Molina, *De Iustitia et iure Libri Sex*, 2 vols. (Mainz, 1659), 1688–89. The quotation is found in Skinner, *Foundations*, 2:155.
9. *Leviathan*, pt. 1, ch. 13.

social beings rather than solitary brutes (DL I.13.19). Their own nature requires a social life and communication with others (ibid.).

The first form of human society is the family, a society that extends to the servants. Within the family we find the first hierarchy of authority, the first three manners of natural subordination. One is the authority of the parents over their offspring, an authority based exclusively upon natural law given the act of procreation (DL III.1.3). The other is the authority of the husband over the wife, an authority based upon the consent of a man and a woman to contract matrimony according to the terms of a contract as dictated by nature itself (DL I.8.5). The third form of natural subordination is that of servants toward their masters. It was Suárez's unpalatable opinion that people who are free can freely sell themselves as slaves, and that once they are slaves, they are obliged by natural law to abide by the conditions of the contract. The authority of parents, husbands, and masters are for Suárez different expressions of *potestas dominativa* (DL I.1.8), a *potestas* that regulates relations between private individuals and is normally exercised for the sake of the one who holds the authority rather than for the benefit of the one who obeys (DL I.8.5). But the family, including its extension through the servants, is an imperfect society because is not sufficient to satisfy all human needs. To do that, human beings need to congregate into a political body.

The second and perfect human society is therefore political society. Political society is not the consequence of Adam's sin (as Luther taught), but rather a natural necessity which corresponds to a natural propensity. Political society requires a public power capable of imposing its legislative will upon the will of its members and of directing their choices toward a common good (DL I.3.19). This power is what Suárez calls *potestas iurisdictionis*, a much more coercive power than the authority of parents, husbands, and masters (DL I.8.5); an authority which is exclusively exercised for the sake of those who obey the law rather than for the sake of the legislators themselves (ibid.); an authority which must be called "sovereign" because on its own level it is not "subject to another" (*alteri non subjecta,* DF III.5).

At this point Suárez deals with the central issues of political philosophy: one, why do people who are naturally free and subject only to God (DL III.1.1) agree to curtail their natural liberty and to place themselves under the authority of other human beings? And two, what serves to legitimate the act of inaugurating a commonwealth? I think it is fair to say that the great Dominicans of the Age of Discovery did not yet clearly recognize all the implications of these questions. But Molina, Mariana, and Suárez did, and in so doing they laid the foundations for contractual and constitutionalist theories of the state in the seventeenth century.

In answering the first question, Jesuit thinkers found themselves in a thorny dilemma: they had to make clear that human nature requires the coercive power of the state without describing that nature in the pessimistic language of Augustinian-Lutheran, post-lapsarian theology. Not all the Jesuit thinkers were equally successful: Mariana, for instance, used a language which is strikingly similar to that of Rousseau's *Essay on the Origins of Inequality*.[10] Suárez, as always, was sober and eclectic. Human positive law, Suárez says, is necessary first of all to determine more concretely the moral life of the citizens *(magis in particulari;* DL I.3.18). Without the determination of the common good by public legislation, human beings hardly know it and seldom strive after it (DL III.1.5). Without the coercive power of the state, it would be nearly impossible *(vix posset;* ibid.) to preserve peace among families divided from each other. The power that makes a political society possible is therefore as natural as the need for it (ibid., 4). Without explicitly stating it, Suárez evidently admits that the motivation behind the social contract was based not only on moral grounds, but also on a form of oblique self-interest dictated by nature itself.

In the natural order of things God has seen to it that political power be invested in human beings. Political power, however, does not naturally reside in any concrete individual nor in each one of the individuals who make up humanity simply because they are all equal and equally deprived of it (DL III.2.1). To derive political authority from Adam's authority, as the patriarchalist Filmer would do thirty years after Suárez, is to confuse the *potestas dominativa* with the *potestas iurisdictionis*. Adam's authority extended to his wife, children, and servants, but not to other family heads (DL III.2.3). Political power therefore resides in the human community as such. But how does the political power that initially resides in the community become invested in one concrete individual *(una naturali persona)* or in a group *(uno consilio;* DF III.1.5)? It is clear that God must give rational and social creatures the capacity to do what is both possible and necessary to fulfill their own nature. But on the other hand, this power which is indispensable to the preservation of the state is not actually given until human beings freely choose to become a political body. In the moment they decide to aggregate as a political society, Suárez writes, they become a "mystical body" from which the *potestas iurisdictionis* results *(per modum proprietatis*

---

10. Mariana's theory is clearly summarized by Skinner, *Foundations*, 2:345–46, and by Allen, *History of Political Thought*, 360–63.

resultantis ex tali corpore mystico; DL III.3.6) and is invested in the community itself, and not in an individual, whether the name of that individual be Adam, James (the King of England), or Philip (the King of Spain; DF III.2.7). In the *Defensio Fidei*, Suárez was very eager to clarify the sense in which one could say, as King James was wont to, that the royal power proceeds from God. That power proceeds from God not in the sense that God immediately and directly invests such power in the person of the king, but only in the sense that God created human nature in such way that once humans decide to congregate into a political body, they are invested with a sovereign power which they are free to transfer or not to transfer to a king or to an assembly. Against Vitoria, however, Suárez, always bent on highlighting the formative power of human choices, maintained that such sovereign power is not immediately given by nature itself *(a natura profectum)*, but through an institutional act of the human will *(mediante voluntate humana et institutione;* DF III.2.10). Created causes, Suárez teaches in his *Metaphysicae Disputationes*, are true causes even if their power to cause is nothing but a participation of God's infinite power. Political power therefore emanates immediately from an act of the human will without any divine intervention. This will is the will to form a community, which, according to natural law, cannot exist without such a power. In the same way as a free person can renounce his or her freedom or be deprived of it by a just cause, free and equal members of the human community can decide to become members of a political body in which they will submit their own will to the will of a superior properly constituted. Natural reason demands that political power be in fact invested in one person or persons, but to decide whether the ruler be one (monarchy), the best (aristocracy), or all (democracy) has been left to the free choice of the community itself (DF III.2.9).

The asymmetry between the origin of political power and the origin of the Pope's power is strongly emphasized by Suárez. Against King James, Suárez strongly upholds Bellarmine's doctrine that the authority of kings does not proceed immediately from God, like that of the pope. In the case of the pope, human beings merely "designate" the person upon whom the jurisdictional power of the Church will be directly invested by God himself (DF III.2.16). The members of the political body, on the other hand, contractually *(vel quasi contractu humano,* DF III.2.8) transfer to the ruler the political power naturally invested in themselves.

To appraise Suárez's ideas on democracy and popular sovereignty we need to look at the nature of this initial transfer of power. In the early decades of the seventeenth century the questions about the transfer of power from the people to the ruler were normally couched in the language of "the right to rebellion," the right, namely, to reclaim that power, a language which Suárez himself had encouraged with his subjective theory of rights. But here Suárez's thought became generally cautious and moderate. Against the radically populist views of Bartolus and the Ockhamists, Suárez denied that such transfer was only a form of delegation which made the ruler a minister of the people and forever accountable to the people. In his response to King James of England, Suárez adopted a much less polemical and more conciliatory tone than that of Cardinal Bellarmine. Probably to protect the Jesuit order and the Catholic Church from the apprehensions of the King of England (and of other European rulers), Suárez was eager to emphasize that, after the transfer of the power to the king, the people have no power whatsoever (DF III.3.2). Such transfer is not a delegation of power, but a "complete alienation and bestowal of all the power that was in the community (*quasi alienatio seu perfecta largitio totius potestatis quae erat in communitate;* DL III.4.11).

These clearly antipopulist and cautious views were, however, interlaced with less traditional and potentially more democratic views on the nature of the original covenant. That is probably why Suárez's *Defensio Fidei* met the same fate as the writings of Bellarmine: both were publicly burnt in London by order of the Archbishop of Canterbury. In some cases, Suárez taught, people can reclaim their liberty "according to the conditions of the original contract or according to the requirements of natural justice" (DF III.3.3). It is true that all Suárez had to say about those conditions was that they must be contained in "old and authentic documents or sufficiently upheld by ancient custom" (ibid.). The "requirements of natural justice," on the other hand, are inalienably written in the hearts of men. As a general principle, natural law empowers people to do whatever it takes to preserve the state created by the contract itself. Another inalienable right is the right to self-defense. When the king becomes a tyrant, the people have the right to defend themselves because the right to self-defense can never be renounced by the original covenant (ibid.). The inalienable right of the people to self-defense can even justify tyrannicide in certain cases and under stringent conditions, conditions which Suárez painstakingly elaborates in a fastidious and lengthy chapter of *Defensio Fidei* (DF III.4).

Suárez also professed the original and difficult doctrine that no transfer of power was absolutely necessary. It is up to the people to decide which form of government they choose and which person or persons will be invested with political authority. In the hypothetical but not impossible case that the members of the political community made no further decision as to the person or persons of the ruler, Suárez wrote, the authority to rule remains democratically in the entire community (DF III.2.8). Natural law, he writes, does not prescribe democracy, but permits it (*de iure naturali concedente, non praecipiente;* DF III.2.9). The doctrine was original because other thinkers of his age, in particular, Mariana, preferred to think that initially all political communities were absolute and paternalistic monarchies and that constitutional restraints on rulers were later efforts to curb absolute authority. The doctrine was, however, difficult because it implied that what Suárez clearly conceived to be "the most imperfect form of government" (*omnium imperfectissima;* DF III.2.8), namely, democracy or the rule of all, was also the more natural in at least the sense that, unlike monarchy or aristocracy, it did not require any further human choice or institution. Suárez's obvious intention was to make clear that unless the people transfer the authority invested in them, the power remains in the community as such (DF III.2.9). But Suárez never explained how the original intention to congregate into a political body was identical and simultaneous with a choice he himself considered to be the least reasonable one, the choice to retain the "resulting" political authority in the community as a whole.

Whenever Suárez speaks about the origin of political society, he seems to take for granted that different groups of people congregate into different political bodies. In fact, he was convinced that a global body politic embracing all of humanity has never existed, is hardly possible, and is far from convenient. The division of humanity into a plurality of states was to him a historical fact which natural law allows and recommends as the most reasonable alternative (DL III.2.6).

Once humanity has been divided into a plurality of political communities, each one of them ruled by a collective will embodied in different forms of government (monarchies, aristocracies, and democracies and their mixtures), the relations with each other need to be ordered by law as much as the relations between individuals are ordered by the laws of each political body. And in the same way as political jurisdiction results and emanates from the mystical body made up by a community of individual human wills bent upon forming a political society, so too the human authority to legislate international relations emanates from the community of nations.

Suárez's anti-utopian views about the pluralism of states were more than compensated by his emphasis on the unity of an international community, a concept which Suárez articulated and pioneered more explicitly and cogently than any of his contemporaries.[11] Human beings, Suárez taught, are members of a community by the mere fact that they share the same rational nature (DL I.6.8). As such, they are subject in conscience to the same and immutable demands of natural law everywhere and at all times, whether before or after Adam's fall, whether they are members of the Church or not (DL II.8). Furthermore, humanity is not only one in the sense of sharing the same species (*habet unitatem non solum specificam;* DL II.19.9), but also one in a quasi-political and moral sense (*sed etiam quasi politicam et moralem;* ibid.). This quasi-political and moral unity is based, first of all, upon the natural precept of mutual love and compassion (*naturale praeceptum mutui amoris et misericordiae;* ibid.), and, in the second place, in the interdependence of all political bodies (ibid.). Political communities are never so self-sufficient that each one of them can make it without the assistance and communication with the others, not just to survive in a material sense, but mostly to live well and to lead a fuller moral existence (ibid.). Suárez's fusion of ethical and utilitarian reasons, morality and mutual need, in explaining the foundations of the international community was meant to have a lasting influence in the history of international law.

Nations therefore need a law to direct and make the rules which govern their required interaction. This law is the *ius gentium* (DL II.19.8). Suárez's primary concept of *ius gentium* represents a significant advance beyond the traditional use, a use derived from Roman law and limited to those precepts of human positive law which all or most nations share in common. Suárez's *ius gentium* has also been called *ius inter gentes*, but for all practical purposes it can also be referred to by the nineteenth-century expression, "international law." Suárez opposed a strong medieval tradition—still echoed by Vitoria—which envisioned the *ius gentium* as a subdivision of natural law. The *ius gentium* is not part of natural law, Suárez argued, because its precepts are much more concrete and specific than those of natural law and cannot be inferred from them by any reasoning process. Natural law forbids what is evil. The *ius gentium*, as any positive law, makes evil what it forbids (DL II.11.2). Natural law is the same for all human beings. The *ius gentium* is normally the same for most (DL II.19.2). The *ius gentium* therefore is an extension of human positive law, a law that has been introduced by human consent and will to make up for the limitations of natural law regarding

---

11. In the introduction to *Hugo Grotius and International Relations*, ed. H. Bull, B. Kingsbury, and A. Roberts (Oxford: Clarendon Press, 1990), B. Kingsbury and A. Roberts do not hesitate to write (10–11) that "the most eloquent account of the concept of international society" was given by Suárez in *De Legibus*.

international relations, exactly the same as all the laws which regulate the interaction of individuals within the political body (DL II.19.1). Unlike the positive law of the state, however, the *ius gentium*, Suárez thought, is not a law promulgated in a written form by an international legislative authority (as one could expect from the parallelism with municipal law), but has been established by the custom of most nations. As examples of such international customary law, Suárez mentions the law of diplomatic immunity, the freedom of international trade (but not the form of the contract nor the obligation to abide by it; DL II.19.7), and the laws of war and peace. It was left to Hugo Grotius to take a further step, a step which the increasing tensions of international trade among the European seaborne empires in an era of expanding mercantilism made more and more necessary: to attempt what Grotius himself described as "the first comprehensive and systematic" treatment of the law of nations. The fact that Grotius's *De Iure Belli ac Pacis* was neither a comprehensive nor a systematic code of international law only reminds us that the history of international law, in which Suárez occupies a prominent place, has been and promises to be a long and complicated process.

In 1492, two large portions of humanity still unaware of each other became forever associated in the blessed lands of the American continent. As most encounters of this type in the history of humanity, this one too was not without pain and not without violence. But it also unleashed the power of human reflection and thought. Ironically it was Spanish Scholastic thinkers who laid the foundations for modern secular political thought. The encounter with nations which had nothing to do with either the Holy Roman Empire or the pope opened the way to the consideration of the state as a natural entity based upon our rational and social nature, an invention equally independent from Adam's fall and from the Christian revelation. Reason had thus discovered the potentially liberating foundation of human equality and unity, in spite of the historical fact that those who arrived on the American shores entertained for a long time resilient self-images of cultural superiority.

It is true that the vision of most Scholastic thinkers in the Age of Discovery, including that of Suárez, was profoundly theological. To Suárez in particular, human nature provided the norm of moral behavior because God had decreed that our free choices had to conform to it. If God did not exist, Suárez taught, behavior unfitting to human nature would be irrational and imprudent but not the violation of a law; it would be a "philosophical" (*peccatum philosophicum*) but not a "theological sin" (*peccatum theologicum*, DL II.5 and 6). Suárez's philosophy of law embodies the fundamental but not any more fashionable assumption that every law entails a superior who commands and a subject who obeys. Still, these and similar reflections invited less traditional opinions. Suárez's fellow Jesuit, Gabriel Vázquez, and, later, Hugo Grotius, did not hesitate to teach that nature provides both the norm and the obligation to act in a certain way, even if, as they proclaimed to be impossible, God did not exist. The way was prepared for a secular conception of natural law.[12]

It was Suárez's unique achievement to integrate political philosophy and ethics into the philosophy of law and to assign to human reason and will its God-given role in making possible the complete moral ordering of free choices. God provides only the self-evident and general principles of natural law. Human reason and will complete the legislative task by providing the concrete rules enacted by legitimate rulers. The state emerges as a human creation which is at the same a moral and a useful institution. The power to legislate is a sovereign power which God has given directly to the people themselves.

Suárez's views on democracy are both traditional and modern. As a good Aristotelian he considered democracy the worst form of government because, like Aristotle and Philip II, he was convinced that the rule of one, even the hereditary rule of one, was the most efficient and the most reasonable (DL III.4.1). Universal participatory democracy was to him unfeasible and impractical. Representative government was to him identical with aristocracy: the best are able to rule because they are few and they represent all because they are the best. Suárez's views on the right to rebellion were also conservative. Although he upheld the right of the people to rebel and even to kill a tyrant, he never clearly explained what a tyrant was (except to say that a ruler who drags his subjects into heresy is indeed a tyrant; DF III.4.4), nor did he specify the mechanism of rebellion. Suárez's assertion that the power of rulers does not proceed directly from God but from the people probably helped to cast some doubts on the medieval theory of the divine rights of kings, but had no measurable restraining influence upon the wave of royal absolutism in Europe. But Suárez taught the basic principle of the constitutional theory of the state: People are free to impose some limitations upon the power they transfer to the ruler and have some inalienable rights which no human agreement can invalidate. Suárez, however, failed to make explicit which constitutional restraints could have been imposed upon the original contract, considered personal

---

12. On Grotius's famous *etsi daremus* and its relation to Vázquez, see Finnis, *Natural Law*, 54–55.

freedom a right which could be sold to others, and limited the scope of inalienable rights to the right to self-defense.

As one of the founders of international law, Suárez was both a champion of cosmopolitan solidarity based upon interdependence and compassion and a champion of cultural and political pluralism. In his thought, he was able to temper the Aristotelian idea of state self-sufficiency with the Christian emphasis on universal brotherhood and charity. Suárez did not have much to say about international organizations or about international agencies to enforce international law. But his vision of a pluralistic and global community in which the good of each of the interdependent members is and should be subordinate to the higher good of the entire international society and in which the totality of international relations must be subject to the rule of law, is more inspiring than ever in our postmodernist cult of divisive pluralism.

PART V

15 A New Beginning in Philosophy: Poinsot's Contribution to the Seventeenth-Century Search

JOHN DEELY

I. STATING THE QUESTION

A great thinker is, willy nilly, a man of his time. Whether he looks forward or backward in his thought, he does so inevitably through the filter of contemporary eyes—his own. And what he sees is perforce tinted by that filter of experience. Breathing the air of his period, he cannot help but imbibe something of its aspirations, whether to further them or to oppose them, as the case may be.

The reflections of this essay turn around two thinkers of the same age, one in the background, René Descartes (1596–1650), and the other in the foreground, John Poinsot (1589–1644), born seven years and dead six years before Descartes.[1] The purpose of this essay is to propound a single heuristic thesis: There is a way of looking at modern philosophy that is very different from the received opinions, one which profoundly affects our understanding of the contemporary situation in philosophy and the shape of its immediate future. Instead of looking from the work of Descartes to the line of mainstream modern devel-

---

1. Writing under his religious sobriquet "Joannes a Sancto Thoma," Poinsot produced two major series of writings, a five-volume *Cursus Philosophicus* published between 1631 and 1635, and a nine-volume *Cursus Theologicus* published between 1637 and 1667. One of the most complete, authoritative syntheses we have of Latin philosophy and theology in its final stage of development as an indigenous, linguistically homogeneous tradition, Poinsot's work is written explicitly from the point of view of that development as it was inspired by the *opera omnia* of Thomas Aquinas in particular. Poinsot's work was eclipsed historically by the fact that "Francis Suárez, who wrote the other summation [of Latin thought], remained the textbook philosopher of Europe long after Descartes had given philosophy a new *point de depart*. Poinsot, by contrast, was nearly without intellectual issue until he was rediscovered in this century by Jacques Maritain" (Miles 1985).

A complete discussion of Poinsot's person and work is provided in the "Editorial Afterword" to *Tractatus de Signis. The Semiotic of John Poinsot* (Deely 1985, sect. 2, pp. 423–44). On the relation of Maritain to Poinsot, see Deely 1986b.

opment that followed from it in the two streams of classical rationalism and empiricism synthesized by Kant, we are better advised to survey the horizon of mainstream Latin thought as it existed at the time that Descartes undertook his work, in order to see how full and good a use Descartes—and, after him, all the classical moderns—made of the Latin resources available in principle at the time.

What comes into view as soon as one effects such a shift in standpoint is actually quite surprising. For it turns out that there were important speculative developments of the Latin tradition under way, especially in Iberia, of central relevance for the contemporary postmodern context of discourse analysis and culture studies in general. Of these developments Descartes had no knowledge, and the Cartesian influence screened them out of subsequent mainstream development as modern philosophy moved from Latin to the natural languages.[2] In particular, our shift of standpoint reveals that more than a century of late Latin development anticipated John Locke's proposal for a philosophical "doctrine of signs" or "semiotic" which would give us a sort of logic and critique of knowledge different than the mainstream of modern thought presaged, while at the same time providing exactly what the moderns wished for, namely, a new starting point for the philosophical enterprise as a whole rooted directly in the experience of each of us more than in the authority of ancient figures.

The "shift from 'Scholasticism' to 'Modernity', many would say, has its echo in our present shift from 'Modernity' to 'Postmodernity'" (Natoli and Hutcheon 1993, viii). But few indeed have so realized that the echo in question resonates with specific anticipations of the postmodern period as a development based not on a unity of natural language (as in the epochs of ancient, medieval, and classical modern philosophy) but on the achievement of an epistemological paradigm based on the realization that "the highest grade of reality is only reached by signs" (Peirce 1904, 23), a paradigm capable of taking into account the very mechanisms of linguistic difference and change as part of the framework of philosophy itself.

A story must be told before it can be believed, and I have come to think that the story of the closing centuries of Latin Scholasticism's contribution to the understanding of mind that modernity bungled is

---

2. The line of argument in this paper I have expanded into a book, *New Beginnings. Early Modern Philosophy and Postmodern Thought* (1994). But the point here made is far more general than my particular line of argument, as can be seen from the Poinsot Special Issue of the *American Catholic Philosophical Quarterly* published in 1994, especially in the essays of John Doyle, "Poinsot on the Knowability of Beings of Reason," and Norman Wells, "Poinsot on Created Eternal Truths vis-à-vis Suarez, Vazquez, and Descartes."

a story not believed precisely because it has not yet been truly told. Descartes and Poinsot, contemporaries in the glorious seventeenth century, are alike, seen from our vantage today, doorways to the past—to the twelve hundred years of Latin philosophy in Poinsot's case, and to the three hundred and fifty years of modernity's determined effort to present itself as the once and future truth owing nothing to history in Descartes'. But it is not the grand vistas of past history opened through the work of these thinkers that concern us here. Our focus in this essay is on the coevality of Poinsot and Descartes, the overlap of these two thinkers in that magic moment when, at once, modernity was gestated and postmodernity presaged—the former in Descartes' starting from ideas and objects as ideas, the latter in Poinsot's starting from signs and objects as signifieds. For by taking this latter point of departure, Poinsot was able not only to synthesize the Latin past, but to give it a future bearing beyond modernity itself, a bearing on the shaping and substance of the postmodern era nascent today.

By comparison with Descartes, Poinsot's contribution to the seventeenth-century search for a new beginning in philosophy is difficult to access. In his *Rules for the Direction of the Mind* (1628, 17), Descartes proposed, as the necessary solution to the muddle of the Latin past, adoption of a new method without which "the pursuit of learning would, I think, be more harmful than profitable." "By 'a method,'" he explained,

I mean reliable rules which are easy to apply, and such that if one follows them exactly, one will never take what is false to be true or fruitlessly expend one's mental efforts,[3] but will gradually and constantly increase one's knowledge till one arrives at a true understanding of everything within one's capacity. (16)

As to the writings of the ancients, insofar as they contain, by virtue of the natural light, scattered glimmers of the Cartesian method, they perhaps deserve to be read, "but at the same time there is a considerable danger that if we study these works too closely traces of their errors will infect us and cling to us against our will and despite our precautions" (13).

In other words, what is proposed as novel in the Cartesian system is the system itself, in particular the method of analysis of objects into their simplest components, buttressed by methodical doubt maintained at each step of the way. Adoption of the Cartesian approach, moreover, is recommended as necessary from the outset if "the pursuit of learn-

---

3. Hence Descartes' assurance to Mersenne in his letter of February 1637 (cited from Stoothoff 1985, 109; cf. Kenny 1970, 30) that his method "consists much more in practice than in theory" and "extends to every kind of subject-matter."

ing" is not to be (as by implication it has perforce always been) "more harmful than profitable" (Descartes 1628, 17); thus, as Descartes would later confess in his *Discourse on Method*, "When I cast a philosophical eye upon the various activities and undertakings of mankind, there are almost none which I do not consider vain and useless" (1637, 112).[4]

The desire for a new approach to philosophy that characterized the birth of modern philosophy in the seventeenth century, moreover, was not something vague and general, but quite specific. The moderns knew both what they were looking for and where they expected to find it. Descartes spoke for the entire period in asserting that "the most useful inquiry we can make at this stage is to ask: What is human knowledge and what is its scope?," and that the task for such inquiry is "to seek to encompass in thought everything in the universe, with a view to learning in what way particular things may be susceptible of investigation by the human mind" (1628, 31).

Poinsot's approach to the problems of philosophy, including those pertaining to the nature and scope of human knowledge, was in almost every respect contrary to that of Descartes. To begin with, he did not think that there was any sure and easy method, old or new, that would lead to the infallible discovery of philosophical truth. For him, there was no substitute for studying the works of those who had gone before, and the method for doing this was to reduce the arguments to be found in previous authors to their logical core and express this core in strict logical form as the means whereby alone hidden assumptions and unsound premises could be brought to light.[5] Hence he rejected Descartes' view (1628, 37) that "ordinary dialectic is of no use whatever to those who wish to investigate the truth of things," though he agreed completely with Descartes (36) in repudiating those who prescribed the forms of dialectic as a means for taking, "as it were, a rest from considering a particular inference clearly and attentively." The forms of dialectic, for Poinsot—the necessary aspect of even probable syllogisms—are merely the preliminary instrument for positioning ourselves to adjudicate what is philosophically sound or unsound in the views of another, ancient or modern.

The disagreement between Poinsot and Descartes over method ex-

---

4. Philosophy itself in its historical dimension Descartes saw as the very paradigmatic case for dismissal in the search for philosophical truth. Whereas Aristotle's meditations on first philosophy (c. 348–330 B.C.) led Aristotle first to consider the views of his predecessors, the *Meditations on First Philosophy* of Descartes (1641) led Descartes first to dismiss his predecessors, as he had so frankly told us to expect in his earlier *Discourse on Method* (1637, 114–15).

5. See Poinsot's "First Prologue: Wherein is set forth the exercise and practice of dialectical disputation," in *Tractatus de Signis* (hereafter TDS; 1632a), 10/1–13/12.

tended also to the object of our knowledge. Poinsot was not a reductionist. He did not believe that higher orders of difficulty in knowledge could be reduced to complex arrangements of ultimately simple objects, so that the complex could be deduced from the simple merely by a careful observation of the proper ways in which simple objects combine to form complex wholes. Poinsot accepted rather a doctrine of substance according to which ontological unities in nature do not ordinarily correspond and can seldom be made to correspond in one-to-one fashion with objective unities represented in knowledge, as Cajetan before him had best clarified.[6] Knowledge, for Poinsot, consisted essentially in the establishment, for any given case, of a correspondence in relationships between objective representation and ontological reality, allowing in particular for objective states of affairs which have no ontological counterpart existing apart from their being known. The problem of truth in any given case is critically to determine which pattern of objectivity we are dealing with—one that does or one that does not represent an ontological as well as an objective state of affairs—in this or that aspect of experience.[7]

In other words, Poinsot was a quintessential Scholastic, at the very moment historically when the very complexity of the results arrived at by the Scholastic method and the very multiplicity of authorities established in the Scholastic line were experienced by most as a crushing burden more trouble to learn than it was worth. Scholastic logic, the entry into the system of philosophy in the mainstream university curricula against which Descartes and the moderns rebelled, demanded seven years' study in Poinsot's university, three in formal logic and four in so-called material logic, which was the study of logic as an instrument not merely for restating arguments in form but for adjudicating therewith the truth of their contents.

Imbued with the deepest respect for tradition, Poinsot felt charged with a double mission: not only to advance the truth, but to do so in a way that carried with it the whole of past truth. Simonin has described

---

6. In his *Commentariam in summam theologicam. Prima pars* (1507), q. 1, a. 3, where he enunciates the principle that differences among things are quite another matter than differences among objects, a principle which Poinsot takes up as one of the fundamental principles of the doctrine of signs: see the TDS, bk. 1, q. 2, 149/41–151/21; q. 4, 187/28–190/23, and n. 33 thereto; esp. bk. 2, q. 1, 235/36–236/46; and q. 5, 270/37–271/21. See also Cajetan's comments on q. 28, a. 1, of this same part of the *Summa*, partially cited in TDS, 95n18.

7. The Latin context in which Poinsot is concerned to synthesize his views, the landscape he surveys in the area we call epistemology, is rich beyond imagining. "Like some great philosophical Indies, it now lies in wait for its Columbus," wrote a current Marco Polo of studies in Latin philosophy (Doyle 1984a, 121; see also Doyle 1987–88, 1990).

the dilemma well: "Poinsot is determined to let no new achievements be lost, and to profit from the final developments of a scholasticism which had exhausted itself in the plenitude of its refinements" (1930, 145).

II. FINDING A FOCUS

If, therefore, we are to find from Poinsot a contribution to the modern demand for a new beginning in philosophy, it will be hidden among the plenitude of refinements made in the final developments of Scholastic philosophy, the mainstream philosophy of the Latin age. There may of course be more than one such contribution in the vast synthesis of Poinsot's *Cursus Philosophicus*. But the most promising area in which to look would naturally concern the nature and extent of human knowledge. For Poinsot was inevitably a man of his own time as well as a figure of tradition. He worked from one of the most vital centers of seventeenth-century university life, cognizant of all the currents of modernity,[8] and breathing the atmosphere of the period. It is no accident that Latin Scholasticism, no less than the peripheral currents which would replace it as mainstream on the Continent and in England, had undergone in its later development a shift in emphasis from ontological questions to questions of epistemology, as we would call them today.

In this regard, the decisive influence on Poinsot's thought came from the University of Paris, where his predecessor at Alcalá, Domingo de Soto, had done his graduate study.[9] At Paris, Soto had been steeped in the controversy begun by followers of Ockham over the adequacy of Augustine's classical definition of sign, enshrined in the fourth book of Lombard's *Sentences* as the focus for sacramental theology, according to which a sign is something which, on being perceived, brings into awareness another besides itself. The Parisian logicians developed at length a point that Aquinas had qualified in passing in a number of contexts but never thematized,[10] the point that this definition from Au-

---

8. That Poinsot clung to discredited empirical beliefs of the ancients (Lavaud 1928, 416–17) or knew nothing of the works of Galileo and Descartes (Simon 1955, xix) are myths that need to be exploded (Deely 1985, 399–404, esp. n. 8). Suffice it here to point out that the structure Poinsot finally gave to his *Cursus* as published, both in what it omits in natural philosophy and what it incorporates in logic, is inexplicable except on the assumption of Poinsot's intimate awareness of the philosophical trends developing in Italy and central Europe.

9. An excellent brief summary of the general historical context, based on the many works of Muñoz Delgado 1964 and Ashworth 1974, 1978, is provided in Angelelli 1992, esp. sect. 3, "From Montaigu to Alcalá and Salamanca."

10. Hence, in commenting on these various contexts spanning the professorial career

gustine is too narrow, because intellectual notions and phantasms alike—in short, concepts and percepts, ideas and images—function precisely to bring into our awareness something that they themselves are not. And not only, for example, is it the case that an idea of a dog is not a dog, but also is it the case that a dog thought of may or may not be a dog existing. Nascent here is not merely the dyadic distinction emphasized by the Paris logicians between signs as vehicles of awareness themselves, sometimes perceptible and sometimes not, but, more fundamentally, a triadic distinction among concepts as psychological states, objects as apprehended terms of cognitive relations, and things existing physically, whether or not objectively. But the immediate focus of the controversy in Paris was on the question of whether the sign is rightly defined when being perceptible to sense is made part of its definition. To this question, the decisive answer was made in the negative.

From this answer arose a new definition of *signum* as *anything* which brings into awareness what it itself is not, and a corresponding new division into signs which perform the act of signifying only on condition that they are themselves objective terms of apprehension, hereafter called *instrumental signs,* and signs which perform the act of signifying without themselves being objects first apprehended as such, hereafter called *formal signs*. The actual coinage of this terminology historians have yet to attribute to a specific individual. What seems certain is that the terminology was in use in Paris by the time Soto studied there, and it is certain that Soto introduced the terminology and the controversy into the Iberian university world early in the sixteenth century, where it became, over the next century, a matter of daily dispute in the schools (see Poinsot 1632, 194/39–40).

The problem was, from Poinsot's point of view, that Soto had introduced this discussion into the Iberian curriculum in a disruptive fashion. For he had made the discussion of signs a part of the opening chapters in his introductory logic text, or *Summulae* (Soto 1529, 1554), and this example had been followed by other Iberian professors, giving rise to "a vast forest of intractable questions and a thorny thicket of sophisms" which have served mainly "to burden and abrade the minds of students, causing no little harm."[11] For "the grasp of beginners is

---

of Aquinas— the *Commentary on the Sentences of Peter Lombard,* bk. 4, d. 1, q. 1, quaestiunc. 2; the *Disputed Questions on Truth,* q. 4. a. 1, ad 7; and q. 9, a. 4, ad 4 and ad 5; the *Questions at Random,* q. 4, a. 17; and the *Summa theologiae* III, q. 60, a. 4, ad 1—and synthesizing their import, Poinsot concludes only that "in sententia S. Thomae probabilius est signum formale esse vere et proprie signum, atque adeo univoce cum instrumentali" (TDS, bk. 2, q. 1, 225/11–14).

11. Poinsot, "To the Reader of 1631," in TDS, 5: "immensam inextricabilium quaes-

not proportioned to these questions about signs"[12]—"swarming with so many and extraordinary difficulties"[13]—which, "for the slower wits," have "raised a fog."[14] Poinsot's solution to this problem was to remove "the metaphysical and other difficulties from the books *On the Soul* which the ardor of disputants has caused to intrude into the very beginning of the *Summulae* books"[15] and "to publish separately, in place of a commentary on the books *On Interpretation*," a "treatise on signs and modes of awareness."[16] This treatise cannot be appropriately introduced—introduced, that is, without causing undue confusion and perplexity—until mind-dependent being and relation have first been thoroughly treated, for the reason that it is on these two notions, and especially the notion of relation, that successful "inquiry concerning the nature and definable essence of signs principally depends."[17]

Here we see one of the best illustrations of the manner in which the work of Poinsot attempts what Simonin has called "a synthesis of irreconcilables": "On the one hand, Poinsot is determined to let no new achievements be lost," while "on the other hand, he is determined further still . . . to arrange his work in its totality according to the pattern and methods of long-standing tradition" (1930, 145).

Poinsot does not disagree with Soto's emphasis on the importance of a doctrine of signs. "Since the universal instrument of logic is indeed the *sign*," he tells us, "the very foundation of the exposition of logic goes unexamined" until and unless the project of a doctrine of signs

---

tionum silvam et spinosa sophismatum dumeta excidere curavimus, quae audientium mentibus onerosae et pungentes utilitatis nihil, dispendii non parum afferebant."

12. Poinsot remarks "super libros Perihermenias," 642a22–24: "Nec enim tironum captui quaestiones istae de signis proportinatae sunt" (TDS, 28/20–21).

13. ". . . tractatum de signis, pluribus nec vulgaribus difficultatibus scaturientem, ne hic iniectus aut sparsus gravaret tractatus alio satis per se graves . . ." ("To the Reader of 1640," in TDS, 35).

14. ". . . fateor sic me ista tractasse, ut accuratioribus oculis haud quaquam praeluxisse praesumam, at nec tardioribus offudisse caliginem, . . ." (ibid.).

15. "Ad haec metaphysicas difficultates pluresque alias ex libris de Anima, quae disputantium ardore in ipsa Summularum cunabula irruperant, suo loco amandavimus et tractatum de signis et notitiis in Logica super librum Perihermenias expedimus" ("To the Reader of 1631," in TDS, 5).

16. "Quod in prima Logicae parte promisimus de quaestionibus pluribus, quae ibi tractari solent, hic expediendis, plane solvimus, excepto quod iustis de causis tractatum de signis, pluribus nec vulgaribus difficultatibus scaturientem, ne hic iniectus aut sparsus gravaret tractatus alio satis per se graves, seorsum edendum duximus loco commentarii in libros Perihermenias simul cum quaestionibus in libros Posteriorum, et pro commodiori libri usu a tractatu Praedicamentorum seiunximus" ("To the Reader of 1640," in TDS, 35).

17. Poinsot remarks "super libros Perihermenias," 642a22–24: quaestiones istae de signis "nunc autem in hoc loco genuine introducuntur, post notitiam habitam de ente rationis et praedicamento relationis, a quibus principaliter dependet inquisitio ista de natura et quidditate signorum" (TDS, 38/21–39/4).

has been completed.[18] Moreover, as the unfolding of his treatment of the questions on relation and mind-dependent being as they pertain to the doctrine of signs makes clear, in Poinsot's view, interpretation is an activity coextensive with the life of the mind.[19] Hence a treatise on interpretation, strictly and properly so called, cannot be restricted to the logical interpretation of terms and propositions, but must extend itself to the instrument of interpretation as such, whether logical or otherwise, and this instrument is the sign. Hence, in view of the full requirements of philosophical tradition, the proper place for a consideration of signs in their entire amplitude is not merely in connection with or as part of a traditional commentary on Aristotle's *De Interpretatione,* as Poinsot's Coimbra teachers and others in the milieu had essayed, but *instead of* and *supplanting* the traditional commentary entirely.[20]

This solution is brilliant as far as it goes. "One sees there quite clearly the eye and hand of an exceptional artist," as Simonin says of Poinsot's treatment of logic in general (1930: 145). But, "whatever sympathy one may have for the attempt, it seems equally clear that it was not destined to develop and fulfill itself normally." Why not? Because more is at stake than a mere question of respecting the pattern of long-standing tradition. The very determination to let no new achievements be lost itself *guarantees* that the pattern will have to be modified. It is only a question of how far one is to go with such modification. By insisting on *the minimal modification of tradition possible consistent with what has been newly achieved,* Poinsot no doubt achieves at the same time the maximum emphasis on the already achieved, which was his set and constant purpose. Whereas Descartes embodied in his work the modern spirit, loving novelty for its own sake and valuing the newly discovered in principle over the already known, Poinsot embodied in his work exactly the opposite spirit of valuing the integrity of established truths equally with the importance of new discovery. He consequently paid heed to the importance of relating newly discovered truths to what has been established, and had no use for pursuing the lead of new consequences apart from a rather full regard for the landmarks provided by past connections.

18. "... commune siquidem Logicae instrumentum est signum, quo omnia eius instrumenta constant, idcirco visum est in praesenti pro doctrina horum librorum ea tradere, quae ad explicandam naturam et divisiones signorum ..." ("Super libros Perihermenias," in TDS, 38/13–19).

19. See note 30 below.

20. It is plain that to replace entirely the traditional commentary with a treatise on signs is radically different from making the treatment of signs a part of a traditional commentary or introduction to a traditional commentary focused on logical interpretation. See Deely 1988, 55–56.

It is here, I think, that Simonin rightly sees in Poinsot "a synthesis of irreconcilables." The consequences of new truths inevitably lead beyond, as well as bear relations to, the boundaries of what has already been discovered. By emphasizing the boundaries of the already discovered, Poinsot risked having newly discovered truth, in effect, become camouflaged in the landscape of the already known. This, in fact, is exactly what happened with his *Treatise on Signs* (see Deely 1985, 447n76 and esp. 461n97). Moreover, the fixity of the pattern itself of long-standing tradition is not something given once and for all. The "most natural place" for the treatment of signs at the time of Poinsot's confrontation of the problem generated by Soto's *Summulae* vis-à-vis Latin philosophical tradition in general and Thomistic tradition in particular would not remain the "most natural place" after his separate publication of a foundational *Treatise on Signs* that successfully reduced the doctrine newly established to its proper perspective and unity. For such a treatise, if successful, would inevitably alter this situation. At the time he undertook to write his own *Tractatus* on the subject, Poinsot expressly held the opinion that the treatment of signs in the courses introductory to the philosophy curriculum (that is, the courses of "minor," "formal," or "summulist" logic) was bound to appear eclectic and confused, disruptive of the order of traditional introduction without commensurate gain. The problem *then*, that is, at that point of the doctrine's development, was to systematize the treatment of signs and to discover the unity proper to the problematic of *signum* providing the foundations for interpretation in general, and logical interpretation in particular. As a research matter, this is a subject for advanced study, not introductory courses.

But if this problematic could be systematized and the unity and treatment proper to it assimilated, the problems constituting it could then be presented clearly and in their proper relation to logical studies—and to other studies insofar as they are "sign-dependent." *At that point* it would be possible to restore to the introduction a consideration of signs without creating confusion and resorting to eclecticism. This way of handling signs would also require a change in the pattern of traditional introduction, but now the change would be integrative rather than disruptive—it could affect the commensurate gains that clarity and a higher order of synthesis in the subject matter offers to beginning students.

In fact, this is exactly what happened with a logic by Michael Comas published at Barcelona in 1661. Comas, expressly basing his treatment not on questions of pedagogical preparedness but on the requirements proper to the order of doctrine—and, *expressis verbis*, on Poinsot's work in this area—provided a kind of anticipation of the Peircean project of deriving even the traditional concerns of formal logic and syllogistic directly from the prior consideration of the sign in its proper being (further specified as this and that kind of sign—in the case of logic as then conceived, "second intentions"). In other words, Comas uses Poinsot's arguments on the nature of signs in relation to traditional logic to begin the treatment of that very logic, especially for beginners, with the discussion of signs; and Comas does this in a way systematically derived from Poinsot's *Tractatus de Signis*. Comas's derived way offered an alternative both to the way that Poinsot had chosen, following his teachers, and to the way that Poinsot had criticized, chosen by Soto. The alternatives pursued by Poinsot and Comas alike repugned a confused eclecticism. But, compared to one another, the opposition of their ways is sequential, not repugnantial. What we have here is a detail illustrative of the evolution of intellectual culture consistent with long-standing tradition. Today's graduate seminars have a way of shaping even the most traditional among tomorrow's introductory textbooks for undergraduates.

If Poinsot's concern for integrating new achievements according to the pattern and methods of long-standing tradition represents a synthesis of irreconcilables in this sense, this is precisely because, as Simonin also notes, "Poinsot's work reveals itself as a work of transition" (1930, 145). There are ample reasons for suspecting that Poinsot realized he stood at some kind of boundary of the Latin development, and felt charged with the task of preserving a record of its integrity down to the utmost refinement of its developments. He perhaps made a conscious choice to sacrifice the natural development of his own work in favor of preserving for future generations the landscape and organic texture of philosophy in the Latin Age. "Understood in this way," as Simonin suggests, "and given its place in the development of history, the work of Poinsot acquires a particular significance, and perhaps a special interest, at a time"—such as the present volume undertakes to initiate—"when one rediscovers the flavor of an ancient style" (146).

III. ADJUSTING THE FOCUS: UNDERSTANDING WHAT WE HAVE FOUND

Be that as it may, there remains a special problem with regard to the place of Poinsot's treatise on signs in relation to the *Cursus Philosophicus Thomisticus* overall. While there is no doubt that the treatise on signs stands as a new achievement in one of the final developments of the plenitude of refinements of Latin Scholasticism, there is also no doubt that this treatise proves, on Poinsot's handling, to stand also as a definitive fulfillment of Descartes' proposal that we must "seek to encompass in thought everything in the universe, with a view to learning in what way particular things may be susceptible of investigation by the human mind" in order to answer that "most useful inquiry we can make at this stage," namely, what is the nature and extent of human knowledge (1628, 31)? For, as Locke would later agree, "we shall then use our understandings right, when we entertain all objects in that way and proportion that they are suited to our faculties, and upon those grounds they are capable of being proposed to us" (1690, 30). In other words, Poinsot found within the resources of Latin tradition an answer to the modern question concerning "in what way particular things are susceptible of investigation by the human mind." The answer lay in the doctrine of signs.

There are two ways we can look at Poinsot's achievement on the point. We can consider his doctrine of signs specifically within the context of his *Cursus Philosophicus Thomisticus*, or we can consider the *Tractatus de Signis* as a virtually autonomous treatment that can be evaluated on its own terms as an independent whole establishing the sign as the key to a philosophy of experience. Looked at either way, even though his treatment of the sign was so skillfully balanced and qualified by his artistic integration of it into the traditional treatment of logic that this deep tendency escaped the notice of his contemporary readers, Poinsot turns out to have provided us with nothing less than a new starting point for the philosophical enterprise as a whole.

A. The Tractatus de Signis *Viewed from within the* Cursus Philosophicus Thomisticus

Let us consider the novelty of Poinsot's work within the context of his *Cursus Philosophicus* as a whole. The first part of the *Cursus* consists of the treatment of logic, first according to its form, then according to its informing an actual subject matter by way of providing proofs and establishing probabilities. True to his admission that the question of the sign goes to the foundations of the subject matter of logic, we find that the opening two and a half chapters of the first of the introductory logic or *Summulae* books introduce definitions and divisions of all the terms that will form the subject of the discussion in the *Treatise on Signs*, replacing a *Perihermenias* commentary in the second part of logic. Here, in these opening two and a half pages of the *Cursus*, Poinsot manages to list, without discussion, all the terms and distinctions originally used by Soto to introduce into the Iberian-university world the substance as well as the fruits of the Parisian controversy, whereby the definition of the sign proposed by Augustine in the fifth century and used ever since among the Latins is relegated to the subdivision of signs as "instrumental," and a broader definition is proposed in its place as a definition comprehensive enough to cover "formal" signs as well. Thus the doctrine of signs, to be established on its own grounds, will cover the same materials as the opening chapters of the traditional introductory logic text, but at a deeper level and reorganized according to a different point of view which Poinsot calls simply that of a *doctrina signorum*.

Nor is this all. Remember that Poinsot spoke of "the metaphysical and other difficulties from the books On the Soul" as those needing special resolution from the systematic perspective of the *doctrina signorum*. In my edition of Poinsot's *Tractatus de Signis* as an independent work, I included as appendix B the complete table of contents from the *Cursus Philosophicus*, both as it appears in Reiser's edition and in the form of a synoptic table displaying the whole in an organizational chart. If one glances at that appendix, one finds that it is nothing less than the final conclusions of natural philosophy traditionally viewed that become the starting point of the newly demanded *doctrina signorum*. The reason is that the formal sign, which, you will remember, is identified with the products of perceptual and/or conceptual cognitive acts (usually called *species expressae* by the natural philosophers), is not discussed in the traditional natural philosophy until the treatment of material being that is both living and cognizant is reached, and this is at the very end of the order of exposition. What is last in exposition, however, is first in discovery: with the *doctrina signorum* Poinsot professes to have discovered the means of accounting for the origins and structure of experience as irreducible to subjective being, whether physical or psychical.

Dramatically enough, he traces the basic insight of the *doctrina signorum* to Aquinas's treatment of the Trinity as a community of persons, and to Cajetan's interpretation in particular of the notoriously difficult text in his *Summa theologiae* wherein St. Thomas says that the Persons of the Trinity are able to subsist as purely relative beings because of what is unique to relation among all the modes of physical being, namely, that it exists intersubjectively according to a rationale—the rationale of "being toward"—which is indifferent to the fact of being exercised independently of being cognized or known. In other words, every physical being that exists either in itself or in another exists subjectively and must, as such, exist whether or not it is known to exist by some finite mind, that is to say, whether or not it exists objectively as well as physically. But relation, in order to be what it is, exists not subjectively but as an intersubjective nexus or mode, and for this it *makes no difference* whether *the relation* obtains physically as well as objectively or only in the community of knowledge. In either case, whether it exists only as known or physically as well as objectively, it exists in exactly the same way: intersubjectively. By contrast, substance and accidents exist subjectively only when they are not pure objects of apprehension. Indeed, purely as objects apprehended, they are not subjective existents but relative objects *patterned after* what are not relative, namely, physically existent substances with their accidents, which, Poinsot points out, is precisely why there are mind-dependent relations but not mind-dependent substances or mind-dependent accidents other than relations.[21]

In other words, as *isolated* in this or that respect, physical being is determinately subjective, but in whatever respect reality enjoys *communion*, in that respect it is determinately *intersubjective* and as such can be maintained in cognition alone, in physical being alone, or in physical being and in cognition alike. Hence in the case of the Trinity, Aquinas argues, a diversity of Persons subsistent as *relations* is consistent with the unity of God as pure existence subsistent in itself, *ipsum esse subsistens;* hence too, "Comme particularité de la doctrine de Jean de Saint-Thomas, il faut noter encore qu'il place le constitutif formel de la deité dans l'intellection actuelle de Dieu par lui-même" (J.-M. Ramirez 1924, cols. 807–8).

In the case of the *doctrina signorum*, the application of Aquinas's point about the being proper and unique to relation as a mode of being is much humbler and, philosophically, quite independent of the theological doctrine that the interior life of God consists in a communion of three Persons.

By all accounts, Poinsot points out, signs are *relative* beings whose whole existence consists in the presentation within awareness of what they themselves are not. To function in this way the sign in its proper being must consist, precisely and in every case, in a relation uniting a cognitive being to an object known *on the basis of* some sign vehicle. What makes a sign formal or instrumental simply depends on the sign vehicle: if it is a psychological state, an idea or image, the sign is a formal sign; if the sign vehicle is a material object of any sort, a mark, sound, or movement, the sign is an instrumental sign. But whether the sign is formal or instrumental is subordinate to the fact that, as a sign, the being whereby it exists is not the subjective being of its vehicle (psy-

---

21. TDS, Second Preamble, a. 2, 96/1–36).

chological or material, as the case may be) but the intersubjective being of a relation irreducibly triadic.[22]

Many centuries later, Peirce would resume this point under a clearer terminology: every sign, in order to function as a sign, requires an object and an interpretant, and hence consists in a triadic relation.[23] But the point itself, that the *doctrina signorum* has for its subject matter a unified object of investigation in the being of relation as indifferent to originating from nature or mind, debated intensely among the Latins, is found thematically established not in Soto, the Conimbriceneses, or Araújo (see Beuchot 1980), but in Poinsot. For the first time, a definitive resolution is effected of "the possibility," originally suggested by Augustine (Eco et al. 1986, 65), "of resolving . . . the ancient dichotomy between the inferential relations linking natural signs to the things of which they are signs and relations of equivalence linking linguistic terms to the concept(s) on the basis of which some thing 'is'—singly or plurally—designated."[24] This definitive resolution is effected within the *Cursus Philosophicus* of John Poinsot.[25]

In effecting his resolution, Poinsot writes in a typically "medieval" fashion. All the Latin Scholastics of his time use the terminology of *relatio secundum esse* and *relatio secundum dici*, *relatio realis* and *relatio rationis*, *relatio praedicamentalis* and *relatio transcendentalis*,[26] confirming Eco's remark (Eco et al. 1986, 64) that "medieval materials at first glance normally appear to be stubborn repetitions of a common archetype or model, differing not at all or at least not perceptibly." The

---

22. "Unica relatione signi attingitur signatum et potentia, et haec est propria et formalis ratio signi" (TDS, bk. 1, q. 3, 154/28–30).

23. See, e.g., note 50 below.

24. The conclusion derives from that distinguished doctrine in Cajetan's *Commentary on the Summa theologica*, I, q. 1, a. 3, that the differences of things *as things* are quite other than the differences of things *as objects* and in the being of an object; and things that differ in kind or more than in kind in the one line, can differ in the other line not at all or not in the same way. And so, seeing that the rationale of a sign pertains to the rationale of the knowable (the line of thing as object), because it substitutes for the object, it will well be the case that in the rationale of object a mind-independent natural sign and a stipulated mind-dependent sign are univocal signs; just as a mind-independent being and a mind-dependent being assume one rationale in their being as object, since indeed they terminate in the same power, namely, the power of understanding, and can be attained by the same habit, namely, by metaphysics, or at least specify two univocally coincident sciences, as for example, logic and physics. Therefore, in the being of an object specifying, stipulated and natural signs coincide univocally. "So too a cognitive power is truly and univocally moved and led to a thing signified by means of a stipulated sign and by means of a natural sign" (TDS, bk. 2, q. 5, 270/38–271/12).

25. See TDS, bk. 1, q. 2, 135/1–152/7, esp. 141/12–142/13, together with TDS, bk. 2, q. 5, 269/1–277/12, esp. 270/37–271/12, and q. 6, 278/1–283/32, esp. 280/15–43.

26. See, for example, the analytically fragile but textually massive presentation of Krempel 1952.

forest stands out from the trees, but how does one make the trees stand out within the forest? Scholars skilled in the literal appearances have, on precisely literal ground, failed utterly to see the uniqueness of Poinsot's doctrine.[27] These scholars have failed to recall the medieval adage that "the authorities have a nose of wax";[28] for as Eco said of the *topos* of *latratus canis* (1986, 65), so must it be said of the *topos* of *signum:* "beneath literal appearances, every time the *topos* is cited, one has grounds for suspecting that a slight or more than slight shift of perspective has taken place." Nowhere more than in the matter of the *doctrina signorum* do we find that, among the Latin authors, "concealed differences stand out against the background of seeming repetitions— differences of the sort promising to reveal the heart of systems in reality very different."

In the case of his *Tractatus de Signis* vis-à-vis the *Cursus Philosophicus* as a whole, at least two further points need to be noted if we are fully to appreciate in this context Poinsot's contribution to the seventeenth century search for a new beginning in philosophy.

1. From Sensation to Intellection: The Scope of the *Doctrina Signorum*

Not only does the *Treatise on Signs* cover the very materials that make up the opening three chapters of the *Summulae* books, that is, of the traditional *Cursus Philosophicus* as a whole, but one needs to realize that these opening materials of the *Summulae* books concern *the simplest elements of the primary form of cognitive life,* namely, concepts as the forms of, as providing the structure for, simple awareness. In Poinsot's *Libri Summularum* themselves, the *Artis Logicae Prima Pars* of 1631, concepts are envisioned primarily in the narrow sense as restricted to ideas in the understanding or intellect *(species expressae intellectus).* This point I did not emphasize sufficiently in my Second Semiotic Marker (Deely

27. Looking exclusively from the perspective of formal logic in the traditional Latin sense, Muñoz Delgado (1964, 14, 22) expressed a certain puzzlement or even exasperation over the preference among French and American researchers for the work of Poinsot over that of Soto, a view naturally enough echoed in students of Muñoz Delgado's work, such as Ashworth and Angelelli. Indeed, Ashworth (1988, 1990a) not only takes her orientation from Muñoz Delgado's opinion, but seeks to establish him independently by appeal to literal appearances "as one of the few philosophers who has actually read some of the sixteenth-century authors to whom Poinsot was indebted" (not, apparently, Araújo, nor the contemporary studies of Araújo's work by Beuchot 1980, 1983, 1987; see Ashworth 1990b), going so far so far as to proclaim that in Poinsot nothing is to be found which does more than repeat Domingo de Soto's views.

28. No period better than the Latin period verifies Gracia's thesis "that the history of philosophy must be done philosophically" in order to be intrinsically helpful to the philosopher (1992, 332).

1985, 19), since it was written mainly to help the reader anticipate the departure from the established tradition that Poinsot would make in returning to treat this matter of the concept more broadly from the standpoint of the *doctrina signorum* proper *in place of* the traditional Perihermenias commentary which restricts itself to the concept narrowly conceived, that is, to ideas as opposed to images.[29] For in returning to treat this matter from the standpoint of the *doctrina signorum* envisaged fully as such, Poinsot is at pains to establish with his opening sentence that it can no longer be concepts in the narrow sense that are at issue, but precisely concepts in the broadest sense as including the psychological life of animals as well, or, if one prefers, of human beings not only specifically as rational but generically as animals:

> The question holds as much for a concept of the understanding, which is called an expressed specifier and word, as for an expressed specifier of perception or imagination, which is called an icon or phantasm. How does the definition of a formal sign, which is a formal awareness and which of itself and immediately represents something, apply to these?[30]

However, seeing that the *doctrina signorum* resumes and recasts the whole doctrine of *phantasiari*[31] and *intelligere* from the natural philosophy of cognitive organisms in reshaping the foundations of logic as such still does not reveal the full scope of the *doctrina signorum* as it bears on the understanding of experience. Not only intellection and perception are dependent on signs for the total structure of their objective apprehensions, but sensation as well.

As if to emphasize the role of signs in cognitive life, not merely according to the narrow conception of interpretation worked out in the traditional commentaries on the *De Interpretatione*, but according to the

---

29. "Nec est inconveniens, quod de simplicibus et his, quae pertinent ad primam operationem, agatur in Logica bis, quia, ut notat S. Thomas 1. Periherm. lect. 1., de dictionibus simplicibus sub alia consideratione agitur in Praedicamentis, scilicet ut significant simplices essentias, sub alia in libro Perihermenias, scilicet ut sunt partes enuntiationis, sub alia in libris Priorum, scilicet ut constituunt ordinem syllogisticum" (TDS, 16/40–17/2). See following note.

30. "Procedit quaestio tam de conceptu intellectus, qui vocatur species expressa et verbum, quam de specie expressa phantasiae seu imaginativae, quae dicitur idolum vel phantasma, quomodo illis conveniat definitio signi formalis, quod sit formalis notitia, et quod seipso et immediate aliquid repraesentet" (TDS, bk. 2, q. 2, 240/1–242/2, where the passage is extensively annotated). In the face of such a text, even apart from Poinsot's further discussion of the role of signs in external sensation and the life of brute animals which we shall consider shortly, it is fatuous to conjecture "that Poinsot would not have gone beyond the standard debate as to whether *interpretatio* meant an utterance or an assertion" (Ashworth 1988, 132).

31. I.e., the genus of knowing common to brute and rational animals over and above sensation: see Poinsot, *Philosophia Naturalis Quarta Pars in Tres Libros de Anima*, q. 8, a. 2, discussed in editor's note 2 at TDS, 240/4. See also Deely 1971, 55–83.

broadest and fullest conception of cognition established in the traditional commentaries on the *De Anima,* Poinsot expressly frames his concluding question "Concerning the Sign in Its Proper Being"[32] to establish "Whether the True Rationale of Sign is Present in the Behavior of Brute Animals and in the Operation of the External Senses."[33] The importance of such a question in the context of the modern search for a new beginning in philosophy cannot be overemphasized. Even though Descartes turned radically away from sensation in his attempt to re-establish a foundation for philosophy, his attempt was soon countered in the work of John Locke and the empiricists after him who turned precisely to external sense in their attempt to renew philosophy's foundation. Whether we regard sensation as the foundation of knowledge and core of experience or merely as a superficial point of departure from which to turn to inner experience, the matter of sensation became central to the modern search for a new beginning in philosophy.

Modern philosophers distinguish between primary and secondary qualities of objects; Greek and Latin philosophers distinguish rather between proper and common sensibles, and of course it is the latter, traditional viewpoint that Poinsot works with in his *Cursus Philosophicus.* Of course, bearing on the same subject matter, the two viewpoints are not unrelated. In fact, they are in one sense parallel, in another inverse. They are parallel, in that the modern list of qualities collectively taken matches the Scholastic list of qualities. They are inverse, however, in that the qualities listed as primary in the modern list match the common sensibles, which, in the Scholastic list, are dependent on the proper sensibles and so are secondary; while the proper sensibles, which are primary in the Scholastic list, match the qualities listed as secondary in the modern list. The inversion results from the standpoint according to which the two traditions distinguish the sensible characteristics or qualities of objects given in perception. The moderns (ironically, set as they are on a path which leads inexorably to idealism) drew their distinction from an adamantly realist point of view: the primary qualities are those which hopefully will prove to be mind-independently present in objects, while the secondary qualities are those supposed to be easily constructed and inscribed in objects by the mental activity of the perceiver. Of course, as has long become evident, the hopeful realism of the modern distinction was hopelessly misguided. Nor was it long before Bishop Berkeley explicitly pointed out that the two kinds

32. TDS, bk. 1.
33. TDS, bk. 1, q. 6.

of qualities are interdependent in experience in such a way that there is little ground for alleging a difference in status for the two vis-à-vis a supposed order of mind-independent being (1710, 45).[34]

If we employ the terminology of the moderns from the standpoint the Scholastics developed from Aristotle, Berkeley's argument can be much more forcefully stated: the sensible qualities of the objects of experience are so linked in experience that the supposed primary qualities are only known and attained through and on the basis of the qualities supposed secondary, whence, if the latter are constructed by the mind, there is no basis left for alleging the former not to be.[35]

---

34. George Berkeley, *The Principles of Human Knowledge* (1710), 45: "They who assert that figure, motion, and the rest of the primary or original qualities, do exist without the mind, in unthinking substances, do at the same time acknowledge that colours, sounds, heat, cold, and such like secondary qualities, do not, which they tell us are sensations existing *in the mind alone*, that depend on and are occasioned by the different size, texture, and motion of the minute particles of matter. This they take for an undoubted truth, which they can demonstrate beyond all exception. Now if it be certain, that those original qualities *are inseparably united with the other sensible qualities*, and not, even in thought, capable of being abstracted from them, it plainly follows that they exist only in the mind. But I desire any one to reflect and try, whether he can, by any abstraction of thought, conceive the extension and motion of a body, without all other sensible qualities. For my own part, I see evidently that it is not in my power to frame an idea of a body extended and moved, but I must withal give it some colour or other sensible quality which is *acknowledged* to exist only in the mind. In short, extension, figure, and motion, abstracted from all other qualities, are inconceivable. Where therefore the other sensible qualities are, there must these be also, to wit, in the mind and nowhere else."

35. The point was not lost on Hume in his *Enquiry Concerning Human Understanding* (1748, p. 154, par. 15): "It is universally allowed by modern enquirers, that all the sensible qualities of objects, such as hard, soft, hot, cold, white, black, &c. are merely secondary, and exist not in the objects themselves, but are perceptions of the mind, without any external archetype or model, which they represent. If this be allowed, with regard to secondary qualities, it must also follow, with regard to the supposed primary qualities of extension and solidity; nor can the latter be any more entitled to that denomination than the former. The idea of extension is entirely acquired from the senses of sight and feeling; and if all the qualities, perceived by the senses, be in the mind, not in the object, the same conclusion must reach the idea of extension, which is wholly dependent on the sensible ideas or the ideas of secondary qualities."

By this point Hume had already given us in its explicit, thematic form the famous "problem of the external world" (ibid., sect. 12, pt. 1, p. 152, pars. 11–13): "By what argument can it be proved, that the perceptions of the mind must be caused by external objects, entirely different from them, though resembling them (if that be possible) and could not arise either from the energy of the mind itself, or from the suggestion of some invisible and unknown spirit, or from some other cause still more unknown to us? . . .

"It is a question of fact, whether the perceptions of the senses be produced by external objects, resembling them: how shall this question be determined? By experience surely; as all other questions of a like nature. But here experience is, and must be entirely silent. The mind has never any thing present to it but the perceptions, and cannot possibly reach any experience of their connexion with objects. The supposition of such a connexion is, therefore, without any foundation in reasoning.

"To have recourse to the veracity of the supreme Being, in order to prove the veracity of our senses, is surely making a very unexpected circuit. If his veracity were at all con-

The standpoint of the Latin Scholastics, taken up by Poinsot in his *Cursus Philosophicus* and reshaped according to the requirements of the *doctrina signorum*, distinguishes among two types of sense data in a way that, unnoticed by its more recent partisans who want to insist on "realism" in philosophy, does not in fact presuppose realism,[36] because the Latin distinction is not in the first place ontological, but rather epistemological. The question answered in their distinction concerned the relation of environmental things to the channels of sense through and on the basis of which these things become aspectually and in part ob-

---

cerned in this matter, our senses would be entirely infallible; because it is not possible that he can ever deceive. Not to mention, that, if the external world be once called in question, we shall be at a loss to find arguments, by which we may prove the existence of that Being or any of his attributes." Whence "reason," Hume concludes, "can never find any convincing argument from experience to prove, that the perceptions are connected with any external objects" (ibid., par. 16).

36. It is instructive to compare Poinsot with Hume in this area. To Hume's claim that "no man, who reflects, ever doubted, that the existences, which we consider, when we say, *this house* and *that tree*, are nothing but perceptions in the mind" (1748, p. 152, par. 9), Poinsot answers, to the contrary (TDS, bk. 3, q. 2, esp. 309/47–312/6), that the view that external sense (as distinguished from internal sense-perception—*phantasiari*—and understanding) attains as its object an image produced by the mind is not merely subject to doubt, but is furthermore demonstrably incoherent *(implicat)*, both in terms of sense experience as such *(probatur a posteriori)* and in terms of the rational analysis of sense experience *(probatur etiam a priori)*, which shows both through direct argument and through an indirect *reductio* that the view in question is false. How far apart the Latin and the modern mainstreams had drifted in this area is apparent from Poinsot's further remark (TDS, 310/8–9) that his conclusion on this matter (which we may note was at variance with Suárez) "is the more common one among those competent to treat of the question." So much for Hume's "no man, who reflects, ever doubted . . ."

The whole of book 3 of the *Tractatus de Signis* is devoted to these and related issues concerning experience. Notice in particular, at the present juncture, that Poinsot grants that *if* sense were to know in an image, then indeed there would be an insoluble "problem of the external world" (312/2–6: "Quodsi existat in aliquo sui ut in imagine vel effectu, non immediate videbitur, sed ut contentum in imagine, ipsa vero imago est, quae videtur"). But this consequence he takes as a dialectical proof (a *reductio ad absurdum*) of what Latin tradition had established along several independent lines of direct argument, namely, the superfluousness of *species expressae* in external sense as such and the gratuitousness of supposing or positing them there. Thus, the very basis from which Hume (1748, par. 14) concludes that "reason . . . can never find any convincing argument from experience to prove, that the perceptions are connected with any external objects" is the basis from which Poinsot develops rather convincing proofs that perceptions precisely are connected with external objects in the precisely distinguished action of external sense taken as such within the activity of perception and understanding as a global whole.

It is an interesting and particularly instructive illustration of how the same material of experience can be transformed differently in the hands of different philosophers, while providing a common measure for the comparative soundness of their differing views.

See "A Maxim for Semiotics" in *Semiotics 1987* (Deely 1987), iii–v, for a general discussion of the different ways in which the maxim "nil est in intellectu quod non prius fuerat in sensibus" has been understood in ancient, medieval, and modern thought, including a reinterpretation in the line of the present discussion.

jectified: some aspects of the physical environment, namely, the proper sensibles, are objectified, cognized, or known through a single channel of sense only, while other aspects are assimilated to experience through more channels than one: the common sensibles.

What Poinsot in his *Cursus Philosophicus* is able to demonstrate, in effect, is that the requirements of a doctrine of signs are consonant with the epistemological standpoint of the Scholastics, but definitely incompatible with the would-be realist stance of the moderns, for this latter stance begs the question of the physical status of sensed things which experience must rather provide the basis for deciding, if decided it can be. More than this, the Scholastic standpoint needs to be viewed as in the line of the *doctrina signorum* in a very important sense: the Scholastic way of distinguishing provides in this instance the materials for an analysis which results in the conclusion that the manner in which the common sensibles presuppose the proper sensibles is in strict accordance with the defining characteristics of the type of relation in which signification consists:[37]

> *Wherefore we respond simply* that sense cognizes the significate in a sign in the way in which that significate is present in the sign, but not only in the way in which it is the same as the sign. For example, when a proper sensible such as a color is seen together with a common sensible, such as a profile and movement, the profile is not seen as the same as the color, but as conjoined to the color, and rendered visible through that color, nor is the color seen separately and the profile separately; so when a sign is seen and a significate is rendered present in it, the significate is attained there as conjoined to the sign and contained in it, not as existing separately and as absent.[38]

The importance of this point emerges from the following considerations. If indeed experience begins with sensations, as empiricists claim, and sensations are an irreducible mixture of common with proper sensibles, the latter of which are related to the former as sign to signified; and if the elaboration of sensations as perceptions requires, as all agree, the elaboration of images by the mind on the basis of which the sensible qualities are further presented *as* this or that; and if the understanding of what is perceived[39] also requires the elaboration by the mind of ideas or concepts in order for what is objectively per-

---

37. TDS, bk. 1, q. 6, 205/34–209/32, esp. 208/34–47, cited in the text above and note following.

38. TDS, bk. 1, q. 6, "Whether the true rationale of sign is present in the behavior of brute animals and in the operation of the external senses," 208/34–47.

39. E.g., motion as a point of departure for considering the question of whether a being transcendent to the material order might not be required in order for the perceived fact of physical motion to be possible in the first place; or as a point of departure for differentiating between projectiles and falling bodies; and so on.

ceived to be understood in this rather than that manner (not to mention understood at all); and if, in Peirce's formula (1868, 208), as Poinsot and others of his milieu had argued, "all thought is in signs," meaning that all concepts—all images and all ideas—are related to their objects as signs to significates, and every thought must be interpreted in another thought; then indeed the whole of experience, the being proper to it, from its primitive origins in sensation to its elaboration in perception and further development in understanding, all experience from its lowliest origins in sense to its highest attainments in theoretical understanding, is a continuous network, tissue, or web of sign relations. If that be so, then the doctrine of signs—the thematic elaboration of the role of signs in the constitution of knowledge and experience as the only path we have to the apprehension of objects and the truth about things—is not something peculiar or marginal to the philosophical enterprise but rather something central to it and at its core, however long it takes for individual philosophers and philosophy itself to reach that realization.

Even viewed strictly within the traditional confines of the *Cursus Philosophicus*, then, Poinsot's *Tractatus de Signis* establishes nothing less than a comprehensive role according to which signs provide the fabric and structure for experience as a whole, and for the acts of understanding as well in the full range of their theoretical postulations. The role of the sign at the origins and foundations of awareness in sensation as well as in its perceptual and intellectual superstructures is what Poinsot undertakes to envisage in removing the discussion of *signum* from the traditional terminist perspective and recasting it in a unity and perspective proper to itself. The *Treatise on Signs*, then, for all Poinsot's conservative concerns and commitment to tradition in the very sense that post-Cartesian Europe will reject, is of its very nature a radical work: it takes up again the then-traditional point of entry into philosophical study, and reshapes that point of departure according to an understanding of the fundamental activity of mind—namely, awareness as such—which understanding makes of that activity a branch of the doctrine of signs. We have here, in the heart of Poinsot's determinedly traditional *Cursus Philosophicus Thomisticus*, nothing less than the doctrinal beginnings of a revolution in philosophy, a revolution profoundly in sympathy and tune with the modern search for a new beginning in philosophy. Even from within his tradition, Poinsot's *tractatus de signis* constitutes a new beginning in philosophy, where the concerns of logic and the concerns of natural philosophy, of epistemology and ontology, are joined through their common origin in the action of signs within intellection and, more generally, within experience.

2. The Foundation of the Perspective Proper to the *Doctrina Signorum*—Its Point of Departure

The philosophical tradition indigenous to the Latin Age as it culminated in the work of Aquinas and the school that developed after him down to the end of the Latin epoch had a very clear focus: being. If there is one name that exactly characterizes that development overall it is surely the philosophy of being.[40] Being, the proper object of intellect as sound is of hearing or color of sight, is that with the grasp of which understanding begins, and being as first known *(ens ut primum cognitum)* divides first into *ens reale* and *ens rationis*.[41] Each of these further divides into substance and accident, on the one hand, and negation and relation, on the other hand.[42] The study of substance and accident as including the accident of mind-independent relation as a physical mode was the work of natural philosophy, but the study of negation and relation as mind-dependent objective modes had no comprehensive study. Poinsot was able to show that both negations and relations as mind-dependent beings share with mind-independent relation the common rationale of a "being toward," in contrast with all other modes of mind-independent being which share as such the rationale of subjectivity, or "being in" (*esse in se* in the case of substance, *esse in alio* in the case of accidents other than relation formally considered). But, in the main, the only focus in the study of *ens rationis* as such was established in the distinction between "first" and "second intentions," inasmuch as the latter relations were taken to provide the subject matter for formal logic.[43]

---

40. But not "comme si une philosophie de l'être ne pouvait être aussi une philosophie de l'esprit," not "as though a philosophy of being could not also be a philosophy of mind," as Maritain put it (1963, 388); une philosophie véritable épistémologique, as we might also say.

41. Aquinas, *In duodecim libros metaphysicorum Aristotelis expositio* (c.1268–1272), bk. 4, lect. 6, n. 10: "cum duplex sit operatio intellectus: una, qua cognoscit quod quid est, quae vocatur indivisibilium intelligentia: alia, qua componit et dividit: in utroque est aliquod primum: in prima quidem operatione est aliquod primum, quod cadit in conceptione intellectus, scilicet hoc quod dico ens; nec aliquid hac operatione potest mente concipi, nisi intelligatur ens. Et quia hoc principium, impossibile est esse et non esse simul, dependet ex intellectu entis . . . : ideo hoc etiam principium est naturaliter primum in secunda operatione intellectus, scilicet componentis et dividentis. Nec aliquis potest secundum hanc operationem intellectus aliquid intelligere, nisi hoc principio intellecto."

On the order of primitive concepts from being as first known to the point where correspondence truth can be asserted, see Deely 1982, 153–55n1.

42. In my article on First Philosophy (Deely 1987, 8) the text on this point is printed erroneously as "negation and privation" instead of "negation and relation."

43. "But this formality of a second intention is called 'second intention' according to the difference from a first intention, as if a second state or condition of an object were being expressed. For an object can be considered in two states: *First,* as it is in itself,

This distinction appears so straightforward that only the best of the Latin logicians saw much need to make their students aware of the considerable subtleties required to understand its full implications and the considerable complexity glossed over in the order of *ens rationis* adequately considered. Unfortunately, it is just these neglected complexities that are of much greater importance to the *doctrina signorum* than the distinction itself as taken to provide the focus for formal logic. For example, as Poinsot notes, "a first intention can also be found in the case of mind-dependent beings, as are many negations and privations and extrinsic denominations."[44] Thus, social and cultural roles and personality structure, though mind-dependent creations, belong to the order of first intention.[45] Again, "One second intention can even be materially subtended and accidentally denominated by another second intention, and so a second intention assumes the manner of a first intention in respect of the second intention to which it is subtended."[46] Whence a *processus in infinitum,* useless in principle for explaining things at the level of physical causality,[47] is perfectly possible within the objective order,[48] and, as Peirce best pointed out, is the normal condition in the action of signs within cognition.[49]

---

whether as regards existence or as regards definable structure. *Second,* as it is in apprehension, and this state of existing in cognition is second in respect of the state of existing in itself, which is first, because just as knowability follows on entity, so being known follows on that being which an object has in itself. Those affections or formalities, therefore, belonging to a thing according as it is in itself, are called first intentions; those belonging to the thing according as it is known are called second intentions. And because it is the task of Logic to order things as they exist in apprehension, therefore of itself Logic considers second intentions, the intentions which coincide with things as known" (TDS, First Preamble, a. 2, 59/19–6).

44. "... etiam in entibus rationis potest inveniri prima intentio, sicut sunt multae negationes et privationes et denominationes extrinsecae" (ibid., 58n2).

45. In the *Tractatus de Signis,* see the First Preamble, a. 2, 60/15–35; bk. 1, q. 2, 141/28–142/13; and 150n32, at the end.

46. "Potest etiam una secunda intentio materialiter substerni et denominari accidentaliter ab alia secunda intentione, et sic induit quasi modum primae intentionis respectu eius, cui substernitur" (ibid., 464b28–33).

47. Such is the classical foundation for the rational demonstration of the existence of God from our experience of the world in Aquinas, *Summa theologiae* I, q. 3, a. 3. Cf. TDS, Second Preamble, a. 3, "First Difficulty," 102/37–105/13, esp. 103/12–39.

48. "It follows secondly that although a first intention absolutely taken must be something mind-independent or belonging to something in the state of being independent of objective apprehension (for otherwise it would not be simply first, because that which is mind-independent always precedes and is prior to that which is mind-dependent), yet nevertheless *it is not contradictory that one second intention should be founded on another. In such a case, the founding second intention takes on as it were the condition of a first intention in respect of the other or founded intention, not because it is simply first, but because it is prior to that intention which it founds.*

"For since the understanding is reflexive upon its own acts, it can know reflexively the second intention itself and found upon that cognized intention another second intention;

In view of this situation, it is not surprising that Poinsot devotes one of the longest questions in his *tractatus de signis*[50] to showing that the action of signs requires for its explanation the extrinsic formal causality of objective interaction—what Peirce calls "ideal" causality (but also confuses with final causality)[51]—which can be found in nature wherever there is an assimilation through representation of one thing to another in guiding future outcomes.[52] And, as if to underscore the point, Poinsot devotes the following question to showing why the Aristotelian four causes of material interaction do not explain the action of signs.[53]

Equally fascinating is Poinsot's demonstration that brute animals as well as rational animals fashion and deploy mind-dependent structures of objectivity of which they make use in adapting the world to their own interests and needs. This analysis of so-called *entia rationis* materially formed and employed in the use of signs by animals is one of the most important elements in the preambles to Poinsot's *tractatus de signis*, bound up with his argument that percepts as well as concepts are for-

---

for example, the intention of a genus which is attributed to animal, can, as cognized, again found the second intention of species, inasmuch as the intention of genus is a kind of predicable species. And then this founded second intention denominates the founding second intention as prior, by reason of which circumstance it is said that the genus formally is a genus and denominatively is a species. This is something that frequently happens in these second intentions, to wit, that one of them is in itself formally of a certain type, but is of another type as known denominatively. Nevertheless these are all said to be second intentions, even though the one second intention is founded on another second intention, and there is not said to be a third or a fourth intention, because they all belong to (or coincide with) the object as known, but being known is always a second state for a thing. And because one second intention as it founds another takes on as it were the condition of a first intention in respect of that other founded on it, so even that intention which is founded is always said to be second" (TDS, First Preamble, a. 2, 61/31–62/18).

49. Normal, because it is a consequence of the very nature of a sign as "anything which determines something else (its *interpretant*) to refer to an object to which itself refers (its *object*) in the same way, the interpretant becoming in turn a sign, and so on *ad infinitum*" (Peirce 1902, 2.303).

Eco (1990, 28 and 38) makes two important glosses regarding "infinite semiosis." First, "In structuralistic terms, one could say that for Peirce semiosis is potentially unlimited from the point of view of the system but is not unlimited from the point of view of the process. In the course of a semiosic process we want to know only what is relevant according to a given *universe of discourse*." Second, "Semiosis is unlimited and, through the series of interpretants, explains itself by itself, but there are at least two cases in which semiosis is confronted with something external to it. The first case is that of indices. . . . Indices are in some way linked to an item of the extralinguistic or extrasemiosic world. The second case is due to the fact that every semiosic act is determined by a Dynamic Object. . . . We produce representamens because we are compelled by something external to the circle of semiosis."

50. TDS, bk. 1, q. 4, 166/1–192/14.
51. See the "Excursus on Peirce and Poinsot" in Deely 1985, 492–98, esp. 493–94.
52. See Deely 1991 and ch. 6 of Deely 1990, 83–104.
53. TDS, bk. 1, q. 5, 193/1–203/32. See Deely 1991.

mal signs. Animals, remarked Maritain (1957, 53), make use of signs without knowing that there are signs; Poinsot shows further that animals make use of mind-dependent relations without knowing that there are mind-dependent relations.[54]

My concern here, however, is not to show how the *doctrina signorum* brings into a more comprehensive focus the many complexities of the problematic of mind-dependent being which were left in the background and on the margins of traditional logical and ontological analysis. My concern rather is to show exactly how the *doctrina signorum* within Poinsot's *Cursus Philosophicus Thomisticus* relates to *ens reale* and *ens rationis* as terms distinguished within the intellectual grasp of *ens ut primum cognitum*. As Poinsot himself remarks, the doctrine of signs begins with the establishment of the notion of relation as transcending our experience of the objective contrast between *ens reale* and *ens rationis*.[55]

The point is simple, the move based on it is dramatic. Yet the text conveying this feat[56] is framed with so many technical complexities from the analysis of relation as a mode of being, presupposed to the discussion of *signum* as Poinsot is concerned to situate it, that Poinsot's best modern students have missed its thrust,[57] although once just barely.[58] Let me extract from the tangle the key assertion, and then try to explain its import:

---

54. See TDS, First Preamble, a. 3, 65/1–76/45, esp. 66/47–68/31, where Poinsot explains precisely that "sensus interni... repraesentare possint id, ad cuius instar formatur aliquod ens fictum, quod est materialiter formare entia rationis," and 74/39–48; and bk. 2, q. 2, 246/13–247/21. Cf. "Idolum. Archeology and Ontology of the Iconic Sign" (Deely 1986c).

55. TDS, bk. 1, q. 1, 117/28–118/6, included in the quotation in the following note.

56. "*Quaerimus ergo,* an formalis ista ratio signi consistat in relatione secundum esse primo et per se, an in relatione secundum dici seu [see following note] in aliquo absoluto, quod fundet talem relationem.

"Quid sit autem relatio secundum dici et secundum esse, relatio transcendentalis et praedicamentalis, dictum est in q. 17. de Relatione [art. 1. et 2.; see TDS, Second Preamble, aa. 1 and 2, 80/1–99/42]. Et loquimur hic de relatione secundum esse, non de relatione praedicamentali, quia loquimur de signo in communi, prout includit tam signum naturale quam ad placitum, in quo involvitur etiam signum, quod est aliquid rationis, scilicet signum ad placitum. Et ideo praedicamentale ens esse non potest nec relatio praedicamentalis, licet possit esse relatio secundum esse iuxta doctrinam D. Thomae 1. p. q. 28. art. 1. explicatam eadem q. 17 [esp. 93/17–97/36], quod solum in his, quae sunt ad aliquid, invenitur aliqua relatio realis et aliqua rationis, quae relatio manifestum est, quod non sit praedicamentalis, sed vocatur relatio secundum esse, quia pure relatio est et non aliquid absolutum importat" (TDS, bk. 1, q. 1, 117/18–118/18).

57. See the editor's note on the text of TDS, bk. 1, q. 1, at 117/22.

58. Maritain alone in recent times begins to penetrate Poinsot's foundational doctrine in what is original to it, yet never quite cuts fully to its core; see Deely 1986b, esp. 120–22.

We speak here of ontological relation—of relation according to the way it has being, not of categorial relation, because we are discussing the sign in general, as it includes equally the natural and the social sign, in which general discussion even the signs which are mental artifacts[59]—namely, stipulated signs as such—are involved.[60] And for this reason, the rationale *common* to signs cannot be that of a categorial being, nor a categorial relation,[61] although it *could* be an ontological relation, according to the point made by St. Thomas in the *Summa theologiae*, I, q. 28, art. 1, and explained in our Preamble on Relation—to wit, that only in the case of these things which exist toward another is found some mind-independent relation and some mind-dependent relation,[62] which latter plainly is not categorial, but is called a relation according to the way it has being (an ontological relation), because it is purely a relation and does not import anything absolute.[63]

Put as simply and straightforwardly as possible, Poinsot is saying here that the *doctrina signorum* must take its departure from a standpoint that transcends the division of being into *ens reale* and *ens rationis*.[64] This explicit realization is what sets his *Tractatus de Signis* apart within the *Cursus Philosophicus* and Latin tradition as a whole as a virtual demand for a new beginning in philosophy, a beginning in terms of which the division of being into categories, for example, needs to be justified anew in terms of an experiential starting point.[65]

To begin with, what is called "ontological relation" or "relation according to the way it has being" in my translation is called, in Poinsot's

---

59. I.e., which are mind-dependent beings.
60. See the extended discussion of this point at TDS, bk. 1, q. 2, 141/12–142/13.
61. See Poinsot 1632, Logica, p. 2, q. 14, a. 1, "Quid sit praedicamentum et quid requiratur ut aliquid sit in praedicamento" ("What a category is and what are the conditions for anything's belonging to a category"), 500b36–501a2: "Since the distinction of the categories was introduced for this, that the orders and classes of diverse natures might be set forth, to which all the things that participate some nature might be reduced, the very first thing to be excluded from *every* category is mind-dependent being, for being that depends for its existence on being cognized (mind-dependent being) has not a nature nor a true entity, but a constructed one, and therefore must be relegated not to a true category, but to a constructed one. Whence St. Thomas says (in q. 7, art. 9 of his *Disputed Questions on the Power of God*) that only a thing independent of the mind pertains to the categories" (cited in n. 10 to TDS, bk. 1, q. 1, 118).
62. See TDS, Second Preamble, a. 2, esp. 93/17–96/36, but also 89/21–91/28. See further First Preamble, a. 1, 51/37–52/5, 53/32–45; a. 2, 60/7–44; and a. 3 [sic], 70/24–71/19.
63. TDS, bk. 1, q. 1, 117/28–18.
64. See Deely 1977 and 1988, 82–86.
65. Note 16 to TDS, 86/22, was intended to clarify this implication of Poinsot's work, but proved instead to be the single greatest occasion of misunderstanding in the contemporary discussion of Poinsot (Bird 1987, 106–7, followed by Ashworth 1988, 134–36). Accordingly, I found it necessary to clarify the point at some length (Deely 1988, 56–87, esp. 56–69), and this clarification has been incorporated into a much expanded version of note 16 for the electronic version of the *Tractatus de Signis* released by Intelex Corporation in 1992.

Latin, *relatio secundum esse*. Within the Thomistic tradition, the *secundum esse* relative was a *terminus technicus* that had achieved a very high degree of precision thanks to the commentaries of Cajetan, Soto, and Araújo, among others. Categorial or physical relation, *relatio praedicamentalis seu relatio realis*,[66] fits the definition of *relatio secundum esse*, but so does mind-dependent relation or *relatio rationis*.

Now the sign is a peculiar being because our experience of it cannot be reduced to the categories of *ens reale* and *ens rationis*. Our experience and use of *signum* conveys with equal facility phenomena of nature, such as lead us to anticipate a storm, and phenomena of culture, such as lead us to respect a flag for what it symbolizes.

Poinsot emphasizes a twofold point which sets the Thomistic development of *signum* apart within the Latin tradition.[67] The reason that

66. The translation of *relatio realis* as "physical relation" has been the second greatest occasion of misunderstanding in contemporary discussion of the 1985 edition of Poinsot's *Tractatus de Signis*. "'Physical beings' will not do for *entia realia*," D. P. Henry states (1987, 1201), "since theological entities are for Poinsot non-physical (indeed metaphysical) but nevertheless real"; whence Henry deems this a "quite inappropriate" translation of a key term, a criticism in which he is joined by Furton (1987, 767) and Ashworth (1988, 145), who also objects on the ground that "there are places in which the type of real being picked out may well include spiritual beings." The objection stems from ignorance of the details of the philosophical vocabulary in Poinsot's tradition, to be sure, but it also serves to emphasize the need mentioned above to go beyond the literal appearances in reading the authors of mainstream Latin tradition. In this particular, nonetheless, I am surprised to learn that it is apparently little known among contemporary renaissance Latin scholars that, beginning with Aquinas himself (e.g., *Sententia libri ethicorum*, bk. 1, lect. 1, n. 1), the term "physical" extends equally to material and spiritual substances, including the *esse divinum* ("Essentia Dei physica consistit in cumulo omnium perfectionum in gradu infinito et in summa simplicitate, ita ut, quamquam perfectio a perfectione differt plus quam ratione ratiocinante, non distinguantur tamen inter se nisi ratione ratiocinata cum fundamento in re imperfecto" [Gredt 1936, vol. 2, thesis 32]). Thus Poinsot, in his theological *Cursus* (1643a, 38n8), speaks of divine grace as producing a "specialem modum praesentiae realis et physicae respectu Dei," flatly contradicting Henry's assertion that theological entities for Poinsot are nonphysical.

The division of *ens reale* into spiritual and material substances, in the Thomistic tradition, is precisely a division in the order of physical being—the order, that is to say, of being as existing independently of objectification in finite cognition. "Ens physicum" and "ens reale" alike designate this order of being throughout its extent, whence the synonymy drawn upon in the 1985 *Tractatus de Signis* translation is inaptly singled out by the reviewers for criticism. A reliable modern guide to the technical Latin usages in Poinsot's tradition can be found in the two-volume text entitled *Elementa Philosophiae Aristotelico-Thomisticae*, written by the learned Benedictine philosopher-scientist, Joseph Gredt, exactly according to the traditional plan of Poinsot's *Cursus Philosophicus*, but updating the material of natural philosophy pertaining to experimental science (psychology, biology, physics, and so on) and addressing the problems under more current headings: see Deely 1985, 461n97. Originally published in 1899, the work went through seven editions in the author's lifetime, and there have been at least five posthumous editions, of which I have relied primarily on the 1961 posthumous edition by Zenzen.

67. I am indebted to Mauricio Beuchot (1980) for learning that Francisco Araújo's

signum must be identified with *relatio secundum esse* is, first of all, because relation in this precise sense designates the only ontological rationale (*ratio entitatis*) which can be found verified in each of the opposed orders of *ens reale* and *ens rationis:* this much is already clear in the cited text, with its explicit demand that the *doctrina signorum* begin at a point beyond, or prior to, the distinction between *ens reale* and *ens rationis*. The uniqueness of the action of signs that follows from this, however, Poinsot uniquely developed.

Even though others in Poinsot's tradition had identified the sign-relation with *relatio secundum esse,* they had not seen how this identification implied a unified subject matter for the *doctrina signorum*. Sometimes relations are mind-independent, as in the case of natural signs, and sometimes they are mind-dependent, as in the case of conventional signs: this much everyone saw. What Poinsot further saw was that this opposition of natural to conventional signs does not preclude the relation constituting *either* type of sign from being sometimes mind-dependent and sometimes mind-independent.

In the case of natural signs, a natural sign formally as a sign functioning here and now is mind-dependent when the conditions required for the relation to be mind-independent are not realized. As Poinsot put it, "relatio signi naturalis ad suum signatum . . . realis est . . . supponendo . . . conditiones relationis realis," alias rationis.[68]

In the case of conventional signs, the foundation for the sign-relation consists "in the extrinsic denomination whereby it is rendered imposed or appointed for signifying by common usage," inasmuch as "it is through this imposition that something is habilitated and appointed to be a stipulated sign, just as it is through some natural sign's being proportioned and connected with a given significate that there is founded a relation of the sign to that significate."[69] But this original foundation does not prevent that same conventional sign from becoming habituated within a population, and by this means becoming transformed into a sign relatively natural, signifying as such by a mind-independent triadic relation and no longer a mind-dependent one.[70] Thus, just as

---

Commentariorum in Universam Aristotelis Metaphysicam of 1617 provides a direct link in the development from Soto's *Summulae* to Poinsot's *Tractatus de Signis*.

68. TDS, bk. 1, q. 2, 137/9–15. Araújo is even more explicit on the point, as reported in Beuchot 1980, 52–53.

69. TDS, bk. 1, q. 2, 141/16–18, 23–27.

70. TDS, bk. 2, q. 6, 280/26–43: "When speaking of human custom, even though it proceeds from a free cause and so is denominated a free effect, nevertheless, the formal rationale of signifying is not any free deputation, but the very frequency and repetition of acts, and this signifies naturally, because it is not a moral deputation, that is to say, it is not an extrinsic deputation which denominates only morally, but the intrinsic perfor-

circumstances can dictate that a natural sign be realized as such through a mind-dependent relation, so circumstances can bring it about that a conventional sign be realized through a mind-independent relation.[71] And mind-independent relations based on habit constitute signs not only in the order of conventions among human animals, but also in the order of interactions between human beings and other animals or among animals themselves. In Poinsot's terse summary, "not all custom is a human act, but all custom can found a natural sign."[72]

In other words, the status of *signum* as ontologically relative is not that of a genus respecting natural and conventional signs as its determinate species, but an existential condition which can be realized in the mind-independent and mind-dependent orders indifferently according to the role of the fundament together with the circumstances which surround the sign but do not constitute it within cognition as a sign. For only a triadic relation can constitute a sign as such. Whether this relation will be mind-dependent or mind-independent is determined not only by the role of the fundament engendering the sign relation, but also by the circumstances under which that fundament operates in generating the relation. Thus, if the fundament of a sign-relation is a pure stipulation taken as such *prescinding from any custom which has grown up around the stipulation*, the resulting sign will be a conventional sign constituted by a mind-dependent relation. If the fundament of a sign-relation is a natural feature or characteristic of an object, or a psychological condition or state (a concept, be it an idea or an image), *and the terminus of the sign-relation (the object signified) also exists physically*, then the resulting sign will be a natural sign constituted by a mind-independent relation. But the *signum*, whether here and now verified under a determinately mind-independent relation or under a determinately mind-dependent relation, is realized according to the same rationale in either

---

mance of acts and their frequency and multiplication constitutes the customary sign. Therefore a signification attaches to that sign naturally, even as multiplied free acts generate a habit as a natural and not as a free effect, because the very multiplication of the acts does not function freely relative to generating the habit, so neither to the signifying resulting from the force of the repetition of the acts, even though these acts in themselves [i.e., singly taken] may be free."

71. According to Beuchot's report (1980, 47), therefore, we have here an important difference between Poinsot and his two main forebears, Soto and Araújo: "Por eso prefiere la de Soto, quien divide primariamente el signo en natural y convencional y, como subdivisiones del natural, el perfecto y el imperfecto o consuetudinario. Así, al ser imperfecto, no tiene significión real, sino de razon, teniendo fundamento en la costumbre, que imita a la naturaleza."

72. "[G]eneraliter loquendo consuetudo non solum invenitur in hominibus, sed etiam in brutis naturali instinctu operantibus. Unde . . . et ita non omnis consuetudo est actus humanus et [omnis consuetudo] fundare potest signum naturale" (TDS, bk. 2, q. 6, 280/15–23).

case, the rationale of a triadic "being toward" which as such transcends subjectivity in every case and renders objects signified univocal in their being as objects regardless of differences in their status as things physically existing.

This singular ability of the sign to pass back and forth between the orders of mind-independent and mind-dependent being with rationale unchanged uniquely gives the *doctrina signorum* the capacity to explain both the possibility of correspondence truth and the reason why truth as correspondence is needed as a critical check upon experience as constituted from within by a texture of relations commingling real and unreal objects, natural and conventional signs, deceits as well as wisdom. The doctrine of signs has a unified subject matter to investigate precisely because the rationale which constitutes any given sign is the same regardless of the circumstances of its occurrence, even though the circumstances of its occurrence will locate the sameness now as resulting primarily from nature, now as primarily from cognition, usually as an admixture of the two orders as together constituting experience. The very fact that the same being of the *relativum secundum esse* is realized in the diversity of all signs as the common ground of the action proper to signs explains the difference between the objective order as such and the subjective order of physical being, including psychological subjectivity.

Poinsot is not only re-explaining the opening chapters of his traditional *Cursus Philosophicus* in terms of the bearing thereon of the later chapters that conclude the traditional *Cursus Artium,* chapters from the tradition of commentary on the *De Anima;* he is also explaining the nature of experience and the experiential origins of the traditional doctrines of logic and the categories of natural philosophy. But his concern is not to emphasize all this inasmuch as it is assuredly new. On the contrary, his concern is to control, balance, qualify, and restrict by the total concerns of the Latin tradition the *doctrina signorum* that more recent concerns and refinements of the Latin tradition have forced to the foreground.

The question we have now to ask is what would have to be made of this doctrine newly systematized were it free to follow on its own terms its deep tendency and enter history on its own terms, rather than in terms imposed upon it by a traditional superstructure developed in a manner largely oblivious to its own foundations as a sign-dependent structure. In other words, how does the *doctrina signorum* appear when viewed no longer in the context of Poinsot's *Cursus Philosophicus Thomisticus* (and hence, indirectly, as a commentary on Thomas Aquinas), but rather as a pure philosophical possibility in its own right?[73]

---

73. Put otherwise, what would happen were we to put to the *Cursus Philosophicus* and

B. The Tractatus de Signis *Viewed in Terms of Its Own Requirements for Philosophy*

The first thing to be said about Poinsot's *Treatise on Signs* viewed on its own has been said by the grand old man of Peirce scholarship, Max H. Fisch: "it is the most *systematic* treatise on signs that has ever been written" (1986, 180). What Poinsot has presented in his thematization of the sign is a thoroughgoing demonstration that the action of signs is what gives structure to our sensations, perceptions, and understanding, both practical and theoretical—in a word, to our experience as a whole. If this is true, a philosophy based on experience must be based on the sign, and a philosophy of signs must be a philosophy of experience. If philosophy begins with experience, then philosophy begins with signs and remains dependent upon signs in its farthest developments. Philosophy can know objects which are more than signs and, through such objects, something of things as well in their own being, as can science; but nothing of this can come about without signs or other than through the action of signs, albeit critically controlled and adjusted by understanding, both comparative and reflexive.

Viewed in terms of its own requirements for philosophy, therefore, Poinsot's *tractatus de signis* has the same consequences that we have seen it to have for tradition: it requires a re-examination of philosophy's starting point, and an admission that that starting point is rooted in the action of signs which determine the nature and extent of our knowledge. "Poinsot's semiotics," wrote Sebeok, "not only expands our comprehension of communication, but in countless ways of what is communicated, and it suggests possibilities for finding a unity for knowledge that may have seemed lost forever after Descartes" (1986, 15).

In the end, once the traditional terms of its discussion have finally been understood, the most surprising thing about Poinsot's *tractatus de signis* is how modern it clearly is. History has its accidents, but in this

---

existing tradition as a whole the proposal Poinsot put to the logicians of his day? I paraphrase 38/11-19: Nevertheless, because these matters are all treated in those books by way of interpretation and signification, since indeed the universal instrument of awareness is the *sign*, from which all its instruments are constituted, therefore, lest the foundation of the expositions of philosophy itself go unexamined, the project of the present work is to treat of those things concerning the nature and divisions of signs insinuated in the works of traditional philosophy, but which have been reserved for special treatment here. (Sed tamen, quia haec omnia tractantur in his libris per modum interpretationis et significationis, commune siquidem cognitionis instrumentum est signum, quo omnia eius instrumenta constant, idcirco visum est in praesenti pro doctrina horum librorum ea tradere, quae ad explicandam naturam et divisiones signorum in libris traditionalibus insinuata, huc vero reservata sunt.)

case it has also its confluences. The year in which Poinsot brought his *Tractatus* to publication was the year in which John Locke was born. At the age of fifty-eight, Locke, in fathering the second of the two great traditions which defined the development of modern philosophy, concluded his famous *Essay Concerning Human Understanding* by proposing that the answer to the modern question posed by Descartes in launching the rationalist tradition, and posed anew by Locke himself in launching the empiricist tradition, should perhaps be sought instead by launching another tradition, a line of reflection based on "*semiotic* or *the doctrine of signs.*" Neither Locke himself nor any of his successors in the modern period tried out this "way of signs." Instead, as history amply recorded, the "way of ideas" was pursued by modern philosophy down to its classical systematization in the *Critiques* of Immanuel Kant.

Locke's proposal, when it was considered at all, was rejected out of hand—for example, by Leibniz (1704) in his *New Essays Concerning Human Understanding*, on the grounds that natural phenomena and conventional signs have no common denominator, because the latter are arbitrary and the former are not; and that a distinction, one of whose parts, semiotic, virtually absorbs the other two, physics and ethics, is defective.[74] Fraser, in his 1894 edition of Locke's *Essay* (2:463n1), has only disparagement for "this crude and superficial scheme of Locke" wherein it is proposed that the study of signs as providing the means for speculative and practical knowledge alike may hold the key to understanding aright the nature and extent of human knowledge.

As the modern period in philosophy neared its end, a more judicious assessment was made by Charles Sanders Peirce. Directly inspired by his reading of Locke and thoroughly cognizant both of the modern period and of the Greek and Latin periods in philosophy (though not, unfortunately, of the Iberian development of the doctrine of signs except for the work of the Conimbricenses, who adopted all the positions concerning signs which, on Poinsot's demonstration, make a unified doctrine impossible),[75] Peirce was compelled to describe himself as "a pioneer, or rather, a backwoodsman, in the work of clearing and opening up . . . the doctrine of the essential nature and fundamental varieties of possible semiosis." This last was Peirce's term for the action of signs, derived from a reading sometime around 1879 of the remains of an *ante* 79 A.D. Herculaneum papyrus on the subject of signs by the Epicurean philosopher Philodemus (see Fisch 1986a, 329–30).

74. Cf. Winance 1983, 515: "C'est dans la tradition de Peirce, Locke, et Jean de Saint-Thomas que la logique peut devenir une sémiotique qui absorberait l'épistémologie et même la philosophie de la nature."
75. See Doyle 1984b.

Locke's proposal for semiotic, once seen against the backdrop of Poinsot's *tractatus de signis*, surely appears as one of history's confluences within the *Zeitgeist* of the seventeenth century,[76] revealing as it does that the very problem exercising modern thought in its rejection of Latin immersion in Aristotelian philosophy of nature was the problem on which Poinsot brought all the resources of the Latin tradition to bear, namely, the problem, as Locke put it, of "the way and proportion that objects are suited to our faculties, and upon those grounds they are capable of being proposed to us" (1690, 30). This task, in Descartes words, is one which "everyone with the slightest love of truth ought to undertake at least once in his life, since the true instruments of knowledge and the entire method are involved in the investigation of the problem" (1628, 31). That Peirce should have come to be regarded as the father of the semiotic tradition, as Descartes was of rationalist and Locke of empiricist tradition, is, by contrast, rather more of an accident, the historical accident whereby the highest development of Latin thought after Ockham fell into oblivion, and the Iberian influence on university life, except as filtered through Suárez, became lost to modern times.

As the contemporary development enters a post-modern age, this particular accident of history, at least, is being redressed. And in this particular case we have learned enough to now see clearly that, when it comes to the doctrine of signs, it is anything but the case that, as Whitehead could once credibly allege, "A brief, but sufficiently accurate, description of the intellectual life of the European races during the succeeding two centuries and a quarter up to our own times is that they have been living upon the accumulated capital of ideas provided for them by the genius of the seventeenth century" (1925, 57–58). The problem with Whitehead's assertion is that, in the area of the doctrine of signs, the accumulated capital of ideas provided by the genius of the seventeenth century was primarily Hispanic, and by dint of circumstance (not excluding some deep-rooted prejudices), was not available to the European races to draw upon. Whitehead's observation is, in equal parts, sufficiently accurate and sufficiently inaccurate. With the present volume, and I hope in many others to follow, we have been dealing with the part that is inaccurate. If the intellectual life of the European races during the past three centuries had been living upon the complete capital of ideas laid up in the seventeenth century, Peirce would not be the father of semiotic tradition but one of its late systematizers, perhaps in a position respecting the semiotic tradition com-

---

76. See Deely 1986a.

parable to the position in which Poinsot found himself respecting the Latin tradition in logic and natural philosophy.

What is certain is that philosophical doctrine as it developed in the later Latin centuries in the area of what we today call "epistemology," or the theory of knowledge, has an intrinsic relevance to the modern concern voiced by Locke under the name of "semiotic." Locke's concern, anticipated by Poinsot, has been taken up today through the work of Charles Sanders Peirce, whence it bids fair to become the mainstream post-modern development as philosophy, along with the rest of civilization, moves toward the twenty-first century.

IV. CONCLUSION

The independent publication of Poinsot's *Tractatus de Signis* in 1985 indeed had the merit, among others, as Santaella Braga said, "of making evident that the doctrine of signs proclaimed by Locke did not have to wait two-hundred years to rise in the bosom of Peirce's complex and monumental work" (1991, 155). Yet Peirce does not provide the only proof in contemporary philosophy of the value of Poinsot's work to philosophy's future. Jack Miles, in preparing copy for the release by the University of California Press of my 1985 autonomous edition of Poinsot's *Treatise on Signs,* wrote: "That Poinsot's diagnosis of the course of western philosophy was superior to—or at the very least clearly distinct from—the alternative diagnosis of Descartes and of all modern philosophy is proven, Deely argues, by the reemergence in our day of Poinsot's questions as semiotic." I would stand by Miles's formulation, but add in support of it here the following concluding observations.

If we put Poinsot's claim that the doctrine of signs transcends in its starting point the division of being into *ens reale* and *ens rationis* into modern terms, what is being asserted is that semiotic transcends the opposition of realism to idealism. Not until Heidegger in the contemporary period do we encounter such a claim among the philosophers. Heidegger at least recognized that "this problem [of the unity of being prior to the categories] was widely discussed in medieval ontology especially in the Thomist and Scotist schools," and although he did not think that the medieval discussion succeeded in "reaching clarity as to its principles,"[77] neither did Heidegger know of Poinsot's work in this particular. Correspondence truth both Poinsot and Heidegger recog-

---

77. "Die mittelalterliche Ontologie had dieses Problem vor allem in den thomistischen und skotistischen Schulrichtungen vielfätig diskutiert, ohne zu einer grundsätzlichen Klarheit zu kommen" (Heidegger 1927, 3).

nized; but with his doctrine of signs Poinsot was achieving within the Latin tradition the first systematic clarification of the ontological foundations in relation for the possibility of truth as a conformity knowable in the structures of objectivity between thought and things. Such a clarification Heidegger called for as late as 1943 in his essay *Vom Wesen der Wahrheit*.

The difficulty and originality alike of Poinsot's work derive, in short, from his recognition that *the first concern* of anyone who would seek to explain signs, the universal means of communication, must be to pay heed "to Aristotle's *problem of the unity of Being* [as that which is experientially first in human understanding] as over against the multiplicity of 'categories' applicable to things."[78] The experience of signs and of the escape from the subjectivity of the here and now is as fundamental in its own way as is the experience of things in terms of the data which provide experimental justification for the scheme of the categories, as is clear from the fact that the derivation of the categories from experience is itself a function of the use we make of signs in developed discourse.[79]

Poinsot's contribution to the seventeenth-century search for a new beginning in philosophy was nothing less than to show in detail what that new beginning might best be, namely, a setting out in earnest along the way of signs. It was a contribution destined to be overlooked in its day, but privileged to enter into the history of semiotic development anew at a later time, the time when the exploration of the way of signs would be, for the first time, thematically undertaken. By this accident, history achieves another confluence, and the last of the Latins joins the last of the moderns to initiate a post-modern era in philosophy, where experience and the being proper to it become the central occupation of philosophy in exploring the way of signs.

WORKS CITED IN CHAPTER 15

Angelelli, Ignacio. 1992. Logic in the Iberian age of discovery: Scholasticism, Humanism, Reformed Scholasticism. Paper at the "Hispanic Philosophy in the Age of Discovery" conference, 14–17 October, The Catholic University of America, Washington, D.C.

---

78. "Und wenn schliesslich *Hegel* das 'Sein' bestimmt als das 'unbestimmte Unmittelbare' und diese Bestimmung allen weiteren kategorialen Explikationen seiner 'Logik' zugrunde legt, so hält er sich in derselben Blickrichtung wie die antike Ontologie, nur dass er das von Aristoteles schon gestellte Problem der Einheit des Seins gegenüber der Mannigfaltigkeit der sachhaltigen 'Kategorien' aus der Hand gibt" (Heidegger 1927, 3).

79. See the gloss in note 16 to TDS, Second Preamble, a. 1, 86/9–22, especially as expanded in the electronic edition on the basis of Deely 1988.

Aquinas, Thomas. c. 1268–72. *In duodecim libros metaphysicorum Aristotelis expositio*. In *S. Thomae Aquinatis Opera Omnia et sunt in indice thomistico*, edited by Roberto Busa, 4:390–507. 7 vols. Stuttgart-Bad Cannstatt: Frommann-Holzboog, 1980.

Ashworth, E. J. 1974. *Language and logic in the post-Medieval period*. Dordrecht: D. Reidel Publishing Co.

———. 1978. Multiple quantification and the use of special quantifiers in early sixteenth century logic. *Notre Dame Journal of Formal Logic* 19:599–613.

———. 1988. The historical origins of John Poinsot's *Treatise on signs*. *Semiotica* 69, nos. 1/2:129–47.

———. 1990a. Domingo de Soto (1494–1560) and the doctrine of signs. In *De ortu grammaticae. Studies in Medieval grammar and linguistic theory in memory of Jan Pinborg*, edited by G. L. Bursill-Hall, Sten Ebbesen, and Konrad Koerner, 35–48. Amsterdam: John Benjamins.

———. 1990b. The doctrine of signs in some early sixteenth-century Spanish logicians. In *Estudios de historia de la logica. Actas del II simposio de historia de la logica: Universidad de Navarra Pamplona 25–27 de Mayo 1987*, edited by Ignacio Angelelli and Angel d'Ors, 13–38. Pamplona: Ediciones EUNATE.

Berkeley, George. 1710. *The principles of human knowledge*. In *The works of George Berkeley, Bishop of Cloyne*, edited by A. A. Luce and T. E. Jessop. London: Nelson, 1948ff.

Beuchot, Mauricio. 1980. La doctrina tomista clásica del signo: Domingo de Soto, Francisco de Araújo y Juan de Santo Tomás. *Critica* 36.

———. 1983. Lógica y lenguaje en Juan de Sto. Tomás. *Diánoia* 17.

———. 1987. *Metafísica: La ontología Aristotelico-Tomista de Francesco de Araújo*. Mexico City: Universidad Nacional Autónoma de Mexico.

Bird, Otto A. 1987. John of St. Thomas Redivivus ut John Poinsot. *The New Scholasticism* 61, no. 1 (Winter): 103–7.

Cajetan, Thomas de Vio. 1507. *Commentaria in summam theologicam. Prima pars*. Reprinted in *Sancti Thomae Aquinatis Doctoris Angelici Opera Omnia*, vols. 4 and 5. Rome: Leonine, 1888–89.

Deely, John. 1971. Animal intelligence and concept-formation. *The Thomist* 35, no. 1 (January): 43–93.

———. 1977. "Semiotic" as the doctrine of signs. *Ars Semeiotica* 1/3: 41–68.

———. 1982. *Introducing semiotic: Its history and doctrine*. Bloomington: Indiana University Press.

———. 1985. "Editorial Afterword" to *Tractatus de signis: The semiotic of John Poinsot*, 391–514. Berkeley: University of California Press.

———. 1986a. John Locke's place in the history of semiotic inquiry. In *Semiotics 1986*, edited by Jonathan Evans and John Deely, 406–18. Lanham, Md.: University Press of America.

———. 1986b. Semiotic in the thought of Jacques Maritain. *Recherche Sémiotique/Semiotic Inquiry* 6, no. 2: 1–30.

———. 1986c. Idolum. Archeology and ontology of the iconic sign. In *Iconicity: Essays on the nature of culture*, festschrift in honor of Thomas A. Sebeok, edited by Paul Bouissac, Michael Herzfeld, and Roland Posner, 29–49. Tübingen: Stauffenburg Verlag.

———. 1987. On the problem of interpreting the term "first" in the expression "first philosophy." In *Semiotics 1987*, edited by J. Deely, 3–14. Lanham, Md.: University Press of America.

———. 1988. The semiotic of John Poinsot: Yesterday and tomorrow. *Semiotica* 69, nos. 1–2 (April): 31–127.
———. 1990. *Basics of semiotics*. Bloomington: Indiana University Press.
———. 1991. Semiotics and biosemiotics: Are sign-science and life-science coextensive? In *Biosemiotics. The semiotic web 1991*, edited by Thomas A. Sebeok and Jean Umiker-Sebeok, 45–75. Berlin: Marton de Gruyter.
———. 1994. *New beginnings. Early modern philosophy and postmodern thought*. Toronto: University of Toronto Press.
Deely, John N., Brooke Williams, and Felicia E. Kruse, eds. 1986. *Frontiers in semiotics*. Bloomington: Indiana University Press.
Descartes, René. 1628. *Rules for the direction of the mind*, translated by Dugald Murdoch. In *The philosophical writings of Descartes*, edited by John Cottingham, Robert Stoothoff, and Dugald Murdoch, 1: 9–78. 2 vols. Cambridge: Cambridge University Press, 1985.
———. 1637. *Discourse on the method of rightly conducting one's reason and seeking truth in the sciences*, translated by Robert Stoothoff. In *The philosophical writings of Descartes*, 1:111–51.
Doyle, John P. 1984a. The Conimbricenses on the relations involved in signs. In *Semiotics 1984*, edited by John Deely, 567–76. Lanham, Md.: University Press of America.
———. 1984b. Prolegomena to a study of extrinsic denomination in the work of Francis Suarez, S.J. *Vivarium* 22, no. 2: 121–60.
———. 1987. Suarez on beings of reason and truth (1). *Vivarium* 25, no. 1: 47–76.
———. 1988. Suarez on beings of reason and truth (2). *Vivarium* 26, no. 1: 51–72.
———. 1990. "Extrinsic cognoscibility": A seventeenth century supertranscendental notion. *The Modern Schoolman* 68 (November): 57–80.
Eco, Umberto. 1990. *The limits of interpretation*. Bloomington: Indiana University Press.
Eco, Umberto, et al. 1986. Latratus canis or: The dog's barking. In Deely, Williams, and Kruse 1986: 63–73.
Fisch, Max H. 1986. Review of *Tractatus de signis: The semiotic of John Poinsot*, edited by John Deely. In *New Vico Studies*, edited by Giorgio Tagliacozzo and Donald Phillip Verene, 4:178–82. New York: Humanities Press International.
Furton, Edward J. 1987. Review of *Tractatus de signis: The semiotic of John Poinsot*, edited by John Deely. *The Review of Metaphysics* 40, no. 4: 766–767.
Gracia, Jorge J. E. 1992. *Philosophy and its history. Issues in philosophical historiography*. Albany: State University of New York Press.
Gredt, Josephus. 1936. *Elementa philosophiae Aristotelico-Thomisticae*. 7th ed. 2 vols. Barcelona: Herder.
Heidegger, Martin. 1927. *Sein und Zeit*. Tübingen: Max Niemeyer Verlag.
Henry, Desmond Paul. 1987. The way to awareness. Review of *Tractatus de signis: The semiotic of John Poinsot*, edited by John Deely. *Times Literary Supplement*, 30 October–5 November, p. 1201.
Hume, David. 1748. *Enquiry concerning human understanding*, edited by P. H. Nidditch. 3d ed. Oxford: Oxford University Press, 1975.
Kenny, Anthony, ed. and trans. 1970. *Descartes, Philosophical letters*. Oxford: Clarendon Press.

Krempel, A. 1952. *La doctrine de la relation chez saint Thomas. Exposé historique et systématique.* Paris: J. Vrin.

Lavaud, M.-Benoît. 1928. Jean de Saint-Thomas, l'homme et l'oeuvre. Appendix 2 to *Introduction à la théologie de saint Thomas,* Lavaud's French translation of Poinsot's "Isagoge ad D. Thomae Theologiam," 411–46. Paris: André Blot.

Locke, John. 1690. *An essay concerning human understanding.* Collated and annotated by Alexander Campbell Fraser. 2 vols. Oxford, 1894.

Maritain, Jacques. 1957. Language and the theory of sign. Originally published as chapter 5 of *Language: An enquiry into its meaning and function,* edited by Ruth Nanda Anshen, 86–101. New York: Harper & Bros. Reprinted in Deely, Williams, and Kruse 1986, 51–62, to which reprint page references are keyed.

———. 1963. *Distinguer pour unir: Ou, les degrés du savoir.* Paris: Desclée de Brouwer. Page refers. are to the French text of the 7th ed. as reproduced in *Jacques et Raïssa Maritain oeuvres completes,* 4:257–1110. Fribourg: Éditions Universitaires Fribourg Suisse et Éditions Saint-Paul Paris).

Miles, John Russiano. 1985. Text of the original announcement by the University of California Press of the publication of *Tractatus de signis: The semiotic of John Poinsot.*

Muñoz Delgado, Vicente. 1964. *Lógica formal y filosofía en Domingo de Soto.* Madrid.

Natoli, Joseph, and Linda Hutcheon. 1993. Reading *A postmodern reader,* introduction to *A postmodern reader,* edited by Joseph Natoli and Linda Hutcheon, vii–xiv. Albany: State University of New York Press.

Peirce, Charles Sanders. 1868. Questions concerning certain faculties claimed for man. *Journal of Speculative Philosophy* 2:103–14. Page refs. are to reprinted edition in the *Writings of Charles S. Peirce. A chronological edition, Volume 2,* ed. Edward C. Moore et al., 193–211. Bloomington: Indiana University Press.

———. 1902. S.v. "sign." In *Dictionary of psychology and philosophy,* edited by J. M. Baldwin, 2:527. 3 vols. New York: Macmillan.

———. 1904. Letter of 12 October from Peirce to Lady Welby. In *Semiotics and significs. The correspondence between Charles S. Peirce and Victoria Lady Welby,* edited by Charles S. Hardwick, 22–36. Bloomington: Indiana University Press, 1977.

Poinsot, John. 1631. *Artis Logicae Prima Pars.* In *Cursus Philosophicus Thomisticus,* edited by B. Reiser, 1:1–247. Turin: Marietti, 1930. The opening pages 1–11a14 of this work and the "Quaestio Disputanda I. De Termino. Art. 6. Utrum Voces Significant per prius Conceptus an Res," pages 104b31–108a33, relevant to the discussion of signs in the *Secunda Pars* (1632), have been incorporated in the 1632a entry below for the independent edition of that discussion.

———. 1632. *Artis Logicae Secunda Pars.* In *Cursus Philosophicus Thomisticus,* edited by B. Reiser, 1:249–839. Turin: Marietti, 1930.

———. 1632a. *Tractatus de signis: The semiotic of John Poinsot,* extracted from the *Artis Logicae Prima et Secunda Pars* and arranged in bilingual format by John Deely in consultation with Ralph A. Powell. Berkeley: University of California Press, 1985. Pages in this volume are set up in matching columns of English and Latin, with intercolumnar numbers every fifth line. (Thus, references to the volume are by page number, followed by a slash and the appropriate line number of the specific section of text referred to—e.g., 287/3-26.)

———. 1643. *Tomus Secundus Cursus Theologici.* In *Cursus Theologicus,* edited at Solesmes, 2:531–end and 3. Paris: Desclée, 1934 and 1937.

Ramirez, J.-M. 1924. S.v. "Jean de St. Thomas." *Dictionnaire de théologie catholique,* 8:803–8. Paris: Letouzey. (Note: This work is not reliable for chronology.)

Santaella Braga, Lúcia. 1991. John Poinsot's doctrine of signs: The recovery of a missing link. *The Journal of Speculative Philosophy,* New Series, 5, no. 2: 151–59.

Sebeok, Thomas A. 1986. A signifying man. Review of *Tractatus de Signis: The semiotic of John Poinsot,* edited by John Deely. *The New York Times Book Review,* 30 March 1986, pp. 14–15.

Simon, Yves R. 1955. Foreword and notes to *The material logic of John of St. Thomas,* translated by Yves R. Simon, John J. Glanville, and G. Donald Hollenhorst, ix–xxiii and 587–625. Chicago: University of Chicago Press.

Simonin, H.-D. 1930. Review of the 1930 Reiser edition of Poinsot's *Ars Logica. Bulletin Thomiste* (September): 140–48.

Soto, Domingo de. 1529, 1554. *Summulae.* Facsimile of 3d ed. Hildesheim, N.Y.: Georg Olms Verlag.

Stoothoff, Robert. 1985. Translator's preface to Descartes 1637, 1:109–10.

Whitehead, Alfred North. 1925. *Science and the modern world.* New York: Macmillan.

Winance, Eleuthère. 1983. Review of *Introducing semiotic* (Deely 1982). *Revue Thomiste* 80 (juillet–août).

Contributors

Rafael Alvira studied at the Universities of Madrid, Navarre, Rome, and Münster-Westphalia, and at the Universidad Complutense de Madrid and the Lateran (Rome). He has taught at the University Complutense (Madrid) and at the State University of La Laguna in Spain. He is currently Ordinary Professor at the School of Philosophy, University of Navarre (Spain). He has been a lecturer and visiting professor in a number of countries and universities. He has published several books and over eighty articles. He is a member of the boards of the European Democratic Forum (Strasbourg), the Business and Humanism Institute (Pamplona), and the International Association for Christian Teaching (Geneva).

Eduardo Andújar received his Ph.D. in philosophy from the University of Ottawa. After post-doctoral studies at the École Pratique des Hautes Études in Paris, he returned to Ottawa, where he teaches at the Collège dominicain de Philosophie et de Théologie. His essays include "Aequitas, Aequalitas et Auctoritas chez les maîtres de l'École espagnole du XVIe siècle," in *Aequitas, Aequalitas, Auctoritas. Theoretical Reason and Legitimation of Authority in XVIth Century Europe* (1992), and "De la nature et par la volonté à l'histoire," in *Moral and Political Philosophies in the Middle Ages* (1995). He is also co-editor of *Moral and Political Philosophies in the Middle Ages.*

Mauricio Beuchot, O.P., received his Ph.D. from the Universidad Iberoamericana de México. He is professor and researcher at the Universidad Nacional Autónoma de México, and is co-ordinator of its Center of Classical Studies. Among his books concerning the colonial period are: *Filósofos dominicos novohispanos* (1987), *La filosofía social de los pensadores novohispanos* (1990), *Estudios de historia y de filosofía en el México colonial* (1991), *La querella de la conquista. Una polémico del siglo XVI* (1992), *Los fundamentos de los derechos humanos en Bartolomé de las Casas* (1994), *Filosofía y ciencia en el México dieciochesco* (1996), and several translations, from Latin, of colonial thinkers.

Alfredo Cruz-Prados received his Ph.D. from the University of Navarre (Spain) and has been on the faculty of that university since 1985. He has published *La sociedad como artificio. El pensamiento político de Hobbes* (1986, 1992) and *Historia de la Filosofía Contemporánea* (1987, 1991), as well as a number of articles, including "La Política de Aristóteles y la democracia," in *Anuario Filosófico* (1988), "Para un concepto de guerra de una filosofía de la paz. Actualidad del pensamiento de Vitoria," in *Anuario de Filosofía del Derecho*, and "Sobre los fundamentos del nacionalismo," in *Revista de Estudios Políticos*.

Jean De Groot is Assistant Professor of Philosophy at The Catholic University of America. She received her Ph.D. in history of science at Harvard University, where her specialty was Aristotelian natural philosophy. She has received fellowships from Harvard University and from Dumbarton Oaks Center for Byzantine Studies in Washington D.C. Her publications include *Aristotle and Philoponus on Light* (1991), and "Form and Succession in Aristotle's Physics," in Proceedings of the Boston Area Colloquium for Ancient Philosophy (1996).

John Deely is Professor in the Department of Philosophy, Loras College, Dubuque, Iowa. His publications include *Introducing Semiotic: Its History and Doctrine* (1982), *Tractatus de signis: The Semiotic of John Poinsot* (1985), *Basics of Semiotics* (1990), and *New Beginnings: Early Modern Philosophy and Postmodern Thought* (1994).

John P. Doyle received his Ph.D. from the University of Toronto in 1966. After teaching at St. Michael's College in Vermont he went to St. Louis University, where he has been Professor of Philosophy since 1973. He has published *Francisco Suárez, S.J.: On Beings of Reason* (1995), plus twenty-three articles reflecting his interest in late Scholastic philosophy, especially that of Suárez. He is preparing for publication *Francisco De Vitoria: On Homicide* and "Two Thomists [Cajetan and Vitoria] on the Morality of a Jailbreak," scheduled for *The Modern Schoolman* (1997).

Yves Floucat is both Doctor of Philosophy and Doctor of Letters. Professor of Metaphysics and Morals at the Centre Indépendant de Recherche Philosophique (CIREP) in Toulouse (France), he is also founder and director of the Centre Jacques Maritain in Toulouse and member of the Pontifical Academy of St. Thomas in Rome. Since 1988 he has directed the series Croire et Savoir for the publisher Pierre Téqui in Paris. As well as numerous articles in French and other journals, and chronicles of philosophy for the *Revue Thomiste*, he has published the following: *Pour une philosophie chrétienne: Eléments d'un débat fondamental* (1983), *Vocation de l'homme et sagesse chrétienne* (1989), *Métaphysique et Religion: Vers une sagesse chrétienne intégrale* (1989), *L'Etre et la Mystique des saints: Conditions d'une métaphysique thomiste* (1995), *Jacques Maritain ou la fidélité à l'éternel* (1996). He is co-director of *Jacques Maritain et ses contemporains* (1991), a collective work of CIREP. He has collaborated on publications of the Centre de Philosophie Ibérique et Ibéro-Américaine at the University of Toulouse-Le Mirail; on the *Encyclopédie Philosophique Universelle* (1992); and on the *Petit Dictionnaire des philosophes de la religion* (1996).

Jorge J. E. Gracia, Distinguished Professor, State University of New York at Buffalo, is author of the following books: *Suarez on Individuation* (1982), *Introduction to the Problem of Individuation in the Early Middle Ages* (1984, 1988), *Individuality: An Essay on the Foundations of Metaphysics* (1988; winner of the John N. Findlay Prize in Metaphysics), *The Metaphysics of Good and Evil According to Suarez* (1989; with D. Davis), *Philosophy and Its History: Issues in Philosophical Historiography* (1992), *A Theory of Textuality: The Logic and Epistemology* (1995), and *Texts: Ontological Status, Identity, Author, Audience* (1996). He is also author of over 150 articles and editor of over a dozen volumes, primarily on metaphysics, medieval philosophy, and Latin American thought.

Stephen Menn received a Ph.D. in mathematics from Johns Hopkins University in 1985 and a Ph.D. in philosophy from the University of Chicago in 1989. He has taught at Princeton and is now Associate Professor of Philosophy at McGill University. He is author of *Plato on God as Nous* (1995) and *Descartes and Augustine* (forthcoming). He is working on a book called *The Aim and the Argument of Aristotle's Metaphysics*, and, with Calvin Normore, on a book called *Nominalism and Realism, from Boethius to Hobbes*.

Carlos G. Noreña is Professor Emeritus of Philosophy and Provost Emeritus of Stevenson College at the University of California, Santa Cruz, where he taught for twenty-nine years. He has also taught at the Catholic University in Tokyo and at the University of California, San Diego. His educational background includes master's degrees in classics, philosophy, theology, and civil law, from universities in Spain, West Germany, and the United States. He is author of two books on Spanish Renaissance thought, an English translation of *Vives: De Anima et Vita, Book Three*, a Vives bibliography, and many articles dealing with Vives, Suárez, John Huart, Ockham, and Francisco de Vitoria.

Contributors

Marcelo Sánchez Sorondo studied at the National University of Buenos Aires and the Catholic University of Argentina before receiving the S.T.D. from the University of St. Thomas Aquinas in Rome and the Laureate in Philosophy from the University of Perugia. He is former Dean of the Faculty of Philosophy at the Lateran University (Rome), where he is currently Professor of the History of Philosophy. His areas of research have included Thomistic anthropology and the affinities between Aristotle and Hegel. Among his many publications, the following are of particular note: *La gracia como participación de la naturaleza según Santo Tomás de Aquino* (1979), *Aristotele e San Tommaso* (1981), *Aristóteles y Hegel* (1987), "L'energeia noetica aristotelica come il nucleo speculativo del *Geist* hegeliano," in *L'atto aristotelico e le sue ermeneutiche* (1990), "Per un servizio sapienziale della filosofia nella chiesa," *Aquinas* (1994), and "La teologia di Aristotele," in *Dizionario teologico* (in press).

Mirko Skarica studied at the University of Heidelberg before receiving his Ph.D. from the University of Navarre. He has been Fulbright Visiting Scholar at the University of Texas at Austin. He is head of the Graduate Division of the Institute of Philosophy at the Universidad Católica de Valparaíso, where he has worked since 1965. He has translated into Spanish St. Thomas's commentary on Aristotle's *Peri Hermeneias* (1990). On the problem of future contingents he has written "Predeterminación y libertad en Fray Alonso Briceño," *Philosophica* (1993), and "Anmerkungen zum Kommentar von Boethius zu *De interpretatione* 9 von Aristoteles," in *Zur Modernen Deutung der Aristotelischen Logik*, vol. VII (forthcoming).

William A. Wallace is a Dominican priest with doctorates in philosophy (1959) and theology (1962) from the University of Fribourg, Switzerland. He is Professor Emeritus of Philosophy and History at The Catholic University of America and Adjunct Professor of Philosophy at the University of Maryland, College Park. He is best known for his discoveries relating to Galileo's early notebooks, on which he has published eight books. Less known is the fact that he was led to Galileo from research on the physics of Domingo de Soto, which he conducted at Harvard University in 1965–67. He has written extensively on the history and philosophy of medieval and Renaissance science and recently has been appointed Associate Editor for philosophy and science of the *Encyclopedia of the Renaissance*, forthcoming from Scribners'. Among his seventeen books the latest is *The Modeling of Nature: Philosophy of Science and Philosophy of Nature in Synthesis* (1966).

Norman J. Wells received his licentiate in medieval studies from the Pontifical Institute of Medieval Studies in 1953 and his Ph.D. from the University of Toronto in 1955. After teaching one year at Fordham University (1954–55), he went to Boston College in 1955 and has been there ever since. The bulk of his research has been focused on late Scholasticism represented by Francisco Suárez, S.J., and the relationship of that late Scholastic perspective to René Descartes and the origins of early modern thought.

Juan Antonio Widow received his Ph.D. from the Universidad Complutense de Madrid in 1968. He has been on the faculty of the Universidad Católica de Valparaíso since 1961, and served as Director of the Instituto de Filosofía of that university from 1973 to 1980. He is editor of *Philosophica*, a review published by the Instituto de Filosofía. He is author of *El Hombre, Animal Político* (1984) and has collaborated on several other books. Among his other publications are some thirty-five articles on metaphysics, epistemology, and political philosophy.

Index Nominum

Abelard, 228n
Abellán, José Luis, 4n, 7n, 10n, 12n, 83, 83n
Abril-Castelló, Vidal, 69, 83n, 85n, 92n, 94n, 99n
Acuña, R., 38n
Adams, Marilyn, 236n
Albert the Great, Saint, 117, 202, 203, 209, 227n
Alcalá, Luis de, 141
Alexander VI, Pope, 41, 89
Allen, J. W., 258n, 264n
Almain, 259
Anawati, M. M., 176n
Angelleli, Ignacio, 280n, 290n
Anscombe, G. E. M., 156n
Anselm, Saint, 221
Antonin, Saint, 132, 139, 143n
Araújo, Francisco, 211n, 289, 290n, 302, 302n, 303n, 304n
Arches, Petrus, 121
Arcos, Miguel de, 39, 40–42, 62
Argote, Francisco de, 85n
Arias, Antonio, 13
Aristotle, 20, 46, 48n, 56n, 63n, 66, 76–77, 78, 79, 100, 104n, 106–10, 106n, 110n, 115, 116, 117, 118, 119, 121, 123, 125, 126, 155–58, 181, 183, 192, 192n, 227, 227n, 228n, 242, 251–55, 270, 278n, 283, 293, 310
Arnauld, 223, 223n
Arquillière, H. X., 65n
Ashworth, E. J., 6n, 21n, 280n, 290n, 291n, 301n, 302n
Augustine, Saint, 18, 20, 65, 85nn, 92n, 205, 216, 219, 221, 280–81, 287, 289
Auroux, Sylvain, 176n
Averroes, 14, 177, 252, 252n, 254
Avicenna, 228n
Azpilcueta, Martin de, 132

Baeza, Francisco, 5n

Báñez, Domingo, 13, 46, 143n, 183–86, 187n, 203n, 204n, 210n, 216, 229n
Barbier, M., 56
Barcia Trelles, Camilo, 258n
Bartolus, 266
Baruzi, Jean, 160
Bataillon, Marcel, 42n, 72, 72n
Baudart, A., 176n
Baudelaire, Charles, 171
Beato, Francesco, 121
Bellarmine, Robert, Saint, 266
Bellasco, Giovanni Battista, 121
Beltrán de Heredia, Vincente, 45n, 51n, 63nn, 70n, 114n, 120, 120n
Benedetti, Giovan Battista, 121
Berger, Gaston, 160n
Bergson, Henri, 160
Berkeley, George, 292–93, 293n
Bernard of Siena, Saint, 132, 139, 143n
Berton, C., 190n
Beuchot, Mauricio, 6nn, 7n, 10n, 18n, 289, 290n, 302n, 303n, 304n
Beuve-Méry, Hubert, 48n
Biermann, Benno M., 39n, 71n
Bird, Otto A., 301n
Blondel, Maurice, 160, 160n
Bodin, J., 258
Boehme, Jacob, 176, 176n, 179n
Boehner, P., 236n
Boethius, 117, 186
Bonaventure, Saint, 17n, 183
Borges, Pedro, 94n
Boulnois, Olivier, 172n
Bouyer, Louis, 148n
Bradwardine, Thomas, 116, 117, 120, 123
Braga, Juan Gomez de, 124
Briceño, Alonso, 6, 6n, 13, 182, 183, 194–98
Brunn, E. Zum, 177n
Bufalo, Stefano del, 124
Bull, H., 268n
Buridan, Jean, 117, 120, 250

321

Burley, Walter, 123, 227n
Burrus, Ernest J., 53n

Cajetan, Cardinal (Thomas de Vio), 33, 37, 38, 39, 40, 43, 183, 203n, 206n, 211n, 227, 228n, 229, 229nn, 243, 243n, 244n, 248, 279n, 289n, 302
Calmette, J., 56n
Campanus of Navarre, 117
Cano, Melchior, 13, 217n
Capreolus, John, 202, 203, 203n, 204, 206, 206n, 207, 209, 210, 211n, 216, 218, 219, 220, 224n, 237n
Carreño, A. M., 31n
Carreras Artau, Joaquin, 258n
Carro, Venancio D., 69, 70nn, 72, 72n, 74n, 92n, 97n, 98n, 110n
Cassiodorus, 21
Cassirer, Ernst, 127
Castelbranco, Antonio del, 124
Castro, Alfonso de, 13
Caterus, 223
Celaya, Juan de, 113, 117, 118, 120, 228n
Cerquiera, Luis de, 124
Chafuen, Alejandro A., 135nn, 137n, 141n
Chamberlin, E. R., 17n
Charlemagne, 55
Charles V, 71n, 74n, 113
Chauvet, F. de J., 31n
Chauvin, Etienne, 226, 226n, 241
Childeric, 55
Christopher à Govea, 251n
Cicero, 228n
Ciruelo, Pedro Sanches, 114, 116
Clagett, Marchall, 119, 119n
Clavius, Christopher, 123, 126
Clement, 148, 148n
Collingwood, R. G., 142n
Columbus, Christopher, 73, 73n
Comas, Michael, 284–85
Copleston, Frederick, 5n
Coronel, Antonio, 113
Coronel, Luis, 113
Courtine, Jean-François, 26n, 172n
Coutagne, J.-J., 160n
Craig, William Lane, 182
Crockaert (Crokaert), Peter, 45n, 117, 227n
Cronin, T. J., 202n, 223n
Crouzel, Henri, 177n
Cruz, Felipe de la, 141n

da Vinci, Leonardo, 60
Davis, Harold E., 4n

De Libera, A., 177nn, 178n
de Lubac, Henri, 173n, 176n, 179n
de Muralt, A., 179n
de Roover, Raymond, 143, 143n
Dear, P., 210n, 224nn
Deely, John, 27n, 275n, 276n, 280n, 283n, 284, 287, 290–91, 291n, 294n, 297nn, 299nn, 300nn, 301nn, 302n, 308n, 309, 310n
Defourneaux, M., 19n
Delahoutre, Michel, 176n
Denzinger, H., 49n
Descartes, René, 7n, 9, 23, 26, 201, 202n, 209n, 213, 214n, 223–25, 275–79, 275n, 276n, 280n, 283, 286, 292, 306, 307, 308
Diego de Covarrubias, 71, 71n, 258
Dominic of Flanders, 251
Doyle, John P., 276n, 279n, 307n
Duhem, Pierre, 114, 114n, 119, 119n, 122, 125, 126, 128
Dullaert, Jean, 116, 117, 118, 126
Dumont, Jean, 74n, 75nn
Duns Scotus, John, 6, 18, 20, 172, 172n, 182, 194, 195, 196, 202n, 203–4, 204n, 213, 228n, 232–39, 241, 244n, 245, 249, 249n, 251

Eckhart, Meister, 175, 176n, 177
Eco, Umberto, 289–90, 299n
Edwards, William F., 126, 126n
Ehrle, Franz, 230n
Eiximenis, Francesc, 21
Elorduy, E., 259n
Ephrem, Saint, 171
Epicurus, 228n
Erasmus, 72
Escobar, Edmundo, 4n
Euclid, 117
Eudaemon, Andreas, 124, 125

Fabié, A. M., 71n
Fantazzi, C., 114n
Ferdinand of Aragón, 3, 73
Fernández Santamaría, J. A., 91n, 99n, 101n
Ferreira Gomes, Joaquim, 226n
Fichte, J. G., 175, 175n
Filmer, R., 264
Finnis, John, 260n, 270n
Fisch, Max H., 306, 307
Fitzralph, Richard, 49, 49n
Fonseca, Pedro de, 13, 24, 226–56
Fontan, P., 173n
Forest, Aimé, 160n, 166, 167n, 168n, 171, 171nn

Francis of Assisi, Saint, 60
Francovich, Guillermo, 8n
Fraser, Alexander Campbell, 307
Freddoso, Fred, 256n
Friede, Juan, 75n
Frondizi, Risieri, 7n, 8n
Furlong, Guillermo, 6n
Furton, Edward J., 302n
Fuster, J., 17n

Galileo Galilei, 114, 119, 122–29, 280n
Gallegos Rocafull, José M., 6, 10n
Gaos, José, 7n, 10n
Garcia de Toledo, 148n
García Icazbalceta, J., 31n
García Menendez, Alberto A., 257n
García Pelayo, Manuel, 71, 71n
García Villoslada, R., 21, 45n
Gardet, Louis, 176n, 177n
Garin, P., 202n
Gassendi, 223
Gentili, Alberico, 46, 46n
Gerson, L. P., 212n
Getino, Luis Alonso, 45nn, 46nn, 50n
Ghini, Luca, 121
Giacon, Carlo, 6n
Gil Fernández, Luis, 16n
Gilson, Etienne, 17n, 21n, 172, 172nn, 180, 201n, 202n
Gómez Camacho, Francisco, 137n
Gomez Robledo, Ignacio, 258n
González, David, 12n
González, Jaime, 92n, 94n
Gracia, Jorge J. E., 8nn, 9n, 16n, 24n, 25n, 26nn, 290n
Gram, M., 206n
Gredt, Josephus, 302n
Gregory of Rimini, 227n
Grotius, Hugo, 46, 46n, 260, 260n, 269, 270, 270n
Grice-Hutchinson, M., 16n
Guevara, 72
Guy, Alain, 4n, 6n

Haakonssen, Knud, 260n
Haase, W., 16n, 21n,
Hadot, Pierre, 159n
Hamilton, Bernice, 57, 57n
Hanke, Lewis, 40n, 69, 71, 71n, 100n, 108n
Hanisch Espíndola, Walter, 6n, 14n, 194n
Hartmann, Nicolai, 7
Harvey Nedellec, 209, 209n
Hegel, G. F. W., 59, 59n, 175, 178n

Heidegger, Martin, 175, 309–10, 309n, 310n
Henninger, Mark, 232n, 236n
Henry of Ghent, 18, 203, 203n, 206, 207, 209, 210, 213, 216, 218, 219, 220, 223, 224, 224n, 232, 239, 240, 246
Henry, D. P., 302n
Heraclitus, 228n
Hernández, Ramón, 49n, 50n, 56n
Herrejón Peredo, C., 32, 32n, 35n
Heytesbury, William, 117, 120, 123
Hobbes, Thomas, 47, 262, 262n
Hume, David, 9, 293n, 294n
Hus, John, 49
Husserl, Edmund, 178n
Hutcheon, Linda, 276

Ignatius of Loyola, 19
Iriarte, J., 23n
Irwin, William, 27n
Isabella of Castile, 3, 73, 74
Isidore of Seville, 21

Jaksi, Iván, 8nn
James I, King, 265–66
Jansen, Cornelius, 182
Jarlot, Georges, 258n
Javellus, 251
John Paul II, Pope, 60
John Poinsot: see John of Saint Thomas
John of the Cross, Saint, 160–80
John of Saint Thomas, 13, 22n, 275–314
Jones, W. T., 5n
Jordanus de Nemore, 117
Juan de Santo Tomás: see John of Saint Thomas

Kaluza, Zenon, 227n
Kant, Immanuel, 9, 66, 206, 276, 307
Katz, Steven, 146nn, 153, 154n
Kavanaugh, Kieran, 147n, 153
Keen, Benjamin, 75n
Kendzierski, Lottie H., 228n
Kennedy, L. A., 201n, 203n, 204n, 210n, 217n
Kenny, Anthony, 277n
Keynes, John Maynard, 142–43, 143n
Kingsbury, B., 268n
Korn, Ernst R., 176n
Koyré, Alexandre, 119, 119n
Krempel, A., 289n
Kretzmann, Norman, 6n, 22n
Kristeller, Paul Oskar, 5n

Lacombe, Olivier, 176n, 177nn

Index Nominum

Lacoste, Jean-Yves, 178n
Landucci, S., 202n
Larroyo, Francisco, 4n
Las Casas, Bartolomé de, 13, 25, 32, 34, 36, 37, 38, 40, 42, 69–87, 88–110, 258
Lauterpacht, Hersch, 260n
Lavaud, M.-Benoît, 280n
Lavelle, Louis, 160n
Lawrence, Jeremy, 47n, 50n, 258n
Lax, Gaspar, 116, 117, 118, 125
Laywine, Alison, 256n
Ledesma, Pedro de, 203n
Leibniz, G. W., 26, 307
Leo X, Pope, 17n
Lerner, Ralph, 229n, 233n
Lessius, 182
Lewis, Christopher, 123
Liceti, Fortunio, 128
Locke, John, 26, 276, 286, 292, 307–9, 307n
Lohr, Charles H., 6n, 26n, 254n
Losada, Angel, 69, 89n, 94n
Louis XIV, 57
Lugo, Juan de, 133, 133n, 137, 137n
Luther, Martin, 90, 101n, 263
Lynch, John, 258n

Machiavelli, N., 258, 259
Mahdi, Muhsin, 229n, 233n
Mahoney, Edward, 27n
Mahn-Lot, Marianne, 69, 71, 71nn
Maimonides, 14
Major (Mair), John, 113, 117, 227n, 259
Mancio del Cuerpo de Cristo, 203n
Manuel á Lima, 124
Maravall, José Antonio, 258n, 261n, 262, 262n
Marc, André, 166, 166n
Marenbon, John, 25n
Mariana, Juan de, 13, 25, 258, 263, 264, 264n, 267
Mariátegui, José 5n
Marín, Higinio, 108n
Marinho, José, 4n
Marion, J.-L., 202n, 223n, 224
Maritain, Jacques, 160, 160n, 166, 166n, 167, 167n, 168n, 169, 169n, 171n, 175n, 275n, 297n, 300, 300n
Martín Hernández, F., 40n
Martínez, Manuel M., 75n
Marx, Karl, 178, 178n
Maurer, Armand, 180n, 204n, 220n
McGinn, Bernard, 145n, 148n
Medina, Bartolomé de, 203n
Mendoza, Antonio de, 32, 36
Menéndez y Pelayo, Marcelino, 72n

Menu, Antonius, 123
Mercado, Manfredo Kempff, 4n
Mercado, Tomás de, 13
Mersenne, 210n, 224, 224nn, 225, 277n
Mesnard, Pierre, 48n, 57, 57n
Meurisse, Martin, 223, 223n, 224
Michael de Bay, 182
Michalski, K., 18n
Miles, John Russiano, 275n, 309
Mill, John Stuart, 143n
Mingay, J. M., 155n
Miranda, F., 35n, 36n
Molina, Luis de, 13, 23, 25, 136–37, 137n, 141n, 182, 183, 186–89, 190–91, 192, 193, 194, 196, 227, 228n, 258, 262, 262n, 263
Montaigne, Michel de, 18
Moscoso, 72
Motolinía (Toribio de Benavente), 71n, 74, 74n, 91, 100n
Muñoz Delgado, Vicente, 21n, 280n, 290n

Natoli, Joseph, 276
Naszalyi, Emilio, 48n, 49n
Nicol, Eduardo, 3n, 7n, 8n,
Nicholas of Cusa, 178n
Nietzsche, F., 180n
Nifo, Agostino, 127, 251
Noreña, Carlos, 21n
Normore, Calvin, 256n

O'Gorman, Edmundo, 78n
O'Meara, D. J., 128
Origen, 148, 148n
Ortega y Gasset, José, 7, 8n, 10, 12
Oviedo, Fernández; 77

Pagden, Anthony, 47n, 50n, 78, 78n, 92n, 257n
Palacios Rubio, 32
Paliard, Jacques, 160n
Paul, Saint, 49
Paul III, Pope, 75
Paul VI, Pope, 71
Paul of Venice, 117, 227n, 251n
Paulus, J., 203n
Paz, Matías, 257
Pedro de Valencia, 137n
Peers, E. Allison, 161n
Peirce, Charles Sanders, 276, 285, 289, 296, 298, 299, 299n, 306, 307, 307n, 309
Pereira, Benito (Pererius, Benedictus), 13, 123

Index Nominum   325

Pereña, Luciano, 16n, 49n, 71n, 72n, 74n, 77n, 86n, 258nn, 259n
Perez Prendes, J. M., 49n, 258n
Périco, Y., 160n
Pernoud, Régine, 131, 131nn, 132n, 138–39, 139n
Peter Aureole, 237n
Peter Lombard, 280
Peter of Spain, 114, 118, 125
Philip II, King, 270
Philip III, King, 258
Philodemus, 307
Pierre d'Ailly, 116, 236n
Pike, Nelson, 146n, 153–54, 154nn
Pinta Llorente, M. de la, 19n
Pippin, 55
Plancarte, Gabriel Méndez, 6n
Plato, 149n, 159, 161, 177, 260
Plotinus, 161, 176–77, 176nn, 177nn
Popkin, Richard, 18
Poupard, Paul, 176n
Powell, Ralph A., 27n
Price, James R., III, 146n
Protagoras, 59
Pseudo-Dionysius, 148, 148n, 149, 149nn
Putallaz, F.-X., 177n

Quesada, Vicente G., 19n
Quintana, Manuel, 71
Quiroga, Vasco de, 13, 31, 35–42

Ramirez, J.-M., 288
Ramos, D., 84n, 92n
Ramos, Samuel, 7, 7n, 8n
Randall, John Hermann, Jr., 127
Recasens Siches, Luis, 258n
Redmond, Walter, 6n, 10n
Reiser, B., 287
Richard of Middleton, 49n
Roberts, A., 268n
Rodis-Lewis, G., 202n
Rodrigues, Otilio, 147n, 153
Rodríguez, Ramón Insúa, 4n
Romero, Francisco, 7n, 9,
Romeyer, B., 258n
Rousseau, J.-J., 262, 264
Rovira, María del Carmen, 4n
Rubio, Antonio, 10, 10n, 13, 24
Rugerius, Ludovicus, 123, 126

Sacrobosco, 116, 123
Salazar, Francisco de, 13
Salazar Bondy, Augusto, 15n, 24n
Santaella Braga, Lúcia, 309
Santullano, Luis, 147n

Saranyana, Josep-Ignasi, 39n, 98n
Scheler, Max, 7
Schmidt, Peter L., 21n
Schmitt, Charles B., 5n, 6n, 26n, 254n
Schmitz, Heinz R., 176n, 178n, 179n
Schönmetzer, A., 49n
Schutte, Ofelia, 8n
Scorraille, Raoul, 10n
Scott, James Brown, 257n
Sebeock, Thomas A., 306
Seneca, 14
Sepúlveda, Juan Ginés de, 69–87, 88–110, 257
Shorris, Earl, 12n
Siegfried, H., 206n
Sierra, Vicente D., 73n
Sierra Bravo, R., 16n, 133nn, 137n, 138n, 141n
Silíceo, Juan Martínez, 116, 117
Simon, Yves R., 280n
Simonin, H.-D., 279–80, 282, 283, 284, 285
Sisebutus, 67
Skinner, Quentin, 254n, 258n, 260n, 262n, 264n
Smith, Adam, 143n
Soder, Josef, 258n
Sokolowski, Robert, 152
Solana, Marcial, 4n, 45nn
Sombart, Werner, 142, 142n, 143n
Soncinas, 202n, 205n, 209, 210n, 216, 218, 251
Soto, Domingo de, 13, 32, 69, 69n, 70, 76n, 78, 79n, 83nn, 89, 93, 113–29, 132–33, 133n, 134, 134n, 136, 136nn, 137–38, 137nn, 138n, 139–40, 140nn, 141n, 203n, 210n, 217n, 226n, 227, 227n, 228nn, 229n, 231nn, 232n, 244, 245, 255–56, 256n, 258, 280–82, 284, 285, 286, 289, 290n, 302, 303n, 304n
Spencer, Aguayo, 36n
Spinoza, Baruch, 175
Stace, Walter, 146n, 153–54, 153n
Stoothoff, Robert, 277n
Suárez, Francisco de, 5n, 9, 10, 10n, 13, 21–22, 23, 25–26, 26n, 123, 172n, 182, 183, 189–93, 194, 195, 201–25, 226–56, 257–71, 275n, 276n, 308
Suetonius Pratum, 21
Swineshead, Richard, 117, 123
Sylvester of Ferrara, 205n, 210n, 216

Taton, René, 119n
Teresa of Avila, Saint, 145–59
Thierry of Freiberg, 178n

Index Nominum

Thomas Aquinas, Saint, 6, 20, 37, 38, 43, 45n, 46, 48n, 59, 60, 60n, 61n, 62, 65, 65n, 66, 66n, 67, 67n, 79, 79n, 80, 80nn, 84, 92n, 117, 118, 132, 132n, 139, 140n, 161, 161nn, 164, 165, 165nn, 167, 167n, 169, 169n, 180, 182, 183–85, 186, 187, 187n, 194, 204, 206, 209, 210, 216, 220, 227, 228nn, 229, 229nn, 233n, 238n, 245, 250, 252, 252n, 260, 260n, 275n, 280, 281n, 287–88, 291n, 297, 297n, 298n, 300n, 301n, 302n, 305n
Thomas of Strasbourg, 240n
Thomas of Villanova, 113
Thomaz, Alvaro, 118
Toletus, Francisco, 13, 122–25, 127, 243, 244
Torres, Alberto María, 63n
Torquemada, 39
Trentman, John, 22n
Tresmontant, Claude, 163, 163n, 175n, 179n
Trombeta, 228n
Truyol Serra, Antonio, 257n

Urdánoz, Teofilo, 45nn, 46n, 50n

Valdéz, R., 36n
Valerio Maximo, 84
Vallius, Paulus, 123, 125, 126–27
Varchi, Benedetto, 121
Vargas Uribe, G., 42n
Vasconcelos, José, 5n
Vázquez, Gabriel, 13, 195–96, 258, 270, 270n, 276n
Vera Cruz, Alonso de la, 6, 6n, 13, 52n
Villanueva, E., 24n
Vincent of Beauvais, 21
Vitelleschi, Mutius, 123, 126
Vitoria, Diego de, 72
Vitoria, Francisco de, 5n, 7, 13, 23, 25, 31, 32, 35, 37, 43, 45–58, 59–68, 72, 92n, 93, 95, 96, 97, 113, 114, 117, 118, 120, 132, 133, 133n, 135, 135n, 136, 138, 138n, 141–42, 141n, 142n, 203n, 217n, 227n, 228n, 257–58, 257n, 258, 258n, 265, 268
Vives, Juan Luis, 13, 21n, 114–15, 114n, 117, 126, 133–34, 134n
von Hayek, Friedrich, 142n, 143n
von Mises, Ludwig, 143n
von Wright, G. H., 156n

Wade, Francis C., 228n
Wallace, William A., 26n, 114n, 119n, 121n, 122n, 123n, 124nn, 125n, 126n, 127n, 128n, 228n
Waltzer, R. R., 155n
Warren, F. B., 35n
Wehrle, Joannnes, 160n
Wells, Norman, 201n, 202n, 203nn, 206n, 210n, 211n, 217n, 221n, 225nn, 232n, 276n
Whitehead, Alfred North, 308
William of Ockham, 182, 227n, 230, 230n, 231, 235–39, 241–42, 243, 243n, 280, 308
Winance, Eleuthère, 307n
Windelband, Wilhelm, 5n
Wittgenstein, Ludwig, 9, 9n, 156n
Wolff, Christian, 26
Wolter, Alan, 18n
Wycliff, John, 49

Zaballa, Ana de, 100n
Zabarella, Jacopo, 127
Zacharias, Pope 55
Zavala, Silvio, 38n, 39, 39n, 40, 100n, 105n
Zea, Leopoldo, 8n
Zumárraga, Juan de, 13, 31–35, 37
Zumel, Francisco, 201–25

www.ingramcontent.com/pod-product-compliance
Lightning Source LLC
Chambersburg PA
CBHW032302300426
44110CB00033B/271